T0316856

Globalization, the Human Condition and Sustainable Development in the Twenty-first Century

Globalization, the Human Condition and Sustainable Development in the Twenty-first Century

Cross-national Perspectives and European Implications

Arno Tausch and Almas Heshmati

ANTHEM PRESS
LONDON · NEW YORK · DELHI

Anthem Press
An imprint of Wimbledon Publishing Company
www.anthempress.com

This edition first published in UK and USA 2012
by ANTHEM PRESS
75-76 Blackfriars Road, London SE1 8HA, UK
or PO Box 9779, London SW19 7ZG, UK
and
244 Madison Ave. #116, New York, NY 10016, USA

British Library Cataloguing-in-Publication Data
A catalogue record for this book is available from the British Library.

Library of Congress Cataloging-in-Publication Data
Tausch, Arno, 1951-
Globalization, the human condition, and sustainable development in
the Twenty-first century : cross-national perspectives and European
implications / Arno Tausch and Almas Heshmati.
p. cm.
Includes bibliographical references and index.
ISBN 978-0-85728-410-5 (hardback : alk. paper)
1. Globalization. 2. Sustainable development. 3. Poverty. 4.
European Union countries–Economic integration. 5. European Union
countries–Economic policy. I. Heshmati, Almas. II. Title.
HF1365.T38 2012
337–dc23
2012007077

ISBN-13: 978 0 85728 410 5 (Hbk)
ISBN-10: 0 85728 410 X (Hbk)

This title is also available as an eBook.

In memory of the Austrian political economist Kurt W. Rothschild,
21 October 1914 – 15 November 2010

CONTENTS

Appendices

Let me start by saying that for Europe openness is a 'congenital condition'. For Europe, openness is like breathing. It has been an integral part of our values since the beginning. Fifty years ago the Treaty of Rome foresaw an open market and an area of freedoms which have expanded enormously over time. Today, the four freedoms of movement in the single market are deeply rooted in the life of our continent and its citizens.

—*José Manuel Durão Barroso, President of the European Commission, from 'Europe: An open society in a globalised world', International Forum 'The economy and the open society', Milan, 8 May 2007*[1]

'Nobody can fall in love with the single market,' Jacques Delors used to say. That the single market is not loved is normal and even reassuring. A market is an instrument, not an end in itself. When the market is regarded as a superior entity, as if it were always able to deliver efficiently and did not need appropriate regulation and rigorous supervision, dangers are likely to lie ahead, as shown by the financial crisis. It was forgotten by many that the market 'is a good servant but a bad master'. Yet the single market is a crucial servant for the European Union. First, it is a necessary – though not sufficient – condition for a good performance of the European economy, just as well-functioning domestic markets are for national economies. Secondly, and even more importantly, a robust single market is key to the overall health of the European Union, because it represents the very foundation of the integration project. But today the single market not only is not loved. It is seen by many Europeans – citizens as well as political leaders – with suspicion, fear and sometimes open hostility....

The single market and its four freedoms embodies an ideal: that of a space across national boundaries within which citizens can move, work, do research or start up a business without any discrimination. As the single market grew in scope and size, it was felt that this was not always the case. Market opening would widen the horizons for big business, but would not work for the many and the small: citizens, consumers, or SMEs. Surveys show that attitudes towards the single market today range from lack of interest to open rejection. In part, economic integration and its benefits have

---

1 Available at: http://europa.eu/rapid/pressReleasesAction.do?reference=SPEECH/07/293& format=HTML&aged=0&language=EN&guiLanguage=en (accessed 13 November 2011).

become business as usual and thus undervalued. Much of the disillusionment, however, comes from frustration with remaining barriers or the feeling of disempowerment that citizens experience when dealing with the single market.

—Mario Monti, 'A New Strategy for the Single Market: At the Service Of Europe's Economy and Society', report to the president of the European Commission José Manuel Barroso, 9 May 2010[2]

In the future days, which we seek to make secure, we look forward to a world founded upon four essential human freedoms. The first is freedom of speech and expression – everywhere in the world. The second is freedom of every person to worship God in his own way – everywhere in the world. The third is freedom from want – which, translated into world terms, means economic understandings which will secure to every nation a healthy peacetime life for its inhabitants – everywhere in the world. The fourth is freedom from fear – which, translated into world terms, means a world-wide reduction of armaments to such a point and in such a thorough fashion that no nation will be in a position to commit an act of physical aggression against any neighbour – anywhere in the world. That is no vision of a distant millennium. It is a definite basis for a kind of world attainable in our own time and generation. That kind of world is the very antithesis of the so-called new order of tyranny which the dictators seek to create with the crash of a bomb.

—President Franklin D. Roosevelt, excerpted from the State of the Union Address to the Congress, 6 January 1941

---

2 Available at: http://ec.europa.eu/internal_market/strategy/index_en.htm (accessed 13 November 2011).

LIST OF ABBREVIATIONS

CEE	Central and Eastern Europe
CO$_2$	Carbon dioxide
DYN	A measure of dynamic change over time
ELF85	Electoral fractionalization in 1985
EMU	European Monetary Union
EPI	Environmental Performance Index, developed by Columbia and Yale universities
ERT	European Roundtable of Industrialists
ESI	Environmental Sustainability Index, developed by Columbia and Yale universities
ETH Zurich	Swiss Federal Institute of Technology, Zurich
EU	European Union
EU-15	Refers to the 15 members of the European Union before the last round of EU extensions in 2004 and 2007: Austria, Belgium, Denmark, Finland, France, Germany, Greece, Ireland, Italy, Luxembourg, Netherlands, Portugal, Spain, Sweden and the United Kingdom.
EU-25	In 2004, the following 10 countries joined the European Union: Cyprus, Czech Republic, Estonia, Hungary, Latvia, Lithuania, Malta, Poland, Slovakia and Slovenia.
EU-27	Bulgaria and Romania were the last two countries to join the European Union.
EU-2020	European Union in the year 2020. According to the European Commission, the EU's growth strategy for the coming decade until the year 2020 is aimed at a smart, sustainable and inclusive economy.
euro	European currency
Euro-Lex	Internet information system on European Union law, organized by the European Commission
Eurostat	Official Statistics Office of the European Commission
F	A statistical test, mostly used in connection of 'F-test' and 'F-value' to evaluate the overall quality of statistical procedures, such as multiple regression, which explains variations in a dependent variable by one or several independent variables. The name was coined by George W. Snedecor, in honour of Sir Ronald A. Fisher. Fisher initially developed the statistic as the variance ratio in the 1920s.

FDI	Foreign direct investment
FPZ	Free production zones
GDP	Gross domestic product
GLI	Global Lisbon Index
GNP	Gross national product
HDI	Human Development Index, developed by the UNDP
HDR	*Human Development Report*, an annual survey on the state of human development and the Human Development Index, published by the UNDP
HPI	Happy Planet Index
HLY	Happy life years
IBM	International Business Machines (IBM), a multinational technology and consulting firm headquartered in Armonk, New York
IHT	*International Herald Tribune* (newspaper)
ILO	International Labour Organization
IMF	International Monetary Fund
ISI Web of Knowledge	A bibliographical database run by the Institute for the Study of Scientific Information It exists as an online academic citation index provided by the company Thomson Reuters, and is nowadays also increasingly referred to by the term 'Web of Science'.
KOF	Business cycle research institute at **ETH Zurich**
ln	Natural logarithm
MILEX	Military expenditure per GDP
MNC	Multinational corporations, mostly used in connection with MNC outward investments (stock) per GDP
MNC PEN	Stock of inward FDI per GDP, a measure of the penetration of a country by multinational corporations
MPR	Military personnel rate
NIDL	New International Division of Labour
NUTS	Nomenclature of territorial units for statistics, or nomenclature of units for territorial statistics (European Union)
OECD	Organisation for Economic Co-operation and Development, an international economic organization of 34 countries founded in 1958
OIC	Organisation of Islamic Cooperation (OIC). It currently has 57 member states, and changed its name from the Organisation of the Islamic Conference on 28 June 2011.
OMC	Open method of coordination (of policies in the European Union)
R&D	Research and development expenditures
SAR	Special administrative regions (SARs) of the People's Republic of China (PRC), comprising Hong Kong and Macau
SPSS	A computer program used for statistical analysis. It now belongs to the computer company **IBM**.

t-test	A statistical hypothesis test, used, among others, to measure whether the individual coefficients contributing to slope of a regression line differs significantly from 0
UN	United Nations
UNCTAD	United Nations Conference on Trade and Development (UNCTAD)
UNDP	United Nations Development Programme (UNDP), the United Nations' global development network
UNIDO	United Nations Industrial Development Organization (UNIDO)
USSR	Soviet Union (1922–1991)
UTIP	University of Texas Inequality Project
WVS	World Values Survey of the University of Michigan

GLOSSARY OF KEY TERMS

Absolute latitude. Absolute latitude is the absolute geographical position of a country, away from the earth's equator.

Annual population growth rate. The annual population growth rate (1975–2005) as a percentage measures long-term population growth since the mid-1970s.

At-risk-of-poverty rate (Eurostat indicator). The at-risk-of-poverty rate is the share of people with an equivalized disposable income (after social transfer) below the at-risk-of-poverty threshold, which in the European Union is set at 60 per cent of the national median (equivalized disposable) income after social transfers and taxes.

Avoiding net trade of ecological footprint gha per person. This measures the degree of independence (as a desirable status) a nation has from the international footprint trade, be it on the giving or on the receiving end.

Bretton Woods institutions. From 1 to 22 July 1944, 730 delegates from 44 Allied nations gathered at the Mount Washington Hotel in Bretton Woods, New Hampshire, USA, to draw up the postwar monetary and financial global order after World War II. The agreements signed set up the International Bank for Reconstruction and Development (IBRD), the General Agreement on Tariffs and Trade (GATT) and the International Monetary Fund (IMF).

Brussels/Paris/Washington Consensus. This is sometimes also called the 'Brussels/Frankfurt/Washington Consensus'. Globalization critics and sceptics of European integration maintain that the **Washington Consensus** has now also become the main policy goal of the European Union (seated in Brussels), the Organisation of Economic Co-operation and Development (seated in Paris) and the European Central Bank (seated in Frankfurt) –hence together they now make up the 'Brussels/Paris/Frankfurt/Washington Consensus'.

Business investment (Eurostat indicator). Business investment is gross fixed capital formation by the private sector as a percentage of GDP and is a Eurostat indicator for the EU Lisbon Strategy (= '14 structural indicators'). This indicator is defined as total gross fixed capital formation (GFCF) expressed as a percentage of GDP, for the private sector.

Carbon emissions per capita (from ESI). This measures metric tons of carbon emissions per capita, and is based in turn on United Nations Statistics Division's Millennium Indicator Database.

Carbon emissions per million US dollars GDP (from ESI). This indicator measures metric tons of carbon emissions per million US dollars, in constant 1995 US dollars.

Civil and political liberties violations index, 2003 (from ESI). This index measures the average of political and civil liberties indices, each ranging from 1 (high levels of liberties) to 7 (low levels of liberties) and is based on the US-based social science think-tank Freedom House. Each country and territory was awarded from 0 to 4 raw points for each of 10 questions grouped into three subcategories in a political rights checklist, and for each of 15 questions grouped into four subcategories in a civil liberties checklist. The total raw points in each checklist correspond to two final numerical ratings of 1 to 7. These two ratings are then averaged to determine a status category of 'Free', 'Partly Free', or 'Not Free'.

Combined development indicator. In this work, this term – sometimes also called the **single development indicator,** or **combined, final EU-2020 development index**, or **overall development index** (for 176 countries), or **global development index** – refers to our index of democracy, economic growth, environment, gender, human development, R&D, and social cohesion. The performances of all the countries of our investigation for all the dependent variables were standardized along a scale, ranging from 0 to 1. Zero is the worst, and 1 is the best in terms of performance. High numerical values for the following items constitute a development debacle: Combined Failed States Index; civil and political liberty violations; ecological footprint (gha per capita); infant mortality (2005); the quintile share income difference between richest and poorest 20 per cent; the unemployment rate; ln (number of people per million inhabitants 1980–2000 killed by natural disasters per year + 1); carbon emissions per million US dollars GDP; and carbon emissions per capita. High numerical values for the other indicators (10–35) are a blessing. The components of this overall development index are:

1. Combined Failed States Index
2. Civil and political liberty violations
3. Ecological footprint (gha per capita)
4. Infant mortality (2005)
5. Quintile share income difference between richest and poorest 20%
6. Unemployment rate
7. ln (number of people per million inhabitants 1980–2000 killed by natural disasters per year + 1)
8. Carbon emissions per million US dollars GDP
9. Carbon emissions per capita
10. Closing economic gender gap
11. Closing educational gender gap

12. Closing health and survival gender gap
13. Closing of global gender gap overall score 2009
14. Closing political gender gap
15. Corruption avoidance measure
16. Country share in top world 500 universities
17. Crisis Performance Factor
18. Democracy measure
19. Economic growth, IMF predicted growth rate in 2009
20. Economic growth, IMF predicted growth rate in 2010
21. Economic growth in real terms per capita per annum, 1990–2005
22. Environmental Performance Index (EPI)
23. Environmental Sustainability Index (ESI)
24. Female survival, probability of surviving to age 65
25. Gender empowerment index value
26. Global tolerance index
27. Happy life years
28. Happy Planet Index (HPI)
29. Human Development Index (HDI) value 2004
30. Life expectancy (years)
31. Life satisfaction (0–10)
32. Per capita world-class universities
33. Rule of law
34. Tertiary enrolment
35. Avoiding net trade of ecological footprint gha per person

Combined Failed States Index (Fund for Peace). The index is a combined measure of 12 critical phenomena, ranging from the delegitimization of the state to uneven economic development. The higher the numerical value, the greater is the danger of combined state failure.

Comparative price levels (US = 1.00). These were calculated from the UNDP *Human Development Report 2000*. The GDP at current international exchange rate is simply divided by the GDP at real purchasing power parity for each country of the world. The USA is the international standard, with the US achieving the value of 1.0. For **Eurostat**, comparative price levels are comparative levels of final consumption by private households including indirect taxes (EU-27 = 100). If the index of the comparative price levels shown for a country is higher or lower than 100, the country concerned is relatively expensive or cheap as compared with the EU average. Dependency theories and world-systems theories assume that low comparative price levels are an indicator of 'unequal exchange' between the countries of the centre and the periphery and that comparative price levels should be high, while neoliberal theories and the European Commission aim at low comparative price levels (low comparative price levels as an indicator of economic reform) .

Correlation coefficient. A correlation coefficient ranges from -1 to 1 and measures the relationship between two variables (linear relationship).

Corruption avoidance measure (from ESI). This index, measured for the year 2002, is based on a standardized scale (a so-called z-score), with high scores corresponding to effective control of corruption, and is based on figures from the World Bank. It is based on multi-pronged, experiential surveys of households, firms and public officials, which were used to measure social and economic costs of corruption. The quality of public service delivery, business, environmental, and public sector vulnerability were also examined, and the indicators on institutions, expenditure flows, and procurement were then added to yield the standardized score.

Council of the European Union. The Council of the European Union (Council of Ministers) is the European Union's main decision-making body. Its meetings are attended by member state ministers, and it is thus the institution which represents the member states. The council's headquarters are in Brussels, but some of its meetings are held in Luxembourg. Sessions of the council are convened by the rotating EU presidency, which sets the agenda. The council meets in different configurations (nine in all), bringing together the competent member state ministers: general affairs and external relations; economic and financial affairs; employment, social policy, health and consumer affairs; competitiveness; cooperation in the fields of justice and home affairs (JHA); transport, telecommunications and energy; agriculture and fisheries; environment; education, youth and culture. Each country of the European Union presides over the council for six months, by rotation. Decisions are prepared by the Committee of Permanent Representatives of the member states (Coreper), assisted by working groups of national government officials. The council, together with the European Parliament, acts in a legislative and budgetary capacity.

Country share in top world 500 universities. This is based on the University of Shanghai's world university rankings; the *Academic Ranking of World Universities* is compiled by Shanghai Jiao Tong University. It is one of the two most prominent world university rankings in the world, along with the *Times Higher Education World University Rankings*. The ranking compared 1,200 higher education institutions worldwide according to a formula that took into account alumni winning Nobel Prizes and Fields Medals (10 per cent), staff winning Nobel Prizes and Fields Medals (20 per cent), highly cited researchers in 21 broad subject categories (20 per cent), articles published in *Nature* and *Science* (20 per cent), the Science Citation Index and Social Sciences Citation Index (20 per cent), and the per capita academic performance (on the indicators above) of an institution (10 per cent).

Crisis Performance Factor. This was calculated from IMF and UNDP data. The idea was to develop a measure of the resilience of economic growth in the current world recession. It is based on the following: (1) the IMF predicted growth rate in 2009 (issued April 2009); (2) the IMF predicted growth rate in 2010 (issued April 2009); (3) residual measure, the crisis recovery of 2010 vis-à-vis 2009 (based on IMF prognosis, April 2009); and (4) the resilience of economic growth during the crisis (regression residuals: UNDP documented economic growth 1990–2005 led to the growth of 2009, based on IMF prognosis in April 2009). All four indicators were transformed according to the UNDP methodology, with the best country value scoring 1.0, and the worst country value scoring 0.0.

Democracy measure (from ESI). This index is based on the averages of 1993–2002 from the Polity IV Project of the University of Maryland. The Index is based on the trend-adjusted 10-year average score with high values corresponding to high levels of democratic institutions. The averages of the Polity IV scores for 10 years between 1993 and 2002 were adjusted for trend: if the trend was positive, the average was increased by 1, if the trend was negative, the average was reduced by 1. The purpose of the adjustment was to reward improvements.

Dependency theory. Dependency theory maintains that ever since the capitalist world system evolved (by around the discovery of the Americas in 1492 at the latest), there has been a stark distinction between the nations of the centre and the nations of the periphery.

Disaster risk (from UNDP, 2004). This indicator is based on the single, combined overall UNDP Disaster Risk Index. The UNDP disaster indicator measures the number of people per a million inhabitants (1980–2000) who were killed by cyclones, droughts, earthquakes, and floods. The formula used was the number of people per million inhabitants between 1980 and 2000 who were killed by natural disasters each year (+ 1 for logarithmic transformation).

Dispersion of regional employment rates by gender (Eurostat indicator). This is defined as the coefficient of variation of employment rates (of the age group 15–64) across regions (NUTS Level 2) within countries. It is a Eurostat indicator for the EU Lisbon Strategy (= '14 structural indicators'). The dispersion of regional (NUTS Level 2) employment rates of the age group 15–64 shows the regional differences in employment within countries and groups of countries (EU-25, euro area). The employment rate of the age group 15–64 represents employed persons aged 15–64 as a percentage of the population of the same age group.

Early leavers from education and training by gender (Eurostat indicator). This indicator is used by Eurostat as an indicator for the EU-2020 strategy. It measures early leavers from education and training by gender – as a percentage of the population aged 18–24 with at most lower secondary education and not in further education or training.

Ecological footprint (gha/cap) (from Happy Planet Index website). The measure was developed by the ecologists Mathis Wackernagel and William Rees, and championed by a range of organizations including the Global Footprint Network and the World Wide Fund for Nature (WWF). The ecological footprint of an individual is a measure of the amount of land required to provide for all their resource requirements plus the amount of vegetated land required to sequester (absorb) all of their CO_2 emissions and the CO_2 emissions embodied in the products they consume. This figure is expressed in units of 'global hectares'. The advantage of this approach is that it is possible to estimate the total amount of productive hectares available on the planet. Dividing this by the world's total population, we can calculate a global per capita figure on the basis that everyone is entitled to the same amount of the planet's natural resources. Using the latest footprint methodology, the figure is 2.1 global hectares. This implies that a person using up to 2.1 global hectares is, in these terms at least, using their fair share of the world's resources. In 2005, the per capita footprint for the rich OECD nations was 6.0 global hectares.

Economic freedom (score for 2000). This is the key international indicator for economic liberalism and was published, amongst others, by the Heritage Foundation, the CATO Institute and other leading global liberal think-tanks. The basic assumption of the indicator is that economic freedom is the fundamental right of every human to control his or her own labour and property. In an economically free society, the assumption is that individuals are free to work, produce, consume, and invest in any way they please, with that freedom both protected and unconstrained by the state. In economically free societies, the root assumption is that governments allow labour, capital and goods to move freely, and refrain from coercion or constraint of liberty beyond the extent necessary to protect and maintain liberty itself. The index measures ten components of economic freedom, assigning a grade in each using a scale from 0 to 100, where 100 represents the maximum freedom. The ten component scores are then averaged to give an overall economic freedom score for each country. The ten components of economic freedom are: business freedom, trade freedom, fiscal freedom, government spending, monetary freedom, investment freedom, financial freedom, property rights, freedom from corruption, and labour freedom. We time-lagged the index somewhat to allow the study of the more long-term effects.

Economic growth, IMF predicted growth rate in 2009. Since autumn 2008, the world economy faces the deepest recession since the 1930s. For this reason, data, estimates or even qualified and well-being based international predictions on the comparative impact of the recession on the countries of the world are enormously important for a world-system analysis of the dynamics of the global crisis.

Economic growth, IMF predicted growth rate in 2010 (see above). The data refer to the year 2010, and is based on well-informed predictions, published by the statistical services of the IMF.

Economic growth in real terms per capita per annum, 1990–2005 (UNDP). These figures about economic growth per capita in real terms from UNDP sources refer to the 'heyday' of the 'Clinton boom' years and the onset of a decline-phase (B-phase) in the world economic cycle. The UNDP *HDR 2007–8* were available for a free Excel format download from the UNDP HDR website, and are based on relevant World Bank figures in turn.

Employment rate by gender, age group 20–64 (Eurostat indicator). This is a Eurostat indicator for the EU-2020 strategy. The employment rate is calculated by dividing the number of persons aged 20 to 64 in employment by the total population of the same age group. The indicator is based on the EU Labour Force Survey.

Employment rate of older workers by gender (Eurostat indicator). This is a Eurostat indicator for the EU Lisbon Strategy (= '14 structural indicators'). The employment rate of older workers is calculated by dividing the number of persons aged 55 to 64 in employment by the total population of the same age group. The indicator is based on the EU Labour Force Survey.

Energy intensity of the economy (Eurostat indicator). This measures the gross inland consumption of energy divided by GDP (kilogram of oil equivalent per 1,000 euro gross domestic product (GDP) for a given calendar year. It measures thus the overall energy efficiency.

Environmental Performance Index, 2008 (EPI) (Columbia/Yale EPI Project). The EPI focuses on two objectives: (1) reducing environmental stresses on human health; and (2) promoting ecosystem vitality and sound natural resource management. These broad goals reflect the policy priorities of environmental authorities around the world as well as the environmental dimension of the Millennium Development Goals (MDGs). Success in meeting these objectives is measured by 25 indicators in six policy categories. The 2008 EPI deploys a proximity-to-target methodology. By identifying specific targets and measuring the distance between the target and current results, the EPI provides an empirical foundation for policy benchmarking and a context for evaluating national performance.

Environmental Sustainability Index (ESI). The 2005 Environmental Sustainability Index (ESI) benchmarks the ability of nations to protect the environment over the next several decades. It does so by integrating 76 data sets – tracking natural resource endowments, past and present pollution levels, environmental management efforts, and a society's capacity to improve its environmental performance – into 21 indicators of environmental sustainability. These indicators permit comparison across the following five fundamental components of sustainability: environmental systems; environmental stresses; human vulnerability to environmental stresses; societal capacity to respond to environmental challenges; and global stewardship.

EU-2020 strategy. The European Commission sets out a vision of 'Europe's social market economy' for the twenty-first century. The strategy intends to show how the EU can 'come out stronger from the (current world economic) crisis and how it can be turned into a smart, sustainable and inclusive economy delivering high levels of employment, productivity and social cohesion' (http://ec.europa. eu/eu2020/index_en.htm). The strategy rests on five pillars – social security, labour, education, research and development, and environmental protection.

European Commission. Established by the Treaty of Rome in 1957, the European Commission comprises of 27 commissioners since the accession of Bulgaria and Romania on 1 January 2007. Its main function is to propose and implement the European Community policies adopted by the European Council and the European Parliament. It acts in the general interest of the EU with complete independence from national governments. It enjoys a quasi-exclusive right of initiative in matters where the European Community method applies (matters where member states have transferred a significant part of their responsibilities, such as the Common Agricultural Policy, the Customs Union, the internal market, the euro, etc.). The Lisbon Treaty brings forth to the community issues relating to justice and internal affairs and assigns the European Commission a right of initiative in these areas, which it shares with member states. As 'guardian of the treaties', the European Commission oversees the application of EU law under the control of the Court of Justice of the European Union. It executes the budget and manages the programmes. It exercises coordinating, executive and management functions, as laid down in the treaties. With the exception of the Common Foreign and Security Policy, and other cases provided for in the treaties, it also ensures the EU's external representation. It initiates the EU's annual and multiannual programming with a view to achieving inter-institutional agreements. The European Commission is appointed for a five-year term by the European Council acting by qualified majority in agreement with the member states. It is subject to a vote of appointment by the European Parliament, to which it is answerable. The commissioners are assisted by an administration made up of directorates-general and specialized departments, whose staff are divided mainly between Brussels and Luxembourg.

European Council. With the entry into force of the Treaty of Lisbon, the European Council became one of the European Union institutions. Comprising of the heads of state or government of the member states, it meets at least four times a year and includes the president of the European Commission as a full member. It elects its president for a period of two and a half years. The role of the European Council is to provide the European Union with the necessary impetus for its development and to define the general political guidelines (Article 15 of the Treaty on European Union – the TEU). It does not exercise any legislative function. However, the Treaty of Lisbon provides the option for the European Council to be consulted on criminal matters (Articles 82 and 83 of the Treaty on the Functioning of the European Union) or on social security matters (Article 48 of the TFEU), in cases where a state opposes a legislative proposal in these areas. Decisions are taken following negotiations between member states during European summits. The outcomes of European Council proceedings are recorded in conclusions published after each meeting. An extraordinary meeting can be held whenever necessary.

Eurostat. Official Statistics Office of the **European Commission**.

Failed States Index. The US think-tank Fund for Peace and *Foreign Policy* magazine publish an annual 'Failed States Index'. For each component indicator, the ratings are placed on a scale of 0 to 10, with 0 being the lowest intensity (most stable) and 10 being the highest intensity (least stable). The total score is the sum of the 12 indicators and is on a scale of 0–120. The index combines demographic pressures, massive movement of refugees and internally displaced peoples, the legacy of vengeance-seeking group grievance, chronic and sustained human flight, uneven economic development along group lines, sharp and/or severe economic decline, criminalization and/or delegitimization of the state, progressive deterioration of public services, widespread violation of human rights, security apparatus as a 'state within a state', rise of factionalized elites, intervention of other states or external factors. Scandinavia, Ireland, Switzerland, Australia and New Zealand were the world's most stable countries in 2010 (http://www.foreignpolicy.com/articles/2010/06/21/2010_failed_states_index_interactive_map_and_rankings – accessed 18 November 2011). Also known as the **Combined Failed States Index**.

Female survival, probability of surviving to age 65 (UNDP). These data refer to the period 2000 to 2005 and was taken from the UNDP's statistics facility website from the UNDP *HDR 2007–8* data set. The data measured the percentage probability at birth of a woman surviving to age 65. The probability of a newborn infant surviving to the specified age is subject to the prevailing patterns of age-specific mortality rates.

Foreign savings rate. This was calculated from the UNDP *Human Development Report 2000* for the year 1998. We time-lagged the indicator to evaluate the more long-term effects of the variable. For dependency authors, especially Paul Israel Singer, foreign savings rates show the weight that foreign savings, mostly from the global centres and richer semi-peripheries, have in the accumulation process of the host countries in the periphery and semi-periphery. It is calculated by the difference between the share of investments per GDP and the share of savings per GDP.

Free production zones (FPZ). Employment as a percentage of the total population is the indicator best suited to measure the effects of the 'NIDL' (New International Division of Labour). An important sub-school of dependency and world-systems research, most prominently represented by Froebel,

Heinrichs and Kreye (1980), predicted the unfettered rise of the model of 'export processing zones', especially in China and Southeast Asia. More recent studies highlighted the fact that these export processing zones (EPZ) – or 'free production zones' already account for some 80 per cent of the merchandise exports of countries like China, Kenya, the Philippines, Malaysia, Mauritius, Mexico, Senegal, Tunisia, Vietnam. Sixty-six million people are now employed in 3,500 EPZs in 130 countries of the world, 40 million of whom are employed in China.

GDP per capita. Its square was time-lagged and calculated from the UNDP *Human Development Report 2000* for the year 1998. This double logarithmic formulation is a classic in transnational comparative development research, and captures best the theoretical concepts of non-linear progressing development, applied to phenomena of inequality, economic growth and the environment. We introduced such a double logarithmical formulation for all multiple regression equations of this book.

GDP per capita in PPS (Eurostat indicator). This is GDP per capita in purchasing power standards (PPS) (EU-27 = 100). This is a Eurostat indicator for the EU Lisbon Strategy (= '14 structural indicators'). The volume index of GDP per capita in purchasing power standards (PPS) is expressed in relation to the European Union (EU-27) average set to equal 100.

Gender Empowerment Measure (GEM). This is a composite UNDP indicator that captures gender inequality in three key areas: the extent of women's political participation and decision making, economic participation and decision-making power, and the power exerted by women over economic resources. In the calculation of the index, female and male shares of parliamentary seats (first component), female and male shares of positions as legislators, senior officials and managers (the first half of the second component) and female and male shares of professional and technical positions (the second half of the third component) and female estimated earned real income expressed in international purchasing power parities (the third component) enter into the calculation.

Global tolerance index. This index is based on data from the World Values Survey (WVS). To assess the totality of tolerance in Europe and in the world, we propose to construct a non-parametric index of 'global tolerance', which combines the following WVS data with sufficient availability on the percentages per total population overcoming xenophobia and racism. More specifically, five population shares are taken account of: (1) people who are tolerant of neighbours of a different race; (2) people considering tolerance and respect for other people as important qualities; (3) people not saying men should have more right to a job than women; (4) people tolerant of immigrants and foreign workers as neighbours; and (v) people tolerant of homosexual neighbours. The country values are projected onto a scale from 0 to 1, with 0 representing the least tolerant countries and 1 representing the most tolerant countries, according to standard UNDP methodology. See also: A. Tausch, 'Towards an Index of Global Tolerance: A quantitative analysis, based on the "World Values Survey" data'. *Islamic Perspective* 4 (2010): 263–79, available at: http://iranianstudies.org/journals/islamic-perspective-journal-number-4-2010/ (accessed 18 November 2011).

Greenhouse gas emissions, base year 1990 (Eurostat indicator). This is a Eurostat indicator for the EU-2020 strategy. For greenhouse gas emissions, the base year is 1990. This indicator shows trends in the total volume of man-made emissions of the 'Kyoto basket' of greenhouse gases. It presents the total annual emissions in relation to the 1990 emissions. The 'Kyoto basket' of greenhouse gases includes: carbon dioxide (CO_2) methane (CH_4), nitrous oxide (N_2O), and the so-called F-gases (sulphur hexafluoride (SF_6), hydrofluorocarbons and perfluorocarbons). These gases are aggregated into a single unit using gas-specific global warming potential (GWP) factors. The aggregated greenhouse gas emissions are expressed in units of CO_2 equivalents. The indicator does not include emissions and removals related to land use, land-use change and forestry (LULUCF); nor does it include emissions from international aviation and international maritime transport. CO_2 emissions from biomass with energy recovery are reported as a memorandum item according to UNFCCC guidelines and are not included in national greenhouse gas totals.

Gross domestic expenditure on R&D (GERD) (Eurostat indicator). This is a Eurostat indicator for the EU-2020 strategy. The indicator provided is GERD (gross domestic expenditure on R&D) as a percentage of GDP).

Growth of MNC penetration over time. The dynamic effects of multinational corporations penetration (DYN MNC PEN) from 1995 to 2005 is based on UNCTAD sources. Several global sociologists, such as Volker Bornschier and associated authors, expected short-term dynamic effects from such increases of MNC penetration.

Happy life years (HLY) (from Happy Planet Index). The Happy Planet Index Organization used data from the life satisfaction question: 'All things considered, how satisfied are you with your life as a whole these days?' Responses were made on a numeric scales from 0 to 10, where 0 is dissatisfied and 10 is satisfied. In HPI 2.0, the HPI Organization takes advantage of new data collected by Gallup. Gallup's world poll has, in the last two years, included a question on life satisfaction, which has been asked in the 112 countries included. Gallup's intention is to continue polling the countries of the world on a regular basis so as to monitor how life develops. To augment these 112 countries, the authors also included data from the two most recent waves of the World Values Survey (WVS, from 2000 and 2005). This survey asks the exact same question regarding life satisfaction, albeit with a slightly different response scale (1–10 as opposed to 0–10). The two waves cover

84 countries. HPI used well-documented econometric and polito-metric methods to augment the database where Gallup public opinion survey data were missing and where World Values Survey data were available.

Happy Planet Index (HPI). The HPI is a measure that shows the ecological efficiency with which a human well-being is delivered around the world. It is the first ever index to combine environmental impact with well-being to measure the environmental efficiency (country by country) of people's lives. It shows the relative efficiency with which nations convert the planet's natural resources (footprint per capita) into long and happy lives for their citizens. The nations that top the index aren't the happiest places in the world, but the nations that score well show that achieving long, happy lives without overstretching the planet's resources is possible.

Human Development Index (HDI) value 2004 (UNDP). The data were taken from the UNDP's statistics facility website, and the data are from the UNDP *HDR 2006* data set. The HDI sets a minimum and a maximum for each dimension, called goalposts, and then shows where each country stands in relation to these goalposts, expressed as a value between 0 and 1. The educational component of the HDI is comprised of adult literacy rates and the combined gross enrolment ratio for primary, secondary and tertiary schooling, weighted to give adult literacy more significance in the statistic. Since the minimum adult literacy rate is 0 per cent and the maximum is 100 per cent, the literacy component of knowledge for a country where the literacy rate is 75 per cent would be 0.75; the statistic for combined gross enrolment is calculated in an analogous manner. The life expectancy component of the HDI is calculated using a minimum value for life expectancy of 25 years and maximum value of 85 years, so the longevity component for a country where life expectancy is 55 years would be 0.55. For the wealth component, the goalpost for minimum income is $100 (PPP) and the maximum is $40,000 (PPP). The HDI uses the logarithm of income to reflect the diminishing importance of income with increasing GDP. The scores for the three HDI components are then averaged in an overall human development index.

Immigration – share of population (2005). The data for this percentage were also directly taken from the UNDP *HDR 2009* statistics facility.

Infant mortality (2005) (UNDP). Infant mortality rates are calculated per 1,000 live births. Data were taken from the UNDP's statistics facility on the internet, and is from the UNDP *HDR 2007–8* edition.

Kuznets curve. Economics Nobel laureate Simon Smith Kuznets (1901–1985) ventured the hypothesis that along the path of development, a nation will experience first a rising, and later a falling rate of economic inequalities.

Labour productivity per person employed (Eurostat indicator). Labour productivity per person employed is the GDP in purchasing power standards

(PPS) per person employed relative to the EU-27 (EU-27 = 100). It is a Eurostat indicator for the EU Lisbon Strategy (= '14 structural indicators'). GDP per person employed is intended to give an overall impression of the productivity of national economies expressed in relation to the European Union (EU-27) average. If the index of a country is higher than 100, this country's level of GDP per person employed is higher than the EU average and vice versa.

Life expectancy (years) (Happy Planet Index). We used the HPI data series for life expectancy. Average life expectancy at birth was taken by the HPI Organization from the 2007–8 UNDP *Human Development Report*, which provides figures for the year 2005.

Life satisfaction (0–10) (Happy Planet Index). See **Happy life years.**

Long-term unemployment rate by gender (Eurostat indicator). This figure is the number of long-term unemployed (for 12 months or more) as a percentage of the total active population. It is a Eurostat indicator for the EU Lisbon Strategy (= '14 structural indicators'). Long-term unemployed persons are those aged 15 or over not living in collective households who are without work for the next two weeks but are available to start work within the next two weeks and who are actively seeking work (i.e. have actively sought employment at some time during the previous four weeks or are not seeking a job because they have already found a job to start at a later date). The total active population (labour force) is the total number of the employed and unemployed population. The duration of unemployment is defined as the duration of the search for a job or as the length of the period since an individual's last job was held (if this period is shorter than the duration of the search for a job).

Matthew effect. Most economists assume that economic growth at middle-income levels is most rapid. There is a well-established tradition to control for these effects by introducing a double-logarithmic function (ln GDP per capita) in all cross-national multiple regression equations, explaining economic growth rates. This curve-linear function of growth, being regressed on the natural logarithm of development level and its square, is sometimes called the 'Matthew effect', following Matthew 13:12 in the Bible: 'For whosoever hath, to him shall be given, and he shall have more abundance: but whosoever hath not, from him shall be taken away even that he hath.'

Membership of the Islamic Conference. This is a very clear and simple measurement concept for the hypothesis by the US political scientist Samuel P. Huntington (1927–2008) that – *inter alia* – Islam will be a development blockade in the twenty-first century. Our indicator is simply a dummy-variable (1 for membership, 0 for non-membership), based on the website of the Organisation of the Islamic Conference (2009).

Military expenditures per GDP. These were taken from the UNDP Human Development Report Office Statistics facility, *HDR 2007–8*, and were time-lagged to take into account the very long-term effects of military spending rates. The time-point chosen was the beginning of the 1990s.

Military personnel rate. This measures a country's army personnel per 1,000 population, and due to the skewness of the indicator, there is a strong and well-founded research tradition, founded by the eminent German sociologist Erich Weede, to calculate the natural logarithm of the original number plus the number 1 ($\ln(MPR + 1)$). The statistical source of our data were the official website of the US Central Intelligence Agency. The data refer to the first decade of the new millennium.

MNC headquarter status (MNC HEADQU). This was measured in our analysis by the time-lagged indicator MNC outward investments (stock) per GDP by around 1995. It is thus an indicator of the power or weakness of the 'national' capital in question on the world markets. Bornschier and his school expected that a high headquarter status mitigates against the long-term negative effects of MNC penetration (the value of the stock of cumulated foreign direct investment per GDP of the host country).

MNC penetration (MNC PEN). This is the key variable of most quantitative dependency and world-systems theories, and it measures the weight that cumulated foreign capital investments had in the host countries, i.e. the percentages of the cumulated stocks of multinational corporation investments per total host country GDP. We time-lagged our indicator and used the values for the year 1995, to take the long-term societal consequences of foreign direct investment penetration into account. The Swiss sociologist Volker Bornschier and his school predicted a strong long-term negative determination of development by a high MNC penetration, due to the negative consequences that monopolies have on the long-term development trajectory of countries.

Multiple regression. See **Regression equation.**

Muslim population share per total population. This was taken from the University of Sydney's NationMaster statistics facility.

Net exports of ecological footprint gha per person (Global Footprint Network). The ecological footprint of consumption for a given country measures the bio-capacity demanded by the final consumption of all the residents of the country. In contrast, a country's primary production ecological footprint is the sum of the footprints for all resources harvested and all waste generated within a country's geographical borders. The difference between the production and consumption footprint is trade. In order to measure the footprint of imports and exports, one needs to know both the amounts traded as well as the embodied resources (including carbon dioxide emissions) in all categories. The embodied footprint is measured as the number of global hectares required to make a tonne per year of a given product. The footprint intensity of any primary product is by definition the same anywhere in the world since it is expressed in global hectares. However, the embodied footprint of secondary products will depend on transformation efficiencies ('extraction rates'), and these vary between countries. The National Footprint Accounts (2009 edition) track the embodied ecological footprint of over 700 categories of traded crop, forest, livestock and fish products. The embodied carbon dioxide emissions in 625 categories of product are used with trade flows from the United Nation's Comtrade database (UN Commodity Trade Statistics Database 2007) to calculate the embodied carbon footprint in traded goods. Throughout the National Footprint Accounts, the embodied footprint of trade is calculated assuming world average footprint intensities for all products. The differences between exports and imports for the ecological footprint gha per person are then the net exports of ecological footprint gha per person.

NUTS. Nomenclature of territorial units for statistics or nomenclature of units for territorial statistics is a geo-code standard for referencing the subdivisions of countries for statistical purposes. The standard is developed and regulated by the European Union, and thus only covers the member states of the EU in detail.

OMC. This stands for the open method of coordination of policies in the European Union. European decision makers hope that the OMC provides a new framework for cooperation between the member states, whose national policies can – they hope – thus be directed towards certain common objectives. Under this intergovernmental method, the member states are evaluated by one another (in Euro-speak: 'peer pressure'), with the European Commission's role being limited to surveillance. The European Parliament and the Court of Justice play virtually no part in the OMC process. The open method of coordination takes place in areas which fall within the competence of the member states, such as employment, social protection, social inclusion, education, youth and training. It is based principally on jointly identifying and defining the objectives to be achieved (adopted by the European Council); jointly establishing the measuring instruments (statistics, indicators, guidelines); benchmarking, i.e. comparison of the member states' performance and exchange of best practices (monitored by the European Commission). Depending on the areas concerned, the OMC involves so-called 'soft law' measures which are binding on the member states in varying degrees but which never take the form of directives, regulations or decisions. Thus, in the context of the Lisbon Strategy, the OMC required the member states to draw up national reform plans and to forward them to the European Commission.

Openness Index. This is time-lagged for the year 1990, and measures the very long-term, two-decade effects of export shares per GDP + import shares per GDP. It was taken from the UNDP Human Development Report Office statistics facility, *HDR 2007–8*. The countries with the greatest openness in 1990 were the small states and territories including Hong Kong, China (SAR),

Bahrain, Luxembourg, Malta, Antigua and Barbuda, Slovenia, Panama, Croatia, Swaziland and St. Lucia.

Partial correlation. This is the method used to describe the relationship between two variables while excluding the effects of another variable, or several other variables, on this relationship.

Per capita world-class universities. This is calculated from UNDP and University of Shanghai world university rankings. The indicator relates the figures, used in the country share in top world 500 universities (based on University of Shanghai world university rankings), to our UNDP figures about total population. The indicator is world-class universities per million inhabitants.

Persons at risk of poverty after social transfers (Eurostat indicator). This is a Eurostat indicator for the EU-2020 strategy.

Persons of the age 20 to 24 having completed at least upper secondary education by gender. This is a Eurostat indicator for the EU Lisbon Strategy (= '14 structural indicators'). It is the percentage of the population aged 20 to 24 who have completed at least secondary upper education by gender. The indicator is defined as the percentage of young people (of both genders) of the age bracket 20–24 years who have attained at least an upper secondary level education, i.e. with an education level ISCED 3a, 3b or 3c long minimum (numerator). The denominator consists of the total population of the same age group, excluding 'no' answers to the questions 'highest level of education or training attained'. Both the numerators and the denominators come from the EU Labour Force Survey (LFS).

Population at risk of poverty or exclusion (Eurostat indicator). This is one of Eurostat's measures of social cohesion. The Europe 2020 strategy promotes social inclusion, in particular through the reduction of poverty, by aiming to lift at least 20 million people out of the risk of poverty and exclusion. This indicator summarizes the number of people who are either at risk of poverty and/or are materially deprived and/or are living in households with very low work intensity. Persons who are at risk of poverty are persons with an equivalized disposable income that is below the risk of poverty threshold, which is set at 60 per cent of the national median equivalized disposable income (after social transfers). The Eurostat collection for 'material deprivation' covers indicators relating to economic strain, durables, housing, and environment of the dwelling. Severely materially deprived persons have living conditions severely constrained by a lack of resources, and experience at least four out of the nine following deprivations: they cannot afford (1) to pay rent or utility bills, (2) to keep their home adequately warm, (3) to face unexpected expenses, (4) to eat meat, fish or a protein equivalent every second day, (5) a week's holiday away from home, (6) a car, (7) a washing machine, (8) a colour TV, or (9) a telephone. People living in households with very low work intensity are people aged 0–59 living in households where the adults have worked less than 20 per cent of their total work potential during the past year.

Population at risk of poverty or exclusion – as a percentage and per 1,000 persons (Eurostat indicator). This is a Eurostat indicator for the EU-2020 strategy. This indicator summarizes the number of people who are either at risk of poverty and/or are materially deprived and/or are living in households with very low work intensity.

Population density. This was taken from the US CIA World Factbook. It measures population density per square kilometre by around the first decade in the new millennium.

Predictor variables. Suppose a public health researcher wants to study factors influencing the life expectancy of a population. He or she uses the quantity of alcohol and tobacco consumed, the daily amount of physical exercise, and the daily intake of vitamin C as the variables in the statistical (multiple regression) model. In this model, alcohol, tobacco, exercise and vitamin C are the predictors of life expectancy. The statistical analysis determines which of these factors wields a significant influence, and which of these factors does not contribute significantly to the explanation of life expectancy. The term 'multiple regression' applies to the linear prediction of one outcome from several predictors.

Principal components. Principal components analysis is a very common data reduction technique for selecting a subset of 'highly predictive' variables from a larger group of variables. For example, in order to select a sample of 50 development indicators, one could use this method to find a subset that gave the 'best overall summary' of the 50 indicators. There are many different mathematical methods to extract and calculate these components; the most common is the one, based on the correlations between the variables. The components then reproduce in a mathematically optimal way the underlying correlation matrix. Usual statistical software procedures, implemented at major universities and research centres around the world, offer standard procedures to calculate such components.

Public education expenditure per GDP. This, for the middle of the first decade of the new millennium, was taken from the UNDP's Human Development Report Office statistics facility on the internet (UNDP *HDR 2000*), and refers to the time-lagged data for 1995 to 1997 to measure the long-term effects of public education expenditures.

Quintile share income difference between richest and poorest 20 per cent (Eurostat indicator). The income quintile share ratio, or the S80/S20 ratio, is a measure of the inequality of income distribution. It is calculated as the ratio of total income received by the 20 per cent of the population with the highest income (the top quintile) to that received by the 20 per cent of the population with the lowest income (the bottom quintile). Our global data were taken from the UNDP's statistics facility on the internet, and refer to the UNDP HDR 2006. The data show the ratio of the income or expenditure share of the richest 20 per cent to that of the poorest 20 per cent, and are based on the relevant World Bank data.

Regression equation. A regression equation is the mathematical expression of the relationship between two (or more) variables. It indicates how well you can predict some variables based on the knowledge of other variables. A regression line represents the regression equation on a scatter plot. Multiple linear regression aims to find a linear relationship between a dependent variable and several predictor variables. The residual represents the unexplained variation in the dependent variable. Usual statistical software procedures, implemented at major universities and research centres around the world, offer standard procedures to calculate such equations.

Rule of law (2002) (from ESI). This index is based on a standardized score (z-score), where high values correspond to high degrees of rule of law. It is originally based on World Bank data. The rule of law is important in terms of establishing the 'rules of the game' for civil society, the private sector and the government; for ensuring that violations of environmental regulations are enforced; and for promoting stable expectations that facilitate long-range planning. The indicators measuring rule of law are defined as the extent to which agents have confidence in and abide by the rules of society. They are the perceptions of the incidence of crime, the effectiveness and predictability of the judiciary, and the enforceability of contracts.

Severely materially deprived persons (Eurostat indicator). This is a Eurostat indicator for the EU-2020 strategy.

Share of renewables in gross final energy consumption (Eurostat indicator). This is a Eurostat indicator for the EU-2020 strategy. It measures the share of renewable energy in gross final energy consumption as a percentage.

Share of women in government. At all levels this is one of the UNDP's long-term lead indicators of the institutionalization of political feminism. We time-lagged the variable and measured it circa 1998. It was documented in the UNDP *HDR 2000*. The idea of the indicator is to capture the real advance of women not only at the level of the top political administration of a given country, but also at the general level of the central government, i.e. taking the important decision-making ministerial bureaucracies into account as well.

Share of world population. This was calculated from UNDP *HDR 2007–8* statistics, and reflects the enormous differences in size of the nations of the earth, and the demographic weight of a nation in world society.

Social security expenditure per GDP. This is an average figure for the 1990s (International Labour Organization, ILO). The social security expenditure ratio is generally to be considered as the best single indicator of the existence of a tight social net.

Socio-liberal strategies. Since the 1990s, it has become common to talk about the combination of the goals of social equality and a market economy. The British Labour Party under the leadership of former PM Tony Blair was a political movement thought by many to be typical of that tendency. However, it has been shown in the literature (Tausch and Prager 1993) that the intellectual roots of attempts to combine social justice and a liberal society, which became very popular throughout the world in the 1990s, go back to the ideas of social democratic reformers in Europe in the 1920s and 1930s. In contrast to the social democratic movements of the 1990s, their ideas about the redistribution of wealth were more far-reaching.

Tertiary educational attainment by gender, age group 30–34 (Eurostat indicator). This is a Eurostat indicator for the EU-2020 strategy. It measures the share of the population aged 30–34 years who have successfully completed university or university-like (tertiary-level) education with an ISCED 1997 (International Standard Classification of Education) education level of 5–6.

Tertiary enrolment rate (from Nationmaster Sydney). Tertiary enrolment rate is the sum of all tertiary-level students enrolled at the start of the school year, expressed as a percentage of the mid-year population in the five-year age group after the official secondary school leaving age.

Time-lagged. In quantitative development analysis, it is often assumed that certain predictors have an effect on the dependent variable only after a certain time period. So, a public health researcher could test the effects of tobacco consumption on health, by relating life expectancy data to tobacco consumption ten or twenty years ago.

UNDP's Education Index. This is a compound measure of the performance of the education system within primary, secondary and tertiary level, measured for the middle of the new decade of the millennium, and taken from the UNDP *HDR 2007–8*. It is comprised of adult literacy rates and the combined gross enrolment ratio for primary, secondary and tertiary schooling, weighted to give adult literacy more significance in the statistic.

Unemployment rate (United Nations Statistics, data refer to around 2003/2004). The adult unemployment rate refers to the proportion of the adult (aged 15 years and older) labour force that is unemployed, unless otherwise specified. The unemployed are persons who are currently without work, who are currently available for work, and who are seeking or have sought work recently. The base for these statistics is the labour force (that is, the economically active portion of the population), not the total population.

Volume of freight transport relative to GDP (Eurostat indicator). This is an index of inland freight transport volume relative to GDP (2000 = 100). This was a Eurostat indicator for the EU Lisbon Strategy (= '14 structural indicators'). This Eurostat indicator is defined as the ratio between tonne-kilometres (inland modes) and GDP (chain-linked volumes, at the exchange rates of the year 2000). It is indexed on the year 2000. It includes transport by road, rail and inland waterways. Rail and inland waterways transport are based on movements on national territory, regardless of the nationality of the vehicle or vessel. Road transport is based on all movements of vehicles registered in the reporting country.

Washington Consensus. The term was coined in 1989 by the economist John Williamson to describe a set of ten relatively specific economic policy prescriptions that he considered constituted the 'standard' reform package promoted for developing countries by the two Washington DC–based Bretton Woods institutions – the IMF and the World Bank. The Washington Consensus recommends macroeconomic stabilization, economic opening with respect to both trade and investment, and the expansion of market forces within the domestic economy. The term is increasingly used to describe overall neoliberal policies.

Worker remittance inflows as a percentage of GDP. This was directly taken from the UNDP *HDR 2009* statistics facility.

World Economic Forum Gender Gap Indices (2007). These were designed to measure gender-based gaps in access to resources and opportunities in individual countries rather than the actual levels of the available resources and opportunities in those countries. The Global Gender Gap Report 2007 by the World Economic Forum measures the size of the gender gap in four critical areas of inequality between men and women: (1) economic participation and opportunity – outcomes on salaries, participation levels and access to high-skilled employment; (2) educational attainment – outcomes on access to basic and higher level education; (3) political empowerment – outcomes on representation in decision-making structures; (4) health and survival – outcomes on life expectancy and sex ratio.

FOREWORD

We are presently facing a multiple crisis. It features an economic and financial dimension, as well as ones dealing with climate change and the erosion of biodiversity, energy shortages and the volatility of basic-food prices, and political representation and integration. To deal with such a crisis successfully we need sophisticated analyses of the world we inhabit and the root causes of our present predicament.

We also need to consider dominant crisis diagnoses which might lead to false policies. However, they are quite powerful. There has been much talk about the 'return of the state' over the last three years. Politicians from the centre-right to the centre-left – accompanied by a handful of neoliberals – agree with the diagnosis that, while markets do essentially have certain positive effects, the markets have run out of control and must be now re-regulated in some form or other. Either the state or the intergovernmental system, like the EU, should be made responsible for the crisis. Most opinions regard the state as a more or less neutral actor that is responsible for the common good of society, and which deals with collective problems. According to this perspective, markets are rather unconnected to political power and authority; they are considered mainly as mechanisms of allocation which have become partially ineffective. This interpretation fails to take account of the way that the state has transformed itself over the last years and expedited the neoliberal metamorphosis of society.

What many analyses of the economic and financial crisis conveniently ignore is that we are dealing with a structural crisis with no clear outcome at present, even if many banks are managing to rake in large profits once more. What has become clear over the last two years is that powerful economic actors are able to prevent stricter political regulations.

The different dimensions of this multiple crisis have obviously diverging priorities. The climate crisis is highly politicized but almost nothing changes, whereas the financial crisis is dealt with by means of considerable public funding. My main point is that the interconnectedness of the various aspects is not seen. We need to understand in greater detail the dynamics that develop from the collision of the energy and climate crisis, the famines caused by the crisis of food provision, the crises in many regions of the world which result in forced migration, the crisis of representation and decision making which leads in many European countries to a strengthening of extreme right-wing political forces.

In order to comprehend the internal relationship between these crisis dimensions, we need to consider the following aspects contained in the dominant interpretations.

First, the current dynamic of this multiple crisis is the result of a neoliberal reconstruction of capitalism since the 1970s that affects not only worldwide economic relations but also politics, the environment and agriculture. The instruments designated to deal with the crisis are insufficient because they do not recognize the interconnected character of the crisis and its root causes, i.e. neoliberal politics. Secondly, the crisis is the expression of a socially problematic and environmentally disastrous mode of production and living. Mobility, meat consumption, and the use of electronic devices like mobile phones and personal computers are deeply inscribed in the everyday practices of production, distribution and consumption, and they are connected with dominant economic and political interests. This aspect goes beyond neoliberal politics. Thirdly, the assorted crisis dimensions are characterized by intense asynchronicity. The climate and energy crises are crises of industrial civilization. In other areas, such as economics and finance, the crises are a result of the ongoing process of neoliberal globalization which began 30 years ago and gained momentum after 1989. We still do not know if the economic crisis is more conjunctural or structural. Given the multiple and overlapping character of the crisis the assumption that we can counter the economic crisis with existing means would be wrong and would not be politically adequate. There is simply the danger that short-term dealing with the crisis will be at the expense of a deepening social and environmental crisis.

This study by Arno Tausch and Almas Heshmati should be read against this background. The title itself, 'Globalization, the Human Condition and Sustainable Development in the Twenty-first Century: Cross-national Perspectives and European Implications', indicates a multi-dimensional perspective. It deals with issues such as democracy, growth, environment, gender equality, human development, research and development, and social cohesion.

From the very beginning, the book's theoretical perspective – which focuses on a world-systems approach and dependency theory, though the authors refer also to Keynes and his successors – opens up a truly global perspective, i.e. it overcomes any Eurocentrism, and it avoids the naivety of a cosmopolitan view which usually denies that globalization has to do with power and interests, with polarization and exclusion, with structural and long-term problems which cannot be solved with short-term policies.

The study is full of important and well-sustained insights. I want to emphasize just a few, such as the important role of women in progressive politics when they are in positions of power, or the enormous implications that globalization, i.e. the deepening of the international division of labour, has for ecology. Moreover, the book is an excellent basis upon which to review some of the self-evident assumptions of critical research and action on globalization, especially with regard to thinking critically about what economic freedom means and is concretely about, and to consider the contradictory effects in international migration (termed the 'big unknown').

The book is full of lessons for policymakers, scholars and interested members of the public. Its overall 'message' is that the dominant pro-globalization strategy of the

European Commission, as well as the Lisbon Strategy and its successor, the EU-2020 strategy, is highly problematic.

In the field of scholarship, this book starts with the assumption that times of crisis are historical moments that demand 'reconsidering basic principles of economics and the social sciences'. This is true! However, I do not see such a reconsideration happening yet. This book, and many others, will contribute to a shifting ground in economics and the social sciences.

In January 2011, I was appointed as a member of the Enquete Commission of the German Bundestag on 'Growth, well-being and life-quality'. In the next 30 months, until summer 2013, we will have debates about concepts, strategies and practices around these themes, and we will develop scientifically grounded policy advice. This commission was established as a response to the crisis and the universalized impression prevailing among policymakers, business leaders, the media, civil society organizations and others that we should take the lesson of the crisis and related instabilities seriously. This book will equip me, and others, to argue that we need to go beyond the growth and competitiveness paradigm, first, in measuring wealth and development differently – this volume is full of alternative approaches – and secondly, in reorienting policies and social practices.

The insights of the book are not only important as such, but they are also a good basis for further studies. The comparative analysis of 175 nations emphasizes in a nuanced way the ambiguous effects of the manifold structures and processes of globalization. Starting from here, we also need insights into the complexity of transnational dynamics and social forces. The book focuses mainly and importantly on transnational economic dynamics, which are at the same time the result and condition for developments at the national level. This study gives us important insights into the strategies of the EU – the EU being its focus – and this might be complemented by other studies which reveal political developments beyond it.

I conclude this foreword by underlining that this study is not only an analytical one but one which takes a clear normative position: Europe needs to develop in a more social and environmentally sustainable direction. Arno Tausch und Almas Heshmati show convincingly that this is not just an attractive vision beyond 'real politics', but that the conditions for such a Europe in the sense of a real utopia do exist and must be strengthened.

Ulrich Brand
Vienna, March 2012

PREFACE

The present book is a quantitative study of world development in both space and time.[1] In space, for we study contemporary global development since the end of communism in Central Eastern Europe and the former USSR in up to 175 nations, using 26 predictor variables to evaluate the determinants of 35 processes of development on a global scale. In time, because we study the logic of global world economic trends at the level of the world system for the last four decades with a time series analysis of inequality and globalization.

Our study has clear implications for the study of global development; but it is also clear that it has many politically highly controversial implications for current debates about the future of Europe in the global economy. Presented with signs of failure and decay all around, European decision makers should start finally to take serious lessons on why some countries in the world system develop better than others. We severely criticize the hitherto existing pro-globalization strategy of the European Commission, and maintain that it is to be held responsible for the failure of the attempt to make Europe the world's leading economy by 2010, the so-called Lisbon Strategy. To judge from the results of this study, the successor strategy (the so-called EU-2020 strategy) will also fail, just like the Lisbon Strategy 2010.

Weighting the overall effects of our independent variables on a combined development indicator, putting together all our chosen measures of democracy, growth, environment, gender equality, human development, research and development and social cohesion, we come to the conclusion that political-institutional feminism, measured by the percentage of power positions at all levels of government, which women control in a country, positively affects the overall development process, and certainly feminism is a driver, not a bottleneck for all countries concerned. In accordance with socio-liberal strategies of development, we also consider the positive effects of economic freedom; in fact, the effects are highly significant. Among the other significant drivers of a positive development scenario we find the indicator MNC outward investments (stock) per GDP, which measures the power position that national capital wields on the world markets; and the UNDP Education Index, which is the best available measurement of a society's human capital formation effort. The good message for European integration is that years of membership in EMU (2010) also wield a positive influence on the overall development performance indicator,

---

1 The authors would like to thank Ms Dominique Eira Adey Balinova from the United Nations in Vienna for her thorough remarks on earlier versions of the text.

but the effect is not as strong as Euro-optimists would have hoped. *Summa summarum*, the size of annual population growth is also a significant bottleneck for combined development. Most importantly, it also emerges that core capital penetration (MNC PEN – stock of inward FDI per GDP) and world economic openness (the time-lagged Openness Index, 1990 (sum of export and import share per GDP)) are both significant bottlenecks of satisfactory overall development performance, thus qualifying important aspects of the current European Commission's global strategy. Passive globalization is not a viable strategy.

Our detailed studies, based on 30 multiple regressions, further confirm the assumptions by research traditions, sympathizing with the anti-globalization movements for the different indicators of the development process:

- The clear contradictions of world economic openness are on the educational and social levels. On the educational level, because open systems tend to perform badly on the per capita world-class universities index and the tertiary enrolment ratio. World economic openness also has a significant negative effect on the Human Development Index, which in many ways is the general master variable for the social situation of a country.
- High comparative price levels, and hence, implicitly, a high level of services of general interest, are a good and sound precondition of global tolerance, of a levelling of the income differences between rich and poor, and per capita world-class university performance. Neoliberals often hold that low comparative price levels indicate 'economic reform'. However, it would be a disastrous idea to aim at lower comparative price levels (as the European Commission demanded from member governments with their 14 Lisbon Strategy indicators).
- Further apprehensions of research that is critical of globalization are fully vindicated by the significant effects of the foreign savings rate. High foreign savings are indeed a driver of unemployment, income inequality, global footprint (gha), and are a blockade against a satisfactory Happy Planet Index performance.
- The new worldwide division of labour, which transplants significant parts of industrial production into the so-called 'export processing zones' or 'free production zones', especially in China and Southeast Asia, is characterized by its very significant negative ecological effects. The New International Division of Labour (NIDL) model is one of the prime drivers of high CO_2 per capita emissions.
- As was already correctly predicted by quantitative dependency and world system research of the 1980s and 1990s, core capital penetration (MNC penetration) has a very significant negative impact on the social development of the host countries of foreign direct investments; but these negative effects are mitigated by the positive effects of MNC headquarter status. The positive effects of MNC headquarter status on per capita world-class universities and on the rule of law vindicate such reasoning.
- MNC penetration increases income polarization and infant mortality, and blocks democracy, desired environmental performance, and the rule of law.

- Increases in MNC penetration over time had a negative effect on the rule of law, and equally had a negative effect on economic growth in the period 1990–2005. A good and plausible reason for this is the process of 'creative destruction' in the less fortunate regions of the world economy, and partially also in several regions of Eastern and Central Europe.

Exactly 50 results from our multiple regressions, explaining 30 process variables, are significant at least at the 10 per cent level. However, of these 50 results, 20, i.e. 40 per cent, did not conform to the theoretical explanations offered by the mainstream of globalization-critical research. Seventeen of the 20 contradicting results stem from just three weak dimensions of the globalization-critical paradigm – (1) the insufficient understanding of the role of economic freedom, especially in advanced countries, (2) the inability to comprehend existing problems in the areas of democracy and tolerance, gender equality, and employment in the 'real existing Muslim countries' and in the parallel worlds of Muslim 'diasporas' in the West, and finally (3) the inability to formulate a proper framework of the interaction between the public and the private, especially in higher education. Four of these contradicting results stem from the positive effects of Economic Freedom on development, and eight contradictions stem from the negative effects of membership in the Organisation of the Islamic Conference (OIC) or from Muslim population shares on such phenomena as democracy and tolerance, gender equality, and employment. The remaining five contradictions stem from the fact that different development theories, including the globalization-critical development consensus, overlook the crowding-out of public education expenditures on employment, growth, and human development. We also have to concede that the understanding of research traditions, sympathizing with the anti-globalization movements, of the global migration process is rather deficient. We can reasonably assume that the import of labour in the world economy, measured by the reciprocal value of the worker remittances scale, has detrimental effects on life quality (Happy Planet Index, life expectancy, life satisfaction, happy life years), and gender relations (closing the political gender gap; closing the overall gender gap). The percentage of the population with an 'immigration background' also has a negative effect on some other key indicators of the environment and gender justice. Immigration, and all the transport activities it causes, increases the CO_2 output of a given society, and it also increases the ratio of carbon emissions per GDP. But there hold other important effects as well, which tend to confirm the optimistic pro-migration policy liberal consensus, inherent in the UNDP *HDR 2009* analysis.

Yes, there are not only Hiob's messages for inward migration. Yes, the share of people with migration background per total population seems to coincide with a weakening of the role of traditional, local, native elites, and income inequality even tends to be lower due to the effects of this variable. Also, current migration phobias and migration pessimism are contradicted in another very important way: there is no significant effect of any migration variable on the unemployment rate. Liberals are right in assuming that inward migration is a driver of economic growth: net international migration rates, 2005–2010, are significantly and positively influencing current economic growth rates, and also the ratio of closing the political gender gap.

For the share of public education expenditure per GDP, the results are rather dire and tend to confirm some of the basic assumptions of the current mainstream Brussels/Paris/Washington Consensus in the field of education policy. Privatization and deregulation, and the restructuring of the public sector in education policy seem to be called for, because public expenditure is one of the main drivers of an unsatisfactory employment performance, the economic growth rate, and three other hardcore survival and basic needs indicators (most probably due to crowding-out effects with other government expenditure components): the female survival probability rate, life expectancy, and the Human Development Index. The only two positive effects of public education expenditure are on per capita world-class universities, and the rule of law.

There is a positive trade-off of effective demand on development. High inequality rates must be regarded in their own right as blockades against female survival rates, and life expectancies. With Galbraith (1999, 2007, 2009) we diagnose such an empirical effect of income distribution on employment as well. The higher the inequality rate, the higher the unemployment rate.

Our analysis of the time series perspectives of globalization and development also revealed astonishing results. Our data analysis for the last four decades highlights the following main trends:

- Rising economic globalization is the defining element of the development trajectory of humanity in the 1970s, 1980s, and 1990s until the beginning of the new millennium – from Spain with the most rapid globalization process to Burkina Faso. 90.57 per cent of humanity, living in 108 countries of the 117 countries with complete data, was affected by that process.
- Only in nine countries were we confronted with a negative time series correlation between the time axis and economic globalization. These countries amount to just 1.90 per cent of the world's population.
- The brave new world of rising economic globalization is a world of rising inequalities. 75.92 per cent of the global population live in countries in which there was a rising linear trend towards inequality over time. For 54.05 per cent of humanity, this trend was especially strong, and the time series correlation coefficient of the time axis with inequality was 0.500 or above. Among the EU-27 countries, there are 13 nations corresponding to this very strong trend towards rising inequality over time.
- 79.61 per cent of humanity also experienced the dire fact that, according to the available time series, globalization in their countries was positively correlated with higher inequality.
- For 48.97 per cent of humanity, living in 55 countries, this trend was especially strong. The time series correlation was 0.500 or above. 13 of the 27 EU countries

are among them and their experience gives testimony to the Latin Americanization of the European continent.

- Only 35 countries experienced some positive promises of globalization, i.e. a negative time series correlation between globalization and inequality. The inhabitants of these countries are a fortunate global minority, and comprise 12.86 per cent of the global population. Only seven EU-27 countries are among them

Under these circumstances, the management of the global migration process becomes one of the most important phenomena to handle politically.

Chapter 1

SHOULD THE MUSICIANS CONTINUE TO PLAY?

Look around, and Europe is in crisis. At the time of writing, Greece, Ireland and Portugal are on the verge of an economic and social abyss, severe doubts about the very future of the European Monetary Union are growing, and austerity packages are being implemented across the European continent. Centrifugal political forces are on the rise, just as are xenophobia, racism and social exclusion. The promised lands of the most competitive and dynamic knowledge-based economy in the world, an economy capable of sustainable economic growth with more and better jobs and greater social cohesion – as envisaged by the European heads of governments in March 2000 at their European Council meeting in Lisbon, Portugal – seem to be further away than ever before. It would be difficult to find believers in this noble vision of a sustainably growing and socially coherent Europe nowadays in any country of the EU, let alone in countries like Greece, Ireland, Italy, Spain and Portugal. Even in the richer, developed European countries of the old economic centres, pessimism is on the rise. However, for the quantitative social scientist, profound economic crises (the Great Depression of the 1930s, the 'oil crisis' of the 1970s, the current world recession) always seem to be appropriate times for reconsidering basic principles of economics and the social sciences.[1]

Always, such times were also propitious to discover or rediscover the fact that unequal relationships profoundly characterize the world economy and that the effects of dependency and the role a nation plays in the world system profoundly affect the economic and social trajectory of a country.[2] On 27 February 2007, we read – among the already visible, terrible icebergs of the looming current economic crisis – the following truly 'Titanic scenario' about the mindset of European central bankers in the *International Herald Tribune* (IHT): they, according to the IHT, think that the European Central Bank may be forced to raise interest rates if higher wage demands fan inflation (*International Herald Tribune*, 27 February 2007).

---

1 See especially the contributions by the great Austrian economist Kurt W. Rothschild, listed in the references section at the end of this volume.
2 To cut a long story short, it might suffice to state here that dependency and world-systems theories predicted (with Cardoso 1979) the following processes:
   • There is a financial and technological penetration by the developed capitalist centres of the countries of the periphery and semi-periphery;
   • This produces an unbalanced economic structure both within the peripheral societies and between them and the centres;

Should the musicians then continue to play? Like on the Titanic on 15 April 1912? This book starts from the assumption that the world can learn a lot from the empirical and theoretical debates and research results of dependency and world-systems research. The European 'political class' seems to not react at all to the implications of the global economic crisis. In a strategic document of the European Union, or if you wish in Brussels newspeak, an 'EU presidency country non-paper' (what jargon!) produced in 2009 by the Swedish government, then holding the rotating EU presidency, we even read that trade and economic integration, combined with new technology, brings new markets, competitors and trade partners closer. They help to decrease poverty, promote democratic values and increase international stability.[3]

If there is continuity in Brussels' thinking ever since the mid-1990s, it is this credo about openness as the main precondition of global ascent. What about the role of, say, internal consumption and investment? The promised lands of free and open markets, always hidden somewhere in the foggy mists of the today's, are at the real centre of European policymaking. Already in March 2000, the EU aimed at its Lisbon 'European Council' to make the EU 'the most competitive and dynamic knowledge-based economy in the world capable of sustainable economic growth with more and better jobs and greater social cohesion'. The very same neoliberal agenda, already then the strategy to achieve this ambitious goal within a decade, is now being applied again. The European Commission at Brussels itself now freely acknowledges that this 'Lisbon agenda' or 'Lisbon Strategy' largely failed, but it does not provide any real more far-reaching explanations for this failure.[4] Instead, it applies the same old medicine again to the ailing patient.

The European Commission itself conceded in one of its main documents on the subject recently[5] that even before the crisis of 2008–9, there were many areas in which Europe was not progressing fast enough relative to the rest of the world. The strategy, proposed by the European Commission in this document on a 'strategy for smart, sustainable and inclusive growth' is relatively simple. The policy package offered by the European Commission has only three pillars. Guess what pillar number one is? Open economies! We go on to read that Europe will continue to benefit from

---

- This leads to limitations on self-sustained growth in the periphery;
- This favours the appearance of specific patterns of class relations; and
- These require modifications in the role of the state to guarantee both the functioning of the economy and the political articulation of a society, which contains, within itself, foci of inarticulateness and structural imbalance.

3 'Eco-efficient Growth in the Age of Globalisation', Swedish non-paper on the Lisbon Strategy post-2010, Stockholm, 2009.

4 http://ec.europa.eu/eu2020/index_en.htm (accessed 26 January 2012).

5 European Commission, 'Communication from the Commission: Europe 2020. A strategy for smart, sustainable and inclusive growth,' COM (2010) 2020, 3 March 2010. Available at http://eur-lex.europa.eu/Notice.do?mode=dbl&lang=en&ihmlang=en&lng1=en,de&lng2=bg,cs,da,de,el,en,es,et,fi,fr,hu,it,lt,lv,mt,nl,pl,pt,ro,sk,sl,sv,&val=509103:cs&page= (accessed 26 January 2012).

being one of the most open economies in the world but competition from developed and emerging economies is intensifying.[6]

In this book, we will systematically confront this type of thinking with macro-quantitative evidence on a global scale to show that a strategy, based on unlimited openness is not the solution, but very often part and parcel of the very problem of the European decline vis-à-vis its major global competitors. We will try to find out by macro-quantitative comparisons how the neoliberal agenda will most probably affect policy outcomes during the next decade, judging by the knowledge of cross-national research on how the main drivers and bottlenecks under scrutiny here have already affected these processes over the last decade or two.

Analysing the policy failure of the 'Lisbon Strategy' 2000–10 and the prospective policy failure of the 'EU-2020 strategy' has important implications not only for Europe, but for other major regions of the world economy as well, such as East and South Asia, advanced countries in the Middle East and North Africa and in Latin America, still confronted with the a semi-peripheral status in the world economy. Is the opening of markets the only viable strategy to catch -up with richer countries?

So, we will start the debate by comparing the trajectory of the EU-15 with the USA and some other highly developed Western democracies in terms of their globalization, their economic growth performance, their unemployment performance, and their inequality. New, universally recognized and reliable time series data, now available in the comparative social sciences, make such comparisons possible. The use of time series data and methodology about globalization and social performance opens up depths of analytical insights, hitherto unknown in the debate.

Graph 1, accordingly, highlights the development history of the old core of the European Union[7] by comparison with the USA as the centre of the world economy and some other developed Western democracies.[8] Globalization refers to the time series data, provided by the ETH Zurich KOF Globalization Index Project.[9] Data for economic growth were taken from the IMF in Washington. Our inequality data are Theil indices of inequality, based on payment inequality in 21 industrial sectors, calculated from UNIDO data sources by the University of Texas Inequality Project, while unemployment refers to unemployment as a per cent of the civilian labour force, documented by the OECD in Paris.

As a first approximation to the subject, our graph uses simple unweighted averages for each of the three groups of countries (the EU-15, the USA and some of the other

---

6 Again, see European Commission, 'Communication from the Commission'.
7 Austria; Belgium; Denmark; Finland; France; Germany; Greece; Ireland; Italy; Luxembourg; Netherlands; Portugal; Spain; Sweden; the United Kingdom.
8 Australia; Canada; Israel; Japan; New Zealand; Norway.
9 Referring to 'actual globalization flows', combining trade (per cent of GDP), foreign direct investment (flows, per cent of GDP); foreign direct investment (stocks, per cent of GDP); portfolio investment (per cent of GDP); and income payments to foreign nationals (per cent of GDP), projected onto a single 0–100 scale.

major developed Western democracies). As stated, the four compared dimensions are economic growth, globalization flows, inequality and unemployment.[10]

Our first analysis yields already clear results, which might provide a possible new input for the entire 'Lisbon Strategy' debate. The USA throughout much of the 1980s, the 1990s and the first decade of our century had a lower unemployment and a higher economic growth than the European centre, i.e. the 15 countries making up the European Union before the last extensions (in the EU jargon, the EU-15). This fact is well known in the political debate about the subject, and really belongs to the canon of contemporary analysis on the subject. Also however – and this is indeed a startling fact – globalization inflows are smaller than in the EU-15, and – most importantly – the tendency towards sectoral inequality as a proxy for overall inequality is less pronounced than in the EU-15. The average, unweighted performance of the other Western democracies[11] rather resembles the European performance of rising globalization, and rising inequality:

Policy pointer

From the viewpoint of this analysis, the main difference between the USA and Western Europe is not only the USA's lower unemployment and higher economic growth throughout much of the 1980s, the 1990s and the first decade of our century, but also its less intensive and less passive globalization.

These phenomena led two neo-Keynesian European economists (Marterbauer and Walterskirchen 2006, i.e. already before the onset of the current crisis) with good reason to diagnose correctly the European political economic predicament as follows:

> The economy of the euro area has been in a poor situation since 2000, with the lowest growth rate of the industrialized world. In contrast to the USA, economic policy in the euro area was not able to initiate a self-sustaining economic upswing. Given unchanged policy guidelines, no lasting improvement can be expected. Mainstream economists explain the weak economic performance of the EU by 'structural problems'. The growth rates of potential output are low due to a lack of reforms on the supply side of the economy. Labour markets are not flexible enough, deregulation and privatisation are lagging behind and the cut in state expenditures especially concerning the welfare state is taking on too slowly. However, potential output commonly is measured as the trend

---

10 In order to visualize our time series in a single graph and on a single easily comprehensible left hand scale, we had to multiply the University of Texas time series inequality (Theil indices of the inequality of wages by sectors) data by a factor of 250 and to divide the ETH globalization flow data by a factor of 10, to produce scales which range from 0 to 12 on a single graph.
11 Australia; Canada; Israel; Japan; New Zealand; Norway.

Graph 1. Economic globalization and social performance in (A) the core states of Europe (EU-15); (B) the USA; and (C) other highly developed OECD countries

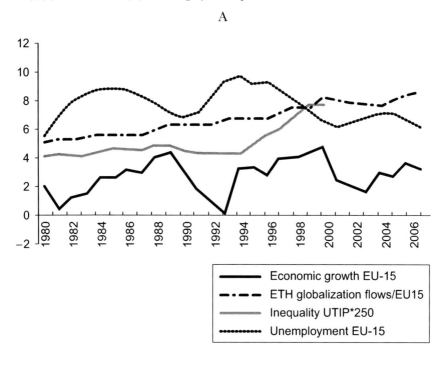

A

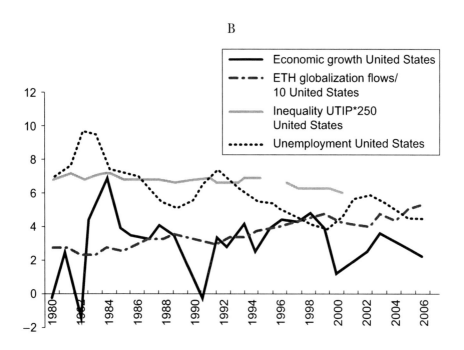

B

C

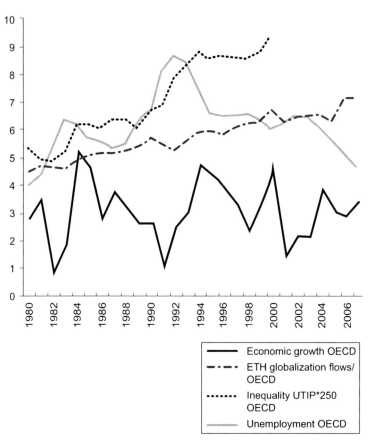

Source: Our own compilations from the data of Appendices 4 and 5. The EU-15 countries in our sample were: Austria; Belgium; Denmark; Finland; France; Germany; Greece; Ireland; Italy; Luxembourg; Netherlands; Portugal; Spain; Sweden; United Kingdom. The other developed Western democracies comprised: Australia; Canada; Israel; Japan; New Zealand; Norway. Economic growth: IMF economic growth data (real GDP per annum) and growth predictions, http://www.imf.org/external/datamapper/index.php (accessed April 2009). Globalization: ETH Zurich globalization time series data, http://globalization.kof.ethz.ch/static/rawdata/globalization_2010_short.xls (accessed January 2010). The Zurich data used in this study refer only to the ETH economic globalization time series which covers 'actual flows', combining: trade (percentage of GDP); foreign direct investment (flows, percentage of GDP); foreign direct investment (stocks, percentage of GDP); portfolio investment (percentage of GDP); and income payments to foreign nationals (percentage of GDP). Inequality: Theil index of inequality, based on payment in 21 industrial sectors; calculated from UNIDO sources in the University of Texas Inequality Project, http://utip.gov.utexas.edu/data.html (accessed January 2010). Unemployment: unemployment as a percentage of the civilian labour force: http://stats.oecd.org/Index.aspx (accessed 26 January 2012). In order to visualize our time series data in a single graph and on a single, easily comprehensible left-hand scale, we had to rescale the data by multiplying the University of Texas time series inequality (Theil indices of the inequality of wages by sectors) data by a factor of 250 and to divide the ETH globalization flow data by a factor of 10 to produce scales that range from 0 to 12.

output of the recent past. This completely overlooks cyclical and demand factors, in particular the effect of supply-side policies on demand. It is always the study of cyclical problems that sheds light on the importance of effective demand. Cycle and trend cannot be separated mechanically by time-series analyses, they are interacting. Following Kalecki, the long run is just a series of cycles. 'In fact, the long run trend is but a slowly changing component of a chain of short-period situations: it has no independent entity.' (Marterbauer and Walterskirchen 2006, citing Kalecki 1968b)

The rest of this study is organized as follows. In Chapter 2, the main critical theories are outlined, and it looks back on earlier major studies on the subject, while Chapter 3 presents the data and the research design. The main results are presented in Chapter 4, while Chapter 5 debates the final results, based on our non-parametric index of development and its multivariate determinants. Chapter 6 probes into time series relationships. Chapter 7 finally summarizes the study, while the appendices document our results and represent an invitation to the research community to further use and test our explanations.

Policy pointer

As critics of the current European political economy correctly remark, the euro area has the lowest growth rate of the industrialized world (Marterbauer and Walterskirchen 2006). Given current austerity policies, no lasting improvement can be expected. In accordance with Marterbauer and Walterskirchen, cyclical and demand factors have to be reconsidered as well.

Chapter 2

BACKGROUND

As pointed out in Chapter 1, for the European Commission the world is relatively simple, and according to its current vision of the world, an answer to the question why Europe is currently more severely affected by the current economic downturn than other regions of the world economy is relatively quickly given: significant fiscal deficits, rising debt ratios, inability of regulators to regulate the financial market and greedy and speculative banking sector are to blame for the current crisis. These, together with the costs of ageing populations and unemployment, pose a significant challenge for fiscal sustainability. A stable and well-functioning financial sector is necessary. Large current account imbalances rooted in a persistent lack of competitiveness or due to other reasons must be addressed by acting on fiscal policy, on wage developments, on structural reforms relating to product and financial services markets (including the flow of productivity enhancing capital), and on labour markets.[1] Member states should encourage the right framework conditions for wage bargaining systems and labour cost developments consistent with price stability.

Policy pointer

For the European Commission, the world is relatively simple: significant fiscal deficits and rising debt ratios are the main problem together with the costs of ageing populations and unemployment, which pose a significant challenge for fiscal sustainability. A stable and well-functioning financial sector is necessary. However, as followers of the countervailing Kalecki–Steindl paradigm correctly emphasize, full employment as the main political concern, demand as a growth driver, higher effective demand to raise employment, technology and educational policy, lower household savings, a stable or rising wage share, an anti-cyclical policy (cycle and trend have the same determinants), a rise of the public sector (which promotes growth through effective demand), tax coordination and international cooperation should be the basis of EU economic policymaking.

---

1 European Commission, 'Recommendation for a Council Recommendation of 27.4.2010 on broad guidelines for the economic policies of the Member States and of the Union. Part I of the Europe 2020 Integrated Guidelines', COM(2010) 193 final, Brussels, 27.4.2010, SEC(2010) 488 final. http://ec.europa.eu/eu2020/pdf/Brochure Integrated Guidelines.pdf (accessed 26 January 2012).

According to the European Commission, states with large current account surpluses should pursue measures aimed at implementing structural reforms conducive to strengthening potential growth and underpinning domestic demand. Member states, which do not tap their full employment and productivity growth potential because of sectors with low competition, a weak business environment and obstacles to employment and labour reallocation, must act coordinately to achieve the desired. Appropriate labour market reforms are needed in a number of countries so as to increase wage flexibility, reduce segmentation and improve incentives to work for all; and member states face challenges regarding increasing productivity and facilitating transition towards higher value added production and exports, and in several cases a diversification of the industrial base. An efficient regulatory business environment, administrative efficiency as well as promoting a higher degree of competition must be provided. Member states face important challenges regarding the human capital endowment and upgrading of their economies.[2]

The five targets for the EU in 2020[3] are:

1. *Employment*
   75 per cent of the 20–64 year-olds to be employed.
2. *R&D / innovation*
   Of the EU's GDP, 3 per cent (public and private combined) is to be invested in R&D and/or innovation.
3. *Climate change / energy*
   Greenhouse gas emissions are to be 20 per cent (or even 30 per cent, if the conditions are right) lower than 1990; 20 per cent of energy should come from renewables; there should be a 20 per cent increase in energy efficiency.
4. *Education*
   School drop-out rates should be reduced to below 10 per cent; at least 40 per cent of 30 to 34-year-olds should be completing third level education.
5. *Poverty / social exclusion*
   There should be at least 20 million fewer people in or at risk of poverty and social exclusion by 2020.

The European Commission maintains[4] that Europe has identified new engines to boost growth and jobs. These areas are addressed by seven flagship initiatives. Within each initiative, both the EU and national authorities have to coordinate their efforts so they are mutually reinforcing. Most of these initiatives have been presented by the European Commission in 2010.

- Smart growth
- Digital agenda for Europe

---

2 Council of the European Union, 'Note, from: The General Secretariat of the Council, to: Delegations', 10731/10, ECOFIN 345, COMPET 191, SOC 404, 4 June 2010.
3 http://ec.europa.eu/europe2020/targets/eu-targets/index_en.htm (accessed 26 January 2012).
4 http://ec.europa.eu/europe2020/targets/eu-targets/index_en.htm (accessed 26 January 2012).

- Innovation Union
- Youth on the move
- Sustainable growth
- Resource-efficient Europe
- An industrial policy for the globalization era
- Inclusive growth
- An agenda for new skills and jobs
- European platform against poverty

The European Union also set out its strategy until the year 2020 (the so-called 'Europe 2020 strategy') in the form of ten guidelines, on which progress must be achieved by the member countries. Unlike the now deceased and safely buried Lisbon Strategy or 'Lisbon agenda', spelt out in 2000 and relevant for the decade 2000 to 2010, the aim is now far more low-key. No more talk about becoming the most competitive and dynamic knowledge-based economy in the world within the next decade. The aim is now simply to set out a vision of 'Europe's social market economy' for the twenty-first century. It pretends to show how the EU can 'come out stronger from the crisis and how it can be turned into a smart, sustainable and inclusive economy delivering high levels of employment, productivity and social cohesion. To deliver rapid and lasting results, stronger economic governance will be required.'[5] The strategy now has ten main guidelines:

Guideline 1:   Ensuring the quality and the sustainability of public finances
Guideline 2:   Addressing macroeconomic imbalances
Guideline 3:   Reducing imbalances in the euro area
Guideline 4:   Optimizing support for R&D and innovation, strengthening the knowledge triangle and unleashing the potential of the digital economy
Guideline 5:   Improving resource efficiency and reducing greenhouse gas emissions
Guideline 6:   Improving the business and consumer environment and modernizing the industrial base
Guideline 7:   Increasing labour market participation and reducing structural unemployment
Guideline 8:   Developing a skilled workforce responding to labour market needs, promoting job quality and lifelong learning
Guideline 9:   Improving the performance of education and training systems at all levels and increasing participation in tertiary education
Guideline 10: Promoting social inclusion and combating poverty

Since guidelines 1 to 3 are focused only on the rather short-term strategies from the current global recession (ensuring the quality and the sustainability of public finances;

---

5 http://ec.europa.eu/eu2020/index_en.htm (accessed 26 January 2012).

addressing macroeconomic imbalances; and reducing imbalances in the euro area), the real long-term development goals of the European Union are summarized by guidelines 4 to 10.

Amidst all the variety of aims, goals, targets, terms, but also indicators and guidelines, we present to our readers two boxes, which summarize all those variables, which the European Commission aimed to maximize ever since the European Council meeting in Lisbon in March 2000. These variables were/are the 'official' yardsticks for the success or failure of a state in the Lisbon Strategy/EU-2020 strategy. Unlike in international social science, where debates about indicators are open, the indicators, presented in Box 1 and 2 were established by unanimous intergovernmental decision at the level of the Council of the European Union. Once fixed, these indicators remained there to stay, considerable critique by the international social science community notwithstanding (Heinemann et al. 2004). Yet, these variables are also of potential interest not only for European, but for global social science. Performance on these indicators formed the basis for political recommendations by the European Commission to member governments to implement the Lisbon Strategy. The open method of coordination (OMC) required the member states to draw up national reform plans and to forward them to the European Commission.

Can all these startling varieties of indicators be maximized at once by a strategy of open markets? We start our overview by a presentation of the indicators, currently in force, and compare them with the Lisbon 'structural indicators', which guided European policymaking since March 2000, and which were now substituted by European Commission's EU-2020 indicators. However, Eurostat still documents these 'Lisbon structural indicator' data series as well.

Box 1. The current EU-2020 strategy; these indicators should be maximized/minimized in the political process

Headline targets	Indicators	Definition
75% of the population aged 20–64 should be employed	**Employment rate by gender, age group 20–64**	The employment rate is calculated by dividing the number of persons aged 20–64 in employment by the total population of the same age group. The indicator is based on the EU Labour Force Survey.
3% of the EU's GDP should be invested in R&D	**Gross domestic expenditure on R&D (GERD)**	Gross domestic expenditure on R&D (GERD) – % of GDP. The indicator provided is GERD (gross domestic expenditure on R&D) as a percentage of GDP.
Reduction of the greenhouse gas emissions by 20% compared to 1990	**Greenhouse gas emissions, base year 1990**	Greenhouse gas emissions, base year 1990 – index 1990 = 100. This indicator shows trends in total man-made emissions of the 'Kyoto basket' of greenhouse gases. It presents annual total emissions in relation to 1990 emissions ('Kyoto basket').

(Continued)

Box 1. Continued

Headline targets	Indicators	Definition
Increase in the share of renewable energy sources in final energy consumption to 20%	**Share of renewables in gross final energy consumption**	Share of renewable energy in gross final energy consumption – %. This indicator is calculated on the basis of energy statistics covered by the Energy Statistics Regulation.
Increase energy efficiency by 20%	**Energy intensity of the economy (proxy indicator for energy *savings*, which is under development)**	Energy intensity of the economy – gross inland consumption of energy divided by GDP (kilogram of oil equivalent per 1,000 euro). This indicator is the ratio between the gross inland consumption of energy and the gross domestic product (GDP) for a given calendar year.
The share of early school leavers should be under 10% and at least 40% of 30–34-year-olds should have completed a tertiary or equivalent education	**Early leavers from education and training by gender**	Early leavers from education and training by gender – % of the population aged 18–24 with at most lower secondary education and not in further education or training. Both the numerators and the denominators come from the EU Labour Force Survey
	Tertiary educational attainment by gender, age group 30–34	Tertiary educational attainment by gender, age group 30–34. The share of the population aged 30–34 years who have successfully completed university or university-like (tertiary-level) education with an ISCED 1997 (International Standard Classification of Education) education level of 5 to 6.
Reduction of poverty by aiming to lift at least 20 million people out of the risk of poverty or exclusion	**Population at risk of poverty or exclusion (*union of the three sub-indicators below*)**	Population at risk of poverty or exclusion – % and per 1,000 persons. The Europe 2020 strategy promotes social inclusion, in particular through the reduction of poverty, by aiming to lift at least 20 million people out of the risk of poverty and exclusion. This indicator summarizes number of people who are either at risk of poverty and/or materially deprived and/or living in households with very low work intensity. Interactions between the indicators are excluded.
	Persons living in households with very low work intensity	People living in households with very low work intensity are people aged 0–59 living in households where the adults work less than 20% of their total work potential during the past year.

(Continued)

Box 1. Continued

Headline targets	Indicators	Definition
	Persons at risk of poverty after social transfers	Persons at risk of poverty after social transfers – % and per 1,000 persons. The persons with an equivalized disposable income below the risk-of-poverty threshold, which is set at 60% of the national median equivalized disposable income (after social transfers)
	Severely materially deprived persons	The data collection 'material deprivation' covers indicators relating to economic strain, durables, housing and environment of the dwelling. Severely materially deprived persons have living conditions severely constrained by a lack of resources, they experience at least 4 out of 9 following deprivations items: cannot afford (1) to pay rent or utility bills; (2) keep home adequately warm; (3) face unexpected expenses; (4) eat meat, fish or a protein equivalent every second day; (5) a week holiday away from home; (6) a car; (7) a washing machine; (8) a colour TV; or (9) a telephone.

Source: compiled from the website of Eurostat, the EU's official statistical service, available at http://epp.eurostat.ec.europa.eu/portal/page/portal/europe_2020_indicators/headline_indicators (accessed 26 January 2012).

Box 2. The 14 'structural indicators' of the Lisbon Strategy, in force since March 2000, and now substituted by the new EU-2020 indicators of the European Commission; these indicators were intended to be maximized/minimized in the political process, which was thought to result in making Europe the leading economy of the world by 2010

Target	Indicators	Definition
General economic background data	**GDP per capita in PPS**	GDP per capita in PPS – GDP per capita in purchasing power standards (PPS) (EU-27 = 100). Gross domestic product (GDP) is a measure for the economic activity. It is defined as the value of all goods and services produced less the value of any goods or services used in their creation. The volume index of GDP per capita in purchasing power standards (PPS) is expressed in relation to the European Union (EU-27) average set to equal 100.

(Continued)

Box 2. Continued

Target	Indicators	Definition
		If the index of a country is higher than 100, this country's level of GDP per head is higher than the EU average and vice versa. Basic figures are expressed in PPS, i.e. a common currency that eliminates the differences in price levels between countries allowing meaningful volume comparisons of GDP between countries. Please note that the index, calculated from PPS figures and expressed with respect to EU-27 = 100, is intended for cross-country comparisons rather than for temporal comparisons.
	Labour productivity per person employed	Labour productivity per person employed – GDP in purchasing power standards (PPS) per person employed relative to EU-27 (EU-27 = 100). GDP per person employed is intended to give an overall impression of the productivity of national economies expressed in relation to the European Union (EU-27) average. If the index of a country is higher than 100, this country's level of GDP per person employed is higher than the EU average and vice versa. Basic figures are expressed in PPS, i.e. a common currency that eliminates the differences in price levels between countries allowing meaningful volume comparisons of GDP between countries. Please note that 'persons employed' does not distinguish between full-time and part-time employment.
Innovation and research data	**Persons of the age 20–24 having completed at least upper secondary education by gender**	Persons of the age 20–24, having completed at least upper secondary education by gender as a percentage of the population of the age 20–24. The indicator is defined as the percentage of young people of the age 20 to 24 years having attained at least upper secondary education attainment level, i.e. with an education level ISCED 3a, 3b or 3c long minimum (numerator). The denominator consists of the total population of the same age group, excluding no answers to the questions 'highest level of education or training attained'. Both the numerators and the denominators come from the EU Labour Force Survey (LFS).

(Continued)

Box 2. Continued

Target	Indicators	Definition
	Gross domestic expenditure on R&D (GERD)	See Box 1.
Economic reform data	**Comparative price levels**	Comparative price levels – comparative price levels of final consumption by private households including indirect taxes (EU-27 = 100). Comparative price levels are the ratio between purchasing power parities (PPPs) and market exchange rate for each country. PPPs are currency conversion rates that convert economic indicators expressed in national currencies to a common currency, called purchasing power standard (PPS), which equalizes the purchasing power of different national currencies and thus allows meaningful comparison. The ratio is shown in relation to the EU average (EU-27 = 100). If the index of the comparative price levels shown for a country is higher or lower than 100, the country concerned is relatively expensive/cheap as compared with the EU average.
	Business investment	Business investment – gross fixed capital formation by the private sector as a percentage of GDP. This indicator is defined as total gross fixed capital formation (GFCF) expressed as a percentage of GDP, for the private sector. GFCF consists of resident producers' acquisitions, less disposals, of fixed tangible or intangible assets, such as buildings, machinery and equipment, vehicles, or software. It also includes certain additions to the value of non-produced assets realized by productive activity, such as improvements to land. The ratio gives the share of GDP that is used by the private sector for investment (rather than being used for e.g. consumption).
Employment data	**Employment rate by gender**	See Box 1.
	Employment rate of older workers by gender	Employment rate of older workers by gender – in %. The employment rate of older workers is calculated by dividing the number of persons aged 55–64 in employment by the total population of the same age group. The indicator is based on the EU Labour Force Survey.

(Continued)

Box 2. Continued

Target	Indicators	Definition
Social cohesion data	**At-risk-of-poverty rate after social transfers by gender**	See Box 1.
	Long-term unemployment rate by gender	Long-term unemployment rate by gender – long-term unemployed (12 months and more) as a % of the total active population.
	Dispersion of regional employment rates by gender	Dispersion of regional employment rates by gender – coefficient of variation of employment rates (of the age group 15 to 64) across regions (NUTS level 2) within countries.
		The dispersion of regional (NUTS level 2) employment rates of the age group 15 to 64 shows the regional differences in employment within countries and groups of countries (EU-25, euro area). The employment rate of the age group 15 to 64 represents employed persons aged 15 to 64 as a % of the population of the same age group. The dispersion of regional employment rates is zero when the employment rates in all regions are identical, and it will rise if there is an increase in the differences between employment rates among regions.
Environment data	**Greenhouse gas emissions, Kyoto base year**	See Box 1.
	Energy intensity of the economy	See Box 1.
	Volume of freight transport relative to GDP	Volume of freight transport relative to GDP – index of inland freight transport volume relative to GDP (2000 = 100). This indicator is defined as the ratio between tonne-kilometres (inland modes) and GDP (chain-linked volumes, at 2000 exchange rates). It is indexed on 2000. It includes transport by road, rail and inland waterways. Rail and inland waterways transport are based on movements on national territory, regardless of the nationality of the vehicle or vessel. Road transport is based on all movements of vehicles registered in the reporting country

Source: Compiled from the website of Eurostat, the EU's official statistical service, available via http://epp.eurostat.ec.europa.eu/portal/page/portal/eurostat/home/.

It has to be emphasized that optimization of the country indicator performance is (Box 1) or was (Box 2) thought to rest above all on the implementation of a strategy of world economic openness. Critics (see below) of the European Commission strategy will be quick in pointing out that the econometric and comparative social scientific foundation for the hypothesis that a neoliberal strategy will be best to maximize performance on all fronts (employment, R&D, energy and the environment, education, poverty reduction) is rather weak. By contrast, our commented guide to the literature on the major international studies in peer-reviewed social science journals about globalization and other preconditions of policy success or failure for the nine 'European Union 2020 guidelines' (compiled from Cambridge Scientific Abstracts and the Social Sciences Citation Index, see the appendix matter of this study), seems to suggest that rather the contrary seems to be the case. Scheme 1 highlights the political, programmatic and ideological tensions currently characterizing the debate about Europe's future in the context of global society:

Scheme 1. The implied global policy connections of the neoliberal EU-2020 strategy

Neoliberal EU-strategy:

- Decline and restructuring of the public sector (efficiency)
- Deregulation and privatization
- Falling wage share (real unit labour costs)
- Higher labour market flexibility to raise economic growth
- Higher savings (for investment)
- International competition (location)
- International tax competition
- No active anticyclical policy (irrelevant for growth path)
- Price stability and budget consolidation as main political concerns
- Supply as growth driver

Desired policy outcomes, maximizing performance:

- Early leavers from education and training by gender
- Employment rate by gender, age group 20–64
- Energy intensity of the economy
- Greenhouse gas emissions, base year 1990
- Gross domestic expenditure on R&D
- Persons at risk of poverty after social transfers
- Persons living in households with very low work intensity
- Population at risk of poverty or exclusion
- Severely materially deprived persons
- Share of renewables in gross final energy consumption
- Tertiary educational attainment by gender, age group 30–34

Source: Our own compilations from the theoretical literature, surveyed in this study.

The most consistent counter-perspective to this 'Commission approach' is the Kalecki–Steindl paradigm. The Kaleckian–Steindl and current mainstream growth policy characteristics are presented below:

The radical counter-perspective of the Kalecki–Steindl paradigm

Differences in growth strategies	
Kalecki–Steindl growth policy	**Current mainstream policy on growth**
Full employment as a main political concern	Price stability and budget consolidation as a main political concern
Demand as a growth driver	Supply as a growth driver
Higher effective demand to raise employment	Higher labour market flexibility to raise economic growth
Technology and educational policy	Deregulation and privatization
Lower household savings	Higher savings (for investment)
Stable or rising wage share	Falling wage share (real unit labour costs)
Anticyclical policy (cycle and trend have the same determinants)	No active anticyclical policy (irrelevant for growth path)
Rise of public sector promotes growth (through effective demand)	Decline and restructuring of the public sector (efficiency)
Tax coordination	International tax competition
International cooperation	International competition (location)

Source: Guger, Marterbauer and Walterskirchen (2004) and Tausch (2010a, 2010b).

The crisis-prone and cyclical nature of global capitalism has been featured already by many theories in the tradition of political economy.[6] Among the important non-mainstream, non-neoliberal political economies of our time, the first to be mentioned in this context is of course Schumpeter. As is well-known (see Vernengo 2006) Schumpeter already foresaw in his writings published in 1908, 1912, 1939 and 1950 that capitalist development takes the form of 'creative destruction'. The writings of Schumpeter ([1908] 2009, [1912] 1969, 1939) and later world system and dependency analyses were always aware of the emergence of crises, cyclical imbalances, regional shifts, and the rise and decline of entire regions and even continents in the process of capitalist development. Schumpeter strongly believed

---

6 Amin (1976, 1994, 1997); Arrighi (1995); Attinà (2003a, 2003b, 2005); Bauer (1936); Bobróvnikov (2004); Bornschier (1996); Devezas and Corredine (2001); Escudier (1993); Galalp (1989); Goldstein (1988); Jessop (1990), Jessop and Sum (2006); Jourdon (2008); Kalecki (1966, 1968a, 1968b, 1971, 1979, 1996); Kalecki and Feiwel (1972); Korotayev and Tsirel (2010); Louçã (1997, 1999); Louçã and Reijnders (1999); Luxemburg (1964); Mandel (1995); O'Hara (1994, 2000, 2001, 2003a, 2003b, 2003c, 2004a, 2004b, 2003c, 2005a, 2005b); Schumpeter ([1912] 1969, 1939); Tausch (2007a, 2007b); Tausch and Ghymers (2006).

in the long, 50-year business cycles, called Kondratiev waves, which to this day arouse many controversies in economics and political science.[7] Successful innovation is a source of temporary market power, eroding the profits and position of old firms, yet ultimately losing to the pressure of the new inventions, championed by the competitors.[8]

Several world system approaches have taken up the basic idea of the Schumpeterian competition and stipulated that even the international system itself since the 1450s is characterized by hegemonies, international system de-concentration, the de-legitimation of the international order, and recurrent global wars over the hegemony in the system.[9] That currently economic growth dramatically shifts away from the North Atlantic arena and the states very closely linked to them to other regions of the world economy seems to indicate that such a major fundamental shift is taking place with the force of a real tsunami.

At this point, we should refer in a more systematic way to the contribution of the Austrian political economist Josef Steindl (1912–1993), whose work nowadays enjoys a renaissance (see also Lavoie 1996). This rediscovery of the importance of the work of Josef Steindl is especially championed by the Austrian Institute for Economic Research in Vienna. It is perceived by many as the most consistent policy alternative to the current, dominant Brussels/Paris neoliberal consensus of the European Commission and the OECD. In Steindl (1946), the author analysed the process of increasing concentration of capital and the oligopoly of the market. In Steindl (1952) he established a relationship between economic stagnation and the growth of oligopoly in advanced capitalist countries. In the words of Guger, Marterbauer and Walterskirchen (2006a):

> In competitive industries, profit margins are highly elastic, and excess capacity is eliminated in the long run by squeezing out surplus capital. In monopolistic industries, on the other hand, price cuts are not practicable. In these industries, demand does not determine prices, but the degree of capacity utilization – also in the long run. The typical producer in the competitive type of industry has low profit margins and rather small chances to survive. In monopolistic industries, on the contrary, producers have substantial profit margins and a high chance of survival. Therefore, it would require a large price cut to eliminate competitors. Hence, oligopolistic or monopolistic firms avoid cut-throat price competition.

Steindl expected a secular tendency to stagnation in mature capitalist economies, brought about by monopolization, and (as Guger, Marterbauer and Walterskirchen remark with justification) the prosperity of the postwar era was a 'big surprise' to Steindl, who published his analysis of US capitalism in 1952. In the introduction to the republication of his book on 'Maturity and Stagnation', Steindl explained

---

7 For empirical studies on Kondratiev waves, see Devezas (2006); Bornschier (1996); Goldstein (1988); Tausch (2007d, 2008b).

8 For a formal model of Schumpeterian growth economics, see Aghion and Howitt (1992).

9 See Devezas (2006); furthermore Arrighi (1995); Goldstein (1988); Tausch (2007d); on the general questions of cycles see also Bakir and Campbell (2006); Kotz (2009); and O'Hara (2003a, 2003b, 2003c).

the extraordinary development of the postwar period in the West by the following factors:

- the rising share of the public sector;
- technical innovations and new products;
- international cooperation in economic policies;
- cooperation between business and trade unions; and
- a favourable political and economic climate.

The postwar boom increased public expenditures, which raised effective demand. These outlays were largely financed by profit taxes. In accordance with Kalecki's arguments, the expansionary effect of public expenditures is even higher, Steindl assumes, if taxes are financed by profits and not mass consumption. Technical innovations stimulated investment. Information and communication technologies, automation and aircraft industries gave a strong impetus. The innovations, due to high military spending, even disseminated to the private sector. In postwar Europe, private investment was further stimulated by the catching-up process with the USA, a process initialled by the Marshall Plan. According to Steindl, the speed of European postwar recovery was greatly enhanced by additional labour supply from agriculture and, later on, from abroad. The change in the secular trend of income distribution since the end of the Second World War in the world's most advanced economies, observed by Steindl, has to be especially noted: since the early 1980s, income distribution has changed in favour of classes with high savings propensities; i.e. in most industrial countries the share of wages and salaries in national income has been declining, while non-wage income, in particular property income, has risen sharply, and income inequality between the rich and the poor has increased considerably.

Policy pointer

As the Austrian economist Josef Steindl correctly explained, the development of the postwar period in the West after 1945 was caused by:

- the rising share of the public sector;
- technical innovations and new products;
- international cooperation in economic policies;
- cooperation between business and trade unions; and
- a favourable political and economic climate.

The postwar economic boom increased public expenditures, which raised effective demand. The expansionary effect of public expenditures is even higher if taxes are financed by profits and not by mass consumption. However, since the early 1980s, income distribution has changed in favour of the classes with

> high savings propensities; i.e. in most industrial countries the share of wages and salaries in national income has been declining, while non-wage income and income inequality between the rich and the poor has increased considerably.

According to Steindl, the burden of taxation has shifted from profits to wages – a process which reduced the expansionary effects of the public sector (Steindl 1979, 5). Assuming that tax revenues are immediately spent, higher profit taxes are paid out of increasing profits (before taxation) due to higher capital utilization, while an increase in wage taxation reduces consumption. The following aspect of Steindl's analysis especially caught the attention of the empirical researchers from the Austrian Institute of Economic Research (Guger, Marterbauer and Walterskirchen 2006a, 2006b): namely, that what Steindl calls a 'policy of stagnation' will continue, since governments are preoccupied with inflation and the public debt (Steindl 1979, 9). Thus the Steindl paper on 'Stagnation Theory and Stagnation Policy' (Steindl 1979, esp. 13) must be regarded, together with Boccara's papers, as one of the first key documents against the current euro-monetarist stagnation policy, which – according to this Kaleckian viewpoint – is the cause of stagnation, unemployment and rising inequality in Europe. The new political and economic landscape, which began to take shape in the late 1970s and 1980s, was characterized by:

- macroeconomic policy being oriented primarily towards price stability and budget consolidation;
- declining international cooperation regarding economic policy (breakdown of the Bretton Woods system and the establishment of a flexible exchange rate system in the early 1970s);
- increasing environmental and energy problems; and
- a political trend against full employment.

Steindl believed in the 'political aspects of full employment'. This hypothesis, first published by Kalecki in 1943, argued that in the long run the entrepreneurs will be losing interest in full employment because of the increasing power of trade unions and employees as a consequence of full employment. As predicted by Kalecki, the end of the period of full employment, which came about in the late 1960s, was politically motivated.

   This new set-up was called by Steindl the 'return of the Bourbons'. The Bourbons' return resulted in a restrictive bias in economic policy, particularly in the EU. For Guger, Marterbauer and Walterskirchen, one of the main consequences for our analysis of the European Union today is the following:

> Steindl identified a persistent and lasting mood against growth and very clearly spoke about a deliberate 'policy of stagnation'. This characterization seems to be even more appropriate for the current development. In the EU a macro-economic policy framework has been established that has a restrictive bias – it

may even be characterized as a 'policy of stagnation' – although it promised stability and growth. In the current macroeconomic policy framework of the EU, institutions to guarantee price stability and sound public finance are extensively developed. However, institutions responsible for aggregate demand and full employment are missing. (Guger, Marterbauer and Waltterskirchen 2006b)

Policy pointer

The restrictive bias of current stagnation policies in the EU increased dramatically in 2011 and 2012. Already before that, institutions guaranteeing price stability and 'sound public finances' wielded and overwhelming power, while aggregate demand and full employment were the 'orphans' of Brussels policies. The currently unfolding Greek tragedy, the fiscal pact, and all the rest of current developments dramatically underline the importance of the Kalecki–Steindl analysis.

According to Steindl, there are currently three main pillars of economic policy in the EU:

1. A 'free' market economy is seen as being stable and improving welfare. Deregulation and establishing free movement of goods, services, capital and labour, and structural reforms especially on product and capital markets are seen as the main element of improving real variables such as economic growth and employment in the long run.
2. Macroeconomic policies are oriented towards ensuring growth and stability by providing stable frameworks. This is seen to be guaranteed by the combination of 'price stability and sound public finance'. For achieving these ends two institutional arrangements have been formed: the European Central Bank, which is primarily oriented on price stability and the Stability and Growth Pact, which aims at budgetary positions 'close to balance or in the surplus' in the medium term.
3. The unemployment problem, seen from a neoclassical perspective, mainly being determined by 'structural factors'.[10] European Union employment policies are oriented towards increasing the adaptability of the workforce and the flexibility of the labour markets.

In view of the current crisis in Greece and in other Southern European countries, Steindl remarked prophetically that it has to be avoided that debtor countries are forced into a painful policy of restrictions, causing low growth and high rates of

---

10 In the medium and long term, unemployment will be unaffected by aggregate demand or productive capacities, but the NAIRU (non-accelerating inflation rate of unemployment) can be reduced by a flexible labour market.

unemployment, from which all countries would suffer. He further pointed out (Steindl 1988) that the record of the EU model of economic policy has been disappointing. Growth rates of GDP are low and unemployment is high in relation to long-run averages and to the USA. Economic policy in the EU seems to have an inherent antigrowth and pro-unemployment bias.

Guger, Marterbauer and Walterskirchen (2006a) thus reach the conclusion:

> What we experienced in recent years was a European economic policy focused on preventing inflation and budget deficits. With the 'Stability and Growth Pact' Steindl's apprehensions were realized: Europe's economic policy got a bias towards stagnation policy from the outset. The Lisbon process – oriented towards economic growth – has not altered this bias so far.

Quantitative social science, especially in the field of sociology and political science, presented increasing dissent to the prevalent neoliberal world-view of the European Commission. In the literature survey reported in the appendix, we summarize the available and most important analyses in the field, relevant for the further theoretical and empirical developments in this book.[11] Faced with the task of presenting our readers our research results in the format of a standard length book below 100,000 words, we refer them to existing and exhaustive introductions to theories that are critical of globalization.[12]

Policy pointer

The point made by the Kalecki–Steindl paradigm about rising monopolistic power is a real one. Of the 108 major international studies on the issue of the social, economic and ecological effects of globalization and the penetration of host countries by foreign transnational corporations since the 1960s in the world economy, surveyed in Cambridge Scientific Abstracts, four out of five clearly showed that the concerns of the Kalecki–Steindl paradigm and social science that is critical of globalization have to be taken seriously, finally, by the political and bureaucratic decision makers. 'It does not deliver the goods'.

For the dependency and world system approaches (see Cardoso 1979), low comparative price levels, high foreign savings, the openings of the national economies to free production zones, a low MNC outward investment presence on the world markets (MNC headquarter status) and a high MNC PEN – stock of inward FDI

---

11 See our 'Commented Guide to the Literature: Major International Studies in Peer-Reviewed Social Science Journals about Globalization and Other Preconditions of Policy Success or Failure for the Nine "European Union 2020 Guidelines"' (compiled from Cambridge Scientific Abstracts and the Social Sciences Citation Index) in the appendix matter of this book.

12 Our theoretical introduction will thus be rather short, and available in-depth presentations of the theory would be Heshmati (2006a, 2006b, 2007); and Heshmati and Tausch (2007).

per GDP,[13] as well as a high world economic openness, measured by the export share per GDP + import share per GDP, will all be possible negative development bottlenecks. Within national and within union effective measures are required to eliminate the negative development bottlenecks with minimal harm to openness.[14] Later tests of the 'foreign capital penetration' arguments, championed by the Bornschier school of thought could only support and refine the original argument, independently from the research design.[15]

Neoliberal economic theory, by contrast, would assume that world economic openness and thus a big share of foreign trade in the GDP would be the key to world economic and social and environmental success. Jeffrey Williamson (2002) surveyed the neoliberal pro-openness arguments in the following way:

> Globalization typically favours all countries which liberalize and penalizes those who do not. There is an abundant literature showing that liberalizing countries have gained from freer trade over the past four decades… Yet, such analysis is vulnerable to the criticism that the effect of trade policies alone cannot be isolated since other policies usually change at the same time. Thus, countries that liberalized their trade also liberalized their domestic factor markets, liberalized their domestic commodity markets, and set up better property-rights enforcement. The appearance of these domestic policies may

---

13 See our glossary and terms, as well as our list of abbreviations.

14 A scientometric analysis of the vast dependency-oriented research literature in the major international (social) science journals – based on the ISI Web of Knowledge (Thomson Reuters), available at Vienna University Library, Austria – revealed that as of 8 March 2012, 406 major international studies quoted the path-breaking Galtung analysis (1971), which was the first to claim by quantitative-statistical methods that dependency and social cohesion are incompatible with one another, and a further 78 major international studies were based on the Sunkel essay (1973), which predicted that the advancement of modernization introduces a 'wedge' along the area dividing the integrated from the segregated segments of societies confronting globalization. Sunkel believed that some sectors of the host countries of transnational investment and globalization will be incorporated and others marginalized. Both Galtung (1971) and Sunkel (1973) must be regarded as the catalyst essays for the two follow-up pioneering quantitative dependency studies authored by Chase Dunn (1975) – which had in turn 235 follow-up studies – and Rubinson (1976) – which yielded 177 follow-up studies. Bornschier, Chase-Dunn, and Rubinson (1978), who then built on the essays by Chase-Dunn (1975) and Rubinson (1976), were the first to study introducing more systematically the concept of the penetration of the host countries of transnational investment (MNC penetration) as a major operationalization of dependency theory. This essay initiated 200 follow-up studies, all published in the major global peer-reviewed social science journals, and the later essay (Bornschier and Ballmer-Cao) devoted to the issue of economic inequality as a consequence of MNC penetration, was followed up by 76 studies.

15 See also our 'Commented Guide to the Literature: Major International Studies in Peer-Reviewed Social Science Journals about Globalization and Other Preconditions of Policy Success or Failure for the Nine "European Union 2020 Guidelines"' (compiled from Cambridge Scientific Abstracts and the Social Sciences Citation Index) in the appendix and literature section of our work.

deserve more credit for raising income while the simultaneous appearance of more liberal trade policies may deserve less.

In this book, we will duly take into account several indicators of globalization and dependency, which are being measured by the following different variables of '(in)/ dependent development', mainly: MNC penetration; the growth of MNC penetration over time; MNC headquarter status (MNC HEADQU); FPZ (free production zones); low comparative price levels; and foreign savings.[16]

For the interested readers, Box 3 summarizes this dependency theory/world-systems theory 'empirical logic':

Box 3. The new logic of dependency and the capitalist world system, challenging neoliberal orthodoxies

MNC penetration (MNC PEN) measures the different degrees of weight that foreign capital investments have in the host countries, i.e. the UNCTAD percentages of the stocks of multinational corporation investments per total host country GDP. This research tradition has been especially developed, as mentioned earlier, by the Swiss sociologist Volker Bornschier and his school. Bornschier and his school predicted a strong negative determination of development by a high MNC penetration, due to the negative consequences that monopolies have on the long term development trajectory of countries.

- We also ascertain the growth of MNC penetration over time (DYN MNC PEN), from 1995 to 2005. The Bornschier school expected short-term dynamic effects from such MNC penetration increases.
- Equally, Bornschier and his school developed a high theoretical and empirical awareness about the long-term consequences of the presence or absence of MNC headquarter status (MNC HEADQU), measured in our analysis by the indicator MNC outward investments (stock) per GDP. Bornschier and his school expected that a high headquarter status mitigates against the long-term negative effects of MNC penetration.
- FPZ (free production zone) employment as a per cent of total population is the indicator best suited to measure the so-called NIDL (New International Division of Labour) school. Early on, Froebel, Heinrichs and Kreye (1980) already predicted the unfettered rise of the model of 'export processing zones', especially in China and Southeast Asia. This first major international study by Froebel, Heinrichs and Kreye (1980) was followed, among others, by Ross (2004) and Singa-Boyenge (2007). Export processing zones (EPZ) or FPZs today already account for some 80 per cent of

(Continued)

---

16 See our glossary and terms, as well as our list of abbreviations.

Box 3. Continued

the merchandise exports of countries like China, Kenya, the Philippines, Malaysia, Mauritius, Mexico, Senegal, Tunisia, and Vietnam. The 3,500 EPZs in 130 countries of the world now employ 66 million people, among these 40 million employees in China. The tendency, correctly foreseen by Froebel, Heinrichs and Kreye (1980), towards this total global re-location of world industries continues unabated. In the present book, we try to determine the quantitative weights that FPZs have in the determination of development performance (percentage of the population working in EPZs versus MNC penetration versus the other dependency/globalization indicators).

- 'Low comparative price levels' (for an exhaustive debate on the underlying issues from a dependency theory/world-systems perspective, see Kohler and Tausch (2003), furthermore Raffer (1987), Yotopoulos (1996) and Yotopoulos and Sawada (2005) from a dependency theory/world-systems perspective, as well as Balassa (1964) and Samuelson (1964) from a more conventional economic theory framework) is operationalized here simply by ERD or ERDI, the exchange rate deviation index, which is calculated by the ratio between GDP at purchasing power parities, divided by GDP at current exchange rates (see also http://epp.eurostat.ec.europa.eu/portal/page/portal/structural_indicators/indicators/economic_reform – accessed 27 January 2012). Dependency theories and world-systems theories assume that low comparative price levels are an indicator of 'unequal exchange' between the countries of the centre and the periphery.[17]

- For dependency authors, foreign savings show the weight that foreign savings, mostly from the centres and richer semi-peripheries, have in the accumulation process of the host countries in the periphery and semi-periphery. It is calculated by the difference between the share of investments per GDP and the share of savings per GDP.

Policy pointer

At the centre of the new thinking, inspired by the Kalecki–Steindl paradigm and also by 'dependency' and 'world-systems' sociology, is MNC penetration. MNC penetration (MNC PEN) measures the UNCTAD percentages of the stocks of multinational corporation investments per total host country GDP. This research tradition has been especially developed by the Swiss sociologist Volker Bornschier

---

17 For an easily readable and available survey of the available and often very complicated literature, as well as the empirics of 'unequal exchange', see Kohler and Tausch (2003) and http://wsarch.ucr.edu/archive/papers/kohlertoc.htm (accessed 27 January 2012).

and his associates. It predicts a strong negative determination of development by a high MNC penetration, due to the negative consequences that monopolies have on the long term development trajectory of countries. Equally, this type of sociology developed a high theoretical and empirical awareness about the long-term consequences of MNC headquarter status (MNC HEADQU), measured by the indicator MNC outward investments (stock) per GDP. It is expected that a high headquarter status mitigates against the long-term negative effects of MNC penetration. In addition, FPZ (free production zone) employment as a percentage of total population, 'low comparative price levels' and foreign savings are thought to wield equally long-term negative effects on growth and development patterns.

The Big Unknown: The Role of Migration in Shaping Development Patterns

The divisive issue of migration divides opinions around the globe, and it also divides opinions among the global social science research community. In dealing with the issue of migration, we first might notice that to our knowledge hardly any theoretically, methodologically or empirically solid cross-national evidence exists[18] about the macro-societal effects of migration on national development.

Policy pointer

While social science has many studies on the determinants of economic growth or income inequality already at its disposal, knowledge about the drivers and bottlenecks of the totality of the processes underlying the EU-2020 strategy is woefully inadequate.

Critics of globalization and the other four freedoms of the internal market, constituting the essence of the EU's neoliberal internal market strategy (freedom of the movement of goods, capital, services and labour) will be as divided on the issue as opinion of the large publics in general in the migration-receiving countries. The World Values Survey as the global opinion barometer par excellence permits a startling testimony about the trend and extent of pro- or anti-immigration opinions in the developed Western democracies.

Looking at the most recent combined national samples of the Western democracies according to the World Values Survey online data facility, we arrive at the following results about migration pessimism today (Box 4).

---

18 With the laudable exception of Sanderson (2010), who analysed the effects of migration on the Human Development Index.

Box 4. The World Values Survey and values of the world of migration

How about people from other countries coming here to work? Which one of the following do you think the government should do? (1) 'Let anyone come'; (2) 'As long as jobs are available'; (3) 'Strict limits'; and (4) 'Prohibit people from coming' (N=19,694 representative respondents in Andorra [2005], Australia [2005], Bulgaria [2006], Canada [2006], Cyprus [2006], Chile [2006], Finland [2005], France [2006], Germany [2006], Great Britain [2006], Italy [2005], Japan [2005], Netherlands [2006], New Zealand [2004], Norway [2007], Poland [2005], Romania [2005], Slovenia [2005], South Africa [2007], South Korea [2005], Spain [2007], Sweden [2006], Switzerland [2007], USA [2006]). *The overall result of this vote in the developed Western democracies was: 'Let anyone come' (7.8%), 'As long as jobs are available' (45.1%), 'Strict limits' (39.3%) and 'Prohibit people from coming' (7.8%).*

Even considering the diverse multicultural communities in the developed world, support for economic migration pessimism is widespread. There is considerable migration pessimism even among Buddhists, Hindus and Muslims, living in the West. Samples below 50 should be interpreted only with extreme precaution.

For one of the 'founding fathers' of dependency and world-systems theory, Samir Amin, successive waves of immigration have also helped to strengthen what he calls 'the American ideology'. Immigrants are certainly not responsible for the misery and oppression that caused their departure. They left their lands as victims. However, emigration also meant renouncing the collective struggle to change the conditions in their country of origin; they exchanged their suffering for the host country's ideology of individualism and 'pulling oneself up by one's boot straps'. This ideological shift also serves to delay the emergence of class-consciousness, which hardly has the time to develop before a new wave of immigrants arrives to help abort its political expression. Migration inevitably weakens class consciousness and active citizenship. American cities provided the stage for a series of murderous wars between gangs formed by successive generations of poor immigrants (Irish, Italian, etc.) and cynically manipulated by the ruling class. Thus, the workers' unions are apolitical, in every sense of the term. They have no links with a party that might share and express their concerns; nor have they ever been able to articulate a socialist vision of their own. Instead they subscribe, along with everyone else, to what the Marxist Samir Amin calls the 'dominant liberal ideology',[19] which thus remains unchallenged.[20]

---

19 Samir Amin uses the term 'liberalism' in a European, not in a US tradition, i.e. he refers to 'liberalism' as an ideology, believing in market forces. In North America, unlike in Europe, the word liberalism often refers to 'social liberalism' in the tradition of President Franklin Delano Roosevelt, and the New Deal.
20 http://www.informationclearinghouse.info/article3681.htm (accessed 27 January 2012).

Box 4. (Continued). Migration pessimism in the West according to the World Values Survey, last wave, 2004–8

		'Let anyone come'	'As long as jobs are available'	'Strict limits'	'Prohibit people from coming'	Total	Migration pessimists ('Strict limits' + 'Prohibit…')
Female	Anglican	-	55.10%	42.90%	2.00%	98	44.90%
Female	Buddhist	1.70%	38.50%	50.70%	9.10%	340	59.80%
Female	Evangelical	6.40%	37.40%	47.80%	8.40%	961	56.20%
Female	Hindu	2.00%	57.90%	33.40%	6.70%	26	40.10%
Female	Jehovah witnesses	0.50%	30.60%	38.20%	30.70%	25	68.90%
Female	Jew	13.60%	69.80%	16.70%	-	27	16.70%
Female	Methodists	-	47.60%	47.60%	4.80%	21	52.40%
Female	Muslim	13.10%	55.60%	26.40%	4.90%	232	31.30%
Female	Orthodox	14.00%	43.60%	32.90%	9.50%	1,573	42.40%
Female	Pentecostal	0.20%	16.00%	69.20%	14.60%	42	83.80%
Female	Presbyterian	1.40%	42.50%	54.80%	1.40%	73	56.20%
Female	Protestant	5.10%	46.60%	39.10%	9.20%	1,965	48.30%
Female	Roman Catholic	5.90%	49.40%	39.00%	5.70%	4,137	44.70%
Female	The Church of Sweden	16.60%	50.80%	31.80%	0.70%	324	32.50%
Female	**Total**	**7.40%**	**45.20%**	**39.50%**	**7.90%**	**10,669**	**47.40%**

Male	Anglican	1.20%	48.10%	46.90%	3.70%	81	50.60%
Male	Buddhist	2.30%	48.10%	46.00%	3.60%	329	49.60%
Male	Evangelical	5.60%	39.80%	45.40%	9.20%	779	54.60%
Male	Hindu	7.30%	46.00%	44.00%	2.70%	34	46.70%
Male	Jehovah's witnesses	9.90%	34.20%	17.10%	38.80%	37	55.90%
Male	Jew	3.50%	77.30%	17.60%	1.70%	31	19.30%
Male	Methodists	7.70%	23.10%	69.20%	-	13	69.20%
Male	Muslim	17.40%	58.90%	19.20%	4.50%	285	23.70%
Male	Orthodox	16.20%	40.60%	34.80%	8.40%	1,326	43.20%
Male	Pentecostal	3.90%	24.00%	57.60%	14.60%	39	72.20%
Male	Presbyterian	1.70%	45.00%	50.00%	3.30%	60	53.30%
Male	Protestant	4.40%	43.50%	42.30%	9.80%	1,627	52.10%
Male	Roman Catholic	6.80%	48.90%	38.20%	6.10%	3,402	44.30%
Male	The Church of Sweden	16.70%	54.20%	28.30%	0.80%	335	29.10%
Male	**Total**	**8.40%**	**45.00%**	**39.00%**	**7.60%**	**9,025**	**46.60%**
Total	**Total**	**7.80%**	**45.10%**	**39.30%**	**7.80%**	**19,694**	**47.10%**

In a similar vein, Immanuel Wallerstein is implicitly highly critical of the migration optimism of large sectors of the European Left. People migrate, legally or illegally, for obvious reasons. Economic betterment and escape from persecution are the two principal ones. They migrate where they can, and where economic and political prospects for them are best. The recipient areas/countries have always been ambivalent about these migrants. Those in favour of stringent state action against migrants (and not only against illegal migrants) express themselves in xenophobic language, and get support based on a generalized sense of economic and social insecurity in the working and middle classes. This group, in the language of Immanuel Wallerstein, tends to favour building walls and expulsions of various kinds. They usually are located in more conservative political forces but attract support from some groups that normally support parties more on the left. Those opposed to stringent state action are in fact two quite different groups. There are the business elites who welcome migrants in the belief that this enables them to keep wage rates down. And to some extent they are right. They thus want migrants to have the right to enter and to work. However, they are not anxious that migrants have political rights, which would enable them to fight for higher remuneration. The second group is quite the opposite. It is composed of the targeted groups plus those on the left who favour increasing, not decreasing, social and political rights for the migrants.[21]

By contrast, Jeffrey Williamson (2002), the great liberal economic historian of global economics and the migration process, analysed the basic facts of international migration in the following way: what he calls North–North migrations[22] between Europe and the New World involved the movement of something like 60 million individuals. Historically, South–North migrations were only a trickle: like today, poor migrants from the periphery were kept out of the centre by restrictive policy, by the high cost of the move, and by their lack of education. World labour markets were segmented then just as they are now. Real wages and living standards converged among the currently industrialized countries. Emigration may contribute to labour scarcity, but it also lowers the GDP. Convergence was driven primarily by the erosion of the gap between the New World and the Old World. In addition, many poor European countries were catching up with the industrial leaders. How much of this convergence in the Atlantic economy was due to North–North mass migration? The labour force impact of these migrations on each member of the Atlantic economy in 1910 varied greatly. Among receiving countries, Argentina's labour force was augmented most by immigration (86 per cent), Brazil's the least (4 per cent), with the USA in between (24 per cent). Among sending countries, Ireland's labour force was diminished most by emigration (45 per cent), France the least (1 per cent), with Britain in between (11 per cent). At the same time, the economic gaps between rich and poor countries diminished. Real wage dispersion in the Atlantic economy declined between 1870 and 1910 by 28 per cent, GDP per

---

21　http://badmatthew.blogspot.com/2006_04_01_archive.html (accessed 10 February 2012).
22　Correctly speaking, Williamson would have to deduce from the number of 60 million individuals the number of migrants who emigrated from Europe to Argentina, Brazil, Chile and Uruguay, the main destination countries of European migration in Latin America in the nineteenth century.

capita dispersion declined by 18 per cent and GDP per worker dispersion declined by 29 per cent. Migration affects equilibrium output, wages and living standards by influencing aggregate labour supply. According to Williamson, in the absence of the mass migration, wages and labour productivity would have been a lot higher in the New World and a lot lower in the Old. In the absence of the mass migration, income per capita would have been a bit higher in the New World and a bit lower in the Old World. Not surprisingly, the biggest impact was on those countries that experienced the biggest migrations. Emigration is estimated to have raised Irish wages by 32 per cent, Italian by 28 per cent and Norwegian by 10 per cent. Immigration is estimated to have lowered Argentine wages by 22 per cent, Australian by 15 per cent, Canadian by 16 per cent and American by 8 per cent (J. Williamson 2002).

Most liberal and left-of-centre–orientated global political discourse would expect that worker remittances have very beneficial effects for the sending countries, and that they amount to a very huge transfer machine of wealth from the rich, migration-recipient countries to the poor, migration-sending countries. Migration is thus seen as a win–win situation. One has to distinguish carefully between migration stocks and migration flow data, and in addition, one has to assess the effects of worker remittances per GDP. In migration-recipient countries, migration stocks and migration flow data will be highly positive, while in the migration-sending countries, these values will be low or – in the case of migration flow data – negative. Worker remittances will be a high percentage of the GDP of the sending countries, and they will be low in most migration-recipient countries, but also in the countries not participating substantially in international migration flows. The available UNDP data, unfortunately, are not based on the concept of net worker remittance balances as a percentage of GDP. The ten countries, whose economies are least dependent on worker remittances are Burundi, Chile, Japan, Laos, Malawi, USA, Gabon, Korea (Republic of), Madagascar and Mauritania. In the following 16 countries, worker remittances make up more than 10 per cent of the current GDP each year: Tajikistan, Moldova, Lesotho, Honduras, Lebanon, Guyana, Jordan, Haiti, Jamaica, Kyrgyzstan, El Salvador, Nepal, Nicaragua, Philippines, Guatemala and Albania. These nations are a real testing case for the hypothesis that outward migration remittances are a driver of development in sending countries.

The recent UNDP *Human Development Report 2009*,[23] devoted to the issue of international migration, quite correctly emphasizes that at the peak of Iberian rule in the Americas, more than half a million Spaniards and Portuguese and about 700,000 British subjects went to the colonies in the Americas. Through the brutal use of force, 11 to 12 million Africans were sent as slaves across the Atlantic between the fifteenth and late nineteenth centuries. Between 1842 and 1900, some 2.3 million Chinese and 1.3 million Indians travelled as contract labourers to Southeast Asia, Africa and North America. At the end of the nineteenth century the fraction of foreign-born residents in many countries was higher than today (UNDP, *HDR 2009*, 28).

For several observers, among them Hatton and Williamson (2009), the current hysteria about inward migration in many industrialized countries has no real

---

basis. For them, the Third World has been undergoing an emigration life-cycle since the 1960s, and, except for Africa, emigration rates have been level or even declining since a peak in the late 1980s and the early 1990s. The current economic crisis will serve only to accelerate those trends. They estimate the economic and demographic fundamentals, which are driving these Third World emigration life-cycles to the US since 1970 – the income gap between the US and the sending country, the education gap between the US and the sending country, the poverty trap, the size of the cohort at risk, and migrant stock dynamics. Their projections imply that pressure on Third World emigration over the next two decades will not increase. In looking at the issue of the drivers of the international migration process, Hatton and Williamson (2009), also cautiously argue on the basis of their econometric evidence, available from 62 countries for the period from 1970 to 2000, that the income ratio (the relationship between income levels in the migration-sending and in the migration-recipient country) and the education ratio (the relationship between education levels in the migration-sending and in the migration-recipient country) are strongly significant.

Hatton and Williamson maintain that the effect of poverty is negative as predicted, but it is attenuated by an increase in the emigrant stock. There is a chain migration effect in the US where for every 1,000 of the stock of previous migrants a further 90 arrive in the following five-year period, or 18 each year. Their study also shows interesting details about the effect of source country poverty. Excluding the interaction with the migrant stock, a doubling of per capita income from US$1,000 to $2,000 (about equivalent to the East and Southeast Asian per capita income level in 1960 and its growth rate between 1960 and 1985, 3.4 per cent) increases the emigration rate by 12 per cent. In contrast, an increase for today's middle-income countries from $10,000 to $11,000 has a negligible effect on the emigration rate (0.03 per cent). Without the migrant stock, economic fundamentals matter much more since migrants tend to be driven by job opportunities rather than family ties.

The UNDP *HDR 2009* maintains that financial remittances are vital in improving the livelihoods of millions of people in developing countries. There is a positive contribution of international remittances to household welfare, nutrition, food, health and living conditions in places of origin. Even those whose movement was driven by conflict can be net remitters, as illustrated in history by Bosnia and Herzegovina, Guinea-Bissau, Nicaragua, Tajikistan and Uganda, where remittances helped entire war-affected communities to survive. In some international migration corridors, money transfer costs have tended to fall over time, with obvious benefits for those sending and receiving remittances. Recent innovations have also seen significant falls in costs at the national level. With the reduction in money transfer costs, families who once relied on relatives and close family friends or who used informal avenues such as the local bus driver to remit are now opting to send money through banks, money transfer companies and even via cell-phones. An important function of remittances is to diversify sources of income and to cushion families against setbacks such as illness or larger shocks caused by economic downturns, political conflicts or climatic vagaries (UNDP, *HDR 2009*, 72).

Similarly, the UNDP also maintains that there should be significant aggregate gains from movement, both to movers and to destination countries. The destination countries will capture about one-fifth of the gains from a 5 per cent increase in the number of migrants in developed countries, amounting to US$190 billion dollars. Immigration increases employment, with no evidence of crowding-out of locals, and investment also responds vigorously to immigration. Population growth due to migration increases real GDP per capita in the short run, one-for-one (meaning that a 1 per cent increase in population due to migration increases GDP by 1 per cent).

Migrants bring broader economic benefits, including higher rates of innovation. Data from the US shows that between 1950 and 2000, skilled migrants boosted innovation: a 1.3 per cent increase in the share of migrant university graduates increased the number of patents issued per capita by a massive 15 per cent, with marked contributions from science and engineering graduates and without any adverse effects on the innovative activity of local people. The USA, in particular, has been able to attract migrant talent through the quality of its universities and research infrastructure and its favourable patenting rules. In Ireland and the United Kingdom the share of migrants with tertiary education exceeds 30 per cent, while in Austria, Italy and Poland it is below 15 per cent. Countries offering more flexible entry regimes and more promising long-term opportunities have done better in attracting skilled people, whereas restrictions on duration of stay, visa conditions and career development, as in Germany for example, limit uptake. The aggregate effect of immigration on the wages of local workers may be positive or negative but is fairly small in the short and long run. In Europe, both multi- and single-country studies find little or no impact of migration on the average wages of local people (UNDP, *HDR 2009*, 84–5).

Summing up the debate, we again should quote from the findings of Jeffrey Williamson (2002):

> Mass migration made an important contribution to late nineteenth-century convergence in the 'North'. In the absence of mass migration, real wage dispersion would have increased by 7 per cent, rather than decreased by 28 per cent, as it did in fact. GDP per capita dispersion would also have decreased by only 9 per cent, rather than by 18 per cent as it did in fact. Wage gaps between New World and Old World would have risen to 128 per cent in 1910 when in fact they declined from 108 to 85 per cent. Real wage convergence before World War I was attributable to migration, about two-thirds of the GDP per worker convergence, and perhaps one half of the GDP per capita convergence. There was an additional and even more powerful effect of the mass migrations on global income distribution. The 60 million European migrants before World War I came from countries whose average real wages and average GDP per worker were perhaps only half of those in the receiving countries. These migrant gains were an important part of the net equalizing effect on world incomes of the mass migrations. North–North mass migrations had a strong levelling influence in the world economy up to 1913. They made

it possible for poor migrants to improve the living standards for themselves and their children. It also lowered the scarcity of resident New World labour which competed with the immigrants, while it raised the scarcity of the poor European labour that stayed home (whose incomes were augmented still further by emigrant remittances). South–South migrations were about the same size as the North–North flows.

Until new research tells us otherwise, I think it is safe to assume that South–South migrations put powerful downward pressure on real wages and labor productivity in Ceylon, Burma, Malaysia, Thailand, East Africa, Manchuria and other labor scarce regions that received so many Indian and Chinese immigrants. Since the sending labor surplus areas were so huge, it is less likely that the emigrations served to raise labour scarcity there by much. (J. Williamson 2002)

Policy pointer

Surveying contemporary social science theory would suggest considering migration as an additional determining factor of social, economic and ecological outcomes of the nations in the global system. The role of migration for the EU-2020 strategy has been insufficiently highlighted up to now.

Worker remittances continue to be an important instrument of wealth transfer from the rich to the poorer countries of the world.[24]

Much of the social scientific debate of the 1990s and especially the first decade of the new millennium following the 9/11 terror attacks in New York dealt with the role, Islam plays and will play in world society. Among the sceptics of Muslim civilization

---

24 Today, the 20 least dependent economies on worker transfers are Burundi; Chile; Japan; Laos; Malawi; USA; Gabon; Korea (Republic of); Madagascar; Mauritania; Oman; Tanzania; Venezuela; Argentina; Congo; Hong Kong, China (SAR); Iceland; Ireland; Italy; and Kazakhstan. The 20 countries with the highest dependency on worker remittances are Tajikistan; Moldova; Lesotho; Honduras; Lebanon; Guyana; Jordan; Haiti; Jamaica; Kyrgyzstan; El Salvador; Nepal; Nicaragua; Philippines; Guatemala; Albania; Bangladesh; Sierra Leone; Dominican Republic; and Cape Verde. It should be recalled here as well that the 20 countries with the highest share of population with an 'immigration background' in global society are Qatar; United Arab Emirates; Kuwait; Jordan; Israel; Bahrain; Singapore; Luxembourg; Brunei; Saudi Arabia; Oman; Switzerland; Australia; New Zealand; Kazakhstan; Canada; Gabon; Lebanon; Latvia; and Armenia. The 20 countries with the lowest share of population with an 'immigration background' are China; Peru; Cuba; Indonesia; Vietnam; Morocco; Myanmar; Madagascar; Lesotho; Haiti; Laos; Colombia; Egypt; Angola; Eritrea; Honduras; Guatemala; Philippines; Mongolia; and Papua New Guinea. The 20 countries with the highest current influx rates are Qatar; Singapore; United Arab Emirates; Iceland; Ireland; Kuwait; Jordan; Luxembourg; Spain; Syria; Burundi; Canada; Cyprus; Norway; Italy; Bahrain; Australia; Austria; Belgium; and Portugal. The 20 countries with the highest migration outflow rates are Georgia; Zimbabwe; Grenada; Guyana; Moldova; Fiji; Jamaica; Lithuania; Tajikistan; Guinea; Armenia; Albania; Ecuador; Mexico; Lesotho; Peru; Kyrgyzstan; Uzbekistan; Dominican Republic; and Congo.

as such, the work of Samuel P. Huntington has to be mentioned especially. The Huntingtonian world-view about Islam as a blockade against development (Huntington 1996) was further advanced *inter alia* by Constant, Gataullina, Zimmermann, and Zimmermann, 2006, with their empirical study about the integration processes of Muslim and Christian immigrants in Germany. Individual data on language, culture, societal interactions, history of migration and ethnic self-identification were used by them to compose measures of the process of cultural adaptation. Their research also attempted to measure social integration, assimilation, separation and marginalization. Their research led them to the conclusion that Christian immigrants adapt more easily to the German society than Muslim immigrants. Immigrants with schooling in the home country and with older age at entry as well as female Muslims remain more strongly attached to the country of origin. Female Muslims integrate and assimilate less and separate more than Muslim men, while there is no difference between male and female Christians. Christians who were young at the time of entering the Federal Republic of Germany were best integrated or assimilated. Christian immigrants with college or higher education in their home country integrated best.

As a further note of caution against the hitherto dominant optimistic views of the effects of inward migration in the social sciences, it cannot be excluded out of hand that the percentage of the population with what today is called an 'immigration background' has a negative effect on some other key indicators of the environment and gender justice. The World Values Survey data in Table 1 show that in most migration-sending countries, materialistic and not post-materialistic and environmentally conscious values tend to be the rule.

Table 1. Protecting environment vs. economic growth – data from the latest wave of the World Values Survey, 2004–2007

> *Here are two statements people sometimes make when discussing the environment and economic growth. Which of them comes closer to your own point of view?* (A) 'Protecting the environment should be given priority, even if it causes slower economic growth and some loss of jobs', and (B) 'Economic growth and creating jobs should be the top priority, even if the environment suffers to some extent'.

Possible answers include:

1. Protecting environment
2. Economy growth and creating jobs
3. Other answer

- Don't know
- No answer
- Not applicable
- Not asked in survey
- Missing; unknown

	Protecting environment	Economy growth and creating jobs	Other answer	Total number of surveyed (per cent)
Ethiopia	23.00%	77.00%	-	1,416 (100%)
South Africa	27.90%	70.80%	1.40%	2,724 (100%)
Zambia	37.40%	61.20%	1.50%	1,362 (100%)
Hong Kong	40.40%	59.60%	-	1,143 (100%)
Poland	42.10%	54.40%	3.40%	875 (100%)
South Korea	35.10%	52.50%	12.50%	1,195 (100%)
Ghana	47.90%	51.70%	0.40%	1,420 (100%)
Iran	48.20%	51.00%	0.80%	2,623 (100%)
Thailand	46.10%	50.40%	3.50%	1,495 (100%)
Germany	36.90%	50.20%	13.00%	1,896 (100%)
Bulgaria	46.40%	50.10%	3.50%	850 (100%)
Uruguay	48.90%	47.90%	3.20%	877 (100%)
Egypt	45.00%	47.40%	7.60%	3,051 (100%)
Mali	49.30%	47.10%	3.70%	1,122 (100%)
Netherlands	50.10%	46.60%	3.30%	981 (100%)
Romania	52.00%	46.10%	1.90%	1,615 (100%)
USA	54.10%	45.90%	-	1,209 (100%)
Jordan	54.30%	45.00%	0.80%	1,138 (100%)
Ukraine	55.60%	43.80%	0.60%	782 (100%)
Taiwan	52.50%	43.30%	4.20%	1,221 (100%)
Turkey	56.80%	42.70%	0.50%	1,259 (100%)
France	54.30%	41.40%	4.30%	961 (100%)
Slovenia	53.90%	41.00%	5.10%	963 (100%)
Russian Federation	55.10%	40.80%	4.10%	1,742 (100%)
Rwanda	59.30%	40.50%	0.20%	1,466 (100%)
World total	**54.60%**	**40.40%**	**5.00%**	**73,461 (100%)**
Malaysia	48.60%	39.90%	11.40%	1,197 (100%)
Trinidad and Tobago	59.90%	38.80%	1.20%	950 (100%)
Burkina Faso	55.70%	38.40%	5.90%	1,228 (100%)
Georgia	57.50%	38.30%	4.20%	1,279 (100%)
Moldova	60.30%	37.90%	1.80%	1,002 (100%)
Great Britain	61.60%	36.10%	2.30%	979 (100%)
Serbia	56.20%	35.90%	7.90%	1,177 (100%)

(Continued)

	Protecting environment	Economy growth and creating jobs	Other answer	Total number of surveyed (per cent)
India	52.50%	35.00%	12.50%	1,424 (100%)
New Zealand	65.00%	35.00%	-	715 (100%)
Australia	65.70%	34.30%	-	1,374 (100%)
Japan	53.20%	34.10%	12.70%	750 (100%)
Guatemala	61.80%	34.10%	4.00%	988 (100%)
Mexico	64.10%	33.60%	2.30%	1,422 (100%)
Cyprus	63.30%	33.60%	3.20%	1,036 (100%)
Sweden	64.70%	33.50%	1.80%	981 (100%)
Spain	64.20%	33.30%	2.50%	1,054 (100%)
Finland	65.90%	33.00%	1.10%	999 (100%)
Peru	65.90%	32.10%	2.00%	1,403 (100%)
Italy	60.90%	31.40%	7.70%	894 (100%)
Brazil	63.60%	31.40%	5.00%	1,433 (100%)
Chile	67.30%	30.90%	1.90%	922 (100%)
China	64.40%	29.50%	6.10%	1,553 (100%)
Colombia	69.90%	28.30%	1.80%	3,017 (100%)
Morocco	54.80%	28.20%	17.10%	1,083 (100%)
Vietnam	59.70%	26.10%	14.20%	1,435 (100%)
Indonesia	34.70%	25.40%	39.90%	1,635 (100%)
Canada	72.20%	22.70%	5.00%	2,041 (100%)
Argentina	74.90%	21.80%	3.30%	922 (100%)
Norway	77.20%	20.90%	1.90%	1,013 (100%)
Switzerland	74.40%	20.00%	5.60%	1,182 (100%)
Andorra	84.00%	9.40%	6.60%	989 (100%)

Source: our own compilations from the World Values Survey, 20 September 2010, online data analysis from http://www.wvsevsdb.com/wvs/WVSAnalize.jsp (accessed 27 January 2012).

Similar data could be produced on the attitudes on gender issues, prevailing in most migration-sending countries. Migration must be considered, *inter alia*, as a process of transferring more conservative value systems on such issues as the environment and gender from the countries of the South and East to the developed centres of the world economy.

Sanderson, 2010, was one of the first consistent attempts to bring in migration as a determining variable of social well-being. Contemporary levels of international migration in less-developed countries are raising new and important questions regarding the consequences of immigration for human welfare and well-being. However, there is little systematic cross-national evidence of how international migration affects human development levels in migrant-receiving countries in the less-developed world. This paper addresses this gap in the literature by assessing the impact of cumulative international migration flows on the Human Development Index, the composite, well-known UNDP measure of aggregate well-being. A series of panel data models are estimated using a sample of less-developed countries for the period, 1970 to 2005. The results indicate that higher levels of international migration are associated with lower scores on the Human Development Index, net of controls, but that the effect of international migration is relatively small.

Education Is Good For Development

Ever since the writings of Coleman (1965), also education should be mentioned among the determining variables of the development performance of a country. Education and human capital formation figure prominently in the *Human Development Reports* of the United Nations Development Programme as variables, which determine positively the development outcome. For the UNDP it has been self-evident over the last decade that gender empowerment and the re-direction of public expenditures away from defence will positively contribute to a positive development outcome. However, neoliberal thought would caution against such premature conclusions. Erich Weede (2002) has shown that standard indicators of human capital endowment – like literacy, school enrolment ratios, or years of schooling - suffer from a number of defects. They are crude. Mostly, they refer to input rather than output measures of human capital formation. Occasionally, Weede and Kaempf believe, these indicators produce implausible effects. They are not robustly significant determinants of growth. They replaced them by average intelligence. This variable consistently outperforms the other human capital indicators in spite of suffering from severe defects of its own.

Weede and his associates maintain that the immediate impact of institutional improvements, i.e. more government tolerance of private enterprise or economic freedom, on growth is in the same order of magnitude as intelligence effects. Public education expenditure is still public expenditure, and it is entirely conceivable that in the end public education expenditure might negatively affect the development chances of a society, not because it is education expenditure, but because it is still public expenditure. For such a theoretical understanding, university reform and university privatization would be important political steps to achieve a more viable development. The UNDP has devoted considerable energies into developing its own kind of human capital and human development approach that quoted large amounts of statistics on how much different countries devoted to their 'unproductive' military efforts and how little they devoted to the 'good' public education expenditures. Such number games suffered from a major scientific handicap by evading the vital question of the comparison of the effects of different types of government expenditures, among them public education expenditures and military expenditures, on indicators of economic growth, human rights, social justice, gender empowerment and ecological well-being (see UNDP *HDR 1998, 2004, 2005*).

Policy pointer

Education is certainly one of the main drivers of a nation's positive development performance. However, does education really have to be publicly financed? The majority of the world's leading universities nowadays are tuition-fee financed institutions in the Anglo-Saxon world. It is depressing to hear all these European debates about 'Lisbon', EU-2020 and research and development expenditures rising to 3 per cent of the GDP without a proper, parallel debate on what to do with our state-owned universities.

The Role of Other Factors

Our account of the other variables, which might yield an influence on the development process, will be rather short. The 'Keynesian' legacy should not be underestimated. 'Keynesians' would expect positive trade-offs to hold between 'government intervention' and the human condition, and not the other way around.[25]

In our macro-quantitative research design, we also include the well-documented 'butter versus guns' dimension of militarization as a development blockade.[26] In our analysis, militarization is considered to be part and parcel of the syndrome of the dependent insertion of the countries of the periphery into the world economy. Especially German inspired peace research underlined this fatal connection, and a number of such studies are available in English on the issue.[27] With some justification, it can be claimed that the highlighting of this point was one of the genuine contributions of peace research in West Germany in the 1970s and 1980s to the international debate on dependency and the world-system.[28]

Military personnel rates were also featured quite frequently in the literature as a driver or bottleneck of development.[29] While some researchers think that military expenditures improve domestic economic performance, others vehemently believe that they crowd out growth-inducing processes.[30] Military expenditures could

---

25 Major Keynesian analyses include nowadays Kalecki (1972, 1979); Modigliani (1987); Stack and Zimmerman (1982); Stack (1978, 1980); and Vickrey (1996).

26 See also Tausch (1986, 1989); Tausch and Prager (1993); and Tausch and Herrmann (2001) for further references on this vast sub-debate of international development accounting.

27 Brzoska and Lock (1992); Brzoska and Ohlson (1986, 1987); Brzoska and Pearson (1994).

28 In addition, also the available studies by Eide and Thee (1980), Kaldor (1983) and Wolpin (1986) would suggest integrating the militarization dimension more closely than has been done hitherto into dependency theory and world-systems research.

29 Among the studies, which claimed a beneficial and positive effect of high military personnel ratios on economic growth were Weede (1980a, 1980b, 1981a, 1981b, 1983, 1985, 1986, 1993); Weede and Jagodzinski (1980a, 1980b); Weede and Tiefenbach (1981a, 1981b, 1981c). More recent research, most notably by Kentor and Kick (2008), however, claimed that recently global military expenditures have escalated sharply despite some worldwide declines in military personnel.

30 Kentor and Kick explore a new dimension of military spending – military expenditures per soldier which measures the capital intensiveness of a country's military organization. The

inhibit national development in part by slowing the expansion of the labour force. Labour-intensive militaries may provide a pathway for upward mobility, but comparatively capital-intensive military organizations limit entry opportunities for unskilled and under- or unemployed people. Deep investments in military hardware also may reduce the investment capital available for more economically productive opportunities.[31] A forceful argument against high military personnel rates and against conscription has come however from a recent, widely circulated study by Keller, Poutvaara and Wagener (2010),[32] which maintains that economic theory as such would predict that military conscription is associated with static inefficiencies as well as with dynamic distortions of the accumulation of human and physical capital. Relative to an economy with an all-volunteer force, the authors think that output levels and growth rates are expected to be lower in countries that rely on military draft to recruit their army personnel. Military conscription has a negative impact on GDP and on its growth is claimed to be robust. OECD countries would be ill-advised to rely on military drafting in their effort to achieve higher economic performance.

The well-known non-linear effects of development levels on development performance (what the social sciences sometimes call the 'acceleration and maturity effects') have to be also qualified in an important way. Ever since the days of the Nobel laureate economist Simon Kuznets, development researchers have applied certain types of mathematical formulations ('curve-linear formulations') in order to capture these effects. One particular formulation, explaining economic growth by a non-linear function of development levels and their square (what is then called, in

---

cross-national panel regression and causal analyses of developed and less developed countries from 1990 to 2003 show, according to Kentor and Kick that military expenditures per soldier inhibit the growth of per capita GDP, net of control variables, with the most pronounced effects in least developed countries.

31 Kentor and Kick also find that arms imports have a positive effect on economic growth, but only in less developed countries.

32 Keller, Poutvaara, and Wagener (2010) maintain that economic theory as such would predict that military conscription is associated with static inefficiencies as well as with dynamic distortions of the accumulation of human and physical capital. Relative to an economy with an all-volunteer force, the authors think that output levels and growth rates are expected to be lower in countries that rely on military draft to recruit their army personnel. The losses in individual lifetime earnings, which a number of microeconometric studies observe for former conscripts, indeed translate into substantial reductions in income and growth on the macroeconomic level, rendering military conscription a socially unnecessarily costly way of military recruitment. The claimed result that military conscription has a negative impact on GDP and on its growth is robust in various specifications. Keller, Poutvaara and Wagener (2010) measured the impact of conscription by a dummy variable, by the labour force share of conscripts, and by the duration of conscription or of alternative service. With all these variables, conscription has a consistently negative and usually statistically significant effect. The variable 'military expenses' however varies in sign. The coefficients are generally of similar magnitude also in smaller samples when potential outliers are excluded or their effects diminished.

technical language, a 'curve-linear function of economic growth'), are sometimes called the 'Matthew effect' following Matthew 13:12:

> For whosoever hath, to him shall be given, and he shall have more abundance: but whosoever hath not, from him shall be taken away even that he hath.

Social scientists interpreted this effect mainly in view of an acceleration of economic growth in middle-income countries vis-à-vis the poor countries and in view of the still widening gap between the poorest periphery nations ('have-nots') and the 'haves' among the semi-periphery countries (Jackman 1982), but they also applied a similar effect to income inequality and more recently, to an 'environmental Kuznets curve'.

Our essay does not only take world economic integration/globalization dimension as a determinant of development performance into account, but also duly considers the dimensions of feminism (see UNDP, *HDR 1995*), culture (membership of a country in the Islamic Conference; see the vast social science debate following Huntington), demography, the economic size of nations, and geography (absolute latitude) into account (see also Easterly 2000). Such control variables are standard practice in cross-national development research and for reasons of space need not be further presented here. Interested readers are referred to the works of Easterly, Heshmati and Tausch for further reference.

There are nowadays rather conflicting views on such factors as population density and population size available on the world market of ideas, which all render themselves for further empirical testing, Already classical Latin American social science, in the works of the Peruvian Marxist José Carlos Mariategui (1894–1930), whose name is hardly ever mentioned in the cross-national development debate, clearly foresaw what he saw as the devastating negative long-term development effects of a low population density on subsequent patterns of development. Mariategui, a very interesting Marxist scholar, who achieved unfortunately posthumous international celebrity by the hijacking of his name by the terrorist group Sendero Luminoso five decades after his death, clearly distinguishes between what he sees as the extensive and wasteful Iberian heritage of colonialism, with its use of the 'abundant production factors' land and fresh, unqualified labour. His account of the rapidly growing labour force in scattered tiny settlements in the Sierra region of the Andes in conjunction with extensive land use and high land concentration make the inclusion of the population density variable in any macro-quantitative account of development performance important.

At the other end of the scale of the views on population density and size, our readers should be reminded that these questions also play an important role in the works of the economists Ernst Friedrich 'Fritz' Schumacher (1911–1977) and Leopold Kohr (1909–1994).[33] Schumacher's critique of Western economies and his proposals for human-scale, decentralized and appropriate technologies led him to call for

---

33 The authors gratefully mention the comments of an anonymous peer-reviewer of this book project on this point. The most important ideas by Kohr and Schumacher were stated in Kohr (1957, 1958, 1960, 1977, 1992) and Schumacher (1973a, 1973b, 1976, 1977).

'Intermediate Size' and 'Intermediate Technology'.[34] Schumacher, in many ways, must be considered as one of the founders of contemporary thinking about 'sustainable development'. The basic logic of the Happy Planet Index, which is extensively used throughout this work, can be traced back to Schumacher's writings.[35] Leopold Kohr's opposition to the 'cult of bigness' in social organization must be also mentioned in this context. Central to Schumacher's concerns is the idea that in rich countries these developments can be partly compensated, as far as incomes are concerned, by an enormous and never ending expansion of welfare payments; in poor countries it produces 'dual societies' – great masses of destitute people on the one side – many of them without work and living in slums – and a small, rich elite on the other, who often 'earn' in an hour more than most of their compatriots earn in a month. A genuine middle class to connect the extremes does not exist; it has disappeared together with the 'disappearing middle' of technology. The loss of social structure is paralleled by the loss of a coherent structure as far as human settlements are concerned: hence the appearance of vast congestion in a few places and a vast (relative) emptiness in all other places (Schumacher 1973b, 1976). Schumacher's alternative strategy is based on the factors of smallness, simplicity, capital-cheapness and non-violence. Schumacher was also among the first to highlight the enormous dependence of modern, industrialized agriculture on fossil fuels. Harvested crops capture solar energy and store it as food or some other useful product. Yet the energy captured is small compared to the energy we burn to capture it. Agriculture, as a result, has become a major consumer of our stores of energy, using more petroleum than any other single industry. If the world is facing a future with rising energy prices, the highly mechanized technology currently used in modern, industrialized agriculture may be inappropriate (Schumacher 1973b).

In Schumacher (1973b) it is already being argued that government effort must be concentrated on sustainable development, because relatively minor improvements, for example, technology transfer to Third World countries, will not solve the underlying problem of an unsustainable economy. 'Buddhist economics', developed in this book, and based on minimum material consumption in relation to life quality, is contrasted with notions like 'growth is good', and 'bigger is better'. Schumacher indeed was one of the first economists to question the appropriateness of gross national product as a measure for human well-being, emphasizing that 'the aim ought to be to obtain the maximum amount of well being with the minimum amount of consumption' (Schumacher 1973b).

For Kohr's approach, the consequences are even more radical;[36] there seems only one cause behind all forms of social misery: bigness. Whenever something is wrong, something is too big. Social problems, have the tendency to grow at a geometric ratio with the growth of the organism of which they are part, while the ability of man to cope with them, if it can be extended at all, grows only at an arithmetic ratio. For Kohr it is clear that if a society grows beyond its optimum size, its problems must eventually outrun the growth of those human faculties which are necessary for dealing with them. A small-state

---

34 For a very good overview of Schumacherian economics, see also http://www.resurgence.org/education/schumacher-circle.html#ne (accessed 27 January 2012).

35 Ibid.

36 See Kohr (1957, 1958, 1960, 1977, 1992).

world would not only solve the problems of social brutality and war; it would solve the problems of oppression and tyranny. It would solve all problems arising from power:

> As regards the scale of socially committed or condoned atrocities, we have so far discovered one fact. Most nations, irrespective of their racial background, the stage of their civilization, their ideology, or their economic system, have managed to roll up an impressively similar record. Mass executions and related monstrosities were perpetrated in Germany under the Nazis, in India under the British, in France under the Catholics, in Russia under some of the most savage, and in Italy under some of the most enlightened, princes. There could not have been a vaster difference of conditions. Yet, if similar excesses occurred everywhere and in all phases and periods of historic development, there must apparently be a common element transcending these differences. This common denominator, as we shall see, seems to be the simple ability, the power, to commit monstrosities. As a result, we arrive at what we might call a power theory of social misery. In part, the proposition seems self-evident. For no one could perpetrate atrocities without the power to do so. But this is not the point. The point is that the proposition operates also in the reverse. Everyone having the power will in the end commit the appropriate atrocities. This sounds somewhat extreme. Clearly, not everybody holding power must necessarily make evil use of it. Which is quite true, but it does not alter the proposition. (Kohr 1957, ch. 2)

Policy pointer

Any good comparative study has to take other possible drivers of development performance into account, including geography, development history and levels, the trajectory of gender emancipation in the country, as well as population size, and population density. Without them, results are simply unrealistic.

We should now briefly comment on how these different theoretical concepts were tested in the hitherto published research literature.

Economic Growth

Typically, Bornschier, Chase-Dunn and Rubinson reached five major conclusions:[37]

1. Direct foreign investment and aid increase economic inequality within countries.
2. Direct foreign investment and aid flows produce short-term increases in relative rates of economic growth within countries.

---

37 The dependency-oriented economic growth theories, most coherently presented in Bornschier, Chase-Dunn, and Rubinson (1978), were maintained, among others, by Alderson and Nielsen (1999); Bornschier (1980a); Clark (2008); Dixon and Boswell (1996); Herkenrath and Bornschier (2002); Kentor (1998); and Mahutga (2006).

3. Stocks of direct foreign investment and aid produce long-term cumulative decreases in economic growth rates.
4. This relationship is a conditional factor for levels of development in countries, the negative effect of investment stocks and of aid stocks being much greater in richer developing countries.
5. These relationships are independent of geographical area.

However, such interpretations did not go uncontested. An influential number of international sociological and political studies vehemently challenged Bornschier's world-view.[38] Certainly, one of the most influential and more recent studies became the one published by Soysa and Oneal (1999). It maintained that by using the latest data and better models of economic growth than those previously used, and considering the role of human capital in the process of economic development, there is no evidence that foreign direct investment harms the economic prospects of developing countries.[39]

---

38 Among them Dutt (1997); Firebaugh and Beck (1994); Firebaugh (1992); Kurzman, Werun and Burkhart (2002); Pattnayak (1999); Soysa and Oneal (1999); Weede and Tiefenbach (1981a, 1981b, 1981c); and Weede (1981a, 1981b). Firebaugh's analysis (1992) was an especially bitter pill to swallow for dependency-oriented theories of economic growth. The article consists of a reanalysis of data from previous dependency studies in 76 less-developed countries in the Bornschier research tradition. Firebaugh shows that, contrary to earlier conclusions, foreign investment spurs rather than inhibits economic growth. Previous studies focused on the coefficient for foreign capital stock, controlling for 'flow' (new investment), and inferred that a negative coefficient for stock reflects dependency effects that retard economic growth. Because capital stock is the denominator for the rate of investment, it follows that the greater the stock, the lower the investment rate for a given level of new investment. Thus, it is concluded that the negative coefficient for capital stock indicates a beneficial rather than a harmful investment effect. In the analysis put forward by Firebaugh and Beck (1994), the authors contend that sociologists have paid little attention to the possible national benefits of economic growth. Instead, they have focused on the possible harm caused by the Third World's dependence on foreign investment and trade. Firebaugh and Beck vehemently question that focus. Based on data for 62 less-developed countries spanning over two decades, they find that the effects of dependence largely vanish when (1) the effects of economic growth are carefully specified, and (2) the 'semi-difference' models currently in vogue in cross-national research are replaced by more appropriate difference or difference-of-logs (growth-rate) models. In light of the common claim that economic growth in the Third World benefits only the rich, Firebaugh and Beck employ measures of national welfare that the rich cannot readily monopolize. The effects of economic growth on national welfare are large and robust, whereas the effects of dependence are hard to find. These findings contradict earlier studies, which had concluded that the effects of dependence dwarf the effects of economic growth.

39 The flow of foreign capital from 1980 to 1991 spurred growth in gross domestic product per capita, while the level of foreign stock, or 'foreign penetration' had no discernible effect. Indeed, new foreign investment was more productive dollar for dollar than was capital from domestic sources. Previous suggestions that foreign investment flows are less beneficial than domestic ones were based, the authors maintain, on a misinterpretation. Moreover, foreign direct investment stimulates investment from domestic sources. Consequently, developing countries have no reason to eschew foreign capital, as dependency theorists urge. No final conclusions for or against dependency-oriented explanations of economic growth can be

Social Cohesion

A great number of empirical studies also maintained, in the spirit of Bornschier, Chase-Dunn and Rubinson (1978), that dependent development, dominated by the transnational corporations, leads to increased socio-economic inequality.[40] A variety of other studies, using a wide array of indicators, ranging from child mortality; child survival, childhood immunization, economic growth, prevalence of health attendants, adequate nutrition, balanced urbanization; female life expectancy; food consumption; infant mortality; infant mortality decline; life expectancy; maternal mortality; mortality, health and welfare; occupational sex segregation and occupational inequality; per capita calorie and protein consumption; physical quality of life index; to population growth and economic development, also maintained that neo-liberal globalization, centred around transnational corporate investment, does not promote, in the language of the European Commission 'social inclusion' and is not an adequate instrument for 'combating poverty and social cohesion'.[11] A very small number of dependency and world-systems–oriented studies also concerned wider aspects of the labour market as constituting part and parcel of the problem of socio-economic inequalities.[12] However, it should be noted that these studies did not measure unemployment rates directly, but only proxy variables for unemployment, i.e. outward migration, and overurbanization.

Neoliberal countervailing studies maintained that the negative consequences of MNC penetration and world market openness for income redistribution are

---

drawn, according to our view, from the studies published by Glasberg and Ward (1993); Kentor and Boswell (2003); Kentor and Jorgenson (2010); and Kick, Davis, Lehtinen and Burns (2000). Kentor and Jorgenson (2010) explored the impact of foreign investment on development from an organizational perspective, by examining the role of foreign subsidiaries in the economic growth of less developed countries between 1970 and 2000. Two aspects of foreign subsidiaries are considered. The first is the total number of foreign subsidiaries located in a given country. The second dimension is 'foreign subsidiary concentration', the percentage of foreign subsidiaries located in a given country owned by corporations headquartered in a single country. Several findings emerge from structural equation models of 41–70 less developed countries between 1970 and 2000. First, overall growth of foreign subsidiaries between 1970 and 2000 has a positive effect on economic growth in less developed countries. Second, relatively high levels of foreign subsidiary concentration in 1970 inhibit this expansion of foreign subsidiaries. Two other aspects of foreign investment, foreign investment concentration and foreign capital dominance, also retard the expansion of foreign subsidiaries. Further analyses suggest that political corruption may, in part, mediate these relationships.

40 This standard theme of quantitative dependency and world-system research was further developed, among others, by Bornschier (1983); Kentor (2001); Lee (2005); Mahutga and Bandelj (2008); Mills (2009); and Morris (1999).

41 Among others Boehmer and Williamson (1996); Bradshaw (1993); Lena and London (1993); Meyer (2003); Moore, Teixeira and Shiell (2006); Ragin and Bradshaw (1992); Rice (2008); Shandra, Nobles, London and Williamson (2004, 2005); Shandra, Shandra and London (2010); Shen and Williamson (1997, 1999 and 2001); Spencer (2006); Timberlake and Williams (1987); Williamson and Boehmer (1997); Wimberley and Bello (1992); and Wimberley (1998).

42 Among them the studies by Bradshaw and Schafer (2000); Sanderson and Kentor (2008); Shandra, London, and Williamson (2003a, 2003b).

non-existent or insignificant, or even positive.[43] Let us look for a moment at the structure of the arguments put forward by the studies constituting the greatest challenge to the dependency/world-systems consensus in the literature. Without going too much into the details (interested readers can follow them in the footnote), we should highlight that the critique of dependency and world-systems theory revolved around the following positions:

a) The German sociologist Erich Weede's contention that Galtung's structural theory of imperialism, in which vertical trade and feudal interaction patterns are seen as impoverishing less-developed countries, Immanuel Wallerstein's world system theory in which the growth performance of economies is seen as being reinforced by state strength; and Volker Bornschier's sociology in which penetration by multinational corporations is viewed as decreasing LDCs' growth rates receive 'little support'. Instead, level of economic development, gross domestic investment, military participation ratio, and some human capital variables contribute to economic growth.

b) The Harvard sociologist Jason Beckfield maintains that not MNC penetration, but regional economic integration raises income inequality.

c) Bussmann, de Soysa and Oneal (2005) indicate that globalization does not increase national income inequality.

d) Tsai (2006a) maintains that besides a country's income level, tropics, landlockedness, population growth, and secondary schooling opportunity are significant predictors of poverty reduction, whereas political factors (democracy, military spending, and war) and government social spending are only weak predictors.[44]

---

43 Among them Beckfield (2006b); Bussmann, de Soysa and Oneal (2005); Crenshaw (1992); and Tsai (2006a), in addition to the earlier studies published by Weede (1981a, 1981b) and Weede and Tiefenbach (1981a, 1981b).

44 Weede (1981a) tests three dependency approaches: (1) Johan Galtung's structural theory of imperialism, in which vertical trade and feudal interaction patterns are seen as impoverishing less-developed countries (LDCs); (2) those of Immanuel Wallerstein in which the growth performance of economies is seen as being reinforced by state strength; and (3) that of Volker Bornschier in which penetration by multinational corporations is viewed as decreasing LDCs' growth rates. These ideas are tested by regressions on a database including information on 97 nations, of which 78 are LDCs. By and large, dependency propositions receive little support. Instead, level of economic development, gross domestic investment, military participation ratio, and some human capital variables contribute to economic growth. Weede (1981b) then attempts to explain cross-national differences in economic growth and income inequality, and data on growth (or decline) of gross national income, and per capita income, by the degree of military participation, by the penetration of multinational corporations, and by the type of economy (capitalist or communist). In Volker Bornschier's version of dependency theory, penetration by multinational corporations has a major negative impact on developing countries. According to 'military sociology', power politics and competition between states positively contribute to growth and distribution of income. Operationally, the military participation ratio is the decisive independent variable. In regression analysis, both 'world system' approaches to explanation of the distribution of income received only marginal confirmation. It is concluded that the military sociology perspective may contribute more than Bornschier's version of dependency theory.

In this survey, we must also mention those studies which could not reach a definitive conclusion, either way, on the social and political imbalances, which dependency and world-systems theories maintain are the consequences of a peripheral position

---

Weede and Tiefenbach (1981c) replicate the Weede (1981a) findings: three different dependency explanations of economic growth are evaluated through cross-sectional regression analyses for 98 countries between 1960 and 1977, using logged per capita gross national product, its square, gross domestic investment, and the military participation ratio as control variables. Johan Galtung's 'A Structural Theory of Imperialism' seems to contain one useful predictor of economic growth, commodity concentration, which hurts the growth prospects of nations; but neither his vertical trade nor his partner concentration has any significant impact. R. Rubinson's 'state strength' approach receives no support at all, since strong states, operationalized by government revenue/gross domestic product, come closer to hurting than promoting economic growth. V. Bornschier's 'investment dependency' approach also fails to explain why some less-developed countries (LDCs) do so much better or worse than others. It is suggested that future research on linkages between the world system and the economic performance of LDCs might profit from broadening the research agenda to include power politics and its military participation effects in addition to political economy variables. Beckfield (2006b) pretends to show that regional economic integration raises income inequality, as workers are exposed to international competition and labour unions are weakened. Regional political integration should also raise income inequality, but through a different mechanism: political integration should drive welfare state retrenchment in market-oriented regional polities as states adopt liberal policies in a context of fiscal austerity. Evidence from random-effects and fixed-effects models of income inequality in Western Europe supports these arguments. Beckfield's results show that regional integration explains nearly half of the increase in income inequality in the Western European countries analysed. The effects of regional integration on income inequality are net of several control variables, including two established measures of globalization, suggesting that a sociological approach to regional integration adds to the understanding of rising income inequality in Western Europe. Bussmann, de Soysa and Oneal (2005), analyse data on inequality and foreign investment for 72 countries, 1970–90, incorporating in their tests the Kuznets (1955) curve, the character of political institutions, and various other aspects of the economy and society emphasized in previous research. The results indicate that globalization does not increase national income inequality. The ratio of foreign direct investment to gross domestic product is unrelated to the distribution of income in both developing and developed countries. The share of income received by the poorest 20 per cent of society is also unaffected by foreign investment. Nor are alternative measures of economic openness – the trade-to-GDP ratio and Sachs and Warner's (1995) measure of free trading policies – associated with greater income inequality. If foreign investment increases average incomes in developing countries, as recent research indicates, and does not increase inequality, it must benefit all strata of these societies, including the poor. Tsai (2006a) conducted a cross-national research on 97 developing countries to test a number of competing hypotheses of poverty. Four major theories from the social sciences were examined, including (1) economic development and openness, (2) geographical and demographical disadvantages, (3) regime characteristics and war; and (4) social policy and human capital enhancement, to determine their explanatory power by modelling the ratio of the poor to total population in those countries. Poverty is defined in the essay by living below an income of US$1 or $2 a day. Both the incidences of poverty and the poor's income shortfall from the non-poor are analysed with ridge regression modelling. Empirical outcomes reveal that besides a country's income level, tropics, landlockedness, population growth and secondary schooling opportunity are significant predictors of poverty reduction, whereas political factors (democracy, military spending and war) and government social spending are only weak predictors.

in the world economy.[45] The startling variety of these inconclusive published major studies concerned: the consequences of dependency for the phenomena of economic and social rights; the Human Development Index; inflation; unemployment; rapid urbanization; state revenue; social spending; human rights; income inequality; manufacturing employment; political exclusion; debt dependence; political instability; political conflict; political violence; instability; and repression.

In a time perspective, one of last substantial empirical research findings on this controversy was the essay by Babones and Zhang (2008). It is widely accepted that higher levels of international trade are associated with higher levels of income inequality. Aggregate trade, however, is not empirically related to income inequality for any panel of countries, and country-level research focusing specifically on 'North–South' trade and national income inequality has generally yielded inconsistent or non-significant results. In this research note, the authors attribute this disconnect between expectations and reality to heterogeneity among the countries typically classed as members of the global 'South'. The authors follow world-systems theorists in identifying two distinct zones in the global South: semi-peripheral and peripheral.[46]

Mahutga and Bandelj (2008) dealt on what they call 'the natural experiment of Central and Eastern Europe (CEE)'. They estimated a series of regression models that relate income inequality to foreign investment and a baseline internal development model. They found that foreign investment has a robust positive effect on income inequality. Further, they show that the effect is observable over the short term, no matter how FDI is measured. They conclude by directing attention to CEE countries as a historically unique opportunity to gauge the effect of exposure to the world economy on many development outcomes.

Policy pointer

For the discipline of political science and sociological comparative development research, recent advances would suggest to work with a wider concept of 'social cohesion', not just analysing income inequality, but also economic and social rights; social spending; human rights; political exclusion and, finally, political repression.

---

45 Among them the studies by Alderson and Nielsen (2002); Babones and Zhang (2008); Bussmann and Schneider (2007); Crenshaw and Ameen (1994); Davenport (1995); Gustafsson and Johansson (1999); Hafner-Burton (2005); Kaya (2010); Kukreja (1991); Lee, Nielsen and Alderson (2007); Moaddel (1994); Payne (2009); Reuveny and Li (2003); Robinson and London (1991); and finally Tsai (2007).

46 Accordingly, they propose a model that divides the countries of the world into three income categories (core/semi-periphery/periphery) rather than the usual two found in the economics literature (North/South). Consistent with their model, they find that the relationship between inequality and trade is consistently conditioned on zone of the world-economy over the period 1980–2000.

Cancun and the Environment

A real 'growth industry' of the last years was the blossoming and booming dependency – and world-systems–oriented study of environmental problems. Notably enough, not one of these studies used the combined Yale/Columbia indices of the environmental situation, the Environmental Sustainability Index (ESI) and the Environmental Performance Index (EPI), available today for a very wide range of countries. They relied instead on a startling variety of approximately 18 major environmental indicators, including carbon dioxide emissions; deforestation; ecological footprint; emission of organic water pollutants; energy use; environmental protection efforts; fertilizer and pesticide consumption; greenhouse gas emissions; growth of ecological footprint; industrial organic water pollution; infant mortality; nitrogen oxides, volatile organic compounds, carbon monoxide, and carbon dioxide gas; nitrous oxide emissions; organic water pollution; pesticide consumption; pesticide and fertilizer use; threatened mammal species; and total carbon dioxide emissions and emissions per unit of production to water pollution. These indicators were often available for only a limited number of developing nations, excluding the experience of the countries of Eastern and Central Europe and the former USSR, and other post-communist nations.

Policy pointer

Neither Eurostat nor the most well-known sociological and political science studies on globalization and the environment make systematic use of the combined Yale/Columbia indices of the environmental situation, the Environmental Sustainability Index (ESI) and the Environmental Performance Index (EPI), which are available for a very wide range of countries. While Eurostat uses its own limited environment data series, the major sociological and political science studies instead relied on a startling variety of approximately 18 major environmental indicators, often available for only a limited number of developing nations, and excluding the experience of the countries of Eastern and Central Europe and the former USSR, and other post-communist nations. To exclude the experience of the heavy industrial and polluted former communist countries is misleading.

From a conceptual viewpoint, this de facto exclusion of the former or continuously communist nations in Eastern Europe, the former USSR and in Asia and Cuba is a major theoretical weakness. The environmental crisis, blamed in most empirical studies on the workings of 'transnational capitalism' was especially severe in the heavy industrial and polluted communist countries before the transformation to some form of capitalism and before the large-scale penetration of these countries by transnational capital.

Nevertheless, the relatively coherent tendency of these studies suggests that there seems to be a strong interaction between transnational capitalist penetration and environmental degradation, especially in third world countries.[17]

To date, the most important neoliberal counter-study to this fledging scientific tradition was the essay by Ehrhardt-Martinez, Crenshaw and Jenkins (2002), which analysed deforestation rates (1980–1995) in the developing countries.[48]

Policy pointer

Although some four out of five of existing studies supported globalization-critical research and the Kalecki–Steindl paradigm, we have to emphasize that the state of the debate on the past empirical studies suggests that a further, thorough investigation about the drivers and bottlenecks of economic growth, social cohesion and the environment on a global level is necessary.

Learning from Advances in the Medical Profession

Decades ago, it would have been unthinkable to find articles on, say, income inequality and life expectancy, in such journals as the *British Medical Journal*. Nowadays, leading and high-impact factor journals of the medical profession are more and more engaged in such debates and the international literature on the determinants of life quality is a growing sub-industry of the development accounting profession in both disciplines. The contradictory array of findings is amazing indeed.[49]

---

47 Most notably Dick and Jorgenson (2010); Jorgenson and Burns (2007); Jorgenson (2003, 2004a, 2004b, 2005, 2006a, 2006b, 2007a, 2007b, 2008, 2009a, 2009b, 2009c, 2009d); Jorgenson and Burns (2004); Jorgenson, Dick and Mahutga (2007); Jorgenson, Kuykendall and Kennon (2008); Lawrence (2009); Longo and York (2008); Mostafa and Nataraajan (2009); Mostafa (2010a, 2010b); Nugent and Shandra (2009); Shandra (2007a, 2007b); Shandra and London (2008); Shandra, Leckband and London (2009); Shandra, Leckband, McKinney and London (2009); Shandra, London, Whooley and Williamson (2004); and finally Shandra, Shor and London (2008, 2009).

48 The authors used ordinary least squares regression with White's correction method for possible heteroskedasticity in the case of less developed countries. Net of controls for initial forest stock and the quality of deforestation estimates, the authors find strong evidence for an environmental Kuznets curve driven by (1) agglomeration effects linked to the level of urbanization, (2) rural-to-urban migration that partially offsets rural population pressure, (3) the growth of services-dominated urban economies, and (4) strong democratic states. The authors find little evidence that foreign debt or export dependence influence the deforestation rate. Although deforestation continues to pose pressing and potentially irreversible environmental risks, there is evidence of self-corrective ecological and modernization processes inherent in development that act to mitigate these risks.

49 Bloom and Canning (2007); Elola, Daponte and Navarro (1995); Franco-Giraldo, Palma, Alvarez-Dardet (2006); Ghobara, Huth and Russett (2004); Jamison, Sandbu and Wang (2001); Jorgenson (2004a, 2004b, 2005, 2009a, 2009b); Jorgenson and Burns (2004); Kawachi and Kennedy (1997); Kawachi, Kennedy and Wilkinson (1999); Kawachi, Kennedy, Lochner et al. (1997); Lynch, Smith, Harper, Hillemeier, Ross, Kaplan and Wolfson (2004); Macinko, Shi and

Thus a variety of approaches can be distinguished today, which ranges from more conventional models of dependency and world system analysis in the tradition of Bornschier and Wallerstein[50] to the alleged detrimental effects of trade union strength and the urban bias on health development.[51] In the leading medical journals of our planet, there is now a very widely received tendency to name inequality as the main causal factor of deficient infant mortality reduction and life expectancy,[52] although also militarism was held responsible for deficient health developments in an influential article of the medical profession, which appeared in one of the international flagship journals, the *Lancet*.[53]

An interesting study in this context is the essay by Furukawa (2005).[54] Using life expectancy and infant mortality rates as health indicators, a multiple regression analysis (regression equation)[55] was established, using these indicators as dependent variables, and with socio-economic environmental data as independent variables. Furukawa arrived at the following conclusions:

1. For improving health of people in recipient countries, it is important to secure safe drinking water, improve literacy, and increase income and the possibility of access to basic medicines.
2. For countries where there are a lot of refugees, it is important to increase the measles vaccine inoculation rate.
3. In countries where there are few refugees, life expectancy will be prolonged by as much as three years if the measles vaccine inoculation rate increases by just 10 per cent.
4. In countries with a high armaments expenditure rate in proportion to GDP, it is important to secure access to sanitary toilet facilities.
5. Life expectancy in countries tends to shorten if life expectancy in their neighbouring countries is short.
6. The rate of public health expenditures in proportion to GDP has no affect on health.
7. If the literacy rate rises 10 per cent, life expectancy will be prolonged by about 1.2 years and the infant mortality rate will decrease about 6 per cent.

Starfield (2004); Mackenbach, Kunst, Cavelaars et al. (1997); Marmot and Wilkinson (2001); McGuire (1998); Navarro and Shi (2001); Owen and Wu (2007); Palma-Solis et al. (2009); Papageorgiou, Savvides and Zachariadis (2007); Preston (2007); Soares (2007); Wickrama, Bikask and Wickrama (2003); Wilkinson (1992a, 1992b, 1997); Wilkinson and Picket (2006); Williamson and Boehmer (1997); and Woolhandler and Himmelstein (1985).

50 Jorgenson (2004a, 2004b, 2005, 2009a, 2009b); Jorgenson and Burns (2004).
51 McGuire (1998).
52 Kawachi and Kennedy (1997); Kawachi, Kennedy and Wilkinson (1999); Kawachi, Kennedy, Lochner et al. (1997); Marmot and Wilkinson (2001); Wilkinson (1992a, 1992b, 1997); Wilkinson and Picket (2006).
53 Woolhandler and Himmelstein (1985).
54 The essay presents a factor analytical and multiple regression research design. Using data from the World Bank World Development Indicators 2002 and 2003, and Human Development Indicators 2002, published by the United Nations Development Programme, Furukawa analysed 68 countries classified as middle and low income countries by the World Bank.
55 See our glossary of terms of concepts.

Recent econometric or polito-metric attempts to identify the determinants of cross-country mortality changes generally support the view that world economic openness significantly contributes towards decreasing mortality in developing countries.[56] Jamison et al. (2001) observed furthermore that landlocked countries and countries in tropical areas tend towards smaller improvements in life expectancy. Papageorgiou et al. (2007) showed that medical imports originating from the ten countries responsible for the bulk of medical research and development worldwide are systematically related to lower mortality. They also associate female schooling, calorie intake, and physician availability with mortality reduction outcomes. The very wide range of causal factors being mentioned as well as the very wide array of mostly very limited samples and research designs[57] in the widely received journal articles[58] make a new analysis of the underlying causes of life expectancy and infant mortality highly necessary.

From the standpoint of the empirical social scientist, working in the field of cross-national development research, especially Wilkinson's widely received hypotheses about the causal trade-off between inequality and low health, manifesting itself in various social indicators, such as life expectancy and infant mortality, sound reasonable. However, Beckfield (2006a) came to the conclusion that the relationship between health and inequality shrinks when control variables are included. Much of the research, published by Wilkinson and his school over the past decades, looks merely into the bi-variate correlations between inequality and social performance at the level of OECD democracies. However, current global social science has data about inequality from practically all over the globe at its disposal. Limiting his research to relatively small samples is error number one in Wilkinson's approach. Error number two is that Wilkinson overlooks the curve-linear trade-off between development levels and inequality levels.[59] Error number three consists in overlooking what colleague Joshua Goldstein, already back in 1985,[60] called the 'plateau curve of basic human needs'.[61]

---

56 Bloom and Canning (2007); Ghobara, Huth and Russett (2004); Jamison, Sandbu and Wang (2001); Owen and Wu (2007); Papageorgiou, Savvides and Zachariadis (2007); Preston (2007); Shaw, Hoorace and Vogel (2005); Soares (2007).

57 Bi-variate analysis versus multiple regression analysis.

58 Elola, Daponte and Navarro (1995); Franco-Giraldo, Palma and Alvarez-Dardet (2006); Kawachi and Kennedy (1997); Kawachi, Kennedy and Wilkinson (1999); Kawachi, Kennedy, Lochner et al. (1997); Lynch et al. (2004); Macinko, Shi and Starfield (2004); Mackenbach, Kunst, Cavelaars et al. (1997); Marmot and Wilkinson (2001); Navarro and Shi (2001); Palma-Solis et al. (2009); Wickrama, Bikask and Wickrama (2003); Wilkinson (1992a, 1992b, 1997); Wilkinson and Picket (2006); Williamson and Boehmer (1997); Woolhandler and Himmelstein (1985).

59 This effect is common knowledge for economists and social scientists ever since the path-breaking article by Kuznets (1955). Bi-variate correlations between inequality and life expectancy tell us next to nothing if we do not control for the interactions with development level.

60 This article, written in one of the true flagship journals of the social science profession, the *International Studies Quarterly*, should be well known by members of the medical profession who dare to venture deeply into fundamental questions of the social science discipline.

61 Like inequality, life expectancy depends on development levels, and the trade-off is again in the shape of an inverted 'U'. Still, the hypotheses, forwarded by Wilkinson and his school, deserve further empirical attention, and we could show their relevance in some of our own

---

Policy pointer

Increasingly, the public health profession also looks at the cross-national drivers and bottlenecks of such variables as infant mortality and life expectancy. The consensus of most published research on the subject in that discipline seems to support those who aim to curb socio-economic inequalities. One of the consequences of these research trends is the inclusion of inequality as a possible driver or bottleneck of mortality and life expectancy variables in future studies. These public health studies are potentially an additional motive for decision makers to look more objectively at the long-term costs and benefits of economic policies, resulting in large scale socio-economic inequalities.

More Holistic Approaches

It is no wonder that several studies opted for a more 'holistic' approach to the problem, in view of the startling variety of indicators and results. If, say, the planned and full-fledged integration of a country into the mechanisms of the New International Division of Labour is such a development policy 'cardinal sin', the percentage of the national population or workforce employed in free production zones must negatively affect not only a single, but an entire variety of development indicators, ranging from social cohesion to gender, economic growth, human rights, poverty and the environment. The untiring efforts of the United Nations Development Programme and its global *Human Development Reports*, which published each year, from 1995 to the mid 2000s, a major new development indicator in addition to the Human Development Index, contributed towards a more – if you wish – 'catholic attitude' towards development indicators, submitted to the tests of the determining factors in multiple regression analysis.[62]

---

final results (see Chapter 4 and Appendix 1). We think a way forward in this debate would be a true dialogue between medicine, public health and the social sciences. Neoclassical economists (like Barro, Durlauf and associates, and Sala-i-Martin) and world system scholars (like Herkenrath and Bornschier, and Jorgenson and associates), who stress the importance of the globalization factor in blocking long-run socio-economic development, are correct in showing that nowadays social science has to take a variety of factors into account to explain the paths of socio-economic development and decay.

62 The existing studies, published by Tausch (2003a, 2003b, 2004, 2005, 2007a, 2007b, 2007c, 2008a, 2008b), Tausch and Ghymers (2006), Tausch and Herrmann (2001), Tausch and Heshmati (2005), Tausch and Prager (1993), were one step in that direction, and studied the effects of dependency and controlled for a larger number of variables on up to 14 key indicators of socio-economic performance, including the Yale/Columbia environment indicators, the UNDP 'gender empowerment index value', and the Freedom House combined data on civil rights and human rights violations. That most other current dependency and world-system oriented research simply overlooked to date to present articles explaining the Yale/Columbia Environmental Performance Index and the Yale/Columbia Environmental Sustainability Index by patterns of the world system position of countries, or transnational capitalist penetration, is a major and real weakness of the literature under survey here.

Already, Van Rossem (1996) had shown that much of the literature on development uses the world system model as a grand conceptual scheme rather than as a theory of development. Van Rossem tested the world system paradigm as a general theory of development by focussing on three central constructs: world system role, dependency, and development. Data for five networks among 163 countries were used to operationalize the world system role. Van Rossem's findings indicate that world system role can be operationalized in terms of role equivalence, yielding results closer to the theoretical model than the more commonly used structural equivalence measures. Contrary to theoretical expectations, world system role was more a function of absolute size of the economy than of level of development. The results weakly supported the world system model of economic performance during the period 1980 to 1989. During this period, world system role had weak to moderate effects on several dependency indicators but did not directly affect economic performance. Dependency had a moderate effect on economic performance. In the following chapter, we will now apply this theoretical knowledge towards developing a valid research design for our study.

Policy pointer

All methodological and theoretical arguments evaluated up to now seem to suggest a new, multi-disciplinary approach regarding both the choice of independent as well as dependent variables. As the EU-2020 policy assumptions, made by the European Commission, correctly assume, development today has many dimensions, not just the economic one, and includes employment, research and development, the environment, education, and poverty and social exclusion. However, to exclude the dimensions of democracy, gender and human development is a fatal misconception of the EU-2020 strategy. Democracy itself might be under stress in Europe (and not just in the new member states); corruption and the rule of law have to be closely monitored around the world and also in Europe, and it is absolutely thinkable that core-nations of the old European Union 15 member countries, under the weight of the current crisis, develop one or several 'failed states syndromes'. The exclusion of the gender dimension is also a glaring misconception, and human development indicators, like life expectancy or the further reduction of infant mortality reduction, are conspicuously absent from the list of EU-2020 indicators.

Chapter 3

METHODS

3.1 Introduction

In this chapter we present a review of the research methodology and discuss its strengths and limitations.[1]

The interest in and the amount of research on the relationships between sub-processes of development and their predictors have been increasing in recent years due to increased availability of secondary data and improvements of the methodology. The growing interest is a result of the rapid development of international relations and the speed at which the recent wave of openness is proceeding. The theoretical literature on each aspect of development is vast but the empirical evidence on the nature and causal relationship between the different interrelated factors of interest remains poorly investigated. Thus, there is an urgent need for further research and methodological development at different levels and on different aspects of development to allow to shed light on these issues and to improve our understanding of the problems, policies and their outcomes.

Globalization and its impacts on inequality and poverty have been intensively studied in recent years. Concerning measurement of globalization, Heshmati (2006a, 2006b) introduces two composite indices of globalization. The first index is based on the A. T. Kearney/*Foreign Policy* magazine report (2002) and the second is obtained from a principal component analysis. They indicate the level of globalization and show how globalization has developed over time for different countries. The indices are composed of four components: economic integration, personal contact, technology and political engagement, each generated from a number of indicators. The indices were also used in a regression analysis framework to study the causal relationships between income inequality, poverty and globalization. The results show evidence of a weak and negative relationship between globalization and income inequality and poverty. An important index of globalization based on similar methodology but comprehensive data is the KOF index (see Dreher, Gaston and Martens 2008).

---

1 We are well aware that this chapter might be of limited use for the general public readers of this book. The chapter is indeed intended for use by graduate students of the social sciences, academic research and teaching personnel, statisticians at national governments or international organizations, analytical research officers, working at transnational corporations or NGOs etc. Readers finding difficulties in comprehending the text could skip it at first, while the authors hope that they will return to the text later.

3.2 The Index Methodology

In recent years there is a more rich literature on the quantitative measurement of previously not measurable outcomes. These outcomes are often multi-dimensional and represented by several indicators with both positive and negative effects. The objective in this study is not only to evaluate the effects of certain policy programs but also to quantify the state of the outcome. The multi-dimensionality of the outcome requires the creation of composite indices to have a single measure of performance and also to aggregate the indicators. In this study, the focus is on the construction of indices of development process that are multi-dimensional and decomposable. Such indices will be a useful tool in the quantification of the state of development and the evaluation of predictors' impacts on development. In this section, we introduce the two main approaches of non-parametric and parametric indices and their extensions frequently used in the construction of such indices.

3.2.1 Non-parametric index

The non-parametric index is a composite index constructed to aggregate a number of indicators of a certain process or outcome. Such indices are used for the measurement of many technological, economic or social phenomena such as globalization,[2] the state of the environment,[3] human development,[4] the trajectory of the development strategy, technology and research,[5] child well-being[6] and other areas of application. The globalization index is a simple combination of forces driving the integration of ideas, people, and economies, worldwide. In existing studies it is often composed of a composition of three to five major components: economic integration, personal contact, internet technology, political engagement, and social development, where each in turn is being generated from a number of determinant variables. This index serves as a model for computation of our sub-indices of development.

In constructing the composite indices, each of the variables introduced is transformed to an index on a scale of one to a hundred, where a hundred is the maximum value and one is the minimum value. Higher values denote a greater level of the index. The weights for calculating the sub-indices are determined parametrically using principal component analysis for the entire data. The analysis partitions the variance of the variables used in each sub-group. The weights are then determined in a way that maximizes the variation explained by the resulting principal component, so that the indices capture the variation as fully as possible. The same

---

2 Heshmati (2006a); Heshmati and Tausch (2007); Tausch and Heshmati (2006); Andersen and Herbertsson (2003); Dreher (2006); A. T. Kearney (2002, 2003); Lockwood (2004); Lockwood and Redoano (2005).
3 Kang (2002).
4 Noorbakhsh (1998).
5 Heshmati and Oh (2007); Archibugi and Coco (2004); Archibugi et al. (2009); Grupp and Mogee (2004); Al-Mutavakkil et al. (2009).
6 Heshmati et al. (2008).

procedure is applied to the sub-indices in order to derive the overall index. The components and the overall index are calculated employing the weighted individual data series instead.

The index is computed non-parametrically based on the normalization of the different indicators and their subsequent aggregation using an ad hoc weighting system

$$(1) \quad INDEX_i = \sum_{j=1}^{J} \sum_{m=1}^{M} \omega_{jm} \{(X_{jmi} - X_{jm}^{min})/(X_{jm}^{max} - X_{jm}^{min})\}$$

where i indicates the country; m and j are within and between component variables; ω_{jm} are the weights attached to each contributing X-variable within a component and weights attached to each of the major components; and min and max are minimum and maximum values of respective variables across countries in a given year. The index is similar to the very commonly used index, the United Nations Development Programme (UNDP) Human Development Index (HDI), which is based on educational attainment, life expectancy and real GDP per capita.

It is important to note that the index in (1) is suitable for indicators with an expected positive effect on the index outcome. In cases where the indicators are expected to have a negative impact on the outcome, the corresponding index is written as

$$(2) \quad INDEX_i = \sum_{j=1}^{J} \sum_{m=1}^{M} \omega_{jm} \{(X_{jm}^{max} - X_{jmi})/(X_{jm}^{max} - X_{jm}^{min})\}$$

where the two indices differ only by the numerator of the ratio. Alternatively, prior to the normalization in (1) and aggregation, the negative indicators are transformed to inverses, $(1/X)$ reversing their expected impact from negative to positive.

The index component's weights in equations (1) and (2) are chosen on an ad hoc basis and are constant across countries.[7] In this study, we choose the weighting approach similar to the commonly used Human Development Index, where all indicators are given equal weight (see Noorbakhsh 1998).

Ideally, the weights attached to each component should differ by indicators, countries as well as over time. In certain cases on an ad hoc basis the researchers assign some indictors a double weight. A heterogeneous weighted system is important as countries are differently dependent on their resources endowments and this dependency changes over time as well. A simple weighting system is to use the square of the normalized indices as a base for the aggregation to obtain the composite index. This weighted system implies that the higher normalized values receive a higher

---

7 However, this non-parametric index can be used as a benchmark index. Lockwood (2004), in computation of a globalization index, finds the ranking of countries to be sensitive to the way the indicators are measured, normalized and weighted (see also Decancq and Lugo 2008).

weight than the lower ones. It is a reasonable assumption as the higher normalized values are considered to be the result of specialization and higher outcome. In the event of opposite expected effect in similarity with the convergence literature one could use the inverse of the normalize values giving more weigh to lower values.

3.3 Parametric Index

The literature on such index numbers is diverse and voluminous. There are at least two other alternative but parametric approaches to the non-parametric index above for computing an index of development process; using the principal component (PC) or factor analysis (FA). In this study we adopt the PC approach. Since the two methods in normalized form give PC scores with unit variance, we use only the PC results in the analysis of development process.[8]

Principal component analysis is a multivariate technique for examining relationships within a set of interrelated quantitative variables. Given a dataset with P numeric indicators, at most P principal components can be computed; each is a linear combination of the original indicators with coefficients equal to the eigenvectors of the correlation of the covariance matrix. The principal components are sorted according to the descending order of the eigenvalues, which are equal to the variance of the components. In short, PC analysis can be viewed as a way to uncover approximate linear dependencies among variables. This method gives a least square type solution to the following model

(3) $Y = XB + E$

in which Y is an $n \times p$ matrix of the centred observed variables, X is the $n \times j$ matrix of scores of the first j principal components, B is a $j \times p$ matrix of eigenvectors or factor patterns, E is an $n \times p$ matrix of residuals, n is the number of observations, p is the number of partial variables, and j the number of variables or indicators of development process. Unlike in a traditional least squares estimation method case, where the vertical distance between the observed and the fitted line is minimized, here the sum of the squared residuals is measured as distances from the point to the first principal axis.

The eigenvalues and eigenvectors of the correlation matrix of the development process indicators are investigated. The eigenvalues bigger than 1.00 are subsequently used in computation of the development process index. These often together explain

---

8 PC analysis was originally developed by Pearson (1901) and further improved by Hotelling (1933). For recent applications of this class of indices, see Heshmati (2006b) and Andersen and Herbertsson (2003). The method has been employed in many areas including the computation of an environmental index (Kang 2002) and in the computation of a simple globalization index using trade and financial openness by Agénor (2003). Heshmati and Oh (2007) used the method for computation of the Lisbon development strategy index and Heshmati et al. (2008) used it to study child well-being in the high- and middle-income countries.

a large percentage share of the total variations. The contribution of the components to the explanation of the variance is declining from the first component to other components. By looking at the eigenvectors, it becomes evident which indicators are forming a specific component and the nature of their effects. In each sub-component, an indicator with an eigenvector exceeding 0.30 is considered statistically as a significant contributor to the principal component.

In practice the researchers used only the first principal component in computation of the parametric index and in ranking the countries studied. This method has the disadvantage in that it ignores information in the remaining variables. One alternative to account for information embodied in all principal components with an eigenvalue bigger than one is to use a weighted average principal component index whereas weight in aggregation of the principal components with eigenvalues greater than one is to use their share of the total variance explained by each component. This method of aggregation will allow utilization of information from all indicators of an outcome.

Each of the parametric and non-parametric indices and in weighted or unweighted forms has its own advantages and disadvantages. In this study, they are used to measure the state of development among the sample countries and attribute it to the possible underlying causes of development. A breakdown of the index into major components provides possibilities to identify positive and negative factors contributing to development. The parametric approach in which a single composite index is provided in comparison with the non-parametric does not provide decomposition of sub-components, rather only principal components which may not be of the same structure as that defined in non-parametric case determined by the researcher. The advantage of the parametric approach is that the components' distribution is determined by the indicators' statistical relationship rather than based on experience or an ad hoc selection of indicators. The results can be used in the design of economic policy measures to bring about desirable changes in national and international development policies. It could be also useful in the evaluation of development policy measures.

In applying the principal components method, we should be well aware of the possible limitations of the method used. It should be emphasized that the method is generally a very useful method to reduce the complexity of the data with multi-dimensions such as development process. However, the linear combinations of the different dimensions of interest may not be always easy to interpret, less so is the complex aggregate index. In addition it might be of little help in determining weights embedding a personal or collective value judgment. In sum, a main limitation of the method could be that what is statistically reasonable may be neither economically nor normatively reasonable in the evaluation of development. This is more evident in particular in cases with data limitations.

The two indices, non-parametric and parametric PC analysis, are computed at each observation of the data. For instance in the context of globalization, they indicate which countries have become most globalized and quantify the state of inequality in globalization among countries and regions. They show how globalization has developed for different countries and regions over time. A breakdown of the index into major components provides possibilities to identify sources of globalization. It is valuable to associate this information with economic policy measures to bring about desirable changes in national and international policies. The indices can also be used to study the causal relationship between globalization, inequality, poverty, growth and a number of other variables frequently found in the development literature, such as openness, wages, and trade liberalization.

3.4 A New Parametric Composite Index

The non-parametric index can serve as a benchmark index in comparison of performance of different indices. The unweighted indices are further computed in weighted forms for the purpose of sensitivity analysis of ranking countries. We call this index an unweighted index as the weights attached to each of the indicators is identical and equal to one. However, as mentioned previously in some studies, some variables are given double weights in the alternative differentiated weighted index. In comparative analysis, the correlation between the different indices provides information about their ranking performance, similarity and differences.

In previous studies the causal links between globalization, inequality, poverty and growth have been investigated in a two-step procedure. In the first step the globalization index is computed as described above non-parametrically or parametrically, and in the second step the latter three variables are regressed on globalization to investigate the impact of independent variable of globalization on the three dependent variables. A two-step procedure has the disadvantage in that it often ignores the directions of causality and simultaneity issues which are important in proper estimation of the causal relationships.

Heshmati and Lee (2010) introduced a new approach which is distinguished from the previous ones in that both of these steps are estimated parametrically and in a single step. The model is based on a multi-dimensional analysis of globalization, while some previous studies often based it on single and trade-related factors. In the new index, the contribution from each indicator, the shares of individual components and the aggregate composite index are configured by their relationship with economic development. For the matter of sensitivity analysis, two different methods, decomposed and composite models estimated iteratively, are used to compute the new globalization index and explain its variations. The indices are used to investigate their impacts on the economic growth and income inequality of the sample countries. The comprehensive and systematic regression analyses show that globalization is positively linked to economic growth, while it has a negative relationship with inequality, but the effects are confounded with unobserved regional effects.

The new model is using two approaches: composite single index and decomposed four component index. In the empirical part, Heshmati and Lee adopt the same index structure and components of the non-parametric and parametric principal component indices described above for the purpose. In the decomposed index approach the impact of each of the globalization components on different economic growth (EG) measures is written as follows,

$$\text{(4)} \quad \log EG_{it} = a_0 + a_1 \log ECON_{it} + a_2 \log PERS_{it} + a_3 \log TECH_{it} + a_4 \log POLI_{it} + u_{it}$$

where each of the main components is specified as

$$\text{(5)} \quad \log Comp_{it} = \sum_{j=1}^{J-1} b_j \log X_{jit} + (1 - \sum_j b_j) \log X_{Jit}$$

In (4), the log EG is represented by the logarithm of four different measures of GDP including GDP, GDP growth, GDP per capita, and growth in GDP per capita, and each is specified as a function of the logarithm of the four globalization components: *ECON, PERS, TECH* and *POLI*. Each of the globalization components in (5) is estimated as a function of J normalized indicators (X) specific to that component. The component *ECON* includes economic variables, *PERS* includes personal variables, *TECH* includes technology variables, *POLI* includes political variables, u is an error term and subscripts j, i and t refer to indicator, a country and time periods.

Each indicator variable has its own parameters (b) reflecting its share contribution to the globalization component as in the non-parametric index, although here they are estimated and not assigned equal weights on an ad hoc basis. For example, the economic factor, *ECON*, has four sub-indicators such as trade, foreign direct investment, portfolio investment, and income payments and receipts. However, because the sum of $b_j s$ is assumed to be unity, we only need three coefficients to calculate the *ECON* value. The b_4 can be derived by $1-b_1-b_2-b_3$. The parameters, a_0-a_4 in model (4) are obtained through regression analysis of economic growth variables and globalization sub-components, and these represent the weights of each component or the effects of globalization on economic growth. Here, no restrictions are imposed on the total sum of the effects. The model is non-linear in parameters and the estimation is conducted in an iterative procedure where the parameters of the globalization components are estimated in the first step and their effects on economic growth are estimated in the second step.

The second approach which is based on the principal component analysis does not distinguish between the four globalization components and lumps all 13 indicators into one single index. It allows estimation of the weights and several principal components that can be distinguished by their contributions to the composite index. The model corresponding to (4) and (5) is written as

$$\text{(6)} \quad \log EG_{it} = a_0 + a_1 \log Index_{it} + u_{it}$$

where log EG is again representing the different GDP measures, and *Index* is specified as a function of all 13 globalization indicators without distinguishing the four components: economic, personal, technology and political components, u is an error term.

$$(7) \quad \log Index_{it} = \sum_{j=1}^{7-1} b_j \log X_{jit} + (1 - \sum_{j=1}^{7-1} b_j) \log X_{7it}$$

Parameters b_1-b_3, c_1-c_2, d_1-d_2, e_1-e_2 are the coefficients of globalization indicators associated with different components of the index. This model is also estimated in an iterative procedure where the whole 13 indicators are employed to estimate the composite globalization index (7) and then estimate its impacts on economic growth (6). From the estimation of (4) through (7), we could obtain estimates of the contributions of each indicator on the globalization index and the effects of globalization on the economic growth of countries. Thus, the combination of the disaggregated and aggregated globalization index and different economic growth definitions leads to the estimation of several different models.

With the help of the adjusted R^2 values and root mean square errors (RMSE), one can distinguish evidence of more adequate specifications of the relationships, and explain variations in GDP levels and their growth rates. Another key difference among the models is attributed to the structure of combining the underlying globalization indicators into a single index or an index with several main components.

The new globalization indices of countries are calculated based on the coefficients obtained from (5) and (7) as shown below in (8):

$$(8) \quad Gind\hat{e}x1j_i = \hat{a}_0 + \hat{a}_1 ECON_i + \hat{a}_2 PERS_i + \hat{a}_3 TECH_i + \hat{a}_4 POLI_i$$
$$Gind\hat{e}x2j_i = \hat{a}_0 + \hat{a}_1 INDEX_i, \quad j = 1,2,3,4$$

In this computation, j represents the type of economic growth values. In the $Gindex1j$ and $Gindex2j$, the first digit (1 or 2) represents the composed/decomposed group type and the second digit (j) represents the type of economic growth variable.

3.5 Distribution of the Indices

The distribution of different indices can be studied in different dimensions such as countries, regions and over time, or by level of development. Information about different sub-components, components and the overall index as well as the indices which are measured in metric efficiency terms where countries are compared with the best country in a given year are provided. Analysis of the distribution of the indices and their components might be more useful than point observations. A disaggregation of the sample into different regions will allow the capturing of the effects of changes and heterogeneity in countries' responses to both within-region internal and external shocks.

Concerning the efficiency indices, where the individual observations are compared to the best globalized country in a given year, this method is better than the standard index as it provide better metric information than the simple ranking. The level of the index and its components are somewhat higher than the globalization indices but the positive trends in general and the breaks in the political components are observed in a similar way. The positive trend shows that despite yearly frontiers the mean level is increasing constantly, suggesting both a shift in the frontier and also a catching-up of the sample countries to the frontier countries. The standard and efficiency mean values are very close and positively developing over time. The range and standard deviation is shrinking largely from 1991, suggesting convergence among countries with relatively high economic component values.

Policy pointer

What is certain is that the hitherto existing debate on the EU-2020 strategy and the earlier Lisbon Strategy debate, in the framework of the larger discussions about Europe's perspectives in the changing world economy, did not or do not use methodological advances in social science indicator construction sufficiently well. The ranking of countries in 'beauty contests' about the Lisbon Strategy may be popular, but it simply does not correspond to the present 'state of the art' in the social sciences nowadays. Our work introduces some of this more recent methodology to evaluate progress in implementing policy goals.

3.6 Simple, Multiple and Stepwise Regression Analysis

The multiple linear regressions model is used to study the relationship between a dependent variable like development outcome and several independent variables like indicators of development. If the set of independent variables consists of only one we have a simple regression case, else a multiple case. In the context of development, the linear regression model is the single most useful method in analysis of relationships between indicators of development and the outcome of development process. In empirical research it is used as a departure point for deeper analysis where the linear models are extended to non-linear formulation and testing of their causal relationships. Here the movement in the dependent development process is defined as a response to changes in some independent or exogenous stimulus factors identified as determinants of development. The added disturbance term is expected to capture the random factors disturbing the stable relationship, omitted variables and measurement errors in the development process.

In analysis of the development relationship the primary focus is on the functional form of the model and hypothesis testing to improve the specification of the model to enable drawing useful inference about the population of countries. Broader techniques are used by researchers in their set of alternative competing models and choice of a specific selected model. This will help the specification analysis and model building to avoid omission of relevant variables and inclusion of superfluous variables. The former leads to omitted variable bias, while over-fit of the model in the latter case leads to reduced precision of the estimates. For more information see Greene (2008).

There are two common strategies in model building: general-to-simple and simple-to-general. In maintaining simplicity, model builders begin with a small model specification and gradually build up the model by adding more explanatory variables. This approach due to the risk of omitted variable bias is not recommended. The increased computational power has led to the alternative general-to-simple model strategy involving long and complex lag structures, but downward reduction of the model to preferred specification is becoming increasingly attractive. This approach has been automated in some statistical packages to ease their implementation. For instance in the 'kitchen sink' regression, every relevant variable is included in which some variables turn to become significant by accident. The same problem arises in stepwise model building where elements of unexplainable effects may affect the result.

In specification and selection of models a number of criteria are frequently used. One is the theoretical relationship between the explanatory variables and the dependent variable which justifies their incorporation. Another is their empirical relevance not necessarily supported by the theory. A third is the nature of the relationship in form of flexible functional forms. The following are used as model specification, estimation and selection criteria: adjusted R^2; the mean-squared error criterion; the pretest estimator; the Akaike information criterion; the Schwartz or Bayesian information criterion; the encompassing principle; and the non-nestedness of models. In this research we use the abovementioned approaches described in Chapter 4 to investigate the globalization, human condition and sustainable development in the twenty-first century with European implications.

3.7 Introduction to the Data

The 'horizon' of the sociological and political science literature, surveyed in Chapter 2, is defined by the following independent and dependent variables sorted alphabetically. The major variables, also featuring as dependent variables in the literature, are printed in indented letters in the list of independent variables.

3.8 The Potential Determinants

Independent variables in cross-national comparative sociological and political science research used as determinants of economic growth, social cohesion and the environment include:

1. A. T. Kearney's globalization index
2. Age at first marriage (women)
3. Agricultural density
4. Agricultural production
5. Anocratic regimes
6. Capital intensity
7. Character of political institutions
8. Debits on investment incomes
9. Debt accumulated from foreign aid
10. Debt service ratios
11. Decentralized states
12. Decreased industrial sector

13. Democracy
14. Domestic investment
15. Ecological footprint
16. Economic growth
17. Economic liberalization
18. Economic restructuring
19. Educational enrolment ratios
20. Elite divisions
21. Environmental NGOs
22. Ethnic separatism
23. Export commodity concentration
24. External economic dependence
25. Female level of education relative to men
26. Female life expectancy
27. Feudal interaction patterns of trade (trade partner concentration)
28. Financial flows from the IMF
29. Flows of foreign aid
30. Flows of MNC investment
31. Food supply
32. Foreign investment concentration
33. Foreign subsidiary concentration
34. Foreign trade structure
35. Forest stocks
36. Geographical and demographical disadvantages
37. Government expenditures per GDP
38. Health expenditures per capita
39. Human capital
40. Industrial sector, industrialism
41. Inequality
42. International food aid
43. International trade in agricultural products
44. Interventionist and restrictive economic policies
45. Kuznets curve
46. Land inequality
47. Landlockedness
48. Limited democracies
49. Literacy rates
50. Manufacturing intensity
51. Migration
52. Military dependency
53. Military expenditures
54. Military influence
55. Military personnel rate
56. Military technological power
57. MNC penetration
58. MNC penetration in agriculture/ primary sector
59. MNC penetration in industry
60. NGOs (various aspects)
61. NIDL (New International Division of Labour)
62. Non-democracies
63. Organic water pollution
64. Political corruption
65. Political democracy
66. Population growth
67. Public sector expansion
68. Public sector size
69. Regime ideology
70. Regime repressiveness
71. Regime types
72. Reproductive autonomy of women
73. Rural–urban migration
74. Sachs and Warner index of free trade policies
75. Secondary schooling
76. Sectoral pattern of direct foreign investment
77. Service sector economy
78. Service-dominated urban economies
79. Social cohesion
80. Social organization of rural areas
81. Social spending
82. Social structure
83. Social unrest
84. State coercive capacity
85. State strength
86. Status of women (relative and absolute indicators)
87. Stocks of direct foreign assistance
88. Stocks of foreign debt
89. Structural adjustment policies

90. Trade with developing countries
91. Tropics
92. Urbanization
93. Vertical trade
94. War
95. Women's NGOs
96. Women's status
97. World economic openness
98. World system position (centre/ semi-periphery/periphery)

3.9 The Potentially Explained Variables

Dependent variables in cross-national comparative sociological and political science research explained by the determinants of economic growth, social cohesion and the environment include:

1. Balanced urbanization
2. Carbon dioxide emissions
3. Carbon monoxide emissions
4. Censorship
5. Changes in income distribution over time
6. Child mortality
7. Childhood immunization
8. Civil war
9. Collective political violence
10. Consumption of synthetic compounds
11. Deaths from political violence
12. Deforestation
13. Domestic capital formation
14. Ecological footprint
15. Economic growth
16. Food consumption
17. Forestry export flows from poor to rich countries
18. Gender pay gap
19. Gender stratification
20. Government respect for human rights
21. Greenhouse gas emissions
22. Health attendance
23. Human Development Index
24. Human rights
25. Income inequality
26. Industrial organic water pollution
27. Infant mortalities
28. Insufficient exploitation of growth potentials
29. Labour standards
30. Life expectancies
31. Maternal mortalities
32. National welfare
33. NOx emissions
34. Nutrition
35. Occupational sex segregation
36. Opportunities for women in the workplace
37. Organic water pollution
38. Per capita calorie and protein consumption
39. Pesticide and fertilizer consumption
40. Political freedom
41. Political restrictions
42. Poverty (below $1 or $2 a day per capita)
43. Protected land area
44. Protest
45. Rebellion
46. Share of income received by the poorest 20 per cent
47. Tertiary school expansion
48. Threatened mammal species
49. Violent protest
50. Volatile organic compounds

3.10 Cross-discipline Communication

Unfortunately, the communication between the discipline of sociological and political science theories of economic growth and development and the discipline of economics is not well established. A joint effort in development of theory and generation of empirical result could help in disciplining unbiased advancement of our knowledge about growth and development and its causal factors and estimation of their impacts. An example worth mentioning is that not a single essay mentioning the catch-words 'MNC penetration' and 'economic growth' was ever published in a leading journal of the global economics profession (such as the *American Economic Review*) throughout the period of the entire and intensive debate on the effects of 'foreign capital penetration' on economic growth from the late 1970s onwards to this day. Instead of concentrating on the ever more complex modelling of the effects of 'foreign capital dependence', the economics profession, by contrast, developed its mathematical models side by side with an ever growing amount of many different variables, which featured as 'control variables' in the literature. An attempt, like the one by Sala-i-Martin (1997), to filter out the most robust predictors of economic growth by applying Bayesian techniques and combining dozens of predictor variables in all mathematically possible different combinations is a very legitimate one from the viewpoint of the advancement of social science and statistical methodology. By contrast, sociologists used to the published articles in journals like the *American Sociological Review* most probably would be shocked by Sala-i-Martin's successful attempt to run 2 million regressions (in a scientific paper version of his 1997 essay, he even speaks about 4 million regressions). Availability of computer power, common databases and search engines for online journal services may finally bring the three disciplines of sociology, politics and economics closer.

The problem, which led Sala-i-Martin to perform his 2 million regressions, exists and remains unresolved. The fact that independent variable x_1 is significantly determining the dependent variable y, the growth rate, or for that matter, income inequality, infant mortality, or environmental indicators under the inclusion of predictors or conditional variable x_2 and x_3, but losing the statistical significance when variable x_4 is included in the regression, is all too-well known in the empirical literature and is indeed, a relevant statistical problem. With a few exceptions, empirical sociology and political science have not yet provided a coherent and reliable answer to this problem of correlation and confounded effects. The application of Kohonen's self-organizing maps for selecting the relevant predictor variables, another advance in the methodological literature, is only at the beginning of its application in the field. The methodology has been first attempted by Mostafa and associates in his papers, all published in 2010. Additional applications are required to assess its performance and robustness concerning limitations above.

Touching upon the relationship of this literature to the traditions in economics, we may summarize with Crowly, Rauch, Seagrave and Smith (1998):

> For more than two decades, economists and sociologists have pursued parallel cross-national quantitative investigations of the determinants of economic

development. These investigations have proceeded in mutual ignorance despite the often large overlap in statistical methods and data employed. Apparently contradictory findings have resulted, especially regarding the impacts of international trade and foreign direct investment.

The question of the geographic, demographic and other independent variables in development accounting found much more attention in the recent economic literature.[9] According to this type of research,[10] we currently are facing around one hundred popular independent variables in the current econometric literature on the determinants of economic growth. Sala-i-Martin, Doppelhofer and Miller (2004) arrived at the following list of robust growth predictors, which keep their significance after all possible relevant changes in the research design, applying their Bayesian estimation techniques:

1. East Asian dummy
2. Primary schooling (1960)
3. Investment price
4. GDP (1960) (log)
5. Fraction tropical area
6. Population density coastal (1960s)
7. Malaria prevalence (1960s)
8. Life expectancy (1960)
9. Fraction Confucian
10. African dummy
11. Latin American dummy
12. Fraction GDP in mining
13. Spanish colony
14. Years open
15. Fraction Muslim
16. Fraction Buddhist
17. Ethno-linguistic fractionalization
18. Government consumption share (1960s)

In their *American Economic Review* article of 2004, Sala-i-Martin and associates highlight the point that the strongest effects on growth are found for good primary schooling enrolment, the low price of investment goods and a low initial level of income where the latter reflects the concept of conditional convergence. Other important variables, according to this study, include regional dummies (such as East Asia, Sub-Saharan Africa, or Latin America), some measures of

---

9 Just to mention Ciccone and Jarocinski (2008); Gylfason (2001); Hodler (2004); Masters and McMillan (2000); Sachs and Warner (2001); and Sturm and de Haan (2005).
10 Presented by Ciccone and Jarocinski (2008); Sala-i-Martin, Doppelhofer and Miller (2004); and Sturm and de Haan (2005).

human capital and health (such as life expectancy, proportion of a country in the tropics and malaria prevalence), religious dummies, and some sectoral variables such as mining. Interestingly enough, and in contrast to current contemporary Islamophobic reasoning, Sala-i-Martin and his team even found quite strong and positive effects of the predominance of the Islamic faith on economic growth, with a likewise positive effect of Buddhist and Confucian cultures on economic growth, while the initial income levels and government consumption levels also quite strongly affected the growth rate.

Policy pointer

Econometricians have used an astonishing number of growth predictors, combining them in an equally astonishing variety of research designs. Among the most robust predictors the econometric literature – which is more and more based on methodological advances like (Bayesian) combination techniques – mentions many variables beyond the political action of governments, like geography or colonial history. Since most of these econometric variables cannot be changed, only some neoliberal policy prescriptions (lowering the investment price; the number of years, an economy was open to world markets, and lowering the government consumption share) or opening up our labour markets to immigrants from East Asia and other regions or cultures (Confucian, Muslim or Buddhist) would be robust contributions to a new economic growth strategy.

3.11 The Current Combined Variable List

Thus, the list of the combined drivers and blockades of development, mentioned in the published social science literature (economics, political science and sociology) among which some were mentioned above, currently includes some 191 variables (our count from the materials above) and is thus approaching 200.

To start with, we have made our data completely and freely available on the internet, so that the global research community can have free access to our data and the opportunity to check our results or to conduct new research (http://www.hichemkaroui.com/?p=2017). This internet site offers not only the Microsoft Excel data (Table 2 of the Excel file) and a list of the sources (Table 2 of the Excel file), but also a codebook in PDF format. A brief description of our data is also contained in Appendix 7 of this work.

Our investigation duly acknowledges many of the key determinants of economic growth, mentioned in the economic literature, like current shares of the country's inhabitants in total world population, calculated from UNDP data; the famous Heritage Foundation 2000 economic freedom score; absolute geographical latitude, adapted from Easterly's growth theory; the UNDP figures for long-term annual population growth rate, 1975 to 2005 (per cent); the trade-off between development level and development performance, otherwise also known in economics as 'conditional convergence' (ln GDP per capita; ln GDP per capita^2); the simple Huntingtonian fact of whether a country is a Muslim country, to be measured by Organisation of the Islamic Conference (OIC) membership or by the Muslim population share (Nationmaster); UNDP data on the simple geographical fact of population density (based on the CIA's World Factbook); UNDP data on public education expenditure per GDP; and the UNDP Education Index, combining the enrolment rates at the primary, secondary and tertiary education levels. We also take into account UNDP figures on military expenditures per GDP and the openly available CIA data on military personnel rate, which are key variables of contemporary political science international relations theory and peace research. In our analysis, we also show the theoretical and practical (political) potential of the following two drivers of development, which are somewhat a 'terra incognita Australis' in the hitherto existing macro-sociological debate, like migration and European (Monetary) Union membership.

The present book will thus duly confront the underlying, pro-globalist logic of the Lisbon Strategy or 'Lisbon agenda' or 'EU-2020 agenda' as the unhappy successor of the failed 2000 to 2010 strategy with what we perceive as the essence of an argument critical of globalization. As we already mentioned, and as we should highlight here especially, recent comparative sociological literature investigated the implications of foreign capital penetration for patterns of development.[11] The choice of a country to be included in the final analysis (175 countries)[12] was determined by

---

11 Cheol-Sung, Nielsen, and Alderson (2007); Crowly, Rauch, Seagrave and Smith (1998); Jorgenson (2006a, 2006b); Moran (2005); Nomiya (2007); Rennstich (2002); Sanderson and Kentor (2009); Shandra (2007a, 2007b); Tausch (2003a, 2003b, 2004, 2007c).

12 Albania; Algeria; Angola; Antigua and Barbuda; Argentina; Armenia; Australia; Austria; Azerbaijan; Bahamas; Bahrain; Bangladesh; Barbados; Belarus; Belgium; Belize; Benin; Bhutan; Bolivia; Bosnia and Herzegovina; Botswana; Brazil; Brunei; Bulgaria; Burkina Faso; Burundi; Cambodia; Cameroon; Canada; Cape Verde; Central African Republic; Chad; Chile; China; Colombia; Comoros; Congo; Congo (Democratic Republic of); Costa Rica; Côte d'Ivoire; Croatia; Cuba; Cyprus; Czech Republic; Denmark; Djibouti; Dominica; Dominican Republic; Ecuador; Egypt; El Salvador; Equatorial Guinea; Eritrea; Estonia; Ethiopia; Fiji; Finland; France; Gabon; Gambia; Georgia; Germany; Ghana; Greece; Grenada; Guatemala; Guinea; Guinea-Bissau; Guyana; Haiti; Honduras; Hong Kong, China (SAR); Hungary; Iceland; India; Indonesia; Iran; Ireland; Israel; Italy; Jamaica; Japan; Jordan; Kazakhstan; Kenya; Korea (Republic of); Kuwait; Kyrgyzstan; Laos; Latvia; Lebanon; Lesotho; Libya; Lithuania; Luxembourg; Macedonia (FYR); Madagascar; Malawi; Malaysia; Maldives; Mali; Malta; Mauritania; Mauritius; Mexico; Moldova; Mongolia; Morocco; Mozambique; Myanmar; Namibia; Nepal; Netherlands; New Zealand; Nicaragua; Niger; Nigeria; Norway; Oman; Pakistan; Panama; Papua New Guinea; Paraguay; Peru; Philippines; Poland; Portugal; Qatar; Romania; Russian Federation; Rwanda; St. Kitts and Nevis; St. Lucia; St. Vincent and the Grenadines; Samoa; São Tomé and Príncipe; Saudi Arabia; Senegal; Seychelles; Sierra Leone; Singapore; Slovakia; Slovenia; Solomon Islands; South Africa; Spain; Sri Lanka; Sudan; Suriname; Swaziland; Sweden; Switzerland; Syria; Tajikistan; Tanzania (United Republic of); Thailand; Timor-Leste; Togo; Trinidad and Tobago; Tunisia; Turkey; Turkmenistan; Uganda; Ukraine; United Arab Emirates; United Kingdom; USA; Uruguay; Uzbekistan; Vanuatu; Venezuela; Vietnam; Yemen; Zambia; and Zimbabwe.

the availability of a fairly good data series for these independent variables (if not mentioned otherwise, UNDP data for the middle of the first decade of the new millennium). In the final regressions, we applied the 'listwise deletion of missing values' routine (i.e. only entering countries with complete data into the statistical analysis). This investigation partly builds on an earlier analysis, published in 2008.[13]

The statistical design of our study is thus based on the usual, SPSS XV ordinary least square standard regression analysis of the 'kitchen sink type' (Durlauf et al. 2008) of economic growth and economic, social and political performance in the research tradition of Barro (2003).[14] Surveying the vast econometric literature on the subject of the possible drivers and bottlenecks of the EU-2020 process and overall development performance of a given country, one indeed finds support for the inclusion of geographic and demographic variables in the comparative analysis of development success or failure.[15]

3.12 The List of Independent Variables

Our main independent variables are:

1. 2000 economic freedom score
2. Absolute latitude
3. Annual population growth rate, 1975–2005 (percentage)
4. Comparative price levels (US = 1.00)
5. Foreign savings rate
6. FPZ (free production zones) employment as a percentage of the total population
7. ln GDP per capita

---

13 The results in Tausch (2008a, 2008b) are based on Microsoft Excel multiple regressions. The SPSS XV regressions reported in the present study are a continuation and refinement of the earlier research results, reported in that mentioned publication. On the reliability problems of common statistical software programs, like Microsoft Excel, especially when collinearity of the predictor variables is higher (as is the case in the present regression equations), see Altman and McDonald (2001), our tests revealed the basic validity of the argument, put forward by Altman and McDonald, which has vast and serious implications for the entire social science profession. SPSS and Microsoft Excel regressions reveal, our tests showed, the same R^2, regression constants, and overall F-tests, but the significance of the predictors changes in Microsoft Excel regressions is not stable, depending on the ordering of the independent variables, while SPSS results are stable, regardless of the ordering of the independent variables.

14 To our knowledge, the term 'kitchen sink regression', commonly used in econometrics of economic growth, was re-introduced in more recent standard social science journal vocabulary in Laver and Shepsle (1999).

15 See Ades and Glaeser (1999); Alesina and La Ferrara (2005); Barro and Sala-i-Martin (2003); Barro (1991, 1996, 1998); Bloom and Sachs (1998); Chanda and Putterman (2007); Dowrick and Quiggin (1997); Easterly and Levine (1997); Frankel and Romer (1999); Gallup and Sachs (1999); Grier and Tullock (1989); Hall and Jones (1999); Kamarck (1976); Kormendi and Meguire (1985); Levine and Renelt (1992); Mankiw, Romer and Weil (1992); and Rodriguez and Rodrik (2001).

8. ln GDP per capita[2]
9. Membership of the Islamic Conference
10. Military expenditures per GDP
11. Military personnel rate ln (MPR + 1)
12. MNC outward investments (stock) per GDP
13. MNC PEN – stock of inward FDI per GDP
14. MNC PEN: DYN MNC PEN 1995–2005
15. Openness Index, 1990 (export share per GDP + import share per GDP)
16. Percentage of women in government, all levels
17. Percentage of world population
18. Population density
19. Public education expenditure per GNP
20. UNDP Education Index
21. Worker remittance inflows as a percentage of GDP
22. Immigration – share of population (2005)
23. Muslim population share per total population
24. Net international migration rate, 2005–2010
25. Years of membership in the EU, 2010
26. Years of membership in the EMU, 2010

Policy pointer

Our independent variables duly acknowledge many of the key determinants of development patterns mentioned in the economic literature, such as current shares of the country's inhabitants in total world population, the Heritage Foundation economic freedom score; absolute geographical latitude, long-term annual population growth rates, the trade-off between development level and development performance (otherwise also known in economics as 'conditional convergence') the influence of Muslim culture or Muslim statehood on development patterns, population density, public education expenditure per GDP, the UNDP Education Index (combining the enrolment rates at the primary, secondary and tertiary education levels), military expenditures per GDP and military personnel rates, migration patterns, and European (Monetary) Union membership. We also properly take a variety of globalization variables into account, ranging from comparative price levels and foreign savings to free production zones, transnational corporations (MNC outward investments (stock) per GDP; MNC PEN – stock of inward FDI per GDP; DYN MNC PEN 1995–2005) and the Openness Index (1990, export share per GDP + import share per GDP). We also consider the possible influence of feminism in power on development. Thus, our choice of the possible 'drivers' and bottlenecks' of development can be regarded as a fair compromise between the leading econometric and the sociological/political science approaches on the subject.

3.13 The List of Dependent Variables

The main dependent variables for this analysis also correspond to standard knowledge in comparative political science and sociology. An ever-growing number of more recently published investigations not only look into the effects of MNC penetration on economic growth, but into the more social and ecological conditions in general.[16,17]

These variables in a way correspond to most of the ten guidelines published by the European Commission in the context of the EU-2020 strategy debate, which rest on the five pillars of social security, labour, education, research and development, and environmental protection (ensuring the quality and the sustainability of public finances; addressing macroeconomic imbalances; reducing imbalances in the euro area; optimizing support for R&D and innovation, strengthening the knowledge triangle and unleashing the potential of the digital economy; improving resource efficiency and reducing greenhouse gases emissions; improving the business and consumer environment and modernizing the industrial base; increasing labour market participation and reducing structural unemployment; developing a skilled workforce responding to labour market needs, promoting job quality and lifelong learning; improving the performance of education and training systems at all levels and increasing participation in tertiary education; promoting social inclusion and combating poverty).

The final and summarizing index, developed by our research to measure Europe's progress towards the goals of the EU-2020 strategy is the 'global Lisbon 2020 index'[18] or (GLI). It is a single non-parametric index, which was finally extracted from the following variables:

1. Avoiding net trade of ecological footprint gha per person
2. Carbon emissions per capita
3. Carbon emissions per million US dollars GDP
4. Civil and political liberty violations
5. Closing economic gender gap

---

16 Beckfield (2006b); de Soysa and Neumayer (2005); Jenkins and Scanlan (2001); Jorgensen (2003, 2005); Kentor (2001); Kentor and Boswell (2003); Lee (2005); Li and Resnick (2003); Meyer (2003); Reuveny and Thompson (2004); Richards, Gelleny and Sacko (2001); Schofer, Ramirez and Meyer (2000); Shandra, London and Williamson (2003); Sumner (2005).

17 Although we presume many of the indicators to be known, we refer our readers especially to the brief summary of the ever more important Happy Planet Index indicator, relating happy life years to ecological footprint, available from http://www.happyplanetindex.org/list.htm, and the very comprehensive Yale/Columbia environmental data series, available at http://sedac.ciesin.columbia.edu/es/esi/ and http://epi.yale.edu/Home, which up to now were practically neglected by cross-national comparative dependency and world-systems research. The important new grammar of the footprint discourse can be found at http://www.footprintnetwork.org/en/index.php/GFN/page/glossary/ (all accessed 27 January 2012).

18 We should, for reasons of clarity, re-iterate here that throughout this work, this term, sometimes also called the single development indicator, or combined, final EU-2020 development index, or overall development index for 175 countries or global development index, refers to our index, which combines democracy, economic growth, environment, gender, human development, R&D, and social cohesion. The performances of all the countries of our investigation for all

  6. Closing educational gender gap
  7. Closing health and survival gender gap
  8. Closing of global gender gap overall score 2009
  9. Closing political gender gap
10. Combined Failed States Index
11. Corruption avoidance measure
12. Country share in top world 500 universities
13. Crisis Performance Factor
14. Democracy measure
15. Ecological footprint (gha per capita)
16. Economic growth IMF prediction growth rate in 2009
17. Economic growth IMF prediction growth rate in 2010
18. Economic growth in real terms per capita, per annum, 1990–2005
19. Environmental Performance Index (EPI)
20. Environmental Sustainability Index (ESI)
21. Female survival, probability of surviving to age 65
22. Gender empowerment index value
23. Global tolerance index
24. Happy life years
25. Happy Planet Index (HPI)
26. Human Development Index (HDI) value 2004
27. Infant mortality (2005)
28. Life expectancy (years)
29. Life satisfaction (0–10)
30. ln (number of people per million inhabitants 1980–2000 killed by natural disasters per year + 1)
31. Per capita world-class universities
32. Quintile share income difference between richest and poorest 20 per cent
33. Rule of law
34. Tertiary enrolment ratio
35. Unemployment rate

The list of variables entered into the final multiple stepwise regressions, consists of the following key variables:

  1. Avoiding net trade of ecological footprint gha per person
  2. Carbon emissions per million US dollars GDP

----

the dependent variables were standardized along a scale, ranging from 0 to 1. Zero is the worst, and 1 is the best performance. High numerical values for the combined failed states index, civil and political liberty violations, ecological footprint (gha per capita), infant mortality (2005), the quintile share income difference between richest and poorest 20 per cent, the unemployment rate, ln (number of people per million inhabitants 1980 to 2000 killed by natural disasters per year + 1), carbon emissions per million US dollars GDP, and carbon emissions per capita, are a development debacle, while high numerical values for the other indicators are regarded as a blessing.

3. Civil and political liberty violations
4. Closing overall gender gap
5. Closing the economic gender gap
6. Closing the political gender gap
7. CO_2 per capita
8. Combined Failed States Index
9. Crisis Performance Factor
10. Democracy measure
11. Economic growth IMF prediction growth rate in 2010
12. Economic growth, 1990–2005
13. Environmental Performance Index (EPI)
14. Environmental Sustainability Index (ESI)
15. Female survival, probability of surviving to age 65
16. Gender empowerment index value
17. Global footprint
18. Global tolerance index
19. Happy life years
20. Happy Planet Index (HPI)
21. Human Development Index (HDI) value 2004
22. Infant mortality (2005)
23. Life expectancy (years)
24. Life satisfaction (0–10)
25. ln (number of people per million inhabitants 1980–2000 killed by natural disasters per year + 1)
26. Per capita world-class universities
27. Quintile share income difference between richest and poorest 20 per cent
28. Rule of law
29. Tertiary enrolment ratio
30. Unemployment rate

Policy pointer

Our investigation not only brings together the most important possible determinants of global development, it also presents the most complete collection of dependent variables in the literature to date, ranging from the dimensions of democracy and economic growth to the environment, gender equality, human development, R&D, and social cohesion. Thus, it is truly universal in orientation and conception, and does not avoid the thorny issues of democracy gender equality, and human development, hitherto excluded from current debates about the EU-2020 strategy and its possible global implications.

Chapter 4

CROSS-NATIONAL RESULTS: BEYOND THE PRO-GLOBALIST DEVELOPMENT APPROACH OF THE EUROPEAN COMMISSION

We will now present the results of our multiple regression analyses in Table 2. In our view, the regression results, presented in Appendix 1 of this work, present the best available choice of variables from both the theoretical as well as empirical statistical perspectives. In testing the implications of the competing paradigms, we arrive at the following list of multiple regressions with significant statistical results:

Table 2. The final results from multiple regression analysis. The properties of the statistical investigations

Dependent variable	Explained variance (adj R^2)[1]	Degrees of freedom (df)[2]	Statistical quality test for the entire equation (F-test value)[3]	Error probability of the entire equation
Human Development Index (HDI)	0.950	133	425.085	0.000
Combined Failed States Index	0.830	119	97.634	0.000
Gender empowerment index value	0.815	70	77.895	0.000
Global footprint	0.812	135	117.592	0.000

(*Continued*)

---

1 In lay language, one might say: 'how much of reality is explained by the model'. It is important to remind our readers that 80 per cent might also be written as the number 0.80, 50 per cent as the number 0.50, and 20 per cent as the number 0.20 etc.

2 The number of observations used to calculate the regression equation is always degrees of freedom + 1. For an easily readable guide to SPSS multiple regression equations, we refer our readers to the following document, prepared by the University of California, Los Angeles: http://www.ats.ucla.edu/stat/spss/output/reg_spss.htm (accessed 27 January 2012).

3 Readers, not particularly interested in statistics, might skip this particular column on the F-values. The more important column is the one stating the error probability of the entire equation, emerging from the overall statistical quality testing. The smaller the error probability, the better.

Table 2. Continued

Dependent variable	Explained variance (adj R^2)[1]	Degrees of freedom (df)[2]	Statistical quality test for the entire equation (F-test value)[3]	Error probability of the entire equation
Infant mortality (2005)	0.794	152	117.921	0.000
Environmental Performance Index (EPI)	0.789	140	88.259	0.000
Happy life years	0.771	102	86.653	0.000
Life expectancy (years)	0.748	105	63.293	0.000
Tertiary enrolment ratio	0.737	136	64.501	0.000
CO_2 per capita	0.727	159	71.594	0.000
Life satisfaction (0–10)	0.694	113	64.990	0.000
Civil and political liberty violations	0.675	143	43.443	0.000
Female survival, probability of surviving to age 65	0.668	114	46.815	0.000
Global tolerance index	0.663	64	34.516	0.000
Per capita world-class universities	0.649	107	25.749	0.000
Crisis Performance Factor	0.640	144	52.963	0.000
Rule of law	0.638	115	34.748	0.000
Closing overall gender gap	0.587	109	26.796	0.000
Democracy measure	0.550	142	29.885	0.000
Economic growth IMF prediction growth rate in 2010	0.521	149	27.974	0.000
Avoiding net trade of ecological footprint gha per person	0.409	138	20.111	0.000
Closing the economic gender gap	0.401	122	21.380	0.000
Happy Planet Index	0.380	119	19.217	0.000
Economic growth, 1990–2005	0.363	111	8.921	0.000
Unemployment rate	0.354	103	10.416	0.000
Carbon emissions per million US dollars GDP	0.350	144	16.535	0.000

(*Continued*)

Table 2. Continued

Dependent variable	Explained variance (adj R²)[1]	Degrees of freedom (df)[2]	Statistical quality test for the entire equation (F-test value)[3]	Error probability of the entire equation
Environmental Sustainability Index (ESI)	0.345	121	13.720	0.000
Quintile share income difference between richest and poorest 20%	0.255	119	6.098	0.000
Closing the political gender gap	0.249	113	7.243	0.000
ln (number of people per million inhabitants 1980–2000 killed by natural disasters per year + 1)	0.144	159	7.713	0.000

Consistent with the paradigms of critical political economy, introduced in this work, we would first of all expect that, contrary to contemporary neoliberalism, economic freedom harms development, and that world economic openness is, unlike the assumptions of neoliberal economics, not a secure remedy to achieve what the European Commission nowadays calls the EU-2020 agenda. We would further expect that instead of low comparative price levels in reality high comparative price levels are quite consistent with Balassa (1964) and Samuelson (1964), a relevant precondition of sound and long-lasting socio-economic success. In accordance with the critical paradigms, presented here, we also expect that too high foreign savings will indeed harm the development process, and that relying on free production zones is not a valid strategy to achieve long-lasting success. In contrast to the neoliberal paradigm, we also expect that a high MNC headquarter status is beneficial and a high foreign MNC penetration and its increases over time are detrimental to the development goals, also featuring in the EU-2020 agenda.

We would also expect with most liberal and left-of-centre–oriented global political discourse that worker remittances have very beneficial effects for the sending countries, and that they amount to a very huge transfer machine of wealth from the rich, migration-recipient countries to the poor, migration-sending countries. Accounting for the total wealth generated by immigrants, migration is thus seen as a win–win situation.

With most opinions of the centre-left, we would reject xenophobic, culturalist or migration pessimistic perspectives and we would in addition strongly expect a positive trade-off between public education expenditures and development performance, and equally, we would expect a similar positive trade-off between human capital formation (UNDP Education Index) and development. The Kalecki–Steindl paradigm (see also Tausch 2010b) would also assume that a high inequality between the social strata is detrimental, and a low inequality is beneficial for the development performance.

We would also assume in accordance with wide sectors of the global political discourse of the centre-left that both high military expenditures as well as high military personnel rates are a waste of resources and should be better spent on such outlays as education and research. In addition, feminism, operationalized by the share of women in government at all levels, and not just the ministerial level, is considered to be a very positive asset for the development process, and – as good Europeans, we would finally believe that both years of membership in the EU and in the European Monetary Union have very beneficial aspects for any of the socio-economic development processes under investigation here. What else would be the benefit of European Union membership, if, at the end of the day, your economic growth is slower and your unemployment is significantly higher the longer your country is a member?

We will keep our demographic, geographic and historical variables listed below constant in our multiple regression designs. All regressions were first tested in stepwise regression models, which included the whole array of the 26 predictors; after selecting the most significant predictors by the stepwise regression procedure we used SPSS XV 'forward regression' to arrive at the final models.

- Percentage of world population
- Absolute latitude
- Already achieved development level (ln GDP per capita, ln GDP per capita^2)
- Annual population growth
- Population density

In evaluating our results, we largely exclude here the demographic, geographic and historical variables from the discourse. At the end of the day, they are outside the set of parameters of the action of governments, at least in the short run, and though they may influence substantially development outcomes, they cannot be utilized to attain development goals in the short run.

In presenting our results, we highlighted the outcomes which contradict the theoretical expectations of what could be termed the globalization-critical development consensus, presented above, in grey colour. It should be noted that all the other results of our indicators are not statistically significant.

Exactly 50 results from our multiple regressions, explaining 30 variables, presented at length in Appendix 1 of this work, are statistically significant at least at the 10 per cent level. The negative effects of passive globalization and the positive effects of inward migration on development are often overwhelming. Nevertheless, an important re-direction of the globalization-critical development discourse is necessary. Of the 50 results, 20, i.e. 40 per cent, do not conform to the theoretical explanations, explained above. However, 17 of the 20 contradicting results stem from just three weak dimensions of the globalization-critical paradigm – (1) the insufficient understanding of the role of economic freedom, especially in advanced countries, (2) the inability to comprehend existing problems in the areas of democracy and tolerance, gender equality, and employment in the 'real existing Muslim countries' and in the parallel worlds of Muslim migration abroad, and, finally (3) the inability to formulate a proper framework of the interaction between the public and the private, especially in higher education. Four of these stem from the positive effects of economic freedom on development, and eight contradictions stem from the negative effects of membership in the Organisation of the Islamic Conference or from Muslim population shares on such phenomena as democracy and tolerance, gender equality, and employment. Five contradictions stem from the fact that different development theories, including the globalization-critical development consensus, presented above, overlook the crowding-out effects of public education expenditures on employment, growth and human development. Put in a nutshell, the globalization-critical development consensus would explain development outcomes in today's world much more reliably if it were to upgrade its understanding of the role of:

• economic freedom for development;
• its treatment of the chances and contradictions of multiculturalism, especially regarding the Muslim world; and
• its views on the role of public or private education, especially in advanced Western societies.

Such words, coming from the author of a book entitled *Towards a Socio-Liberal Theory of World Development* published almost two decades ago (Tausch and Prager 1993), re-iterating some basic socio-liberal truths, should not be regarded as a big surprise.

Since we would like our work to be understood not only by economists, sociologists and political scientists, but by a more general, interested public, we introduce at this stage Scheme 2, which explains how our empirical results should be read. Usually, beta weights in multiple regression analysis range from $+1.0$ to -1.0 (except for cases of very high interrelationships between the explanatory variables), and – together with the error probability levels – are a quality indicator of the results achieved. Beta weights bigger than 1.0 could happen, for example, in the case of the well-known non-linear effects of development levels on development performance (what social sciences sometimes call the 'acceleration and maturity effects').

So let us now see the results in detail. In accordance with neoliberal approaches, and in discord with the mainstream of globalization-critical research, economic freedom has a significant positive impact on indicators of the environment, on the reduction of infant mortality and the avoidance of the failed states syndrome. The environmental variables, positively affected by economic freedom, are carbon emissions per GDP and the Yale/Columbia ESI. However, critics of the Washington/Brussels/Paris Consensus are right in emphasizing that

Scheme 2. How our empirical results have to be read

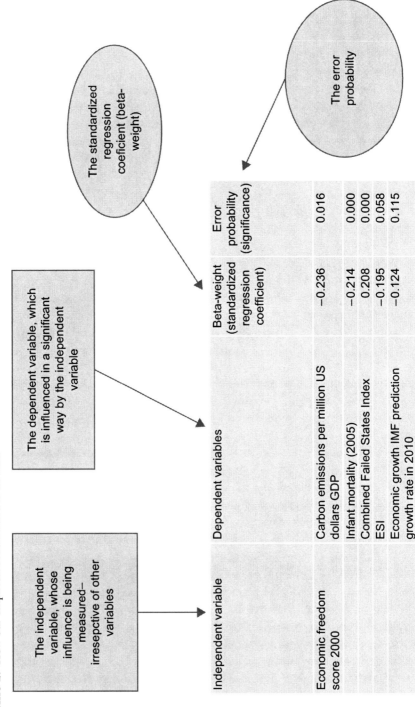

Independent variable	Dependent variables	Beta-weight (standardized regression coefficient)	Error probability (significance)
Economic freedom score 2000	Carbon emissions per million US dollars GDP	−0.236	0.016
	Infant mortality (2005)	−0.214	0.000
	Combined Failed States Index	0.208	0.000
	ESI	−0.195	0.058
	Economic growth IMF prediction growth rate in 2010	−0.124	0.115

in the current period of world economic development, the impact of economic freedom on economic growth is negative:

Independent variable	Dependent variables	Beta-weight (standardized regression coefficient)	Error probability (significance)
Economic freedom score 2000	Carbon emissions per million US dollars GDP	−0.236	0.016
	Infant mortality (2005)	−0.214	0.000
	Combined Failed States Index	−0.208	0.000
	ESI	0.195	0.058
	Economic growth IMF prediction growth rate in 2010	−0.124	0.115

Our next analysis deals with the impact of world economic openness on the 30 main indicators of development. Again, it emerges that the impact of liberal policies – just as in the case above – on the quality of environmental policy is not necessarily negative. In the world system, some of the most persistent sinners in terms of CO_2 and SO_2 output, poisoning rivers, and woodland were the communist dictatorships which ruled Central Eastern Europe until 1989–90. Thus it is no surprise that world economic openness does not increase, but decreases CO_2 emissions per capita. The contradictions of world economic openness are rather on the educational and on the social level. On the educational level, because open systems, more often than not situated in small, welfare-oriented democracies, tend towards a bad performance on the per capita world-class universities index and the tertiary enrolment ratio. There seem to be important economies of scale at work in the educational system. In accordance with the mainstream of dependency theory and globalization-critical writing, a negative social trade-off of world economic openness also has to be expected. World economic openness does have a significant negative effect on the Human Development Index, and in many ways is *the* master variable for the social situation in a country.

Independent variable	Dependent variables	Beta-weight (standardized regression coefficient)	Error probability (significance)
Openness Index, 1990 (export share per GDP + import share per GDP)	Per capita world-class universities	−0.324	0.000
	CO_2 per capita	−0.164	0.001

(Continued)

Independent variable	Dependent variables	Beta-weight (standardized regression coefficient)	Error probability (significance)
	Tertiary enrolment ratio	−0.133	0.005
	Human Development Index	−0.060	0.005

The significant influence of comparative price levels on our 30 chosen development indicators is equally mixed. Neoliberal theories start from the assumption that low comparative price levels will be an advantage for the development process, and high comparative price levels will impede the development trajectory. Our empirical results again confirm the fact that a liberal framework does not necessarily impede a good ecological performance. It can be shown that high comparative price levels lead necessarily towards a higher involvement in the net trade of ecological footprint gha per person. However, it must be made equally clear that the true deficit of ultra-liberal globalization is the social. High comparative price levels, and hence, implicitly, a high level of services of general interest, are a good and sound precondition of global tolerance, of a levelling of the income differences between rich and poor, and per capita world-class university performance.

Independent variable	Dependent variables	Beta-weight (standardized regression coefficient)	Error probability (significance)
Comparative price levels (US = 1.00)	Avoiding net trade of ecological footprint gha per person	−0.401	0.001
	Global tolerance index	0.366	0.055
	Quintile share income difference between richest and poorest 20%	−0.300	0.099
	Per capita world-class universities	0.204	0.090

Policy pointer

The effects of neoliberal policies on development patterns are mixed at best. Economic freedom has a significant positive impact on indicators of the environment, on the reduction of infant mortality and the avoidance of the failed states syndrome. Critics of neoliberalism are right in emphasizing that in the current period of world economic development, the impact of economic freedom on economic growth (2010) is even significantly negative. The impact of world economic openness on the 30 main indicators of development is also mixed. The negative effects of world economic openness are on the educational and on the social level. The effects of comparative price levels on our 30 chosen development indicators are also equally mixed. High comparative price levels, and hence, implicitly, a high level of services of general interest (Eurostat: Absence of economic reform), are a good and sound precondition of global tolerance, of a levelling of the income differences between rich and poor, and per capita world-class university performance.

The apprehensions of globalization-critical research are fully vindicated by the significant effects of the foreign savings rate. High foreign savings *are* indeed a driver of unemployment, income inequality, global footprint, and are a blockade against a satisfactory Happy Planet Index performance of the sample countries.

Independent variable	Dependent variables	Beta-weight (standardized regression coefficient)	Error probability (significance)
Foreign savings rate	Unemployment rate	0.328	0.001
	Quintile share income difference between richest and poorest 20%	0.251	0.007
	Happy Planet Index	−0.189	0.037
	Global footprint	0.082	0.063

The New International Division of Labour (NIDL) model – featured in critical theories of globalization since the 1970s, most prominently in the works of Froebel, Heinrichs and Kreye – which can be best measured by the indicator free production zones employment as a percentage of total population, is one of the prime drivers of high CO_2 per capita emissions. However, in comparison to the other indicators of globalization and dependency, its influence is not as strong as suggested by this particular globalization-critical theory.

Independent variable	Dependent variable	Beta-weight (standardized regression coefficient)	Error probability (significance)
FPZ (free production zones) employment as % of total population	CO_2 per capita	0.238	0.000

For the globalization-critical paradigm of Volker Bornschier, an important control variable was MNC headquarter status. MNC penetration's negative impacts on the social development of the host countries of foreign direct investments are mitigated by the positive effects of MNC headquarter status. Thus, the relationship of mutual MNC penetration in say, Belgium and the Netherlands is not as negative for social development because both countries are an important location of MNCs, which invest heavily abroad, especially overseas and repatriate profits, retaining the very profitable company command, control, communication and intelligence functions at home. Indeed, the positive effects of MNC headquarter status on per capita world-class universities and the rule of law vindicate such reasoning, but economic growth in the period 1990–2005 was significantly and negatively influenced by MNC headquarter status, suggesting that in the long Kuznets cycle between the end of communism and the current world economic crisis, the growth-inducing effects of outsourcing of production from the core countries to regions like Central Eastern Europe (outsourcing from the EU centre countries), or Mexico and the Caribbean (outsourcing from the USA) were stronger than the mentioned positive effects of the profitability of company command, control, communication and intelligence functions at home.

Independent variable	Dependent variables	Beta-weight (standardized regression coefficient)	Error probability (significance)
MNC outward investments (stock) per GDP	Per capita world-class universities	0.371	0.000
	Economic growth, 1990–2005	−0.286	0.008

MNC penetration, the master variable of most quantitative dependency theories, has had a positive and significant impact on economic growth, 1990–2005, suggesting that economic growth in 1990 to 2005 due to the mentioned growth inducing effects of outsourcing of production from the core countries to some regions in Central Eastern Europe (outsourcing from the EU centre countries), or Mexico and the Caribbean (outsourcing from the USA). However, MNC penetration increases income polarization and infant mortality, and blocks democracy, and environmental performance.

Independent variable	Dependent variables	Beta-weight (standardized regression coefficient)	Error probability (significance)
MNC PEN – stock of inward FDI per GDP	Economic growth, 1990–2005	0.552	0.000
	Quintile share income difference between richest and poorest 20%	0.221	0.013

(*Continued*)

Independent variable	Dependent variables	Beta-weight (standardized regression coefficient)	Error probability (significance)
	Infant mortality (2005)	0.160	0.000
	Democracy measure	−0.147	0.011
	Environmental Performance Index (EPI)	−0.113	0.005

Increases in MNC penetration over time had a negative effect on the rule of law, and equally had a negative, but insignificant effect on economic growth in the period 1990–2005. A good and plausible reason for this is the process of 'creative destruction' taking place in the less fortunate regions of the world economy. This is particularly relevant in Central and Eastern Europe. With devastating force, the 'second league' of 'dependent EU-enlargement' and 'dependent development' (Romania, Bulgaria) is now suffering from the crisis. This contrasts with the successful dependent industrialization in Western Poland, the Czech Republic and Western Hungary, where MNC penetration started immediately after the transformation in 1989–90. These regions today are heavily integrated into the circuits of global capitalism.

Independent variable	Dependent variables	Beta-weight (standardized regression coefficient)	Error probability (significance)
MNC PEN: DYN MNC PEN 1995–2005	Rule of law	−0.199	0.002

Policy pointer

The effects of the globalization variables on development patterns are manifold. High foreign savings are indeed a driver of unemployment, income inequality, global footprint, and are a blockade against a satisfactory Happy Planet Index performance. The New International Division of Labour (NIDL) model is one of the main drivers of high CO_2 per capita emissions. MNC headquarter status, as predicted by the Zurich school of sociology (Volker Bornschier) has some mitigating and positive effects on world development, while MNC penetration generally negatively affects development patterns. MNC penetration increases income polarization and infant mortality, and blocks democracy, and environmental performance. Increases in MNC penetration over time had a negative effect on the rule of law, and equally had a negative but insignificant effect on economic growth in the period 1990–2005.

Worker remittances have a significant positive effect on the Happy Planet Index, life expectancy (years), closing the political gender gap, life satisfaction (0–10), closing the overall gender gap, and happy life years, and the only negative significant effect is on the Environmental Sustainability Index (ESI).

In order to be able to compare the results for worker remittances with the other migration policy variables, we would have to multiply the results by a factor of minus one in order to make them comparable with the results for immigration. We would have to keep in mind, though, that the indicator does not measure net worker remittances, but only worker remittances accruing to the economy of a given country, exporting labour to the world economy. While high worker remittance ratios are very typical for migrant workforce exporting countries, the recipient countries typically will have very low numerical values on this indicator. Also however, poor countries not substantially integrated into the sending and receiving of guest workers have low numerical values on this indicator. We can assume that export of labour to the world economy has beneficial effects on life quality (Happy Planet Index, life expectancy, life satisfaction, happy life years), and gender relations (closing the political gender gap; closing the overall gender gap), while it negatively affects the performance of a country on the ESI. We can then assume that the import of labour to the world economy has detrimental effects on life quality (Happy Planet Index, life expectancy, life satisfaction, happy life years), and gender relations (closing the political gender gap; closing the overall gender gap), while it positively affects the performance of a country on the ESI. The labour market scarcities, brought about by outward migration, significantly improve the position of women in typical guest worker exporting economies. In addition, worker remittances are an important instrument of wealth transfer from the rich to the poorer countries of the world. In addition the high capital intensity in production in receiving countries allow for higher labour productivity and a better utilization of labour force in receiving countries. Part of the positive effects is outweighed by the negative family life quality following separation and guest workers' inhuman treatment in some receiving countries.

Independent variable	Dependent variables	Beta-weight (standardized regression coefficient)	Error probability (significance)
Worker remittance inflows as % of GDP	Happy Planet Index	0.356	0.000
	Life expectancy (years)	0.247	0.000
	Closing the political gender gap	0.194	0.054
	Life satisfaction (0–10)	0.188	0.001
	Closing overall gender gap	0.172	0.012
	ESI	−0.144	0.075
	Happy life years	0.118	0.024

The consensus of a large and ever-growing tradition of research would tend to see the effects of international migration on the recipient countries in very positive terms, the political noise from migra-phobic politicians to the contrary. However, not all of the optimistic forecasts of this liberal school of thought can be maintained empirically or at least on a 1:1 basis. We already hinted at the fact that we can assume from the effects of worker remittances that the import of labour to the world economy has detrimental effects on life quality (Happy Planet Index, life expectancy, life satisfaction, happy life years), and gender relations (closing the political gender gap; closing the overall gender gap), while it positively affects the performance of a country on the ESI. The percentage of the population with what today is called an 'immigration background' has a negative effect on some other key indicators of the environment and gender justice. Immigration, and all the transport activities it causes, increases without question the CO_2 output of a given society, and it also increases the ratio of carbon emissions per GDP. There hold nevertheless some other important effects as well, which tend to confirm the migration policy liberal consensus, inherent in the UNDP *HDR 2009* analysis. A large share of people with migration background per total population seems to coincide with a weakening of the role of traditional, local, native elites, and income inequality tends to be lower when the share of population with a migration background is higher per total population in a given country.

Independent variable	Dependent variables	Beta-weight (standardized regression coefficient)	Error probability (significance)
Immigration – share of population (2005) (%)	CO_2 per capita	0.348	0.000
	Carbon emissions per million US dollars GDP	0.267	0.001
	Closing the political gender gap	−0.225	0.026
	Quintile share income difference between richest and poorest 20%	−0.196	0.044

In the comparative social sciences, stock data – like the already given share of population with an immigration background – need not necessarily and always coincide with the patterns of associations of flow data in the empirical analysis. Net international migration rates, 2005–2010, which is a typical migration flow measure, relating to current and contemporary migration flows, are significantly and positively influencing current economic growth rates, and also the ratio of closing the political gender gap. While stocks of already existing large-scale migration negatively affect the closing of the gender political gap, new inflows positively affect the closing of the political gender gap. Certainly, more detailed research would have to establish whether these results can be partially explained by different and shifting cohorts of migrant populations or by the often profound value change in the migration-sending countries.

Independent variable	Dependent variables	Beta-weight (standardized regression coefficient)	Error probability (significance)
Net international migration rate, 2005–2010	Economic growth IMF prediction growth rate in 2010	0.395	0.000
	Closing the political gender gap	0.208	0.083

Also, the effects of membership of the Islamic Conference (OIC) and Muslim population shares cannot be reduced to a simplistic reasoning. Muslim societies, organized in the OIC, tend towards a significantly higher tertiary enrolment ratio than other comparable societies, and in addition, the beneficial effects of Muslim traditions on reducing the quintile share income difference between richest and poorest 20 per cent, the Crisis Performance Factor for the current global recession, and also the Human Development Index cannot be negated. The real Achilles' heels of the 'really existing' Muslim societies, by contrast, are the poor performances along the following indicators:

• Civil and political liberty violations
• Closing overall gender gap
• Closing the economic gender gap
• Closing the political gender gap
• Democracy measure
• Gender empowerment index value
• Global tolerance index
• Unemployment rate

Independent variable	Dependent variables	Beta-weight (standardized regression coefficient)	Error probability (significance)
Membership of the Islamic Conference	Democracy measure	−0.486	0.000
	Closing the political gender gap	−0.162	0.087
	Tertiary enrolment ratio	0.132	0.015

Independent variable	Dependent variables	Beta-weight (standardized regression coefficient)	Error probability (significance)
Muslim population share per total population	Closing the economic gender gap	−0.493	0.000
	Gender empowerment index value	−0.398	0.000
	Closing overall gender gap	−0.375	0.000
	Global tolerance index	−0.323	0.000
	Civil and political liberty violations	0.304	0.000
	Unemployment rate	0.302	0.001
	Quintile share income difference between richest and poorest 20%	−0.299	0.001
	Crisis Performance Factor	0.098	0.096
	Human Development Index	0.075	0.001

Policy pointer

It seems to be that the migration-sending countries manage to receive a growing and positive share of global development policy outcomes. Received worker remittances have a significant positive effect on the Happy Planet Index, life expectancy (years), the closing of the political gender gap, life satisfaction (0–10), the closing of the overall gender gap, and happy life years, and the only negative significant effect is on the Environmental Sustainability Index (ESI). These results imply mounting environmental and social problems in the migration-recipient countries. It also emerges that the percentage of the population with an 'immigration background' has also a similar and lamentable, negative effect on some other key indicators of the environment and gender justice. Immigration, and all the transport activities it causes, increases the CO_2 output. However, a large share of people with migration background per total population seems to coincide with a weakening of the role of traditional elites, and income inequality tends to become lower. Net international migration rates, 2005–2010, are very positively influencing current economic growth rates. We also show that the Achilles' heels of Muslim societies are the poor performances along the following indicators: civil and political liberty violations; closing the gender gaps, the democracy measure, the gender empowerment index value, the global tolerance index, and the unemployment rate.

For the Kalecki–Steindl paradigm (Tausch 2010a), the following drivers of development hold:

- Full employment as main political concern
- Demand as growth driver
- Higher effective demand to raise employment
- Technology and educational policy
- Lower household savings
- Stable or rising wage share
- Anti-cyclical policy (cycle and trend have the same determinants)
- Rise of public sector promotes growth (through effective demand)
- Tax coordination
- International cooperation

For the share of public education expenditures per GDP, the results are rather dire and tend to confirm some of the basic assumptions of the current mainstream Brussels/Paris/Washington Consensus in the field of education policy. Privatization and deregulation, and the restructuring of the public sector in education policy seem to be called for, because public expenditures are one of the main drivers of an unsatisfactory employment performance, economic growth rate, and three hard core survival and basic needs indicators (most probably due to crowding-out effects with other government expenditure components): the female survival probability rate, life expectancy, and the Human Development Index. The only two positive effects of public education expenditures observed are on per capita world-class universities, and the rule of law.

Independent variable	Dependent variables	Beta-weight (standardized regression coefficient)	Error probability (significance)
Public education expenditure per GNP	Per capita world-class universities	0.197	0.003
	Unemployment rate	0.179	0.049
	Economic growth, 1990–2005	−0.170	0.042
	Rule of law	0.168	0.005
	Female survival, probability of surviving to age 65	−0.152	0.011
	Life expectancy (years)	−0.131	0.019
	Human Development Index	−0.052	0.016

The Kalecki–Steindl paradigm is vindicated, though, predicting a positive trade-off of effective demand on development.[4] We even diagnose a detrimental empirical effect of inequality on employment. The higher the inequality rate, the higher the unemployment rate. This effect is quite robust and highly significant at the 0.9 per cent level.

Independent variable	Dependent variables	Beta-weight (standardized regression coefficient)	Error probability (significance)
Quintile share income difference between richest and poorest 20%	Female survival, probability of surviving to age 65	−0.292	0.000
	Unemployment rate	0.238	0.009
	Life expectancy (years)	−0.156	0.004

The UNDP Education Index as the chosen predictor for the long-standing UNDP human capital propelled development approach has the predicted and significant effects on:

- Environmental Performance Index (EPI)
- Human Development Index
- Tertiary enrolment ratio
- Infant mortality (2005) (reduction of infant mortality)
- ln (number of people per million inhabitants 1980–2000 killed by natural disasters per year + 1) (reduction of disaster risk)
- Female survival, probability of surviving to age 65

However, it emerges that there is a numerically positive trade-off between the UNDP Education Index and civil and political liberty violations. The classical and pessimistic modernization theories, surveyed in, among others, Ake (1974), are thus vindicated in one major respect. In addition, we should not underestimate the fact that more often than not, semi-totalitarian or totalitarian systems show quite high indices of school enrolment at all levels of education.[5]

---

4 Especially, it can be shown that Wilkinson (1992a, 1992b, 1996) and Wilkinson and Picket (2006) are right in maintaining that high inequality rates must be regarded in their own right as blockades against female survival rates and life expectancies. On the disturbing effects on employment, see Galbraith (1999, 2007, 2009); Galbraith and Garcilazo (2004, 2005); Galbraith and Kum (2003, 2005); Galbraith, Conceição and Ferreira (1999); and Galbraith, Giovannoni and Russo (2007).

5 The 30 countries with the highest UNDP Education Index are: Australia; Denmark; Finland; Ireland; New Zealand; Canada; Norway; Netherlands; Spain; France; Korea (Republic of); Iceland; Sweden; Belgium; Slovenia; Kazakhstan; USA; Greece; United Kingdom; Estonia; Austria; Lithuania; Latvia; Hungary; Italy; Barbados; Belarus; Russia; Germany; and Cuba.

Independent variable	Dependent variables	Beta-weight (standardized regression coefficient)	Error probability (significance)
UNDP Education Index	Environmental Performance Index (EPI)	0.560	0.000
	Human Development Index	0.530	0.000
	Tertiary enrolment ratio	0.443	0.000
	Infant mortality (2005)	−0.441	0.000
	ln (number of people per million inhabitants 1980–2000 killed by natural disasters per year + 1)	−0.289	0.018
	Female survival, probability of surviving to age 65	0.202	0.027
	Civil and political liberty violations	0.201	0.030

The significant effects of military expenditure per GDP are rather limited in comparison to the other drivers and bottlenecks of international development, under investigation here. They significantly diminish the number of happy life years, indicating a negative trade-off not with life expectancy, but with life quality as such, as measured by the happy life years indicator. The burden of the military effort thus has a limited effect on life quality, but all the other social negative effects, often portrayed in the literature, empirically, possibly due to data limitations, do not materialize in the present phase of development of the world economy. Also, there is a relatively small effect of the military burden rate on the Combined Failed States Index, indicating that high military outlays cannot halt for themselves the downward and vicious spiral of the failed states phenomenon. Rather, high military burden rates become part and parcel of the downward spiral. However, it should be emphasized that the size of the effect is rather small (error probability 7.1 per cent).

Independent variable	Dependent variables	Beta-weight (standardized regression coefficient)	Error probability (significance)
Military expenditure per GDP	Happy life years	−0.113	0.020
	Combined Failed States Index	0.075	0.071

Our research results suggest that high military personnel rates are a bottleneck of democracy, the civil and political liberties performance, the environmental performance, as measured by the Yale/Columbia EPI, and the closing of the overall gender gap.[6] However, it is clear that high military personnel rates not only have negative effects on the development process. High military personnel rates are still to be regarded as one of the drivers of per capita world-class universities, testifying the close relationship between the military sector and military research and development in the world economy.

Independent variable	Dependent variables	Beta-weight (standardized regression coefficient)	Error probability (significance)
Military personnel rate ln (MPR + 1)	Democracy measure	−0.367	0.000
	Civil and political liberty violations	0.315	0.000
	Per capita world-class universities	0.214	0.003
	Environmental Performance Index (EPI)	−0.174	0.000
	Closing overall gender gap	−0.156	0.037

Neoclassical economists[7] argue that gender inequality is not a good choice for economic growth. Dollar and Gatti, for example argue that the relative status of women is poor in the developing world, compared to developed countries. Increases in per capita income lead to improvements in different measures of gender equality, suggesting that there may be market failures hindering investment in girls in developing countries, and that these are typically overcome as development proceeds. Gender inequality in education and health can also be explained to a considerable extent by religious preference, regional factors, and civil freedom. These systematic patterns in gender differentials suggest that low investment in women is not an efficient economic choice, and in their approach they show that gender inequality in education is bad for economic growth. Societies with a preference for not investing in girls pay a price for it in terms of slower growth and reduced income. These approaches, however, are output oriented, and treat the trade-off between gender equality and growth, while they do not consider the effects of gender-oriented political government interventions on the political, social, ecological and economic development outcomes. The best single measure on the control which women exercise over the structures of national government, arguably, is the indicator 'percentage of women in government, all levels', which goes much beyond the ministerial level and looks at different layers of government, i.e. the top political and administrative sphere,

---

6 Several of our results would tend to confirm the pessimism voiced in the Keller, Poutvaara and Wagener study, and thus counter the earlier optimism inherent in the studies by Weede (1980a, 1980b, 1981a, 1981b, 1983, 1985, 1986, 1993); Weede and Jagodzinski (1980a, 1980b); Weede and Tiefenbach (1981a, 1981b, 1981c).

7 In the tradition of Dollar and Gatti (1999) and Klasen (1999).

where the real decisions on the day-to-day running of a given country are being taken.[8]

The development victories of 'real existing feminism' or 'feminism in power' are the good and predictable performances on the gender policy outcome front, and the positive consequences of feminized structures of power on the Yale/Columbia ESI environment indicator and the university system performance indicator, per capita world-class universities. However, there is also a darker side to the whole story: we can establish with some caution that structures in which 'real existing feminism' plays a certain role are tending towards a higher involvement in the international trade of ecological footprint. Additionally, it should not be overlooked that 'feminism in power' is still a form of government intervention, which might negatively affect – as it empirically does – the quality of democracy in a given country. However, the size of these effects is not too strong suggesting that perhaps further research is needed on this subject:

Independent variable	Dependent variables	Beta-weight (standardized regression coefficient)	Error probability (significance)
Percentage of women in government, all levels	Closing the economic gender gap	0.274	0.001
	ESI	0.209	0.013
	Gender empowerment index value	0.200	0.001
	Closing overall gender gap	0.186	0.009
	Per capita world-class universities	0.164	0.017
	Avoiding net trade of ecological footprint gha per person	−0.125	0.074
	Democracy measure	−0.113	0.052

Our empirical investigations also show that – compared to the veritable hagiography about the beneficial effects of European Union and or European Monetary Union membership on economic growth and well-being, the effects of it are rather small. There are only two significant positive effects to be reported in this context, and both concern a comparable dimension of environmental policy. The results show that the member countries of the European Monetary Union are good at reducing their ecological footprint.

---

8 The 30 countries in the world system with the highest share of women in government at all levels are: Bahamas; USA; Sweden; Dominica ; Grenada; Antigua and Barbuda; New Zealand; Colombia; Cape Verde; Latvia; El Salvador; Slovakia; Norway; Barbados; Seychelles; Macedonia (FYR); United Kingdom; Guyana; Peru; Costa Rica; Botswana; Gambia; Croatia; Jamaica; Luxembourg; Philippines; Trinidad and Tobago; Denmark; Australia; and Estonia.

Independent variable	Dependent variable	Beta-weight (standardized regression coefficient)	Error probability (significance)
Years of membership in EMU (2010)	Global footprint	−0.141	0.003

Likewise, years of EU membership coincide with avoiding net trade of ecological footprint.

Independent variable	Dependent variables	Beta-weight (standardized regression coefficient)	Error probability (significance)
Years of membership in EMU (2010)	Avoiding net trade of ecological footprint gha per person	0.396	0.000

Policy pointer

We show that there exists evidence about a crowding-out effect of the share of public education expenditures per GDP: privatization and deregulation, and the restructuring of the public sector in education policy seem to be called for, because public education expenditures are among the main drivers of an unsatisfactory employment performance, the economic growth rate, and three hard core survival and basic needs indicators: the female survival probability rate, life expectancy, and the Human Development Index. We can even diagnose a detrimental empirical effect of public education expenditures on inequality and on employment. Military expenditure per GDP also has significant detrimental effects on key development indicators (happy life years, the Combined Failed States Index), echoed by the detrimental effects of high military personnel rates on democracy, the civil and political liberties performance, the environmental performance, and the closing of the overall gender gap. Our research also suggests that feminism generally has a positive role in development outcomes, while the only positive effects of the European Union architecture are in environmental policy.

We will now look closer at the significant effects of the geographical, demographical and historical determinants of development performance that a country faces today, which cannot be influenced by short-term or, in many cases, even long-term actions of governments, and which have to be interpreted as 'givens'.

Let us start with the effects of absolute latitude, a variable which often appears in the econometrical literature on drivers and bottlenecks of development performance, but which is outside the domain of interest of the mainstream of empirical dependency and world-systems research. Predictably, and due to climatic reasons, latitude has a very strong and significant effect on carbon emissions per million US dollars GDP, and it has a considerable negative effect on life satisfaction. Latitude significantly reduces the Combined Failed States Index, irrespective of the other effects under scrutiny here.

Independent variable	Dependent variables	Beta-weight (standardized regression coefficient)	Error probability (significance)
Absolute latitude	Carbon emissions per million US dollars GDP	0.544	0.000
	Life satisfaction (0–10)	−0.215	0.005
	Combined Failed States Index	−0.151	0.017

Population density seems to affect the ecological costs of infrastructure, and it significantly reduces CO_2 emissions per capita and global footprint.

Independent variable	Dependent variables	Beta-weight (standardized regression coefficient)	Error probability (significance)
Population density	CO_2 per capita	−0.121	0.007
	Global footprint	−0.089	0.024

This finding of course squarely contradicts the propositions, forwarded by Schumacher (1973a, 1973b, 1976, 1977). The significant CO_2- and global footprint–reducing effects of population density rather suggest a reading of the effects of population density, compatible with the socio-economic theory of the Peruvian Marxist José Carlos Mariategui, who, as we already mentioned, examined the negative long-term development effects of a low population density on subsequent patterns of development. Mariategui's analysis of the capital- and land-extensive and wasteful nature of Iberian colonialism, with its use of the 'abundant production factors' of land and of fresh, unqualified labour, is thus to be applied to two of the most pressing environmental problems of today: CO_2 emissions and global footprint per capita. Low population density, often in connection with a rapidly growing labour force in scattered tiny settlements (like in the Sierra region of the Latin American Andes) in conjunction with extensive land use and high land concentration are really among the real root causes the environmental crisis of today.

The percentage share of a given country in the current world population, and hence, population size, is a very positive asset of economic growth and also crisis performance. The positive, growth-enhancing effect of large markets is valid for both the period 1990–2005, as well as for the current economic crisis, and also for the perspectives of a quick recovery. The independent and negative development effects of large population size are on human rights and the Environmental Performance Index (EPI). Large countries, like China and India, tend towards higher economic growth, but due to their great and increasing world political power, tend to gain the ability and incentive to neglect human rights and the environment.

Independent variable	Dependent variables	Beta-weight (standardized regression coefficient)	Error probability (significance)
% world population	Economic growth, 1990–2005	0.263	0.001
	Crisis Performance Factor	0.205	0.000
	Economic growth IMF prediction growth rate in 2010	0.138	0.017
	Civil and political liberty violations	0.109	0.026
	Environmental Performance Index (EPI)	−0.100	0.012

Our readers should be reminded at this point that Kohr (1957) squarely links civil and political liberty violations to the size of nations.

Annual population growth is one of the most interesting determinants of development performance. In the economic cycle, which ended in the current world recession, it tended to be associated negatively with the economic growth rate. In addition, there are very clear and negative long-term effects on the rates of income inequalities, and civil and political liberty violations. High population pressure increases the Combined Failed States Index, and it significantly reduces the tertiary enrolment ratio. However, economic growth during the current recession, and the Crisis Performance Factor are enhanced by annual population growth rates, reflecting the dramatic world economic shifts away from the economic centres towards the periphery and semi-periphery:

Independent variable	Dependent variables	Beta-weight (standardized regression coefficient)	Error probability (significance)
Annual population growth rate, 1975–2005 (%)	Quintile share income difference between richest and poorest 20%	0.471	0.000
	Tertiary enrolment ratio	−0.308	0.000
	Crisis Performance Factor	0.277	0.000

(Continued)

Independent variable	Dependent variables	Beta-weight (standardized regression coefficient)	Error probability (significance)
	Civil and political liberty violations	0.236	0.000
	Economic growth IMF prediction growth rate in 2010	0.188	0.016
	Economic growth, 1990–2005	−0.172	0.069
	Combined Failed States Index	0.108	0.055

Our empirical results also suggest a new perspective on the curve-linear relationships between development level and development performance. In our research, we could establish that, after taking care of the direction of the indicators, there is a wide array of first improving and then deteriorating performances. They all concern the environment and the health/basic human needs dimensions:

- Avoiding CO_2 per capita
- Avoiding global footprint
- Avoiding infant mortality (2005)
- Avoiding net trade of ecological footprint gha per person
- Environmental Performance Index (EPI)
- Female survival, probability of surviving to age 65
- Happy Planet Index
- Life expectancy (years)

The pessimistic essence of the Kuznets curve with rapidly increasing societal problems and very deficient development performances at middle stages of development holds for the following phenomena of the ecological efficiency of the economy, political stability and democracy, avoiding disaster risk, employment policy, gender justice, and tertiary education. All these effects suggest that 'things get worse before they get better':

- Avoiding carbon emissions per million US dollars GDP
- Avoiding Combined Failed States Index
- Avoiding ln (number of people per million inhabitants 1980−2000 killed by natural disasters per year + 1)
- Avoiding unemployment rate
- Closing the political gender gap
- Gender empowerment index value

- Per capita world-class universities
- Rule of law
- Tertiary enrolment ratio

Thus, the first order effects of modernization (measured as ln GDP per capita) on different development indicators are:

Independent variable	Dependent variables	Beta-weight (standardized regression coefficient)	Error probability (significance)
ln GDP per capita	Human Development Index	0.836	0.009
	Happy Planet Index	7.100	0.000
	Carbon emissions per million US dollars GDP	5.614	0.000
	Unemployment rate	3.949	0.002
	Avoiding net trade of ecological footprint gha per person	3.880	0.003
	ln (number of people per million inhabitants 1980–2000 killed by natural disasters per year + 1)	3.751	0.001
	Female survival, probability of surviving to age 65	3.133	0.001
	Life expectancy (years)	2.810	0.000
	Combined Failed States Index	2.713	0.000
	Environmental Performance Index (EPI)	2.158	0.001
	Happy life years	1.542	0.026
	Life satisfaction (0–10)	1.542	0.046
	Tertiary enrolment ratio	−2.013	0.006
	CO_2 per capita	−2.104	0.001
	Rule of law	−2.456	0.008
	Infant mortality (2005)	−2.592	0.000
	Closing the political gender gap	−3.199	0.018
	Per capita world-class universities	−3.258	0.004
	Gender empowerment index value	−4.744	0.000
	Global footprint	−4.870	0.000

The second order or non-linear effects of modernity (measured as ln GDP per capita^2) in turn are:

Independent variable	Dependent variables	Beta-weight (standardized regression coefficient)	Error probability (significance)
ln GDP per capita^2	Global footprint	5.838	0.000
	Gender empowerment index value	5.285	0.000
	Closing the political gender gap	3.597	0.009
	Per capita world-class universities	3.411	0.004
	Rule of law	3.211	0.001
	CO_2 per capita	2.713	0.000
	Tertiary enrolment ratio	2.328	0.001
	Infant mortality (2005)	2.264	0.000
	Civil and political liberty violations	−1.481	0.055
	Economic growth IMF prediction growth rate in 2010	−1.697	0.059
	Environmental Performance Index (EPI)	−1.750	0.004
	Life expectancy (years)	−1.882	0.019
	Female survival, probability of surviving to age 65	−2.552	0.006
	Combined Failed States Index	−3.271	0.000
	ln (number of people per million inhabitants 1980–2000 killed by natural disasters per year + 1)	−3.741	0.001
	Unemployment rate	−3.774	0.004
	Avoiding net trade of ecological footprint gha per person	−4.195	0.002
	Carbon emissions per million US dollars GDP	−6.024	0.000
	Happy Planet Index	−6.908	0.000

Policy pointer

We also show that unchanging external geographical or only long-term changeable demographic conditions significantly can affect major development outcomes: geographical latitude has a very strong and significant effect on carbon emissions per million US dollars GDP, and it has a considerable negative effect on life satisfaction. Latitude significantly reduces the Combined

Failed States Index, irrespective of the other effects under scrutiny. Population density reduces the ecological costs of infrastructure, and significantly reduces CO_2 emissions per capita and global footprint. Population size is a very positive asset of economic growth and also crisis performance. Large countries, like China and India, tend towards higher economic growth, but due to their great and increasing world political power, tend to neglect human rights and the environment. We suggest here a re-reading of the socio-economic theory of the Peruvian Marxist José Carlos Mariategui, who almost a century ago already captured the negative long-term development effects of a low population density on subsequent patterns of development. Our empirical results also suggest a new perspective on the curve-linear relationships between development level and development performance.

A Specialist's Guide to the Multiple Regression Equations

The following section is intended for use by the specialist readership of this book. It should help graduate students of the social sciences, research and teaching personnel at academic institutions as well as think-tanks, government and international agencies, NGOs and transnational corporations and other interested individuals to test the established empirical relationships on their own and to develop their own research and policy agenda, based on the data and insights presented in this work. We will first quickly draw our readers' attention to the more detailed presentation of the 30 multiple regression analyses, which can be found in Appendix 1 of this work. The seven dimensions of the independent variables are:

- Democracy
- Economic growth
- Environment
- Gender
- Human development
- R&D
- Social cohesion

Our analysis suggests that there is a theoretically very promising field of dependency- and world-systems–oriented studies of democracy, which duly takes the militarization factor into account (the optimistic study by Richards, Gelleny and Sacko (2001) notwithstanding).[9]

---

9 These authors were using ordered logit analysis on a cross-national sample of 43 developing countries from 1981 to 1995, and claimed to discover systematic evidence of an association between foreign economic penetration and government respect for two types of human rights, physical integrity rights and political rights and civil liberties. Of particular interest is the finding that both foreign direct investment and portfolio investment are reliably associated with increased government respect for human rights.

Tsai (2006b) attempted to evaluate the impacts of macro-structural factors on political freedom in less-developed countries (LDCs). Political freedom is conceptualized as civil liberty and political rights the general population of a society can enjoy in influencing public policy. The Freedom House indexes are used as measures of freedom. In explaining the individual countries' differences in political freedom, the study considered regime types, level of development, social structure, fractionalization, the state and military influence and external economic dependence as independent variables. Empirical modelling of 118 LDCs with regression techniques and ordered logit methods demonstrated that besides the regime effects, economic development generates a favourable influence, while a large poor population and military spending produce a negative impact on freedom.

Neumayer and de Soysa (2006) started from the hypothesis that economies that are more open to trade and foreign direct investment (FDI) face greater competitive pressure than closed ones. The article tested the effect of globalization on a new measure of free association and collective bargaining rights. The authors found that countries that are more open to trade have fewer rights violations than more closed ones. This effect holds in a global sample as well as in a developing country sub-sample and holds also when potential feedback effects are controlled via instrumental variable regression. The extent of an economy's 'penetration' by FDI has no statistically significant impact. Globalization might not be beneficial for outcome-related labour standards, but it is likely to promote the process-related standard of a right to free association and collective bargaining.

As we noted above, militarization is considered by us to be part and parcel of the syndrome of the dependent insertion of the countries of the periphery into the world economy.[10] In accordance with several studies,[11] we suggest integrating the militarization dimension more closely than has been done hitherto into dependency theory and world-systems research.

Let us start with the presentation of our results for the Combined Failed States Index.[12] Apart from the negative influence of the constant,[13] economic freedom, absolute latitude and the stabilizing effect of 'modernity' (ln GDP per capita^2) all provide a framework, which enhances stability and reduces the failed states syndrome.[14] However, high population pressure, measured by the annual population growth rate ratio, the de-stabilizing forces of modernization (ln GDP per capita) and military expenditures per GDP all contribute towards the failed states syndrome. Thus, the failed state syndrome has to be explained by the process of militarization, while

---

10 Brzoska and Lock (1992); Brzoska and Ohlson (1986, 1987); Brzoska and Pearson (1994).

11 Eide and Thee (1980); Kaldor (1983); and Wolpin (1986).

12 Our equation explains 83 per cent of the variations in this variable, and the highly significant equation (F=97.634, error p=0.000) was achieved with the 120 countries with complete data.

13 This is significant at the 9.4 per cent level.

14 Readers, finding difficulties with these paragraphs, are referred to http://www.ats.ucla.edu/stat/spss/output/reg_spss.htm (accessed 27 January 2012).

dependency and world-systems theory and their main indicators fail to contribute significantly towards the statistical explanation of this phenomenon.

A total of 55 per cent of variation in the democracy measure is being determined in our equation, which is based on the 143 countries with complete data.[15] Apart from the insignificant effects of the constant and the curve-linear effects of the control variable 'modernization' and 'modernity', it can be shown that the following variables are a significant block against democracy: an excessively institutionalized political feminism, membership of the Islamic Conference, a high military personnel ratio, and a high penetration of a country by the transnational corporations (MNC penetration), again confirming a dependency/world-systems/militarization paradigm of development.

The equation for civil and political rights violations is based on the 144 countries of the world with complete data. 67.5 per cent of variations in this variable are being determined by our equation.[16] Apart from the insignificant effect of the constant, and apart from the insignificant effect of economic modernization, the following variables wield a significant influence on this important human rights indicator. The most important drivers of human rights violations in the countries of the world system are population size, measured by the relative share of a country's population in terms of the entire world population, population pressure, military personnel ratios, societal modernization as measured by the UNDP Education Index, and the Muslim population share. A significant block against human rights violations is being constituted by the non-linear effect of modernity (ln GDP per capita^2). Again, the pessimistic predictions of a dependency/world-systems/militarization paradigm of development are vindicated.

The rule of law is being determined in the 116 countries with complete data to the tune of 63.8 per cent of adjusted variance.[17] The main drivers of the rule of law are, apart from the significant effect of the constant, the MNC headquarter status, as being measured by MNC outward investment stock per GDP, and the share of public education expenditures per GDP. There is a pessimistic effect of things getting worse (modernization), before they get better (modernity), and both the stocks and the flows of MNC penetration are again a major bottleneck for the development of democracy, this time measured by the rule of law.

The following equations deal with the analysis of the drivers and bottlenecks of economic growth. It is important to distinguish between these drivers and bottlenecks during the past long-cycle between the mid-1970s and the current world recession, and the drivers and bottlenecks of growth which will lead the countries of the world out of the current recession. We will deal with these cyclical aspects of our analysis in Chapter 6. For the time being, it will suffice to say that there are important differences in the causal mechanisms of economic

---

15 The F-value is 29.885, and the slope part of the equation is highly significant (error p=0.000).

16 The F-value is 43.443, and again the slope of the equation is highly significant.

17 The F-value for the entire equation is 34.748, and the equation is again highly significant (error p=0.000).

growth between the current period and the period 1990–2005. Confronted with the fact that consolidated economic statistics are usually available with a time-lag of at least two years, and our desire to probe more deeply into the underlying mechanisms of the current crisis, we opted to take the risk of working with the provisional, standard economic forecasts provided by the IMF for the years 2009 and 2010, which are available for a sufficient number of countries. Here, we present the results for the determinants of economic growth in 2010, the determinants of our Crisis Performance Factor (see Appendix 2), and the determinants of economic growth, 1990–2005. As we explain in the Appendix 2, the Crisis Performance Factor weights with factor analytical means the following variables:

• IMF prediction growth rate in 2009 (issued April 2009)
• IMF prediction growth rate in 2010 (issued April 2009)
• Residual measure: crisis recovery 2010 vis-à-vis 2009 (based on IMF prognosis, April 2009)
• Resilience of economic growth during the crisis (regression residuals: growth 1990–2005 → growth 2009, based on IMF prognosis, April 2009)

Our equation for the determinants of economic growth in 2010 is based on 150 countries with complete data.[18] Apart from the insignificant effects of the constant, the economic freedom score and the control variable modernization (ln GDP per capita), it now turns out for this most recent period of global capitalism that the main positive drivers of the economic growth rate are relative population size, annual population growth, and the net international migration rate. Modernity remains a significant growth bottleneck, i.e. independent of the demographic and other variables, used in the equation. MNC penetration and DYN MNC penetration, for not wielding any significant effect, were even dropped from the final model specification.

The determinants of the Crisis Performance Factor were calculated with the complete data from 145 countries in the world system.[19] Apart from the insignificant effects of the constant and the control variables modernization and modernity, it emerges that the demographic and the cultural factors are determining to a significant degree the outcome of the resilience of economic growth during the current world economic recession. The main positive drivers of the Crisis Performance Factor again are, as in the case of economic growth in 2010, relative population size and annual population growth, and the Muslim population share per total population. Only a quick glance at the current world maps of economic growth will convince our readers that in many ways the days of the Western-dominated world system are numbered, and that now we experience

---

18 The adjusted R^2 is 52.1 per cent (without using investment as a growth predictor), and the F-value is 27.974 (error probability 0.000).

19 The R^2 is 64.3 per cent, the F-value is 52.963, and the error p is 0.000.

a gigantic and tectonic shift backwards to the demographically dynamic region of the Indian Ocean and China, a fact, which was already highlighted, among others, by the late Andre Gunder Frank (1998). MNC penetration and DYN MNC penetration, for not wielding any significant effect, were again dropped from the equation.

The determinants of economic growth during the period 1990–2005 were calculated for the 112 countries with complete data;[20] 36.3 per cent of the variance of economic growth during this period is being explained. Apart from the insignificant effects of the constant and the control variables modernization and modernity, and the insignificant effects of the increases of MNC penetration over time (error probability 14.7 per cent), the following significant drivers of economic growth emerged from our multiple regression: market size (percentage of world population), and MNC penetration rates. The following significant bottlenecks of economic growth during this period emerge from our equation: demographic dynamics (annual population growth), the monopoly power of multinational headquarters (MNC outward investment stock per GDP), and the growth crowding-out effects of public education expenditures per GDP. We suggest that economic growth in 1990–2005, due to the growth inducing effects of outsourcing of production from the core countries to some regions in Central Eastern Europe (from the EU centre) or Mexico and the Caribbean (from the USA), was positively associated with higher MNC penetration ratios in this period. Our results thus rendered little support for the dependency-oriented theories of economic growth.[21] However, MNC penetration was found to increase income polarization and infant mortality, and blocks democracy, environmental performance, and the rule of law.

Our next analysis deals with the determinants of the dimension of the environment. More recent cross-national research literature (Ehrhardt-Martinez, Crenshaw and Jenkins 2002) duly took notice of the environmental Kuznets curve (or EKC). The amount of ecological variables, already analysed in world-systems studies, is truly amazing and ranges from carbon dioxide emissions to threatened mammal species and the quality of drinking water. We find studies on more than 200 nations, and studies, only based on the empirical evidence of less than 40 states. However, none of the major studies as yet featured on the Yale/Columbia ESI and EPI project combined development indicators, which are freely available for a number of years now and which are, arguably, the best single environment indicator studies available today. Our main argument will consist in demonstrating

---

20 The F-value is 8.921, which still results in an error probability of 0.000.

21 Bornschier, Chase Dunn and Rubinson (1978); Bornschier (1980a, 1980b); Dixon and Boswell (1996); Kentor (1998); Herkenrath and Bornschier (2003); Kentor and Boswell (2003); Mahutga (2006); Kentor and Jorgenson(2010). Since the monopoly power of multinational headquarters (MNC outward investment stock per GDP), was a significant growth bottleneck in the period 1990–2005, and higher MNC penetration ratios were even a significant driver of the growth process, also the analyses by Weede (1981a, 1981b); Firebaugh (1992); Firebaugh and Beck (1994); Soysa and Oneal (1999) have to be qualified in the light of our new evidence.

that environmental world-systems research in future must urgently integrate the migration factor, apart from the more traditional variables of dependency and world-systems research.

As valuable as these research results may be, they totally overlook newer comparable environmental indicator data series, like the Yale/Columbia ESI and EPI combined environmental indicator project, as well as the disaster risk indicator, developed by the UNDP. Arguably, the best available single environment indicator today is the Yale/Columbia EPI, which was presented in Chapter 3, and whose determinants are presented in Appendix 1 of this work.[22] The positive drivers of sustainable development are modernization and human capital formation (the UNDP Education Index), while the most important and significant bottlenecks are relative population size, modernity, the military personnel rate and – as suggested by the earlier studies, quoted above – MNC penetration. The constant has a significant and negative effect. Our approach maybe is more realistic than the studies referred to above, because it duly considers the environmentally destructive effects of militarization, and is tested for a very great number of countries with completely available data. The studies in the tradition of Jorgensen only receive qualified support here, since MNC penetration indeed is a major bottleneck for sustainable development, as measured by the Yale/Columbia EPI.

Our equation about global footprint per capita is based on 136 countries with complete data.[23] The significant drivers of global footprint per capita are the constant, the world-systems theory/dependency theory indicator foreign savings rate, and the effects of modernity, while the footprint-reducing effects are being wielded modernization, by population density, and also by the ecologically positive effects of years of membership in the European Monetary Union as a measure of belonging to the political core of the European Union.

Our equation for the log-transformed UNDP disaster risk indicator is based on 160 countries.[24] The constant is significantly reducing disaster risk. Also human capital formation (UNDP Education Index) and a larger share of immigrants per total population reduce disaster risk, while there is also a considerable 'Kuznets effect' of first rising and then levelling-off disaster risk. While the connection between the UNDP Education Index and low disaster risk is immediately evident, because a population with a high educational level can be better organized in structures of civil protection, the empirically robust connection between a larger share of immigrants and low disaster risk needs further research. One very plausible explanation would be that immigrant populations across the globe are more experienced than national citizens in dealing with cyclones, droughts, earthquakes, and floods, which happen

---

22 The R^2 in our highly significant equation is 81.2 per cent, the F-test wielded an F-value of 88.259, and the calculation of the multiple regression analysis was carried out for 141 countries with completely available data.

23 The R^2 achieved is 81.2 per cent. The F-test yields a value of 117.592, and the equation is very significant.

24 The R^2 is only 14.4 per cent, and the F-value is also relatively small (7.713), but the error probability of the entire equation is still 0.000.

more frequently in migration-sending than in migration-recipient countries. This fact might also contribute to the empirically observable effect, and might pose a question mark about the real causality of the process.

Our next results are about the determination of the Yale/Columbia ESI.[25] They will be an important argument in favour of a socio-liberal feminism, and will clearly be an evidence against an over-optimistic perspective on the effects of migration on the migration-sending countries. The constant and the eco-social 'Kuznets curve' this time wield no significant effects. Economic freedom, as predicted by neoliberal economics, will be best suited to react to the challenges measured by the 76 variables, which are part and parcel of the ESI indicator. In addition, one of the basic tenets of 'alternative feminism' in the developed countries comes true – government structures, dominated by females, seem to react much better to the challenges of the environment than their male-dominated counterparts. But both liberalism and alternative/green feminism overlooks the fact that migration also plays a major role in determining the environmental situation. Worker remittances per GDP significantly reduce the ESI performance. As we highlighted above, the 2005 Environmental Sustainability Index (ESI) benchmarks the ability of nations to protect the environment over the next several decades. It does so by integrating 76 data sets – tracking natural resource endowments, past and present pollution levels, environmental management efforts, and a society's capacity to improve its environmental performance – into 21 indicators of environmental sustainability. These indicators permit comparison across the following five fundamental components of sustainability: environmental systems; environmental stresses; human vulnerability to environmental stresses; societal capacity to respond to environmental challenges; and global stewardship. Migration-sending countries with very high received worker remittance ratios, like Tajikistan, Moldova, Lesotho, Honduras, Lebanon, Guyana, Jordan, Haiti, Jamaica, Kyrgyzstan, El Salvador, Nepal, Nicaragua, the Philippines, Guatemala, Albania, Bangladesh, Sierra Leone, the Dominican Republic and Cape Verde are worst in precisely providing their populations with an ability of nations to protect the environment over the next several decades. Migration-sending dependent nations will perform badly on the ESI indicator.

Our next equation to be presented here deals with CO_2 emissions per capita.[26] Development quickly reduces CO_2 emissions per capita, but at very high development levels, emissions increase again. Population density significantly reduces CO_2 emissions. Neoliberal economic theory is vindicated in one decisive point: world economically open countries have lower CO_2 emissions than 'closed economies'. Dependency theory and the world-systems paradigm, or more concretely, the school of thought, focusing on the socially disruptive effects of the New International

---

25 Based on 122 countries with complete data and an R^2 of 34.5 per cent, and an F-test, which wielded an F-value of 13.720 for the entire, highly significant equation.

26 Our equation is based on 160 countries, and the R^2 (72.7 per cent) and the F-value (71.594) are very high, and the equation is highly significant. The constant is among the significant drivers of CO_2 emissions per capita, and the eco-social Kuznets curve, first claimed by Ehrhardt-Martinez, Crenshaw, and Jenkins (2002), again is validated.

Division of Labour and export processing zones, first published by Froebel, Heinrichs and Kreye (1980), receive qualified support, because the share of export processing zones employment share per total population is significantly and positively linked to CO_2 emissions. This coefficient is more than five times bigger than the standard error of the estimate. At the same time, the even larger effect of immigration as a share of total population stock as an additional driver of CO_2 emissions cannot be simply overlooked.

The following equation deals with CO_2 emissions per GDP.[27] Absolute latitude significantly increases CO_2 emissions per GDP. Neoliberal economic environmental theory is vindicated in one decisive point again: economic freedom causes lower CO_2 emissions per GDP than 'unfree economies'. Dependency theory and the world-systems paradigm receive no support at all in this equation. At the same time, the considerable effect of immigration as a share of total population stock as an additional driver of CO_2 emissions per GDP again cannot be simply 'talked away'. As we already mentioned above, the immigration/CO_2 trade-off cannot be excluded anymore from the debate; the causality of the process most probably has to be explained by both the high transport intensity of mass migration, the industrial intensity of migration-recipient countries and the materialist value scales of most of the migration cohorts in the developed countries.

Avoiding net trade of ecological footprint gha per person is, as we stated above, a measure of global ecological justice, and is based on the data series about net exports of ecological footprint gha per person. The index intends to measure the degree of independence (as a desirable status) a nation has from the international footprint trade, be it on the giving or on the receiving end. Apart from many developing countries with a very low involvement in the international footprint trade, we also have the notable cases of the following countries with a footprint trade (either direction) of 1.0 per cent or below: Austria, Brazil, Bulgaria, China, Cuba, Czech Republic, Denmark, Estonia, France, Germany, Hungary, Korea (Republic of), Lithuania, Mexico, the Netherlands, Poland, Romania, Slovenia, South Africa, Turkey, and the USA. Our equation is based on 139 countries with complete statistical data.[28] All predictors are significant, including the constant, whose numerical sign is negative. The main drivers of footprint self-sufficiency are modernization and years of membership in the European Union. The main bottlenecks for footprint self-sufficiency are political feminism (percentage of women in government, all levels), comparative price levels, and modernity, i.e. the three-pod of 'modern' political systems of the West (feminism, high levels of services of general interest, and a very high per capita income). The ecological price of these systems is the high

---

27 Our equation is based on 145 countries, and the R^2 (35.0 per cent) and the F-value (16.535) are satisfactory, and the equation is very significant. The constant is among the significant reducing factors of CO_2 emissions per GDP, and an inversely shaped eco-social Kuznets curve, is validated, with modernization making the problem of CO_2 emissions per GDP worse, before modernity makes the problem better.
28 The R^2 is 40.9 per cent, the F-value is 20.111, and the error probability is 0.000.

involvement in the net trade of ecological footprints. Thus, the ecologically oriented dependency approaches, which assume a causal negative effect by dependency on the environmental situation, are only partially to be maintained, and are qualified in several respects.[29]

The next equations to be presented here deal with gender issues, human development, research and development, and social cohesion. The massive evidence, provided by cross-national contemporary comparative social science research on these issues, can only briefly be reviewed here.[30]

---

29 In particular, the studies by Jorgenson (2003) (MNC penetration, effect on footprint); Jorgenson and Burns (2004); Jorgenson (2005) (overall export dependence on per-capita resource consumption); Jorgenson (2007a, 2007b) (carbon dioxide emissions and organic water pollution in less-developed countries driven by foreign investment dependence); Jorgenson and Burns (2007) (export intensity as a driver of growth in per capita ecological footprints of nations); Jorgenson (2009a) (effects of world system dependence on industrial organic water pollution intensity, driven by foreign investment in manufacturing and overall export intensity); and Jorgenson (2009b, 2009c, 2009d) (secondary sector foreign investment as a driver of total carbon dioxide emissions and emissions per unit of production, together with export intensity) receive the following qualifications:
- CO_2 emissions per capita are determined by export processing zones, not by foreign investment dependence; the important predictor economic freedom left out in the Jorgenson articles.
- CO_2 emissions per GDP: contrary to the findings by Jorgenson, dependency theory and the world-systems paradigm receive no support at all. At the same time, the considerable effect of immigration as a share of total population stock as an additional driver of CO_2 emissions per GDP cannot be simply 'talked away'.
- EPI (Yale/Columbia): positive drivers of sustainable development are modernization and human capital formation (the UNDP Education Index), while the most important and significant bottlenecks are relative population size, modernity, the military personnel rate and – as suggested by the earlier studies, quoted above – MNC penetration.
- Footprint is determined by foreign savings, not by MNC penetration; the important predictor – EMU membership been left out in previous research.

30 Let us recall the most important and sometimes conflicting theoretical expectations:
- Bornschier (1983): integration into the world economy will result in increased income inequality in peripheral countries.
- Crenshaw (1992): (1) national wealth does exhibit a direct, curvilinear relationship with income inequality; (2) world-systems/dependency theory finds less support; and (3) agricultural density, has a robust, negative influence on income inequality.
- Ragin and Bradshaw (1992): dependency has a more harmful effect on physical quality of life than on economic development.
- Wimberley and Bello (1992): reduction of primary export dependence in Third World countries promotes food consumption, and transnational corporate (TNC) investment dependence has an exceptionally strong harmful effect on food consumption in the periphery.
- Bradshaw (1993): externally imposed austerity measures have directly or indirectly impeded child survival, childhood immunization, economic growth, prevalence of health attendants, adequate nutrition, and balanced urbanization.
- Crenshaw and Ameen (1994): strongest support in the explanation of inequality for modernization and ecological-evolutionary theories, while the patterns of support for political redistribution and dependency/world-systems theory are more mixed.

Our equation about the determinants of the closing of the overall gender gap, which is based on the World Economic Forum (WEF) data series, is based on the 110 countries with complete statistical data.[31] All predictors, including the constant, are statistically significant. The constant has a numerically positive sign. The major drivers of gender equality, as measured by the WEF data series, are the percentage

---

- Shen and Williamson (1997): Foreign investment and debt dependency have adverse indirect effects on child mortality.
- Wimberley (1998): effects of foreign investment dependence on the satisfaction of basic human needs in the Third World. Satisfaction of nutritional needs was indicated by per capita calorie and protein consumption. Two forms of investment dependence are measured for 1967: MNC penetration and debt accumulated from bilateral foreign aid. Specific effects of MNC investment in the agricultural sector also were examined.
- Morris (1999): based on data from two cohorts of countries with data on income inequality (33 countries, 1968–1973, and 31 countries, 1985–1992, respectively). World-system analysis and some aspects of dependency theory are relevant to explaining income inequality both before and after global changes.
- Shen and Williamson (1999): authors find that women's status, age at first marriage, and reproductive autonomy, are strong predictors of maternal mortality. In addition, article finds that economic dependency, especially multinational corporate investment, has a detrimental effect on maternal mortality.
- Kentor (2001): foreign capital dependence has a positive effect on income inequality, raises fertility rates, accelerates population growth and retards economic development. Trade openness, in contrast, has long-term positive effects on economic development.
- Shen and Williamson (2001): authors establish that foreign trade, investment, and debt dependency have adverse effects on infant mortality, mediated by variables linked to modernization/free trade theory and gender inequality theory. State strength has a beneficial direct effect on infant mortality decline. Women's education and reproductive autonomy have significant direct effects, but also play important roles as mediating variables, as does the rate of economic growth.
- Alderson and Nielsen (2002): total inequality variation is principally affected by the percentage of the labour force in agriculture, followed by the institutional factors union density and de-commodification, and only then by globalization. On the other hand, longitudinal variation in inequality, while still dominated by the percentage of the labour force in agriculture, is also principally affected by aspects of globalization, such as southern import penetration and direct investment outflow, and to a lesser extent by migration. Globalization explains the longitudinal trend of increasing inequality that took place within many industrial countries better than it does cross-sectional inequality differences among countries.
- Reuveny and Li (2003): democracy and trade reduce income inequality, foreign direct investments increase income inequality, and financial capital does not affect income inequality.
- Meyer (2003): global economic forces reduce occupational sex segregation and inequality. Global economic restructuring is a gendered process that transforms and builds on existing gender inequalities.
- Shandra, Nobles, London and Williamson (2004): economic and social modernization has beneficial effects on infant mortality. Multinational corporate penetration fosters higher levels of infant mortality. Interaction effects suggest that the level of political democracy conditions the effects of dependency relationships based upon exports, investments from multinational corporations, and international lending institutions.

of women in government at all levels, modernization and modernity, and worker remittances per GDP. This is a clear sign that the scarcity of labour in migration-sending countries positively affects the chances of women to gain advantages, while at the same time our results implies a worsening situation in the migration-recipient countries, where the influx of labour from poorer parts of the world

---

- Bussmann, de Soysa, and Oneal (2005): results indicate that globalization does not increase national income inequality. The ratio of foreign direct investment to gross domestic product is unrelated to the distribution of incomes in both developing and developed countries. The share of income received by the poorest 20 per cent of society is also is unaffected by foreign investment. Nor are alternative measures of economic openness – the trade-to-GDP ratio and Sachs and Warner's (1995) measure of free trading policies – associated with greater income inequality.
- Shandra, Nobles, London and Williamson (2005): indicators linked to economic and social modernization have beneficial effects on child mortality. Multinational corporate penetration fosters higher levels of child mortality. Interaction effects suggest that the level of political democracy conditions the effects of dependency relationships based upon multinational corporations.
- Beckfield (2006b): regional integration explains nearly half of the increase in income inequality in the Western European countries. The effects of regional integration on income inequality are net of several controls, including two established measures of globalization, suggesting that a sociological approach to regional integration adds to our understanding of rising income inequality in Western Europe.
- Moore, Teixeira and Shiell (2006): study uses network analysis. Periphery is significantly and positively associated with national-level infant mortality rates.
- Spencer (2006): study emphasizes (1) the importance of measuring global stratification according to trading patterns and (2) the strong, negative effects of income inequality on life expectancy among peripheral populations.
- Tsai (2006a): poverty is defined by living below an income of US$1 or $2 a day. Empirical outcomes reveal that besides a country's income level, tropics, landlockedness, population growth, and secondary schooling opportunity are significant predictors of poverty reduction, whereas political factors (democracy, military spending, and war) and government social spending are only weak predictors. No evidence was found to support the effects of economic openness on poverty, as proposed by the neoliberal school.
- Lee, Nielsen and Alderson (2007): most traditional measures of trade dependence have inconsistent or weak positive effects on inequality, while export commodity concentration has a negative effect. They also find that the effects of foreign direct investment on inequality are positive at low to intermediate levels of government size, but that this effect is substantially attenuated or negative in societies with a larger public sector. Conclude that distributional outcomes are dependent upon how the state reacts to growing globalization-related pressures.
- Tsai (2007): significant positive impacts of political globalization, whereas economic and social globalization does not generate favourable influences when development level and regional differences are operated as controls. The overall globalization index is found to generate expected favourable influence on the overall human development index. Several hypotheses about globalization's potential negative effects through increasing societal instabilities and reducing state power and social spending are not supported in the analysis. It is concluded that globalization identified by increased global flows and exchanges contributes rather than hampers progress in human welfare.

economy leads towards a relative marginalization of female labour. Bottlenecks against the closing of the gender gap are militarization (military personnel rate) and the share of Muslim population per total population, underlining the negative gender policy trade-off of real existing Muslim countries, as already predicted by Inglehart and Norris (2003a, 2003b).

Female survival (probability of surviving to age 65) is conditioned in the 115 countries with complete data under scrutiny here to the tune of 66.8 per cent[32] by the following significant predictors: the constant (−), inequality, as measured by the quintile share (−), modernity (−), and the crowding-out of health (female survival probability) by public education expenditures (−) as the major bottlenecks, and modernization (+) and human capital formation (UNDP Education Index, +) as drivers of female survival probability.

Our equation about the determinants of the gender empowerment index value, which is based on the relevant UNDP data series, is based on the 71 countries with complete statistical data.[33] The major drivers of gender equality, as measured by the UNDP data series, are the percentage of women in government at all levels, and modernity. Bottlenecks against the closing of the gender gap are modernization and the share of Muslim population per total population, again underlining the negative gender policy trade-off of real existing Muslim countries, predicted by Inglehart and Norris (2003b).

Our equation about the determinants of the closing of the economic gender gap, which is based on the World Economic Forum (WEF) data series, is based on the 123 countries with complete statistical data.[34] The major drivers of economic gender equality, as measured by the WEF data series, are again the percentage of women in government at all levels, and modernity. Bottlenecks against the closing of the economic gender gap are modernization and, once again, the share of Muslim population per total population, and again underlining the negative gender policy trade-off of real existing Muslim countries, as predicted by Inglehart and Norris (2003b).

- Babones and Zhang (2008): aggregate trade is not empirically related to income inequality for any panel of countries, and country-level research focusing specifically on 'North–South' trade and national income inequality has generally yielded inconsistent or no significant results. Authors attribute this disconnect between expectations and reality to heterogeneity among the countries typically classified as members of the global 'South'. The authors find that the relationship between inequality and trade is consistently conditioned on the zone of the world-economy over the period 1980–2000.

31 Our equation explains 58.7 per cent of the total variance, and the F-value is 26.796, and the error probability of the entire equation is 0.000.

32 F-value 46.815, entire equation significant at the 0.000 level.

33 Our equation explains 81.5 per cent of the total variance, and the F-value is 77.895, and the error probability of the entire equation is 0.000. All predictors, including the constant, are significant. The constant again has a numerically positive sign.

34 Our equation explains 40.1 per cent of the total variance, and the F-value is 21.38, and the error probability of the entire equation is 0.000. All predictors, including the constant, are statistically significant. The constant again, as before, has a numerically positive sign.

Finally, our equation about the determinants of the closing of the political gender gap, which is based on the World Economic Forum (WEF) data series, is based on the 114 countries with complete statistical data.[35] Modernization deteriorates the conditions of political gender equality, and modernity increases it. Among the other significant drivers of political gender equality, as measured by the WEF data series, we find worker remittances per GDP. This is again clear sign that the scarcity of labour in migration-sending countries also positively affects the chances of women to gain political advantages, while at the same time our results implies a worsening political marginalization of women in the migration-recipient countries, where the influx of labour from poorer parts of the world economy leads towards a relative marginalization of feminist politics and female political participation. Other bottlenecks against the closing of the political gender gap are the membership of a country in the Organisation of the Islamic Conference, again underlining the negative gender policy trade-off of real existing Muslim countries, as already predicted by Inglehart and Norris (2003b), and the overall share (= stocks) of immigrant population per total population, while at the same time fresh new inflows of migrant population significantly alleviate the situation.

Our following analyses deal with the indicator series of the Happy Planet Organization and the Global Footprint Network, and all feature of the new, ecologically viable understanding of the development process.

For many, the Happy Planet Index is *the* master variable of the new, environment-conscious development discourse. As we already stated, the HPI is a measure that shows the ecological efficiency with which human well-being is delivered around the world. The index doesn't reveal the 'happiest' country in the world. It shows the relative efficiency with which nations convert the planet's natural resources at their disposal (footprint per capita) into long and happy lives for their citizens. The nations that top the index aren't the happiest places in the world, but the nations that score well show that achieving, long, happy lives without overstretching the planet's resources is possible. The highest HPI score is that of Costa Rica (76.1 out of 100). As well as reporting the highest life satisfaction in the world, Costa Ricans also have the second-highest average life expectancy of the New World (second only to Canada). All this is achieved with a footprint of 2.3 global hectares. Of the following ten countries, all but one is in Latin America. The ranking of the EU-27 countries on the index is as follows:

1. Netherlands	6. Finland
2. Malta	7. Cyprus
3. Germany	8. Belgium
4. Sweden	9. Slovenia
5. Austria	10. Italy

---

35 Our equation explains 24.9 per cent of the total variance, and the F-value is 7.243, and the error probability of the entire equation is 0.000. All predictors, including the constant, are significant. The constant has a numerically positive sign.

11. Romania
12. France
13. Slovakia
14. United Kingdom
15. Spain
16. Poland
17. Ireland
18. Bulgaria
19. Lithuania

20. Hungary
21. Czech Republic
22. Greece
23. Portugal
24. Latvia
25. Denmark
26. Luxembourg
27. Estonia

Regarding the Happy Planet Index, there is a very clear ecological Kuznets curve at work,[36] with modernization increasing, and modernity decreasing the Happy Planet Index performance. Worker remittances significantly enhance, and the foreign savings rate, one of the major dependency theory indicators of our work, significantly reduce the Happy Planet Index performance. Our equation clearly shows that outward migration clearly increases, while inward migration most probably decreases Happy Planet Index performance.

Our next calculation about the drivers of and the bottlenecks against the Happy Planet Organization indicators is our equation about happy life years[37], and again, there is the very clear ecological Kuznets curve at work, with modernization increasing and modernity decreasing the happy life years performance. Again worker remittances significantly enhance and military expenditures significantly reduce the happy life years performance. Our equation clearly shows that outward migration clearly increases, while inward migration most probably decreases happy life years performance.

Our last calculation about the drivers of and the bottlenecks against the Happy Planet Organization indicators concerns life satisfaction.[38] Modernization increases life satisfaction performance. Absolute latitude and thus lack of sunshine intensity decrease, and worker remittances significantly enhance life satisfaction performance. Our equation clearly shows that outward migration clearly increases, while inward migration most probably decreases life satisfaction.

Our next reported equations deal with research and development. The drivers and bottlenecks of per capita world-class universities were calculated for

---

36 Our calculation about the drivers of and the bottlenecks against the Happy Planet Index is based on the 120 countries with complete data, and the R^2 is 38.0 per cent, the F-value is 19.217, and the error probability of the entire equation is 0.000. All predictors, including the constant, are significant; the numerical sign of the constant is negative.

37 Based on the 103 countries with complete data, and the R^2 is 77.1 per cent, the F-value is 86.653, and the error probability of the entire equation is 0.000. All predictors, including the constant, are significant; the numerical sign of the constant is negative.

38 It is based on the 114 countries with complete data, and the R^2 is 69.4 per cent, the F-value is 64.990, and the error probability of the entire equation is 0.000. All predictors, except modernity, are significant; the numerical sign of the constant is negative. Only the first part of the ecological Kuznets curve is significant.

the 108 countries with available data.[39] Our calculations show that the most significant drivers of world-class research performance all belong to the category of feminist and military and power-driven 'Keynesianism', constituted by the percentage of women in government. High comparative price levels, modernity, high military personnel ratios, high MNC outward investments, and high public education expenditures per GDP. Dependency theory and world-systems research is vindicated in so far as time-lagged world economic openness is, together with modernization, the most important bottleneck against a successful world-class university policy.

The drivers and bottlenecks of tertiary enrolment ratios now have to be compared to the above reported drivers and bottlenecks of per capita world-class university performance, and were calculated for the 137 countries with available data.[40] Annual population growth rates and modernization are major bottlenecks against high tertiary enrolment ratios. In agreement with the predictions by dependency theory and world-systems research about a negative trade-off between dependency and development performance, it can be shown that time-lagged world economic openness is a blockade against higher tertiary enrolment ratios. Modernity and the overall strength of the human capital effort, measured by the UNDP Education Index, are significant drivers of higher tertiary enrolment ratios, while at the same time, we can venture the optimistic prognosis that membership of the Islamic Conference is a driver of higher tertiary enrolment ratios.

The next and last six equations now deal with life quality and social cohesion in the wider sense of the term. Our first equation in this context deals with the determinants of our new global tolerance index, which combines the following World Values Survey data with sufficient availability on the percentages per total population overcoming xenophobia and racism (Tausch and Moaddel 2009). More specifically, five population shares are taken account of: people tolerant of neighbours of a different race; people considering tolerance and respect for other people as important child qualities; people not saying men should have more right to a job than women; people tolerant of immigrants/foreign workers as neighbours; and people tolerant of homosexual neighbours. Our equation is based on the 65 countries with complete data.[41] Tolerance, according to our calculations, has only two really significant predictors. The first factor is the achievement of a society with the appropriate level of services of general interest (the comparative price levels),

---

39 All the coefficients are significant, the constant has a numerically positive sign, and the R^2 for the entire equation is 64.9 per cent, the F-value is 25.749, and the error probability of the entire equation is 0.000.

40 All the coefficients are significant, the constant has a numerically positive sign, and the R^2 for the entire equation is 73.7 per cent, the F-value is 64.501, and the error probability of the entire equation is 0.000.

41 The R^2 is 66.3 per cent, the F-value is 34.516, and the error probability of the entire equation is 0.000. The constant, and the Kuznets curve are not to be considered as significant, but we included the Kuznets curve as a control variable.

and this is positive in direction. The other factor is the lamentable negative trade-off between Muslim population share and the global tolerance index, indicating again the negative gender policy trade-off of real existing Muslim countries, as predicted by Inglehart and Norris (2003a, 2003b).

Our equation for the determination of infant mortality was calculated for 153 countries with complete data.[42] Economic freedom and modernization reduce infant mortality significantly, while modernity, lamentably, increases infant mortality again. The overall human capital effort of a society, measured by the UNDP Education Index, reduces infant mortality, while MNC penetration, as correctly predicted by dependency and world-systems theory, increases infant mortality rates.

The equation for the determination of life expectancy was calculated for 106 countries with complete data.[43] Modernity, lamentably, reduces life expectancy again, while modernization increases it. The public education expenditure effort by the government crowds out health, and overall income inequality – as correctly predicted by Wilkinson and his medical school – reduces life expectancy, too. Worker remittances are an important driver of life expectancy rate, which implies that migration-sending countries socially benefit from the migration process.

The equation for the determination of income inequality was calculated for 120 countries with complete data.[44] Annual population growth, the foreign savings rate and MNC penetration increase income inequality, while high comparative price levels and a large share of migration stock reduce income inequality. The functioning social welfare institutions of the Muslim communities also significantly reduce income inequality rates.

The equation for the determination of unemployment was calculated for 104 countries with complete data.[45] Modernization increases unemployment, while modernity reduces it.[46] Foreign savings increase unemployment. The Muslim population share is another driver of increased rate of unemployment.

---

42 The R^2 is 79.4 per cent, the F-value is 117.921, and the error probability for the entire equation is 0.000. All predictors, including the constant, are significant. The numerical sign of the constant is positive.

43 The R^2 is 74.8 per cent, the F-value is 63.293, and the error probability for the entire equation is 0.000. All predictors, including the constant, are significant. The numerical sign of the constant is negative.

44 The R^2 is 25.5 per cent, the F-value is 6.098, and the error probability for the entire equation is 0.000. All predictors, except the Kuznets curve and the constant, are significant. The numerical sign of the constant is negative.

45 The R^2 is 35.4 per cent, the F-value is 10.416, and the error probability for the entire equation is 0.000. All predictors, including the constant, are significant. The numerical sign of the constant is negative.

46 The public education expenditure effort by the government crowds out employment, and reduces the overall income inequality and – in the spirit of Galbraith and his school (Galbraith, 1999, 2007, 2009; Galbraith and Garcilazo 2004, 2005; Galbraith and Kum 2003, 2005; Galbraith, Conceição and Ferreira 1999; Galbraith, Giovannoni, and Russo 2007) – it increases unemployment, too.

Finally, the equation for the determination of the Human Development Index was calculated for 134 countries with complete data.[47] Modernity, lamentably, reduces human development again, while modernization increases it. The public education expenditure effort by the government crowds out health and life quality, and hence the Human Development Index, and world economic openness – as correctly predicted by world-systems research – reduces human development, too. The overall societal human capital formation effort, as measured by the UNDP's Education Index, positively contributes to human development, and the social networks of Muslim communities also have a significant and positive effect on the Human Development Index.

Policy pointer

A thorough re-thinking of basic premises of policymaking in Europe is thus necessary. The neo-Keynesian analysis by Marterbauer and Walterskirchen (2006) highlighted the fact that the main instrument applied by EU countries to reach the Maastricht criteria has been to cut public investment. In the USA, the fiscal deficit is primarily the result of an active anti-cyclical policy, which can be measured in terms of increasing structural deficits in the recession (Marterbauer and Walterskirchen 2006). Our own analysis by contrast showed that the ultra-liberal strategy of opening markets is not the solution, but very much part of the problem of the European malaise. Europe is not engaged in the first Lisbon race of its kind to catch up with America. Much of the nineteenth century and the first half of the twentieth century witnessed a European decline vis-à-vis the US, and only the postwar period after 1945 saw a relative closing of the gap, which began to widen again after 1973 (Tausch 2007c).

Andre Gunder Frank has implied for a long time that Europe's quest has to be seen in the larger perspective of Asia's re-ascent in the world system. The United Nations Economic Commission for Latin America (ECLAC/CEPAL) in its path-breaking essay 'Globalización y desarrollo' (2002)[48] provided estimates that dramatically support such a view that stresses the simultaneity of the ascent of Asia from the 1950s onwards with the decline of Europe after 1973 in the world system. One further important consequence of this analysis is the rediscovery of the issue of European industrial policy in the framework of an otherwise relatively free economy, which determines in the end the coefficients of MNC penetration. Thus, the old critical questions addressed in the direction of neoclassical theory

---

47 The R^2 is 95 per cent, the F-value is 425.085, and the error probability for the entire equation is 0.000. All predictors, including the constant, are significant. The numerical sign of the constant is negative.

48 http://www.eclac.cl/cgi-bin/getProd.asp?xml=/publicaciones/xml/6/10026/P10026. xml&xsl=/tpl/p9f.xsl&base=/MDG/tpl/top-bottom.xsl (accessed 27 January 2012).

by such economists as Celso Furtado, Michal Kalecki, Gunnar Myrdal, Francois Perroux, Raul Prebisch, Paul Rosenstein-Rodan, Kurt Rothschild, Dudley Seers, Hans Singer and others can be taken up anew. De-regulation helps, but it helps the dominant centre to maintain and even increase its leading position, and certainly not the technologically and politically weaker nations of the periphery and semi-periphery. So, it is French former European Commission president Jacques Delors (1992) and not economics Nobel Laureate Professor Paul Krugman who seems to have gained the upper hand in the debate started by Krugman in *Foreign Affairs* in 1994, when he spoke so negatively about Delors and his plans for a European industrial policy (http://www.foreignaffairs.org/19940301faessay5094/paul-krugman/competitiveness-a-dangerous-obsession.html – accessed 27 January 2012). Is European wisdom reduced forever to the magic number of a three per cent budget deficit, i.e. the Maastricht criteria? In our opinion, European policymaking finally should dare to take the globalization-critical organizations of 'civil society' seriously.[19]

---

49 Brand (2000, 2005, 2008).

Chapter 5

FINAL CROSS-NATIONAL RESULTS FOR THE COMBINED DEVELOPMENT INDICATOR

To arrive at informed opinions about the combined effects of our 26 predictor variables on the totality of the reduced list of 30 or extended list of 35 dependent variables, measuring 'development', we have to use multivariate or multi-dimensional index construction. As we mentioned in Chapter 3, the performances of all the countries of our investigation for all the dependent variables were standardized along a scale, ranging from 0 (worst value) to 1 (best value). The chosen variables correspond to seven different dimensions and interact with one another (see also Table 3).

Democracy
Economic growth
Environment
Gender
Human development
R&D
Social cohesion

The performance scores, calculated according to the well-known UNDP index practice, described in Chapter 3, can be now combined into a single index, based on our extended list of 35 dependent variables, or they can be first grouped into seven different dimensions, and only then added together. Such a grouping together of the performance results can be interesting, especially in order to judge whether or not the seven different policy dimensions of the presumed, measured phenomenon 'EU-2020 policy performance' correlate strongly and positively with one another.[1]

---

1 In Appendix 5 and Appendix 6, we present some aspects of our overall non-parametric index. We also show our readers the results of a reduced choice of 30 variables, which we entered into our final multiple regressions, instead of the 35 variables, used in the overall non-parametric index construction. The results for the 30 variable index and the 35 variable index are extremely similar, and in addition, since the weight attached to each variable is the same it makes practically no difference whether we calculate the index based on the unweighted average of the 35 performance scores (as we did for the final results in this chapter), or if we calculate it by first calculating the performance scores for the seven main dimensions, and then add these seven aggregated dimension performance scores together for the final combined index. For reasons of space, we just concentrate here on the most interesting and intriguing aspect of the whole,

In an ideal world, democracy, growth, environment, gender equality, human development, research and development and social cohesion all correlate very strongly and positively with one another. Of course, the EU decision makers assumed such neat and positive correlations at least implicitly all along the failed Lisbon Strategy from 2000 to 2010, and they committed this erroneous assumption anew for the EU-2020 process. In the real existing world of 2010, such positive and neat correlations do not exist. The world is full of contradictions. Above all, economic growth returns to what Karl Marx once called the era of 'primitive accumulation', castigating severely the former leading countries.

In the interpretation of the facts, we will concentrate on the results, which contradict the neat and optimistic world of harmony among development factors and dimensions. Table 3 shows that the combined performance index of the six democracy indicators and the combined performance index of the four economic growth indicators present nowadays a very disturbing and extremely high negative correlation coefficient to the tune of -0.522. Along similar lines, economic growth and environmental performance (based on nine indices) significantly and negatively correlate with one another, as do economic growth and the six combined performance indices of the gender policy performance variables, to the tune of -0.505. Also economic growth and the combined five human development performance indices present a highly significant negative correlation, and also economic growth and the three indices of R&D present strong evidence of a high and significant incompatibility. And to make matters worse, environment performance and social cohesion performance, which is based on two indices, are also negatively and significantly correlated with one another.

Policy pointer

Our calculations present a very disturbing and extremely high negative correlation coefficient to the tune of -0.522 between the dimension of democracy and economic growth. Along similar lines, economic growth and environmental performance also significantly and negatively correlate with one another, as do economic growth and the six combined performance indices of the gender policy performance variables. Also economic growth and the combined five human development performance indices present a highly significant negative correlation, and also economic growth and our three indices of R&D present strong evidence of a high and significant incompatibility. To make matters worse, environment performance and social cohesion performance are also negatively and significantly correlated with one another. In the real world we live in, choices are very tough, and the prospects for the 'liberal West' are bleak.

---

i.e. the fact that, as in the old EU-Lisbon Strategy, the overall goals were statistically not very well compatible with one another, implying that performance maximalization will not be easy (see also Heshmati and Tausch 2007), and leave the interesting further aspects of the index construction, possibly involving also principal components approaches to the EU-2020 process, for further possible publications in scholarly journals.

Table 3. The Pearson correlations between the different EU-2020 policy dimensions

	Democracy	Economic growth	Environment	Gender	Human development	R&D
Economic growth	**−0.522****					
significance (two-tailed)	0.000					
N	175					
Environment	0.350**	**−0.321****				
significance (two-tailed)	0.000	0.000				
N	174	174				
Gender	0.654**	**−0.505****	0.371**			
significance (two-tailed)	0.000	0.000	0.000			
N	134	134	134			
Human development	0.661**	**−0.471****	0.414**	0.417**		
significance (two-tailed)	0.000	0.000	0.000	0.000		
N	174	174	174	134		
R&D	0.681**	**−0.480****	0.072	0.605**	0.594**	
significance (two-tailed)	0.000	0.000	0.344	0.000	0.000	
N	175	175	174	134	174	
Social cohesion	0.092	−0.066	**−0.212****	0.004	0.229**	0.299**
significance (two-tailed)	0.244	0.405	0.007	0.968	0.003	0.000
N	162	162	162	131	162	162

Correlations, marked with an asterisk (*) are significant at the 5% level (two-tailed test); and coefficients, marked with a double asterisk (**) are significant at the 1% level (two-tailed test).

Democracy	Combined Failed States Index
Democracy	Civil and political liberty violations
Democracy	Corruption avoidance measure
Democracy	Democracy measure
Democracy	Global tolerance index
Democracy	Rule of law
Economic growth	Crisis Performance Factor
Economic growth	Economic growth IMF prediction growth rate in 2009
Economic growth	Economic growth IMF prediction growth rate in 2010
Economic growth	Economic growth in real terms per capita per annum, 1990–2005
Environment	Ecological footprint (gha per capita)
Environment	ln (number of people/million inhabitants 1980−2000 killed by natural disasters per year + 1)

Environment	Carbon emissions per million US dollars GDP
Environment	Carbon emissions per capita
Environment	Environmental Performance Index (EPI)
Environment	Environmental Sustainability Index (ESI)
Environment	Happy life years
Environment	Happy Planet Index
Environment	Avoiding net trade of ecological footprint gha per person
Gender	Closing economic gender gap
Gender	Closing educational gender gap
Gender	Closing health and survival gender gap
Gender	Closing of global gender gap overall score 2009
Gender	Closing political gender gap
Gender	Gender empowerment index value
Human development	Infant mortality (2005)
Human development	Female survival, probability of surviving to age 65
Human development	Human Development Index (HDI) value 2004
Human development	Life expectancy (years)
Human development	Life satisfaction (0–10)
R&D	Country share in top world 500 universities
R&D	Per capita world-class universities
R&D	Tertiary enrolment
Social cohesion	Quintile share income difference between richest and poorest 20%
Social cohesion	Unemployment rate

Table 4 now lists the 35 components of our combined, final EU-2020 development index. Our table also lists the direction in which the high numerical values of the indicator had to be interpreted. High numerical values for the Combined Failed States Index, civil and political liberty violations, ecological footprint (gha per capita), infant mortality (2005), the quintile share income difference between richest and poorest 20 per cent, the unemployment rate, ln (number of people per million inhabitants 1980−2000 killed by natural disasters per year + 1), carbon emissions per million US dollars GDP, and carbon emissions per capita, are a development debacle, while high numerical values for the other indicators (10–35) are a blessing. The freely available data from Appendix 7 were standardized, as already mentioned, according to the standard UNDP development indicator practice.

Table 4. Components of the non-parametric overall development index

Negative	1	Combined Failed States Index
Negative	2	Civil and political liberty violations
Negative	3	Ecological footprint (gha per capita)

(*Continued*)

Table 4. Continued

Negative	4	Infant mortality (2005)
Negative	5	Quintile share income difference between richest and poorest 20%
Negative	6	Unemployment rate
Negative	7	ln (number of people per million inhabitants 1980–2000 killed by natural disasters per year + 1)
Negative	8	Carbon emissions per million US dollars GDP
Negative	9	Carbon emissions per capita
Positive	10	Closing economic gender gap
Positive	11	Closing educational gender gap
Positive	12	Closing health and survival gender gap
Positive	13	Closing of global gender gap overall score 2009
Positive	14	Closing political gender gap
Positive	15	Corruption avoidance measure
Positive	16	Country share in top world 500 universities
Positive	17	Crisis Performance Factor
Positive	18	Democracy measure
Positive	19	Economic growth IMF prediction growth rate in 2009
Positive	20	Economic growth IMF prediction growth rate in 2010
Positive	21	Economic growth in real terms per capita per annum, 1990–2005
Positive	22	Environmental Performance Index (EPI)
Positive	23	Environmental Sustainability Index (ESI)
Positive	24	Female survival, probability of surviving to age 65
Positive	25	Gender empowerment index value
Positive	26	Global tolerance index
Positive	27	Happy life years
Positive	28	Happy Planet Index
Positive	29	Human Development Index (HDI) value 2004
Positive	30	Life expectancy (years)
Positive	31	Life satisfaction (0–10)
Positive	32	Per capita world-class universities
Positive	33	Rule of law
Positive	34	Tertiary enrolment
Positive	35	Avoiding net trade of ecological footprint gha per person

Table 5 now lists the performance of the countries of the world system according to the criteria of the non-parametric overall development index, based on 35 variables, with equal weight attached to each indicator.[2] The Nordic countries, the Netherlands, New Zealand, Switzerland and Austria are always ranked highest, and, as Table 5 shows, the USA, the failed Lisbon Strategy's best practice reference country number one, is only ranked ninth. Third World countries with advanced

---

2 Rankings based on 30 variables, also with equal weight, or based on 35 variables, based on their prior combination into seven main dimensions, and only then added together, arrive at practically the same conclusion.

human development, like Costa Rica, Chile, Panama, Uruguay and Argentina, are ranked very favourably, and also the State of Israel (excluding the occupied territories) most definitely belongs to the group of the 30 countries of the world with the highest overall development level, which includes democracy, economic growth, environment, gender, human development, research and development, and social cohesion.

Guyana, Tunisia and Albania are the leading Muslim countries along our scale, but their rank on the combined index, equally weighting the UNDP-standardized performance for six indicators of democracy, four indicators of economic growth, nine indicators of the environment, six indicators of gender equality, five indicators of human development, three indicators of research and development, and two indicators of social cohesion, is rather disappointing, showing that several Eastern European countries still outside the European Union, and Latin American countries are ahead of most member nations of the Organisation of the Islamic Conference.

The five least developed countries according to our scale are Equatorial Guinea, Swaziland, Sierra Leone, Sudan and Zimbabwe. The worst performance in the European Union is to be encountered in Romania, which is placed rank 67 of world society, just ahead of Tunisia, and only 8 ranks ahead of the emerging economy of People's Republic of China. Costa Rica, Israel, Chile, Panama, Uruguay, Argentina, Barbados, the Bahamas, the Philippines, Cuba, Hong Kong, the Dominican Republic, Sri Lanka, Brazil, Peru, Thailand, Mauritius, South Korea, Dominica, Ecuador and Singapore would all be better qualified to run for the EU-2020 targets than the worst placed EU member countries Bulgaria (ranked 54), Estonia (ranked 56), Malta (ranked 62) and Romania (ranked 67). Colombia, Jamaica, Belize, Trinidad, Mexico, Guyana, Nicaragua, El Salvador, Malaysia and Mongolia all are better placed than the worst-placed EU-27 member state, thus shattering once more the tenets of Eurocentrism, which are at the basis of European exclusivity in the policy of EU enlargement, especially vis-à-vis the southern and eastern rim of the Mediterranean.

Policy pointer

Combining the startling variety of all these dimensions of development, Table 5 lists the performance of the countries of the world system according to the criteria of the non-parametric overall development index, based on 35 variables, with equal weight attached to each indicator. The Nordic countries, the Netherlands, New Zealand, Switzerland and Austria are ranked highest, and the USA, the failed Lisbon Strategy's best practice reference country number one, is only ranked ninth. So, the 'Lisbon' strategy in reality should have told the other Europeans: become a little Scandinavia of your own…

Table 5. The non-parametric overall development index – results from 175 countries

	Overall 35 development index	Rank in world society
Sweden	0.815	1
Finland	0.794	2
Norway	0.793	3
Switzerland	0.773	4
New Zealand	0.772	5
Denmark	0.761	6
Netherlands	0.761	7
Austria	0.756	8
USA	0.742	9
Iceland	0.741	10
United Kingdom	0.740	11
Germany	0.740	12
Ireland	0.734	13
France	0.731	14
Australia	0.730	15
Canada	0.729	16
Belgium	0.726	17
Costa Rica	0.716	18
Spain	0.714	19
Slovenia	0.698	20
Israel	0.693	21
Japan	0.685	22
Chile	0.681	23
Portugal	0.677	24
Panama	0.674	25
Italy	0.674	26
Uruguay	0.671	27
Argentina	0.663	28
Poland	0.662	29
Barbados	0.657	30
Hungary	0.653	31
Greece	0.652	32

(Continued)

Table 5. Continued

	Overall 35 development index	Rank in world society
Cyprus	0.649	33
Czech Republic	0.643	34
Slovakia	0.641	35
Lithuania	0.640	36
Croatia	0.640	37
Bahamas	0.635	38
Luxembourg	0.633	39
Philippines	0.631	40
Latvia	0.630	41
Cuba	0.629	42
Hong Kong, China (SAR)	0.626	43
Dominican Republic	0.624	44
Sri Lanka	0.623	45
Brazil	0.623	46
Peru	0.621	47
Thailand	0.620	48
Mauritius	0.619	49
Korea (Republic of)	0.618	50
Dominica	0.617	51
Ecuador	0.616	52
Singapore	0.616	53
Bulgaria	0.615	54
Colombia	0.614	55
Estonia	0.612	56
Jamaica	0.611	57
Belize	0.610	58
Trinidad and Tobago	0.607	59
Mexico	0.607	60
Guyana	0.599	61
Malta	0.599	62
Nicaragua	0.598	63
El Salvador	0.593	64
Malaysia	0.591	65

(*Continued*)

Table 5. Continued

	Overall 35 development index	Rank in world society
Mongolia	0.590	66
Romania	0.590	67
Tunisia	0.588	68
Paraguay	0.588	69
Suriname	0.586	70
Albania	0.585	71
Fiji	0.585	72
Honduras	0.579	73
Guatemala	0.576	74
China	0.575	75
Moldova	0.574	76
Cape Verde	0.571	77
Vietnam	0.571	78
São Tomé and Príncipe	0.570	79
Venezuela	0.568	80
Russia	0.568	81
Bolivia	0.566	82
Samoa	0.565	83
Jordan	0.563	84
Grenada	0.563	85
St. Vincent and the Grenadines	0.562	86
Belarus	0.561	87
Indonesia	0.557	88
Bahrain	0.556	89
South Africa	0.555	90
Antigua and Barbuda	0.554	91
Ghana	0.549	92
Kyrgyzstan	0.549	93
Bhutan	0.548	94
Ukraine	0.544	95
St. Lucia	0.543	96
Morocco	0.540	97
Macedonia, Former Yugoslav Republic of	0.539	98

(*Continued*)

Table 5. Continued

	Overall 35 development index	Rank in world society
Laos	0.538	99
Egypt	0.537	100
Oman	0.536	101
India	0.536	102
Kazakhstan	0.533	103
Papua New Guinea	0.532	104
Senegal	0.525	105
Lebanon	0.525	106
Kuwait	0.524	107
Botswana	0.521	108
Saudi Arabia	0.520	109
Algeria	0.519	110
St. Kitts and Nevis	0.519	111
Maldives	0.516	112
Seychelles	0.516	113
Syria	0.516	114
Uzbekistan	0.514	115
Nepal	0.513	116
Georgia	0.513	117
Madagascar	0.512	118
United Arab Emirates	0.509	119
Armenia	0.509	120
Turkey	0.508	121
Brunei	0.508	122
Namibia	0.508	123
Iran	0.508	124
Gambia	0.504	125
Bosnia and Herzegovina	0.501	126
Azerbaijan	0.499	127
Uganda	0.498	128
Tajikistan	0.497	129
Bangladesh	0.496	130
Libya	0.495	131

(*Continued*)

Table 5. Continued

	Overall 35 development index	Rank in world society
Malawi	0.493	132
Cambodia	0.493	133
Tanzania	0.489	134
Gabon	0.487	135
Myanmar	0.486	136
Vanuatu	0.486	137
Qatar	0.485	138
Benin	0.477	139
Solomon Islands	0.475	140
Pakistan	0.475	141
Lesotho	0.472	142
Mozambique	0.472	143
Mali	0.468	144
Mauritania	0.457	145
Kenya	0.455	146
Burkina Faso	0.452	147
Zambia	0.449	148
Congo, Republic of	0.448	149
Cameroon	0.441	150
Comoros	0.438	151
Nigeria	0.436	152
Rwanda	0.435	153
Côte d'Ivoire	0.434	154
Yemen	0.433	155
Haiti	0.433	156
Ethiopia	0.432	157
Djibouti	0.431	158
Guinea	0.425	159
Eritrea	0.421	160
Turkmenistan	0.420	161
Guinea-Bissau	0.418	162
Timor-Leste	0.417	163
Niger	0.415	164

(*Continued*)

Table 5. Continued

	Overall 35 development index	Rank in world society
Congo, Democratic Republic of	0.410	165
Togo	0.408	166
Burundi	0.400	167
Angola	0.392	168
Chad	0.391	169
Central African Republic	0.390	170
Zimbabwe	0.387	171
Sudan	0.363	172
Sierra Leone	0.362	173
Swaziland	0.354	174
Equatorial Guinea	0.351	175

Table 6 presents a view of the differences in rank, with which European policymakers are being confronted today. Arguably, Sweden is the world leader in the combined terms of democracy, economic growth, environment, gender, human development, research and development, and social cohesion. There are several real internationally high-performing EU-27 countries among the ten best placed countries of the world, and these countries are Sweden, Finland, Netherlands, Denmark, and Austria. The world ranks of the EU founding members range from 7 (Netherlands) to 26 (Italy) and 39 (Luxembourg), especially because of its problematic environmental performance. With all due recognition of the advances of the new EU member states in recent years, like Slovenia, and Poland, the dismal performance of Bulgaria, Estonia, Malta and Romania, which are not even among the world's top 50 classified countries, is a serious question mark for the entire EU-2020 strategy. The further the European Union expands southeastward, the more it is confronted with dismal combined performances of candidate countries in terms of democracy, economic growth, environment, gender, human development, research and development, and social cohesion. Turkey ranks only 121 within world society, while India is ranked at 101.

Table 6. Ranking of European countries on the overall, non-parametric development index

	Rank in world society	Overall 35 development index
Sweden	1	0.815
Finland	2	0.794
Netherlands	7	0.761
Denmark	6	0.761

(Continued)

Table 6. Continued

	Rank in world society	Overall 35 development index
Austria	8	0.756
Germany	12	0.740
United Kingdom	11	0.740
Ireland	13	0.734
France	14	0.731
Belgium	17	0.726
Spain	19	0.714
Slovenia	20	0.698
Portugal	24	0.677
Italy	26	0.674
Poland	29	0.662
Hungary	31	0.653
Greece	32	0.652
Cyprus	33	0.649
Czech Republic	34	0.643
Slovakia	35	0.641
Lithuania	36	0.640
Luxembourg	39	0.633
Latvia	41	0.630
Bulgaria	54	0.615
Estonia	56	0.612
Malta	62	0.599
Romania	67	0.590

Our overall development index also bears a great similarity to the UNDP's Human Development Index (HDI), although the UNDP HDI is only based on three dimensions – education, a long life, and real incomes, while our index is a combination of 35 indicator variables. The high correlation between the two indices (R^2 is about ¾) is again evidence of the fact that the UNDP HDI, despite its simple structure and influence of GDP per capita, is an almost ideal measure of development, which well deserves its place in international social policy and beyond:

---

3 The R^2 is 81.3 per cent, and the equation is based on 115 countries with complete data. The F-value is 50.601; and the equation significant at the 0.000 level. The constant is not significant and its numerical sign is positive, and also the 'Kuznets curve' does not achieve significance, but the other predictors are indeed statistically significant.

Graph 2. The Human Development Index and our non-parametric development index, based on 35 variables

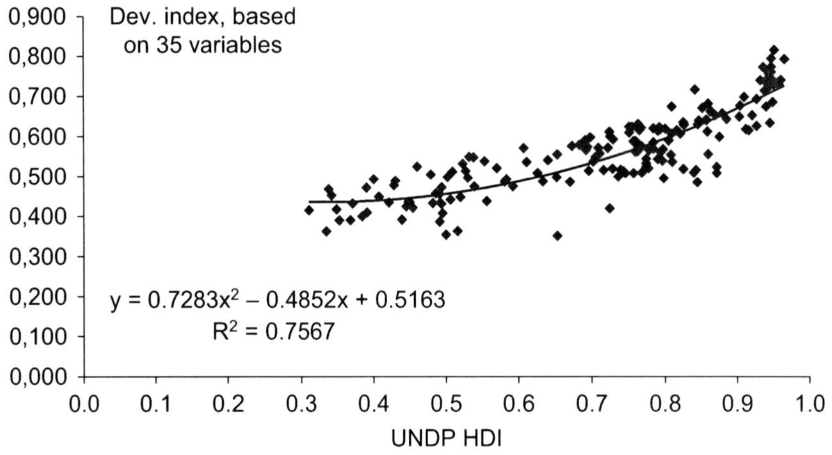

Note: In the non-parametric single index approach the 35 variables are weighted equally. The horizontal x-axis represents the Human Development Index of a given country the vertical y-axis is our development index, based on 35 variables. The dots are the observed country values, the line is the stylized function of the two variables, and the equation expresses the mathematical relationship between the two (for the interested readers: a polynomial function of the second degree).

Table 7 presents the concluding statistical table for our combined results.[3] What are the strategic consequences from Table 7, based on our knowledge about the effects of our independent variables on the combined index of development, based on 35 variables from the dimensions of democracy, growth, environment, gender equality, human development, research and development and social cohesion? Political-institutional feminism, measured by the percentage of power position at all levels of government, which women control in a country, positively affects the overall development process, and certainly feminism is a driver, not a bottleneck for all countries concerned. In accordance with socio-liberal strategies of development, we also have to consider the positive effects of economic freedom; in fact, the coefficient is four times higher than the standard error of the estimate, and the effect is highly significant. Among the other drivers of a positive development scenario we find the indicator MNC headquarter status (MNC outward investments (stock) per GDP), which measures the power position, national capital wields on the world markets, and the UNDP Education Index, which for us is the best available measurement of the human capital formation effort of a society. The good message for European integration is that years of membership in EMU (measured at the year 2010) also wield a positive influence on our overall development performance indicator, but the effect is not as strong, as Euro-optimists would have hoped. *Summa summarum*, the size of annual population growth is a significant bottleneck for the combined development performance. Most importantly, it also emerges that the ultra-liberal globalization strategy of the European Commission is without foundation, and that MNC penetration (MNC PEN – stock of inward FDI per GDP) and world

Table 7. Global determinants of the non-parametric development index[4]

Independent variables	B (unstandardized regression coefficient)	Standard error of the estimate	Beta-weight (standardized regression coefficient)	t-value (statistical test)	Error probability
Constant	0.292	0.331		0.881	0.380
Percentage of women in government, all levels	0.001	0.001	0.090	1.919	0.058
2000 Economic Freedom Score	0.003	0.001	0.283	4.880	0.000
Annual population growth rate, 1975–2005 (%)	−0.021	0.005	−0.237	−4.117	0.000
ln GDP per capita	−0.007	0.078	−0.075	−0.094	0.925
ln GDP per capita[2]	0.001	0.004	0.269	0.342	0.733
MNC outward investments (stock) per GDP	0.002	0.001	0.162	2.968	0.004
MNC PEN – stock of inward FDI per GDP	−0.001	0.000	−0.125	−2.531	0.013
Openness Index, 1990 (export share per GDP + import share per GDP)	0.000	0.000	−0.154	−3.105	0.002
UNDP Education Index	0.147	0.051	0.252	2.880	0.005
Years of membership in EMU (2010)	0.004	0.002	0.090	1.702	0.092

Adj R^2 (adjusted variance explained) = 0,813; df. (degrees of freedom) = 114; F (F-test for the statistical quality of the entire equation) = 50,601; p (error probability of the entire equation) = .000.

4 A very readable and easily available guide to the language of SPSS multiple regression results is to be found again in the following document, prepared by the University of California, Los Angeles: http://www.ats.ucla.edu/stat/spss/output/reg_spss.htm (accessed 27 January 2012).

economic openness (the Openness Index, 1990 (export share per GDP + import share per GDP)) are significant bottlenecks of a satisfactory overall development performance.

Policy pointer

Table 7 presents the concluding statistical table for the determinants of our combined results. What is really the best combined strategy to follow? So that, say, Romania becomes a 'little Sweden'? Political-institutional feminism positively affects the overall development process. In accordance with socio-liberal strategies of development, we also have to consider the positive effects of economic freedom. Among the other drivers of a positive development scenario we find MNC headquarter status, and the UNDP Education Index. Years of membership in EMU also wield a positive influence on our overall development performance indicator. Annual population growth is a significant bottleneck for the combined development performance. Most importantly, it also emerges that MNC penetration and world economic openness are significant bottlenecks of a satisfactory overall development performance. The proper strategy thus combines the following socio-liberal elements, so typical for Scandinavia and the other advanced welfare states of the OECD: social, gender-oriented welfare and a successful human capital policy combined with economic freedom, a strong position of national capital on the world markets, and a selective policy of limited openness and internal demand.

Chapter 6

A TIME SERIES PERSPECTIVE ON GLOBALIZATION, GROWTH AND INEQUALITY

In the present chapter, we leave the somewhat trodden paths of macro-quantitative cross-national development research, and we will venture into the new terrain of time series analysis. New terrain, only insofar as this is an established discipline of economics, especially econometrics, but is rather absent from all the studies claiming to show the pros and cons of globalization for economic growth and social and ecological well-being. Time series analysis of globalization and its impacts is important but neglected in the existing literature on globalization.[1]

In the theoretical chapters above we already highlighted the fact there is a recurring interest in the social sciences to study the long-term swings of global capitalist development. Such studies will be forever linked to the name of Nikolai Kondratiev. The questions, arising out of such research in our context are two-fold. One is the not only academic, but also politically highly relevant and value-charged question, whether there is now, after the global recession, hope for a recovery ('light at the end of the tunnel'), or, as the cruel joke now going around has it, these are just the 'headlamps of an approaching train' we see in the tunnel and thus, there is no recovery in sight. The second question, potentially as alarming as the first, is whether globalization-driven economic cycles in earlier periods and today exhibit the same downward patterns and whether or not they are therefore to be associated with rising global world political tensions – instead of leading the world to the promised lands of prosperity and growth will they result in stagnation and global warfare? Such questions of course are not new in the social sciences: the Marxist classics, especially, are full of references to such catastrophic scenarios, and are a discomforting and strong sound in the chorus of the 'Ode to Joy' we have been hearing ever since the end of communism, 1989.

The return of 'economics as a dismal science' to the debate is also evident from the fact that untransformed world industrial production growth figures since 1947 clearly show in Graph 3 a linear downward trend. In general, in recent decades agriculture and manufacturing sectors have been contracting as a share of the total output, while the service industry has been expanding in major economies. The negative trend shown in Graph 3 does not necessarily reflect the overall decline

---

1 Sutcliffe and Glyn (1999) find that globalization is misinterpreted and its quantitative extent exaggerated, inappropriate statistical measures are used, conclusions are drawn from little data, and no historical comparison is possible.

Graph 3. The linear downward trend of industrial production growth in the world economy since 1947

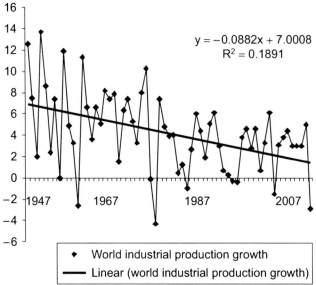

$$y = -0.0882x + 7.0008$$
$$R^2 = 0.1891$$

- ♦ World industrial production growth
- — Linear (world industrial production growth)

in the world economy. Unfortunately, we do not have access to the level and growth rate in the agricultural and service sectors so as to make a comparison with the industrial sector's production. Development of the industrial sector is more relevant as it forms the basis for consumption and demand in the service sector.

Also, the economic growth rates in the major economies of the old kernel of the European Union, i.e. France, Germany and Italy, all point in a downward direction. Ignoring the increasing trend in the 1980s will result in an even steeper decline in economic growth in these countries. This downward trend is captured in Graph 4, while the corresponding Tables 9 and 10 highlight the time series correlation coefficients of the entire world economy and the European Union by international comparison. Indeed, nowhere in Europe are the promised lands of prosperity in sight. Some of the countries which still show a positive correlation between the time axis and economic growth during the period 1980 to 2010, like Greece, Hungary, Ireland, Latvia, Lithuania and Romania, are in the abyss of the current severe economic crisis, and most probably the positive correlation to be observed between the time axis and economic growth is only the consequence of recovery from the very deep recession, which occurred in the 1980s.

Policy pointer

World industrial production growth figures since 1947 clearly show a linear downward trend. Also, the economic growth rates in the major economies of the old European Union, i.e. France, Germany and Italy, all point in a downward direction. Tables 9 and 10 highlight the time series correlation coefficients of the entire world economy and the European Union by international comparison. Europe is in the abyss of the current severe economic crisis, whose long forecasting shadows are all evident from the analysis of the time series data.

Graph 4. The linear downward trend of economic growth in the major old EU member countries France, Germany and Italy since 1980

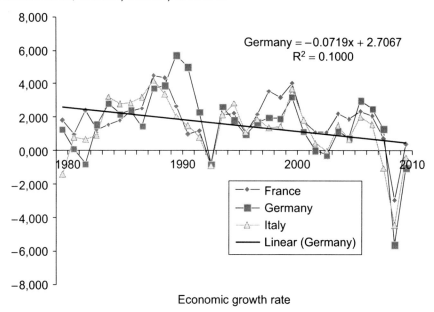

Economic growth rate

Table 8. Time series correlation coefficients of economic growth rates for the countries of the World Economy, based on IMF World Economic Outlook data, 2009 (growth and growth predictions 1980–2010)

	Pearson correlation coefficients of time series growth	Slope of time series growth
Uzbekistan	0.891	0.657
Djibouti	0.880	0.548
Bangladesh	0.803	0.113
Azerbaijan	0.721	1.876
São Tomé and Príncipe	0.670	0.341
Qatar	0.664	0.701
Tajikistan	0.661	1.121
Iraq	0.651	1.354

(*Continued*)

Table 8. Continued

	Pearson correlation coefficients of time series growth	Slope of time series growth
Tanzania	0.645	0.179
Turkmenistan	0.614	1.346
Ukraine	0.609	1.094
Suriname	0.607	0.317
Bolivia	0.592	0.176
Kazakhstan	0.555	0.799
Macedonia, Former Yugoslav Republic of	0.553	0.389
Uganda	0.550	0.226
Russia	0.528	0.667
Moldova	0.514	0.877
Kyrgyzstan	0.508	0.733
Myanmar	0.498	0.310
Samoa	0.496	0.223
Ghana	0.495	0.182
Trinidad and Tobago	0.494	0.311
Guatemala	0.479	0.114
Belarus	0.476	0.669
Greece	0.474	0.116
Poland	0.455	0.228
Mozambique	0.446	0.328
Angola	0.434	0.440
Sudan	0.431	0.197
Libya	0.422	0.346
El Salvador	0.420	0.166
India	0.392	0.078
Guyana	0.372	0.206
Madagascar	0.362	0.178
Ethiopia	0.358	0.278
Zambia	0.355	0.172
Niger	0.347	0.219
Honduras	0.332	0.092
Philippines	0.329	0.131
Sierra Leone	0.313	0.332

(*Continued*)

Table 8. Continued

	Pearson correlation coefficients of time series growth	Slope of time series growth
Nicaragua	0.312	0.132
Malawi	0.309	0.179
United Arab Emirates	0.309	0.260
Kiribati	0.305	0.348
Peru	0.293	0.195
Panama	0.289	0.152
Saudi Arabia	0.285	0.147
Congo, Democratic Republic of	0.281	0.168
Armenia	0.278	0.379
Timor-Leste, Dem Rep of	0.274	0.640
Costa Rica	0.269	0.106
Argentina	0.266	0.175
Senegal	0.255	0.078
Algeria	0.249	0.079
Lithuania	0.249	0.356
Vietnam	0.247	0.071
Benin	0.244	0.073
Brunei	0.243	0.101
Nigeria	0.242	0.183
Burkina Faso	0.239	0.085
Kuwait	0.227	0.418
Mali	0.218	0.111
Albania	0.217	0.191
South Africa	0.214	0.056
Rwanda	0.212	0.287
Solomon Islands	0.202	0.125
Romania	0.194	0.114
Venezuela	0.192	0.130
Bahrain	0.188	0.061
Serbia	0.184	0.270
Montenegro	0.183	0.214
Equatorial Guinea	0.178	0.589
Mauritania	0.175	0.063

(*Continued*)

Table 8. Continued

	Pearson correlation coefficients of time series growth	Slope of time series growth
Chad	0.174	0.147
Iran	0.164	0.128
Hungary	0.163	0.063
Czech Republic	0.160	0.063
Uruguay	0.153	0.079
Nepal	0.143	0.041
Gambia, The	0.139	0.083
Dominican Republic	0.137	0.058
Togo	0.130	0.078
Guinea	0.117	0.018
Mongolia	0.105	0.056
Malta	0.103	0.068
Papua New Guinea	0.100	0.055
Tunisia	0.099	0.025
Bulgaria	0.095	0.060
Morocco	0.093	0.047
Haiti	0.089	0.036
Cape Verde	0.084	0.025
Barbados	0.081	0.027
Jordan	0.069	0.038
Latvia	0.064	0.085
Vanuatu	0.053	0.022
Brazil	0.051	0.019
Ecuador	0.049	0.019
Sri Lanka	0.048	0.010
Lebanon	0.044	0.085
New Zealand	0.033	0.008
Central African Republic	0.025	0.013
Côte d'Ivoire	0.016	0.006
Chile	0.016	0.008
Ireland	0.016	0.007
Gabon	0.014	0.008
Liberia	−0.008	−0.033
Burundi	−0.009	−0.005

(*Continued*)

Table 8. Continued

	Pearson correlation coefficients of time series growth	Slope of time series growth
Colombia	−0.014	−0.004
Congo, Republic of	−0.016	−0.011
Egypt	−0.018	−0.004
Bhutan	−0.023	−0.013
Spain	−0.033	−0.007
Croatia	−0.040	−0.029
Kenya	−0.043	−0.010
Lesotho	−0.043	−0.011
China	−0.051	−0.016
Laos	−0.051	−0.017
Syria	−0.056	−0.031
Slovakia	−0.059	−0.036
Georgia	−0.059	−0.049
Netherlands	−0.068	−0.016
Fiji	−0.071	−0.056
Seychelles	−0.072	−0.042
United Kingdom	−0.088	−0.020
Mexico	−0.112	−0.043
Turkey	−0.114	−0.056
Namibia	−0.116	−0.061
Grenada	−0.118	−0.057
Canada	−0.119	−0.029
Australia	−0.121	−0.026
Sweden	−0.128	−0.030
Austria	−0.133	−0.022
Cambodia	−0.139	−0.088
Iceland	−0.140	−0.060
Finland	−0.145	−0.049
Israel	−0.154	−0.045
Belize	−0.154	−0.098
Guinea-Bissau	−0.165	−0.119
Paraguay	−0.167	−0.060
Mauritius	−0.172	−0.070
Cameroon	−0.172	−0.095

(*Continued*)

Table 8. Continued

	Pearson correlation coefficients of time series growth	Slope of time series growth
Belgium	−0.194	−0.037
Indonesia	−0.201	−0.086
Luxembourg	−0.212	−0.077
Antigua and Barbuda	−0.212	−0.084
USA	−0.229	−0.052
Denmark	−0.238	−0.053
Comoros	−0.244	−0.082
St. Vincent and the Grenadines	−0.247	−0.092
Switzerland	−0.254	−0.051
France	−0.257	−0.041
Bahamas	−0.260	−0.092
Jamaica	−0.262	−0.080
Estonia	−0.263	−0.307
Malaysia	−0.274	−0.125
Norway	−0.289	−0.058
Slovenia	−0.299	−0.115
Cyprus	−0.306	−0.104
Germany	−0.316	−0.072
St. Kitts and Nevis	−0.324	−0.105
Italy	−0.345	−0.067
Hong Kong, China SAR	−0.349	−0.161
Maldives	−0.358	−0.207
Swaziland	−0.363	−0.171
Pakistan	−0.378	−0.084
Yemen	−0.382	−0.094
Thailand	−0.387	−0.195
Botswana	−0.404	−0.263
Singapore	−0.410	−0.225
St. Lucia	−0.417	−0.194
Korea (Republic of)	−0.433	−0.201
Oman	−0.440	−0.222
Eritrea	−0.464	−0.603
Tonga	−0.467	−0.445

(Continued)

Table 8. Continued

	Pearson correlation coefficients of time series growth	Slope of time series growth
Portugal	−0.484	−0.144
Dominica	−0.503	−0.206
Japan	−0.568	−0.151
Afghanistan	−0.619	−1.075
Taiwan	−0.636	−0.274
Zimbabwe	−0.689	−0.509
Bosnia and Herzegovina	−0.715	−1.630

Table 9. Time series correlation coefficients of economic growth rates for the countries of the European Union, based on IMF World Economic Outlook data, 2009 (growth and growth predictions 1980–2010)

	Pearson corr. time series growth	Slope of time series growth
Portugal	−0.484	−0.144
Italy	−0.345	−0.067
Germany	−0.316	−0.072
Cyprus	−0.306	−0.104
Slovenia	−0.299	−0.115
Estonia	−0.263	−0.307
France	−0.257	−0.041
Denmark	−0.238	−0.053
USA	−0.229	−0.052
Luxembourg	−0.212	−0.077
Belgium	−0.194	−0.037
Finland	−0.145	−0.049
Austria	−0.133	−0.022
Sweden	−0.128	−0.030
United Kingdom	−0.088	−0.020
Netherlands	−0.068	−0.016
Spain	−0.033	−0.007
Ireland	0.016	0.007
Latvia	0.064	0.085
Bulgaria	0.095	0.060
Czech Republic	0.160	0.063
Hungary	0.163	0.063
Romania	0.194	0.114
Lithuania	0.249	0.356
Poland	0.455	0.228
Greece	0.474	0.116

Policy pointer

Our rigorous data analysis of the last four decades highlights the following main trends:

- Our time series investigation from 1970 to 2003 covers 92.47 per cent of humanity living in 117 countries and territories of the world.
- Indeed, rising economic globalization is the defining element of the development trajectory of humanity in the 1970s, 1980s, and 1990s until the beginning of the new millennium – from Spain with the most rapid globalization process to Burkina Faso with the lowest. About 90.57 per cent of humanity, living in 108 countries of the 117 countries with complete data, was affected by the globalization process.
- Only in nine countries (Algeria, Malawi, Fiji, Gabon, Oman, Swaziland, Barbados, Bahamas, Iran) were we confronted with a negative time series correlation between the time axis and economic globalization, measured by the KOF index. These countries amount to just 1.90 per cent of the world population.
- The brave new world of rising economic globalization is a world of rising inequalities. About 75.92 per cent of the global population lived in countries, where there was a rising linear trend towards inequality over time. For 54.05 per cent of humanity, this trend was especially strong, and the time series correlation coefficient of the time axis with inequality was 0.50 or above. Ranked by the magnitude of this phenomenon, we find 60 nations, from Lesotho, Portugal and Lithuania at the top right through to El Salvador, Austria and the USA. Among the EU-27 countries, there are 13 nations corresponding to this very strong trend towards rising inequality over time: Portugal, Lithuania, Czech Republic, Romania, the United Kingdom, Slovenia, Slovakia, Bulgaria, Hungary, Germany, Ireland, Poland, and Austria.
- Of humanity, 79.61 per cent also experienced the dire fact that according to the available time series, globalization in their countries was positively correlated with higher inequality.
- For 48.97 per cent of humanity, living in 55 countries, this trend was especially strong. The time series correlation was 0.50 or above. 13 of the 27 EU countries are among them and their experience gives a testimony about the Latin Americanization of the European continent: Romania, Hungary, Czech Republic, Portugal, Poland, Bulgaria, Ireland, Germany, Lithuania, the United Kingdom, Slovenia, Austria and Slovakia.
- Only 35 countries experienced some positive promises of globalization, i.e. a negative time series correlation between globalization and inequality. The inhabitants of these countries are a fortunate global minority, and comprise 12.86 per cent of the global population. Only seven of the EU-27 countries

are among them, namely Latvia, the Netherlands, Spain, Cyprus, Sweden, Finland, and France. Interestingly enough, in globalization-critical France, this effect was strongest, and in Latvia, the effect was weakest. Other highly developed economies with a very notable trend of globalization leading to less inequality over time are South Korea and Singapore.

Our time series analysis evaluated the data from the following 117 countries with complete data:

Albania, Algeria, Angola, Argentina, Australia, Austria, Azerbaijan, Bahamas, The, Bangladesh, Barbados, Belgium, Benin, Bolivia, Botswana, Brazil, Bulgaria, Burkina Faso, Burundi, Cameroon, Canada, Central African Republic, Chile, China, Colombia, Congo (Rep.), Costa Rica, Côte d'Ivoire, Croatia, Cyprus, Czech Republic, Denmark, Dominican Republic, Ecuador, Egypt, El Salvador, Ethiopia, Fiji, Finland, France, Gabon, Germany, Ghana, Greece, Guatemala, Haiti, Honduras, Hungary, Iceland, India, Indonesia, Iran, Ireland, Israel, Italy, Jamaica, Japan, Jordan, Kenya, Korea (Rep.), Kuwait, Kyrgyzstan, Latvia, Lesotho, Lithuania, Luxembourg, Macedonia (FYR), Madagascar, Malawi, Malaysia, Malta, Mauritius, Mexico, Moldova, Mongolia, Morocco, Mozambique, Nepal, Netherlands, New Zealand, Nicaragua, Nigeria, Norway, Oman, Pakistan, Panama, Papua New Guinea, Peru, Philippines, Poland, Portugal, Romania, Russian Federation, Rwanda, Senegal, Singapore, Slovakia, Slovenia, South Africa, Spain, Sri Lanka, Swaziland, Sweden, Syria, Tanzania, Thailand, Togo, Trinidad and Tobago, Tunisia, Turkey, Uganda, Ukraine, United Kingdom, USA, Uruguay, Venezuela, Zambia, Zimbabwe

If the relationship between globalization and inequality is a clear numerically positive trade-off, the time series correlation must be high. A time series correlation coefficient to the magnitude of <0.50 indicates that the 55 countries of the world economy, most devastated by inequality impacts of globalization (in order of descending magnitude of devastation) are:

Romania, Czech Republic, Hungary, Portugal, Angola, Poland, China, Ecuador, Australia, Azerbaijan, Iran, Bulgaria, New Zealand, Ukraine, Ireland, Germany, Mongolia, Zambia, Turkey, Mexico, Lesotho, Croatia, Lithuania, Honduras, Brazil, Côte d'Ivoire, Russian Federation, Trinidad and Tobago, Venezuela, Egypt, Pakistan, United Kingdom, Canada, Chile, Slovenia, Uruguay, Nigeria, Syria, Philippines, Colombia, Austria, Togo, Slovakia, Japan, Senegal, Guatemala, El Salvador, Kuwait, Cameroon, Panama, Peru, Papua New Guinea.

Our data analysis reported in Table 10 now shows the 61 states of the world that must be regarded as the chief victims of globalization (time series correlation (r) globalization with inequality >0.25; globalization with time >0.25, and rising inequality over time (r >0.00)).

Table 10. The 61 chief victim states of current globalization

Country	r, globalization with inequality	r, globalization with time	r, inequality with time
Albania	0.455	0.604	0.341
Angola	0.947	0.981	0.868
Argentina	0.286	0.935	0.462
Australia	0.894	0.967	0.831
Austria	0.662	0.969	0.557
Azerbaijan	0.892	0.926	0.949
Belgium	0.285	0.970	0.399
Bolivia	0.477	0.842	0.677
Brazil	0.821	0.762	0.678
Bulgaria	0.880	0.770	0.840
Cameroon	0.578	0.631	0.928
Canada	0.729	0.878	0.834
Chile	0.723	0.983	0.733
China	0.913	0.923	0.935
Colombia	0.673	0.933	0.600
Côte d'Ivoire	0.808	0.746	0.843
Croatia	0.835	0.686	0.658
Czech Republic	0.966	0.973	0.949
Denmark	0.479	0.945	0.372
Ecuador	0.912	0.952	0.822
Egypt	0.754	0.911	0.863
El Salvador	0.589	0.709	0.566
Germany	0.866	0.941	0.776
Guatemala	0.606	0.937	0.645
Honduras	0.828	0.896	0.662
Hungary	0.966	0.835	0.796
Ireland	0.870	0.967	0.737
Israel	0.403	0.759	0.825
Jamaica	0.446	0.931	0.697
Japan	0.649	0.955	0.785
Kuwait	0.587	0.404	0.637
Lesotho	0.845	0.932	0.977
Lithuania	0.835	0.957	0.955
Mexico	0.851	0.928	0.831
Mongolia	0.864	0.891	0.302
New Zealand	0.872	0.964	0.808
Nigeria	0.700	0.954	0.442
Norway	0.321	0.964	0.377
Pakistan	0.754	0.923	0.774

(*Continued*)

Table 10. Continued

Country	r, globalization with inequality	r, globalization with time	r, inequality with time
Panama	0.573	0.797	0.763
Papua New Guinea	0.503	0.327	0.615
Peru	0.508	0.931	0.609
Philippines	0.686	0.981	0.705
Poland	0.938	0.882	0.723
Portugal	0.950	0.954	0.973
Romania	0.986	0.777	0.922
Russian Federation	0.790	0.984	0.832
Senegal	0.624	0.701	0.744
Slovakia	0.652	0.828	0.846
Slovenia	0.712	0.958	0.856
Sri Lanka	0.281	0.958	0.057
Syria	0.694	0.870	0.725
Togo	0.661	0.400	0.574
Trinidad and Tobago	0.784	0.864	0.837
Turkey	0.854	0.950	0.847
Ukraine	0.871	0.958	0.891
United Kingdom	0.751	0.938	0.859
USA	0.420	0.961	0.513
Uruguay	0.712	0.941	0.851
Venezuela	0.757	0.891	0.576
Zambia	0.855	0.800	0.909

The following 29 countries listed in Table 11 experienced no rising inequality over time, and also their time series correlation coefficient between globalization and inequality was negative. Further research will have to establish why these lucky 29 countries could escape the general deterioration of social conditions, expressing themselves in rising inequality rates.

Table 11. The 29 lucky countries that escaped: No major inequality increasing effect of globalization, no increasing inequality over time

Country	r, globalization with inequality	r, globalization with time	r, inequality with time
Korea, Republic of	−0.791	0.966	−0.888
Cyprus	−0.532	0.722	−0.834
Singapore	−0.938	0.886	−0.833
Benin	−0.795	0.954	−0.816
Ethiopia	−0.394	0.833	−0.788
Finland	−0.668	0.964	−0.779
Kenya	−0.657	0.720	−0.742
France	−0.723	0.980	−0.727
Iceland	−0.653	0.916	−0.720

(*Continued*)

Table 11. Continued

Country	r, globalization with inequality	r, globalization with time	r, inequality with time
Rwanda	−0.707	0.713	−0.680
Sweden	−0.587	0.977	−0.674
Congo, Republic of	−0.875	0.821	−0.649
Indonesia	−0.522	0.897	−0.644
Nepal	−0.689	0.885	−0.563
Thailand	−0.516	0.952	−0.511
Mozambique	−0.453	0.941	−0.475
Mauritius	−0.591	0.908	−0.472
Spain	−0.342	0.986	−0.438
Tunisia	−0.394	0.952	−0.368
Netherlands	−0.340	0.981	−0.314
Haiti	−0.228	0.842	−0.277
Malaysia	−0.306	0.974	−0.239
Moldova	−0.317	0.702	−0.238
Jordan	−0.154	0.851	−0.181
Uganda	−0.023	0.788	−0.168
Latvia	−0.174	0.927	−0.072
Costa Rica	−0.018	0.933	−0.072
Zimbabwe	−0.208	0.847	−0.068
Kyrgyzstan	−0.264	0.738	−0.034

In Tables 13 and 14, we look at some of the drivers of why globalization leads to inequality over time, and why inequality rises over time, by carefully analysing the macro-sociological and economic characteristics of such societies. High foreign savings certainly and significantly coincide with a strong globalization leading to inequality trade-off over time, and public education expenditures mitigate the process, and there is a clear Kuznets curve of income levels at play. The significant drivers of the process of rising inequality over time can be equally named. Apart from the Kuznets curve, we find military expenditure and MNC penetration as the two most important drivers of rising inequality over time, while the net international migration rate mitigates the process.

Table 12. Significant drivers of the process that globalization leads to inequality

	B	Standard error	Beta	t-value	Error prob.
Constant	−7.742	2.853		−2.714	0.008
Foreign savings rate	0.012	0.005	0.268	2.565	0.012
ln GDP per capita	1.792	0.662	3.677	2.708	0.008
ln GDP per capita^2	−0.095	0.038	−3.399	−2.487	0.015
Public education expenditure per GNP	−0.073	0.030	−0.238	−2.441	0.016

Adj R^2 = 13.6%; df = 106; F = 5.161, error prob. = .001.

Table 13. Why does inequality rise over time? What are the significant drivers of this process?

	B	Standard error	Beta	t-value	Error prob.
Constant	−3.763	3.232		−1.164	0.247
ln GDP per capita	0.825	0.766	1.719	1.077	0.284
ln GDP per capita^2	−0.043	0.045	−1.569	−0.966	0.336
Military expenditure per GDP	0.018	0.011	0.162	1.673	0.098
MNC PEN – stock of inward FDI per GDP	0.010	0.004	0.282	2.789	0.006
Net international migration rate, 2005–2010	−0.443	0.169	−0.339	−2.619	0.010

Adj R^2 = 11.3%; df = 103; F = 3.612, error prob. = .005.

Policy pointer

In our study, we also analysed the drivers of why globalization leads to inequality over time, and why inequality rises over time. High foreign savings coincide with to strong globalization/inequality trade-off over time. Military expenditures and MNC penetration are the two most important processes leading towards a rising inequality over time, while net international migration rates mitigate this process.

Chapter 7

CONCLUSIONS

Let us start our survey by looking at the general tendencies of our results. Our detailed studies, which were based on 30 multiple regressions, in many ways confirmed the globalization-critical paradigm:

Main final policy pointers

- The clearest contradictions of world economic openness are on the educational and on the social levels. On the educational level, because open systems, more often than not situated in small, welfare-oriented democracies, tend towards a bad performance on the per capita world-class universities index and the tertiary enrolment ratio. World economic openness does have a significant negative effect on the Human Development Index, in many ways the master variable for the social situation in a country.
- High comparative price levels, and hence, implicitly, a high level of services of general interest, are a good and sound precondition of global tolerance, of a levelling of the income differences between rich and poor, and per capita world-class university performance. They are in fact the very nature of the 'European social model' and the 'European model' in general. Pushing comparative price levels down as a strategy of economic reform[1] – as the European Lisbon Strategy has demanded from EU member states ever since March 2000, when the heads of European governments met at their Lisbon European summit – implies a single-minded strategy towards global intolerance, towards increasing income differences between rich and poor, and towards lowering the per capita world-class university performance. All this has happened in Europe since 2000, sold under the auspices of 'economic reform'.
- The apprehensions of globalization-critical research are fully vindicated by the significant negative effects of the foreign savings rate. High foreign savings are indeed a driver of high unemployment, income inequality, global footprint, and are a blockade against a satisfactory Happy Planet Index performance.
- The New International Division of Labour (NIDL) model is one of the prime drivers of high CO_2 per capita emissions.

---

1 See http://epp.eurostat.ec.europa.eu/statistics_explained/index.php/GDP_per_capita,_consumption_per_capita_and_comparative_price_levels and http://epp.eurostat.ec.europa. eu/portal/page/portal/structural_indicators/indicators/economic_reform (accessed 27 January 2012).

- MNC penetration's negative impact on the social development of the host countries of foreign direct investments is mitigated by the positive effects of MNC headquarter status. Indeed, the positive effects of MNC headquarter status on per capita world-class universities and on the rule of law vindicate such reasoning. However, the EU strategy over recent years completely failed to tackle this issue, while a true European strategy should aim to increase European MNC headquarter status.
- MNC penetration increases income polarization and infant mortality, and blocks democracy, environmental performance, and the rule of law.
- Increases in MNC penetration over time had a negative effect on the rule of law, and equally had a negative effect on economic growth in the period 1990–2005. A good and plausible reason for this is the process of 'creative destruction' in the less fortunate regions of the world economy, partially also in these regions of East Central Europe.

Now let us summarize our results for sustainable development, one of the other main pillars of the EU-2020 strategy. Our empirical investigations showed that – per se – European Union and or European Monetary Union membership have, by global comparison, rather small beneficial effects on the environmental situation. There are only two significant positive effects to be reported in this context, and both concern a comparable dimension of environmental policy. The member countries of the European Monetary Union are good at reducing the ecological footprint. Likewise, years of EU membership coincide with countries avoiding the net trade of their ecological footprint.

High foreign savings, and hence, a reliance on foreign sources of savings, are indeed a driver of global footprint, and are a blockade against a satisfactory Happy Planet Index performance. The New International Division of Labour (NIDL) model, is one of the prime drivers of high CO_2 per capita emissions. MNC penetration, the master variable of most quantitative dependency theories, blocks environmental performance (EPI) and several other socially important processes. We can assume that the import of labour to the world economy has detrimental effects on life quality (Happy Planet Index, happy life years). Also, the percentage of the population with what today is called an 'immigration background' has a negative effect on some other key indicators of the environment. Immigration, and all the transport activities it causes, increases the CO_2 output of a given society, and it also increases the ratio of carbon emissions per GDP.

Now we should systematically evaluate the consequences of our study for social cohesion. Former president of the European Commission, Jacques Delors – a French socialist and Protestant – used to say that nobody can fall in love with the single market. Mario Monti, the Italian, Catholic former European commissioner, and current prime minister of Italy now recognizes that when the market is regarded as a superior entity, as if it were always able to deliver efficiently and did not need appropriate regulation and rigorous supervision, dangers are likely to lie ahead, as shown by the financial crisis. It was – Monti says – forgotten by many that the market 'is a good servant but a bad master'.

'Yet the single market is a crucial servant for the European Union. First, it is a necessary – though not sufficient – condition for a good performance of the European economy, just as well-functioning domestic markets are for national economies. Secondly, and even more importantly, a robust single market is key to the overall health of the European Union, because it represents the very foundation of the integration project'.

However, the most basic vision of the postwar world of peace and prosperity was spelt out by American president Franklin Delano Roosevelt on 6 January 1941, quoted at the beginning of this book. The first of man's four freedoms is the freedom of speech and expression – everywhere in the world. The second is to worship God in his own way everywhere in the world. The third is freedom from want. The fourth is freedom from fear.

Our social cohesion studies, based on 13 multiple regressions, confirmed the globalization-critical paradigm, and showed that current realities of the world economy suggest a Rooseveltian reading of four freedoms, which might be undermined or even threatened by what Mario Monto called the 'bad master', and which is definitely regarded by the European political elites as the superior entity – as if it were always able to deliver efficiently and did not need appropriate regulation and rigorous supervision. Our results, in particular, suggested that:

- World economic openness does have a significant negative effect on the Human Development Index, in many ways *the* master variable for the social situation in a country;
- Low comparative price levels, and hence, implicitly, a low level of services of general interest, are a bad precondition for the levelling of the income differences between rich and poor;
- High foreign savings are indeed a driver of unemployment, and income inequality; and
- MNC penetration increases income polarization and infant mortality.

We can reasonably also assume that the import of labour to the world economy, has detrimental effects on life quality (Happy Planet Index, life expectancy, life satisfaction, happy life years), and gender relations (closing the political gender gap; closing the overall gender gap). The percentage of the population with what today is called an 'immigration background' also has a negative effect on some other key indicators of gender justice. However, there also hold some other important effects as well, which tend to confirm the migration policy liberal consensus, inherent in the UNDP *HDR 2009* analysis.

Yes, there are not only Hiob's messages for inward migration, but the process is a very contradictory one. Yes, the share of people with migration background per total population seems to coincide with a weakening of the role of traditional, local, native elites, and income inequality tends to be lower when the share of population with a migration background is higher per total population in a given country. There is no significant effect of any migration variable on the unemployment rate.

Net international migration rates 2005 to 2010, which are a typical migration flow measure, relating to current and contemporary migration flows, are significant and are closing the political gender gap.

There is one policy area where we fundamentally disagree in the light of our results with current globalization-critical thinking and also the Kalecki–Steindl paradigm of an alternative European political economy. For the share of public education expenditures per GDP, the results are rather dire and tend to suggest that privatization and deregulation, and the restructuring of the public sector in education policy in Europe seem to be called for, because public expenditures are one of the main drivers of an unsatisfactory employment performance, and three hard core survival and basic needs indicators (most probably due to crowding-out effects with other government expenditure components): the female survival probability rate, life expectancy, and the Human Development Index.

There is a positive trade-off of effective demand on development. High inequality rates must be regarded in their own right as blockades against female survival rates, and life expectancies. With Galbraith's (1999, 2007, 2009) approach, we diagnose such an empirical effect for employment as well. The higher the inequality rate, the higher the unemployment rate.

Under such circumstances, Europe must return to the Delors agenda and a social welfare state to manage the multiple tasks of integration and social cohesion. The often-hailed beneficial effects of foreign capital penetration do not materialize, or materialize completely. As correctly predicted by the dependency literature in the tradition of Osvaldo Sunkel, social polarization dramatically increases by a development model, based on a very high foreign capital penetration. One further important consequence of our analysis is the rediscovery of the issue of European industrial policy in the framework of an otherwise relatively free economy, whose absence determines in the end the high coefficients of MNC penetration and the low coefficients of European MNC headquarter status.[2] De-regulation helps, but it helps the dominant centre to maintain and even increase its leading position, and certainly not the technologically and politically weaker nations of the periphery and semi-periphery.[3]

Thus, our results exactly open up, as we stated above, the box of industrial policy. Has Europe such a policy at all, or is European wisdom reduced to the magic number of a 3 per cent budget deficit, i.e. the Maastricht criteria? Or is the single market indeed being regarded as the superior entity, as if it was always able to deliver

---

2 Thus, the old critical questions addressed in the direction of neoclassical theory by such economists as Celso Furtado, Michal Kalecki, Gunnar Myrdal, Francois Perroux, Raul Prebisch, Paul Rosenstein-Rodan, Kurt Rothschild, Dudley Seers, Hans Singer and others can be taken up anew.

3 And so it is the French former European Commission president Jacques Delors (1992), and not economics Nobel Laureate Professor Paul Krugman, who seems to have gained the upper hand in the debate started by Krugman in *Foreign Affairs* in 1994 (http://www.foreignaffairs.org/19940301faessay5094/paul-krugman/competitiveness-a-dangerous-obsession.html – accessed 27 January 2012).

efficiently and did not need appropriate regulation and rigorous supervision, as Mario Monto warned in his quoted report in 2010?

Weighting the overall effects of our independent variables on our some three dozen indicators of development, we came to the conclusion that political-institutional feminism, measured by the percentage of power position at all levels of government, which women control in a country, positively affects the overall development process, and certainly feminism is a driver of development, not a bottleneck for all countries concerned. In accordance with socio-liberal strategies of development, we also have to consider the positive effects of economic freedom.

Among the other drivers of a positive development scenario we find the indicator MNC headquarter status and the UNDP Education Index, which perhaps is the best available measurement of the human capital formation effort of a society. Under these conditions, years of membership in the EMU (2010) would also wield a positive influence on the overall development performance indicator, but the effect is not as strong as Euro-optimists would have hoped. High annual population growth is a significant bottleneck for the combined development performance of democracy, growth, environment, gender equality, human development, research and development and social cohesion. Most importantly, it also emerges that MNC PEN – stock of inward FDI per GDP and the time-lagged world economic Openness Index, 1990 (export share per GDP + import share per GDP) are both significant bottlenecks of a satisfactory overall development performance.

Our analysis of the time series perspectives of globalization and development revealed truly astonishing results, again supporting our globalization-critical cross-national analysis. Our data analysis of the last four decades highlighted the following main trends:

• Rising economic globalization is the defining element of the development trajectory of humanity in the 1970s, 1980s and 1990s until the beginning of the new millennium – from Spain, with the most rapid globalization, process to Burkina Faso. Of humanity, 90.57 per cent, living in 108 of the 117 countries with complete data, were affected by that process.
• Only in nine countries were we confronted with a negative time series correlation between the time axis and economic globalization. These countries amount to just 1.90 per cent of the world population.
• The brave new world of rising economic globalization is a world of rising inequalities. Of the global population, 75.92 per cent lived in countries in which there was a rising linear trend towards inequality over time. For 54.05 per cent of humanity, this trend was especially strong, and the time series correlation coefficient of the time axis with inequality was 0.50 or above. Among the EU-27 countries, there are 13 nations corresponding to this very strong trend towards rising inequality over time.
• Of humanity, 79.61 per cent also experienced the dire fact that, according to the available time series, globalization in their countries was positively correlated with higher inequality.

- For 48.97 per cent of humanity, living in 55 countries, this trend was especially strong. The time series correlation was 0.50 or above. Thirteen of the EU-27 countries are among them and their experience gives a testimony about the Latin Americanization of the European continent.
- Only 35 countries experienced some positive promises of globalization, i.e. a negative time series correlation between globalization and inequality. The inhabitants of these countries are a fortunate global minority, and comprise 12.86 per cent of the global population. Only seven of the EU-27 are among them.

Under such circumstances, Europe must return to the Delors agenda and a liberal social welfare state to manage the multiple tasks of integration and social cohesion. In our opinion, European policymaking should dare finally, to take the globalization-critical organizations of 'civil society' seriously.[4] According to our analysis, industrial policy is the *sine qua non* of a real European answer to the US Keynesian global power strategy that always put the well-being of the US transnational corporation ahead of ideology.

---

4 Brand (2005); Brand and Raza (2003); Brand et al. (2000); Brand et al. (2001).

APPENDICES

Appendix 1: Multiple Regressions – The Dependency Model, Tested against Feminist, Demographic, Neoliberal, Geographic, Cultural, Peace Research and Human Capital Policy Predictors, Migration Theories and Integration Theories

Predictors

2000 economic freedom score

Absolute latitude

Annual population growth rate, 1975–2005 (%)

Comparative price levels (US = 1.00)

Foreign savings rate

FPZ (free production zones) employment as a percentage of total population

Immigration – share of population 2005 (%)

ln GDP per capita

ln GDP per capita^2

Membership of the Islamic Conference

Military expenditures per GDP

Military personnel rate ln (MPR + 1)

MNC outward investments (stock) per GDP

MNC PEN – stock of inward FDI per GDP

MNC PEN: DYN MNC PEN 1995–2005

Muslim population share per total population

Net international migration rate, 2005–2010 (%)

Openness Index, 1990 (export share per GDP + import share per GDP)

Percentage of women in government, all levels

Percentage of world population

Population density

Public education expenditure per GNP

UNDP Education Index

Worker remittance inflows as a percentage of GDP

Years of membership in the EU (2010)

Years of membership in EMU (2010)

The reported equations were chosen from the following dependent variables:

Avoiding net trade of ecological footprint gha per person

Carbon emissions per million US dollars GDP

Carbon emissions per capita

Civil and political liberty violations

Closing economic gender gap

Closing educational gender gap

Closing health and survival gender gap

Closing of global gender gap overall score 2009

Closing political gender gap

Combined Failed States Index

Corruption avoidance measure

Country share in top world 500 universities

Crisis Performance Factor

Democracy measure

Ecological footprint (gha per capita)

Economic growth IMF prediction growth rate in 2009

Economic growth IMF prediction growth rate in 2010

Economic growth in real terms per capita, per annum, 1990–2005

Environmental Performance Index (EPI)

Environmental Sustainability Index (ESI)

Female survival, probability of surviving to age 65

Gender empowerment index value

Global tolerance index

Happy life years

Happy Planet Index (HPI)

Human Development Index (HDI) value 2004

Infant mortality (2005)

Labour force participation rate of migrants (both sexes)

Life expectancy (years)

Life satisfaction (0–10)

ln (number of people per million inhabitants 1980–2000 killed by natural disasters per year + 1)

Per capita world-class universities

Quintile share income difference between richest and poorest 20 per cent

Rule of law

Tertiary emigration rate

Tertiary enrolment

Total unemployment rate of immigrants (both sexes)

Unemployment rate

Dependent variable	Results – stepwise regression: Independent variable	Statistical properties					Development dimension
		B	Standard error	Beta	t-value	Error probability	
1. Combined Failed States Index							Democracy
	Constant	−86.409	51.211		−1.687	0.094	
	2000 economic freedom score	−0.498	0.135	−0.208	−3.696	0.000	
	Absolute latitude	−0.223	0.092	−0.151	−2.428	0.017	
	Annual population growth rate, 1975–2005 (%)	2.311	1.190	0.108	1.942	0.055	
	ln GDP per capita	55.360	11.731	2.713	4.719	0.000	
	ln GDP per capita^2	−3.839	0.689	−3.271	−5.572	0.000	
	Military expenditures per GDP	**0.370**	**0.203**	**0.075**	**1.826**	**0.071**	
	Memorandum item: statistical properties of the equation	adj R^2	df	F	error prob.		
		83.000	119.000	97.634	.000		
2. Democracy measure		B	Standard error	Beta	t-value	Error probability	Democracy
	Constant	−0.970	20.294		−0.048	0.962	
	Percentage of women in government, all levels	−0.310	0.158	−0.113	−1.958	0.052	
	ln GDP per capita	0.667	4.820	0.124	0.138	0.890	
	ln GDP per capita^2	0.089	0.280	0.283	0.317	0.752	
	Membership of the Islamic Conference	−6.529	0.824	−0.486	−7.925	0.000	

Democracy

Independent Variable	B	Standard error	Beta	t-value	Error probability
Military personnel rate ln (MPR + 1)	-3.384	0.589	-0.367	-5.749	0.000
MNC PEN – stock of inward FDI per GDP	-0.053	0.021	-0.147	-2.574	0.011
Memorandum item: statistical properties of the equation	adj R²	df	F	error prob.	
	55.000	142.000	29.885	.000	

3. Civil and political liberty violations	B	Standard error	Beta	t-value	Error probability
Constant	-1.862	5.195		-0.358	0.721
Percentage of world population	0.090	0.040	0.109	2.256	0.026
Annual population growth rate, 1975–2005 (%)	0.371	0.104	0.236	3.576	0.000
ln GDP per capita	1.364	1.242	0.860	1.098	0.274
ln GDP per capita²	-0.136	0.070	-1.481	-1.938	0.055
Military personnel rate ln (MPR + 1)	**0.809**	**0.142**	**0.315**	**5.702**	**0.000**
UNDP Education Index	1.979	0.904	0.201	2.190	0.030
Muslim population share per total population	0.015	0.003	0.304	5.088	0.000
Memorandum item: statistical properties of the equation	adj R²	df	F	error prob.	
	67.500	143.000	43.443	.000	

(Continued)

Dependent variable	Results – stepwise regression Independent variable	Statistical properties B	Statistical properties Standard error	Statistical properties Beta	Statistical properties t-value	Statistical properties Error probability	Development dimension Democracy
4. Rule of law	Constant	6.365	3.521		1.808	0.073	
	ln GDP per capita	−2.208	0.817	−2.456	−2.702	0.008	
	ln GDP per capita^2	0.164	0.047	3.211	3.500	0.001	
	MNC outward investments (stock) per GDP	**0.003**	**0.007**	**0.035**	**0.447**	**0.656**	
	MNC PEN – stock of inward FDI per GDP	**−0.004**	**0.003**	**−0.090**	**−1.388**	**0.168**	
	MNC PEN: DYN MNC PEN 1995–2005	**−0.008**	**0.002**	**−0.199**	**−3.168**	**0.002**	
	Public education expenditure per GNP	0.086	0.030	0.168	2.896	0.005	
	Memorandum item: statistical properties of the equation	adj R^2	df	F	error prob.		
		63.800	115.000	34.748	.000		

	Independent variable	B	Standard error	Beta	t-value	Error probability	Economic growth
5. Economic growth IMF prediction growth rate in 2010	Constant	−4.029	9.049		−0.445	0.657	
	Percentage of world population	0.175	0.073	0.138	2.409	0.017	

Independent variable	B	Standard error	Beta	t-value	Error probability	Economic growth
2000 economic freedom score	−0.031	0.020	−0.124	−1.586	0.115	
Annual population growth rate, 1975–2005 (%)	0.454	0.186	0.188	2.446	0.016	
ln GDP per capita	2.954	2.121	1.222	1.392	0.166	
ln GDP per capita^2	−0.238	0.125	−1.697	−1.900	0.059	
Net international migration rate, 2005–2010	**1.284**	**0.228**	**0.395**	**5.625**	**0.000**	

Memorandum item: statistical properties of the equation

adj R^2	df	F	error prob.
52.100	149.000	27.974	.000

6. Crisis Performance Factor

Independent variable	B	Standard error	Beta	t-value	Error probability	Economic growth
Constant	2.848	2.761		1.031	0.304	
Percentage of world population	0.091	0.022	0.205	4.096	0.000	
Annual population growth rate, 1975–2005 (%)	0.241	0.058	0.277	4.178	0.000	
ln GDP per capita	−0.314	0.646	−0.370	−0.486	0.627	
ln GDP per capita^2	−0.009	0.037	−0.181	−0.238	0.812	
Muslim population share per total population	0.003	0.002	0.098	1.677	0.096	

Memorandum item: statistical properties of the equation

adj R^2	df	F	error prob.
64.300	144.000	52.963	.000

(Continued)

Dependent variable	Results – stepwise regression	Statistical properties	Statistical properties	Statistical properties	Statistical properties	Statistical properties	Development dimension
7. Economic growth, 1990–2005	Independent variable	B	Standard error	Beta	t-value	Error probability	Economic growth
	Constant	−6.961	10.487		−0.664	0.508	
	Percentage of world population	0.216	0.065	0.263	3.308	0.001	
	Annual population growth rate, 1975–2005 (%)	−0.308	0.168	−0.172	−1.839	0.069	
	ln GDP per capita	1.575	2.417	0.793	0.652	0.516	
	ln GDP per capita^2	−0.053	0.138	−0.471	−0.385	0.701	
	MNC outward investments (stock) per GDP	**−0.054**	**0.020**	**−0.286**	**−2.710**	**0.008**	
	MNC PEN – stock of inward FDI per GDP	**0.052**	**0.009**	**0.552**	**6.115**	**0.000**	
	MNC PEN: DYN MNC PEN 1995–2005	**−0.011**	**0.007**	**−0.129**	**−1.461**	**0.147**	
	Public education expenditure per GNP	−0.196	0.095	−0.170	−2.064	0.042	
	Memorandum item: statistical properties of the equation	adj R^2	df	F	error prob.		
		36.300	111.000	8.921	.000		

8. Environmental Performance Index (EPI)	B	Standard error	Beta	t-value	Error probability	Environment
Constant	−66.751	27.623		−2.417	0.017	
Percentage of world population	−0.548	0.216	−0.100	−2.536	0.012	
ln GDP per capita	23.041	6.605	2.158	3.489	0.001	
ln GDP per capita^2	−1.084	0.374	−1.750	−2.898	0.004	
Military personnel rate ln (MPR + 1)	**−3.298**	**0.806**	**−0.174**	**−4.091**	**0.000**	
MNC PEN – stock of inward FDI per GDP	**−0.094**	**0.033**	**−0.113**	**−2.871**	**0.005**	
UNDP Education Index	36.930	4.216	0.560	8.760	0.000	
Memorandum item: statistical properties of the equation	adj R^2	df	F	error prob.		
	78.900	140.000	88.259	.000		

9. Global footprint	B	Standard error	Beta	t-value	Error probability	Environment
Global Footprint Constant	31.026	4.440		6.988	0.000	
Foreign savings rate	**0.017**	**0.009**	**0.082**	**1.872**	**0.063**	
ln GDP per capita	−8.365	1.065	−4.870	−7.851	0.000	
ln GDP per capita^2	0.580	0.063	5.838	9.203	0.000	
Population density	0.000	0.000	−0.089	−2.283	0.024	

(Continued)

Dependent variable	Results – stepwise regression Independent variable	Statistical properties	Statistical properties	Statistical properties	Statistical properties	Statistical properties	Development dimension
	Independent variable	B	Standard error	Beta	t-value	Error probability	
9. Global footprint	Years of membership in EMU (2010)	−0.128	0.042	−0.141	−3.037	0.003	Environment
	Memorandum item: statistical properties of the equation	adj R^2	df	F	error prob.		
		81.200	135.000	117.592	.000		
10. ln (number of people per million inhabitants 1980–2000 killed by natural disasters per year + 1)	Independent variable	B	Standard error	Beta	t-value	Error probability	Environment
	Constant	−15.273	5.398		−2.830	0.005	
	ln GDP per capita	4.262	1.287	3.751	3.312	0.001	
	ln GDP per capita^2	−0.247	0.074	−3.741	−3.355	0.001	
	UNDP Education Index	−2.011	0.839	−0.289	−2.397	0.018	
	Immigration – share of population 2005 (%)	**−0.018**	**0.012**	**−0.124**	**−1.497**	**0.136**	
	Memorandum item: statistical properties of the equation	adj R^2	df	F	error prob.		
		14.400	159.000	7.713	.000		

| 11. ESI | | | | | | |
Independent variable	B	Standard error	Beta	t-value	Error probability	Environment
Constant	45.688	32.605		1.401	0.164	
Percentage of women in government, all levels	0.249	0.099	0.209	2.526	0.013	
2000 economic freedom score	0.158	0.083	0.195	1.912	0.058	
ln GDP per capita	−3.350	7.714	−0.492	−0.434	0.665	
ln GDP per capita^2	0.305	0.454	0.770	0.672	0.503	
Worker remittance inflows as a percentage of GDP	**−0.154**	**0.086**	**−0.144**	**−1.797**	**0.075**	
Memorandum item: statistical properties of the equation	adj R^2	df	F	error prob.		
	34.500	121.000	13.720	.000		

| 12. CO$_2$ per capita | | | | | | |
Independent variable	B	Standard error	Beta	t-value	Error probability	Environment
Constant	32.170	12.138		2.650	0.009	
FPZ (free production zones) employment as a percentage of total population	**0.331**	**0.063**	**0.238**	**5.281**	**0.000**	
ln GDP per capita	−9.438	2.877	−2.104	−3.281	0.001	
ln GDP per capita^2	0.706	0.168	2.713	4.214	0.000	
Openness Index, 1990 (export share per GDP + import share per GDP)	**−0.020**	**0.006**	**−0.164**	**−3.240**	**0.001**	

(Continued)

Dependent variable	Results – stepwise regression	Statistical properties	Statistical properties	Statistical properties	Statistical properties	Statistical properties	Development dimension
	Independent variable	B	Standard error	Beta	t-value	Error probability	
12. CO_2 per capita							Environment
	Population density	−0.001	0.001	−0.121	−2.710	0.007	
	Immigration – share of population 2005 (%)	**0.168**	**0.025**	**0.348**	**6.811**	**0.000**	
	Memorandum item: statistical properties of the equation	adj R^2	df	F	error prob.		
		72.700	159.000	71.594	.000		
13. Carbon emissions per million USD of GDP							Environment
	Independent variable	B	Standard error	Beta	t-value	Error probability	
	Constant	−6595.543	1383.628		−4.767	0.000	
	2000 economic freedom score	−7.988	3.279	−0.236	−2.436	0.016	
	Absolute latitude	12.325	2.012	0.544	6.125	0.000	
	ln GDP per capita	1792.705	325.022	5.614	5.516	0.000	
	ln GDP per capita^2	−111.407	19.201	−6.024	−5.802	0.000	
	Immigration – share of population 2005 (%)	**8.903**	**2.615**	**0.267**	**3.404**	**0.001**	
	Memorandum item: statistical properties of the equation	adj R^2	df	F	error prob.		
		35.000	144.000	16.535	.000		

14. Closing overall gender gap — Independent variable	B	Standard error	Beta	t-value	Error probability	Gender
Constant	0.516	0.216		2.389	0.019	
Percentage of women in government, all levels	0.002	0.001	0.186	2.683	0.009	
ln GDP per capita	0.015	0.050	0.288	0.297	0.767	
ln GDP per capita^2	0.001	0.003	0.193	0.201	0.841	
Military personnel rate ln (MPR + 1)	**−0.014**	**0.007**	**−0.156**	**−2.114**	**0.037**	
Worker remittance inflows as a percentage of GDP	**0.001**	**0.001**	**0.172**	**2.556**	**0.012**	
Muslim population share per total population	−0.001	0.000	−0.375	−5.168	0.000	
Memorandum item: statistical properties of the equation	adj R^2	df	F	error prob.		
	58.700	109.000	26.796	.000		

15. Female survival, probability of surviving to the age of 65 — Independent variable	B	Standard error	Beta	t-value	Error probability	Gender
Constant	−178.454	61.114		−2.920	0.004	
Quintile share income difference between the richest and poorest 20 per cent	**−0.618**	**0.122**	**−0.292**	**−5.052**	**0.000**	

(Continued)

Dependent variable	Results – stepwise regression	Statistical properties	Statistical properties	Statistical properties	Statistical properties	Statistical properties	Development dimension
	Independent variable	B	Standard error	Beta	t-value	Error probability	Gender
15. Female survival, probability of surviving to the age of 65	ln GDP per capita	49.109	14.514	3.133	3.383	0.001	
	ln GDP per capita^2	−2.304	0.820	−2.552	−2.809	0.006	
	public education expenditure per GNP	−1.406	0.546	−0.152	−2.575	0.011	
	UNDP Education Index	19.464	8.692	0.202	2.239	0.027	
	Memorandum item: statistical properties of the equation	adj R^2	df	F	error prob.		
		66.800	114.000	46.815	.000		

Dependent variable	Independent variable	B	Standard error	Beta	t-value	Error probability	Gender
16. Gender empowerment index	Constant	3.834	0.636		6.029	0.000	
	Percentage of women in government, all levels	0.005	0.001	0.200	3.499	0.001	
	ln GDP per capita	−0.845	0.143	−4.744	−5.926	0.000	
	ln GDP per capita^2	0.053	0.008	5.285	6.623	0.000	
	Muslim population share per total population	−0.002	0.000	−0.398	−6.768	0.000	

Memorandum item: statistical properties of the equation	adj R²	df	F	error prob.	
	81.500	70.000	77.895	.000	

17. Closing the economic gender gap						
Independent variable	**B**	**Standard error**	**Beta**	**t-value**	**Error probability**	**Gender**
Constant	1.246	0.469		2.658	0.009	
Percentage of women in government, all levels	0.005	0.001	0.274	3.474	0.001	
ln GDP per capita	−0.136	0.108	−1.349	−1.250	0.214	
ln GDP per capita²	0.007	0.006	1.263	1.169	0.245	
Muslim population share per total population	−0.002	0.000	−0.493	−6.222	0.000	

Memorandum item: statistical properties of the equation	adj R²	df	F	error prob.	
	40.100	122.000	21.380	.000	

18. Closing the political gender gap						
Independent variable	**B**	**Standard error**	**Beta**	**t-value**	**Error probability**	**Gender**
Constant	1.473	0.599		2.459	0.016	
ln GDP per capita	−0.343	0.142	−3.199	−2.413	0.018	
ln GDP per capita²	0.022	0.008	3.597	2.642	0.009	
Membership of the Islamic Conference	−0.044	0.026	−0.162	−1.729	0.087	

(Continued)

Dependent variable	Results – stepwise regression / Independent variable	Statistical properties	Statistical properties	Statistical properties	Statistical properties	Statistical properties	Development dimension
		B	Standard error	Beta	t-value	Error probability	
18. Closing the political gender gap	Independent variable						Gender
	Worker remittance inflows as a percentage of GDP	**0.003**	**0.002**	**0.194**	**1.948**	**0.054**	
	Immigration – share of population 2005 (%)	−0.003	0.002	−0.225	−2.251	0.026	
	Net international migration rate, 2005–2010	0.066	0.038	0.208	1.749	0.083	
	Memorandum item: statistical properties of the equation	adj R^2	df	F	error prob.		
		24.900	113.000	7.243	.000		
19. Avoiding net trade of ecological footprint gha per capita	Independent variable	B	Standard error	Beta	t-value	Error probability	Global ecological justice
	Constant	−85.394	31.144		−2.742	0.007	
	Percentage of women in government, all levels	−0.130	0.072	−0.125	−1.801	0.074	
	Comparative price levels (US = 1.00)	**−8.056**	**2.312**	**−0.401**	**−3.485**	**0.001**	
	ln GDP per capita	22.761	7.550	3.880	3.015	0.003	
	ln GDP per capita^2	−1.436	0.462	−4.195	−3.109	0.002	

	B	Standard error	Beta	t-value	Error probability	Happiness
Years of membership in the EU (2010)	0.234	0.050	0.396	4.716	0.000	
Memorandum item: statistical properties of the equation	adj R²	df	F	error prob.		
	40.900	138.000	20.111	.000		

20. Happy Planet Index (HPI)

Independent variable	B	Standard error	Beta	t-value	Error probability	Happiness
Constant	−280.000	46.695		−5.996	0.000	
Foreign savings rate	**−0.236**	**0.112**	**−0.189**	**−2.105**	**0.037**	
ln GDP per capita	73.912	11.094	7.100	6.662	0.000	
ln GDP per capita²	−4.158	0.649	−6.908	−6.411	0.000	
Worker remittance inflows as a percentage of GDP	**0.587**	**0.135**	**0.356**	**4.346**	**0.000**	
Memorandum item: statistical properties of the equation	adj R²	df	F	error prob.		
	38.000	119.000	19.217	.000		

21. Happy life years

Independent variable	B	Standard error	Beta	t-value	Error probability	Happiness
Constant	−87.614	35.855		−2.444	0.016	
ln GDP per capita	19.100	8.451	1.542	2.260	0.026	
ln GDP per capita²	−0.460	0.490	−0.644	−0.938	0.350	
Military expenditures per GDP	**−0.754**	**0.318**	**−0.113**	**−2.370**	**0.020**	

(Continued)

Dependent variable	Results – stepwise regression / Independent variable	Statistical properties					Development dimension
		B	**Standard error**	**Beta**	**t-value**	**Error probability**	
21. Happy life years	**Worker remittance inflows as a percentage of GDP**	**0.257**	**0.112**	**0.118**	**2.295**	**0.024**	**Happiness**
	Memorandum item: statistical properties of the equation	adj R^2	df	F	error prob.		
		77.100	102.000	86.653	.000		
22. Life satisfaction (0–10)	**Independent variable**	**B**	**Standard error**	**Beta**	**t-value**	**Error probability**	**Happiness**
	Constant	–6.732	3.790		–1.776	0.079	
	Absolute latitude	–0.017	0.006	–0.215	–2.854	0.005	
	ln GDP per capita	1.816	0.899	1.542	2.021	0.046	
	ln GDP per capita^2	–0.036	0.053	–0.528	–0.680	0.498	
	Worker remittance inflows as a percentage of GDP	**0.035**	**0.011**	**0.188**	**3.260**	**0.001**	
	Memorandum item: statistical properties of the equation	adj R^2	df	F	error prob.		
		69.400	113.000	64.990	.000		
23. Per capita world-class universities	**Independent variable**	**B**	**Standard error**	**Beta**	**t-value**	**Error probability**	**Knowledge society**
	Constant	3.509	1.307		2.684	0.009	

Independent variable	B	Standard error	Beta	t-value	Error probability	Knowledge society
Percentage of women in government, all levels	0.007	0.003	0.164	2.431	0.017	
Comparative price levels (US = 1.00)	**0.179**	**0.105**	**0.204**	**1.713**	**0.090**	
ln GDP per capita	−0.911	0.310	−3.258	−2.941	0.004	
ln GDP per capita^2	0.054	0.018	3.411	2.942	0.004	
Military personnel rate ln (MPR + 1)	**0.099**	**0.032**	**0.214**	**3.075**	**0.003**	
MNC outward investments (stock) per GDP	**0.011**	**0.002**	**0.371**	**4.988**	**0.000**	
Openness Index, 1990 (export share per GDP + import share per GDP)	**−0.002**	**0.000**	**−0.324**	**−5.161**	**0.000**	
Public education expenditure per GNP	0.031	0.010	0.197	3.078	0.003	
Memorandum item: statistical properties of the equation	adj R^2	df	F	error prob.		
	64.900	107.000	25.749	.000		
24. Tertiary enrolment ratio						
Constant	1.275	0.540		2.362	0.020	
Annual population growth rate, 1975–2005 (%)	−0.055	0.011	−0.308	−4.989	0.000	
ln GDP per capita	−0.364	0.129	−2.013	−2.815	0.006	
ln GDP per capita^2	0.024	0.007	2.328	3.348	0.001	

(Continued)

Dependent variable	Results – stepwise regression / Independent variable	Statistical properties	Statistical properties	Statistical properties	Statistical properties	Statistical properties	Development dimension
		B	Standard error	Beta	t-value	Error probability	
24. Tertiary enrolment ratio							Knowledge society
	Membership of the Islamic Conference	0.062	0.025	0.132	2.460	0.015	
	Openness Index, 1990 (export share per GDP + import share per GDP)	**−0.001**	**0.000**	**−0.133**	**−2.836**	**0.005**	
	UNDP Education Index	0.492	0.096	0.443	5.116	0.000	
	Memorandum item: statistical properties of the equation	adj R²	df	F	error prob.		
		73.700	136.000	64.501	.000		
25. Global tolerance index	Independent variable	B	Standard error	Beta	t-value	Error probability	Multicultural tolerance
	Constant	1.636	1.019		1.606	0.113	
	Comparative price levels (US = 1.00)	**0.157**	**0.081**	**0.366**	**1.951**	**0.055**	
	ln GDP per capita	−0.285	0.239	−1.817	−1.194	0.237	
	ln GDP per capita²	0.018	0.014	2.071	1.264	0.211	
	Muslim population share per total population	−0.002	0.000	−0.323	−3.987	0.000	
	Memorandum item: statistical properties of the equation	adj R²	df	F	error prob.		
		66.300	64.000	34.516	.000		

26. Infant mortality (2005)	Independent variable	B	Standard error	Beta	t-value	Error probability	Social inclusion
	Constant	576.606	83.129		6.936	0.000	
	2000 economic freedom score	−0.777	0.179	−0.214	−4.337	0.000	
	ln GDP per capita	−87.974	19.619	−2.592	−4.484	0.000	
	ln GDP per capita^2	4.453	1.120	2.264	3.977	0.000	
	MNC PEN – stock of inward FDI per GDP	**0.364**	**0.085**	**0.160**	**4.285**	**0.000**	
	UNDP Education Index	−94.037	12.705	−0.441	−7.402	0.000	
	Memorandum item: statistical properties of the equation	adj R^2	df	F	error prob.		
		79.400	152.000	117.921	.000		

27. Life expectancy (years)	Independent variable	B	Standard error	Beta	t-value	Error probability	Social inclusion
	Constant	−63.159	27.661		−2.283	0.025	
	ln GDP per capita	23.657	6.558	2.810	3.608	0.000	
	ln GDP per capita^2	−0.914	0.383	−1.882	−2.387	0.019	
	Worker remittance inflows as a percentage of GDP	**0.324**	**0.073**	**0.247**	**4.436**	**0.000**	
	Quintile share income difference between richest and poorest 20 per cent	**−0.187**	**0.063**	**−0.156**	**−2.990**	**0.004**	

(Continued)

Dependent variable	Results – stepwise regression	Statistical properties	Statistical properties	Statistical properties	Statistical properties	Statistical properties	Development dimension
	Independent variable	B	Standard error	Beta	t-value	Error probability	Social inclusion
27. Life expectancy (years)	Public education expenditure per GNP	−0.654	0.274	−0.131	−2.389	0.019	
	Memorandum item: statistical properties of the equation	adj R²	df	F	error prob.		
		74.800	105.000	63.293	.000		

Dependent variable	Independent variable	B	Standard error	Beta	t-value	Error probability	Social inclusion
28. Quintile share income difference between the richest and poorest 20 per cent	Constant	9.775	55.216		0.177	0.860	
	Annual population growth rate, 1975–2005 (%)	4.236	1.146	0.471	3.696	0.000	
	Comparative price levels (US = 1.00)	**−8.866**	**5.337**	**−0.300**	**−1.661**	**0.099**	
	Foreign savings rate	**0.203**	**0.074**	**0.251**	**2.730**	**0.007**	
	ln GDP per capita	−3.599	13.441	−0.443	−0.268	0.789	
	ln GDP per capita²	0.394	0.836	0.835	0.471	0.638	
	MNC PEN – stock of inward FDI per GDP	**0.139**	**0.055**	**0.221**	**2.532**	**0.013**	

Independent variable	B	Standard error	Beta	t-value	Error probability	Social inclusion
Immigration – share of population 2005 (%)	**−0.250**	**0.122**	**−0.196**	**−2.042**		**0.044**
Muslim population share per total population	−0.082	0.025	−0.299	−3.344		0.001
Memorandum item: statistical properties of the equation	adj R²	df	F	error prob.		
	25.500	119.000	6.098	.000		

29. Unemployment rate						
Independent variable	B	Standard error	Beta	t-value	Error probability	
Constant	−90.856	27.685		−3.282	0.001	
Quintile share income difference between richest and poorest 20 per cent	**0.161**	**0.061**	**0.238**	**2.656**	**0.009**	
Foreign savings rate	**0.154**	**0.044**	**0.328**	**3.522**	**0.001**	
ln GDP per capita	20.749	6.541	3.949	3.172	0.002	
ln GDP per capita²	−1.141	0.381	−3.774	−2.991	0.004	
Public education expenditure per GNP	0.548	0.275	0.179	1.990	0.049	
Muslim population share per total population	0.053	0.016	0.302	3.369	0.001	
Memorandum item: statistical properties of the equation	adj R²	df	F	error prob.		
	35.400	103.000	10.416	.000		

(Continued)

Dependent variable	Results – stepwise regression	Statistical properties	Statistical properties	Statistical properties	Statistical properties	Statistical properties	Development dimension
30. Human Development Index	Independent variable	B	Standard error	Beta	t-value	Error probability	Social inclusion
	Constant	−0.575	0.202		−2.852	0.005	
	ln GDP per capita	0.127	0.048	0.836	2.657	0.009	
	ln GDP per capita^2	−0.002	0.003	−0.263	−0.852	0.396	
	Openness Index, 1990 (export share per GDP + import share per GDP)	**0.000**	**0.000**	**−0.060**	**−2.874**	**0.005**	
	Public education expenditure per GNP	−0.005	0.002	−0.052	−2.445	0.016	
	UNDP Education Index	0.503	0.031	0.530	16.021	0.000	
	Muslim population share per total population	0.000	0.000	0.075	3.366	0.001	
	Memorandum item: statistical properties of the equation	adj R^2	df	F	error prob.		
		95.000	133.000	425.085	.000		

Appendix 2: The Crisis Performance Index (Factor Analytical), 2009–2010 and After

Based on:

- IMF prediction growth rate in 2009 (issued April 2009)
- IMF prediction growth rate in 2010 (issued April 2009)
- Residual measure: crisis recovery 2010 vis-à-vis 2009 (based on IMF prognosis, April 2009)
- Resilience of economic growth during the crisis (regression residuals: growth 1990–2005 > growth 2009, based on IMF prognosis, April 2009)

Data available via http://www.imf.org/external/pubs/ft/weo/2009/01/weodata/weoselgr.aspx

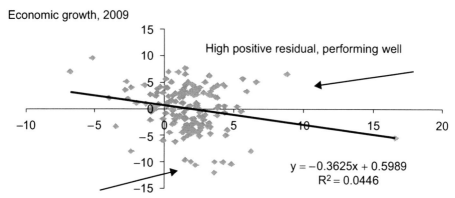

Note: 5,00 equals 5.0, 10,0 equals 10.0 etc.

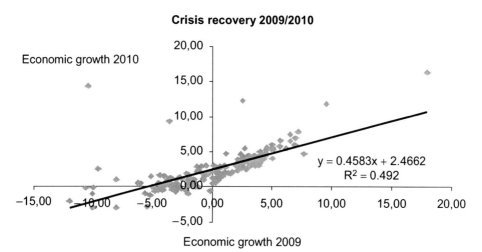

Note: 5,00 equals 5.0, 10,0 equals 10.0 etc.

	Extraction
IMF prediction growth rate in 2009	0.885
IMF prediction growth rate in 2010	0.768
Residual measure: crisis recovery 2009/2010	0.044
Regression residual growth 1990–2005 → growth 2009	0.869

Eigenvalue	% of total variance explained
2,565	64,131

	The factor loadings – crisis performance index
IMF prediction growth rate in 2009	0.941
IMF prediction growth rate in 2010	0.876
Residual measure: crisis recovery 2009/2010	0.210
Regression residual growth 1990–2005 → growth 2009	0.932

The components of the crisis performance index – predicted economic growth 2009

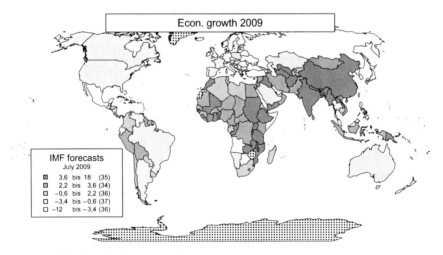

Bis is shorthand for 'ranging from… to…'

The components of the crisis performance index – predicted economic growth 2009

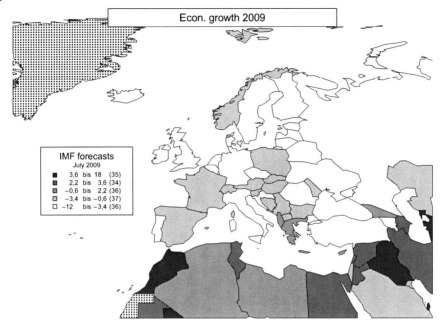

Bis is shorthand for 'ranging from… to…'

The components of the crisis performance index – predicted economic growth 2009

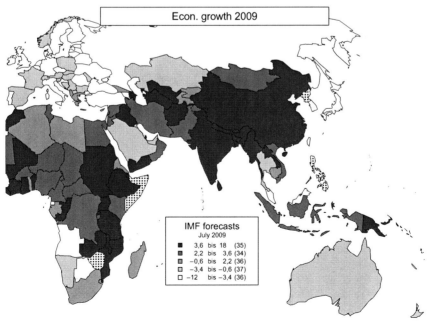

Bis is shorthand for 'ranging from… to…'

The components of the crisis performance index – predicted economic growth 2009

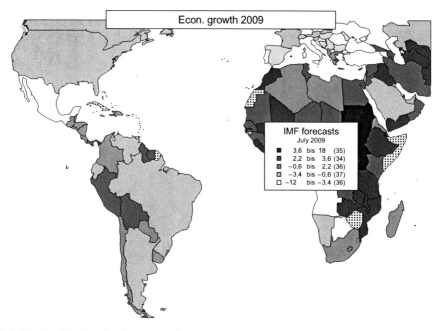

Bis is shorthand for 'ranging from… to…'

The components of the crisis performance index – predicted economic growth 2010

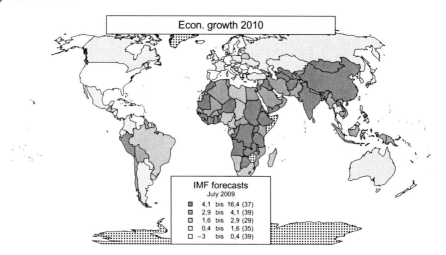

Bis is shorthand for 'ranging from… to…'

The components of the crisis performance index – predicted economic growth 2010

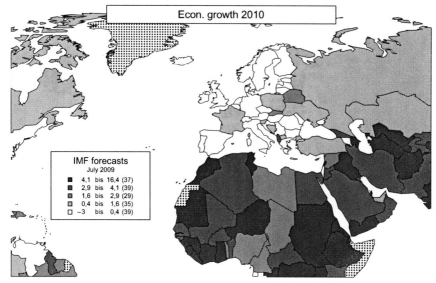

Bis is shorthand for 'ranging from… to…'

The components of the crisis performance index – the resilience of predicted economic growth 2009 vis-à-vis earlier growth

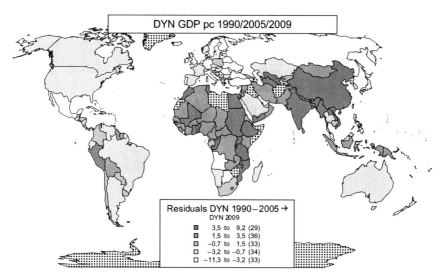

Bis is shorthand for 'ranging from… to…'

The components of the crisis performance index – the resilience of predicted economic growth 2009 vis-à-vis earlier growth

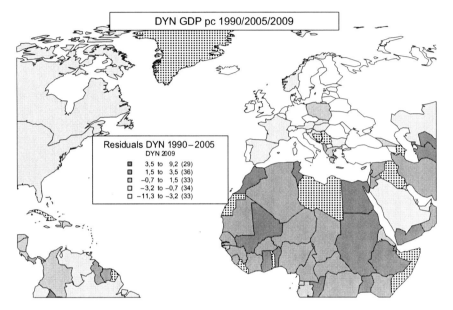

Bis is shorthand for 'ranging from… to…'

Appendix 3: The Dynamics of Globalization since 1980 in 29 Major Economies of the World – The Time Series

Sources

Economic growth: IMF growth data and growth predictions, http://www.imf.org/external/datamapper/index.php (data download April 2009).

Globalization: ETH Zurich globalization time series data, http://globalization.kof.ethz.ch/static/rawdata/globalization_2010_short.xls (data downloaded January 2010). The Zurich data, used in our graphs, refer to the ETH economic globalization time series only, which covers 'actual flows', combining trade (percentage of GDP), foreign direct investment (flows, percentage of GDP); foreign direct investment (stocks, percentage of GDP); portfolio investment (percentage of GDP); and income payments to foreign nationals (percentage of GDP). The ETH Zurich globalization data are weighted according to the following key:

A. Economic globalization		(Economic globalization accounts for 37% of the ETH overall globalization factor)
i) Actual flows		0.50
	Trade (percentage of GDP)	0.19
	Foreign direct investment, flows (percentage of GDP)	0.20
	Foreign direct investment, stocks (percentage of GDP)	0.24
	Portfolio investment (percentage of GDP)	0.17
	Income payments to foreign nationals (percentage of GDP)	0.20

Inequality: Theil index of inequality, based on payment in 21 industrial sectors; calculated from UNIDO sources in the University of Texas inequality project, http://utip.gov.utexas.edu/data.html (data downloaded January 2010).

Unemployment: Unemployment as a percentage of the civilian labour force, http://stats.oecd.org/Index.aspx (1 August 2011).

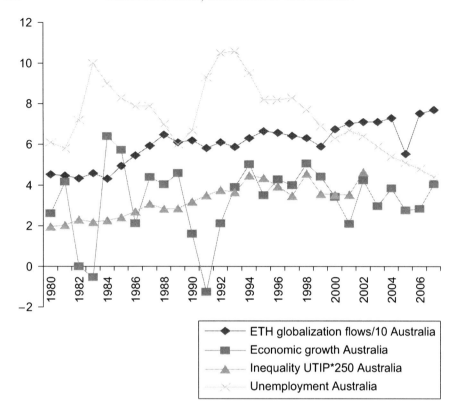

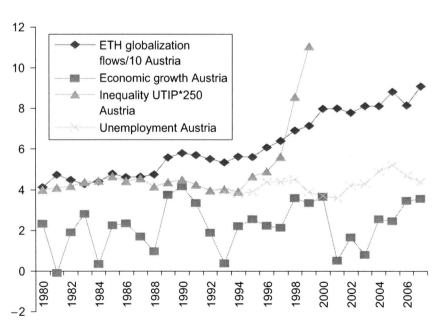

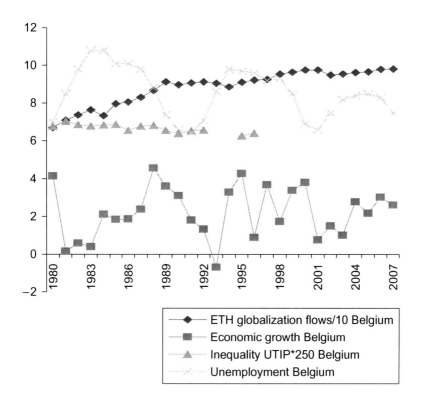

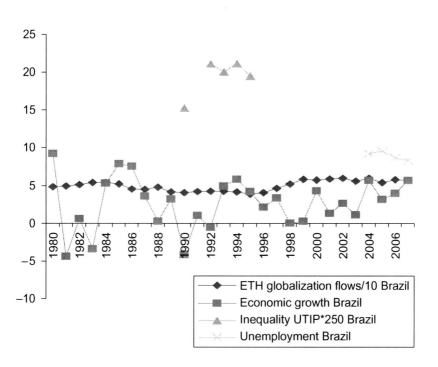

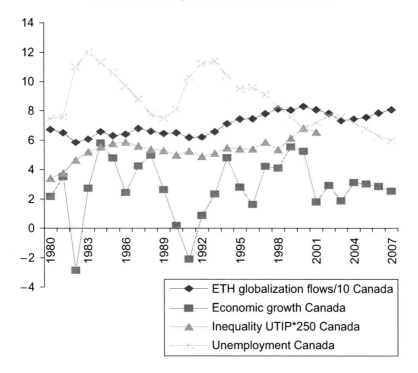

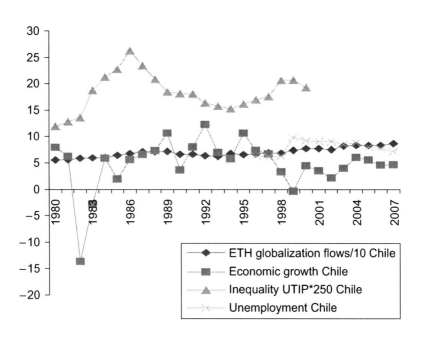

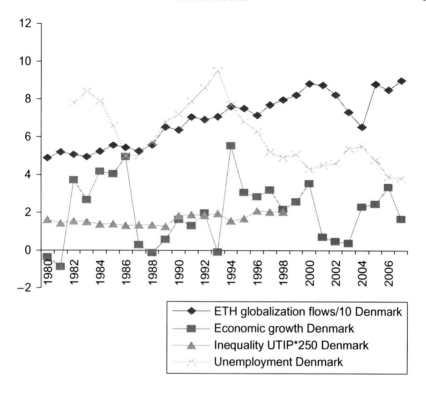

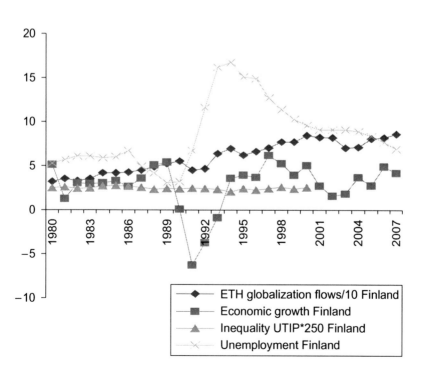

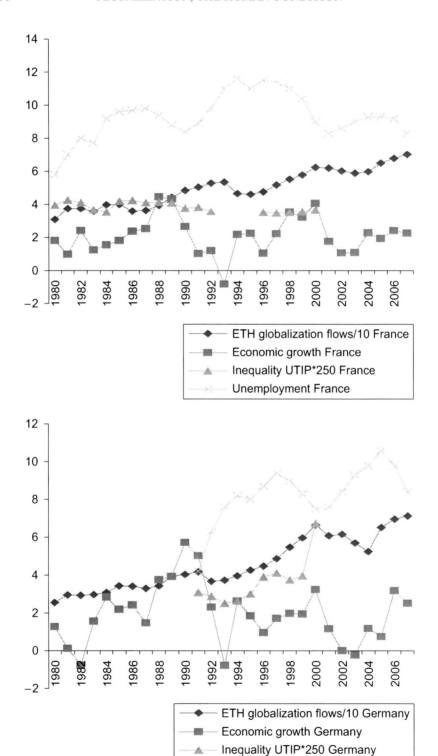

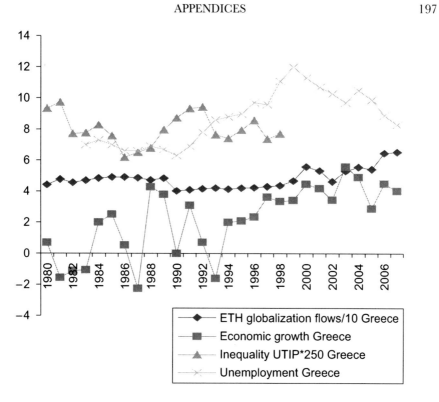

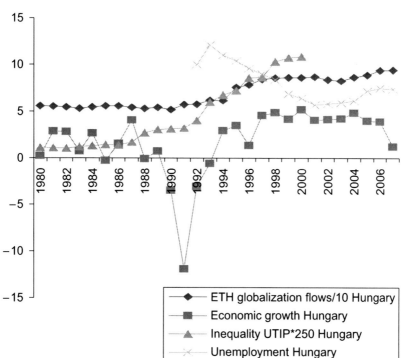

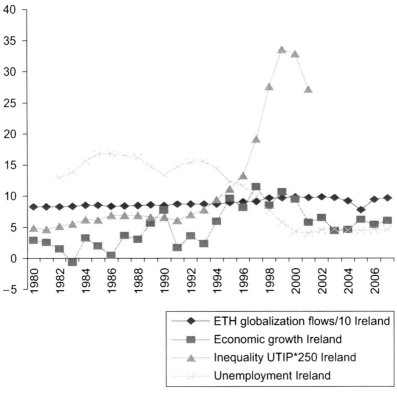

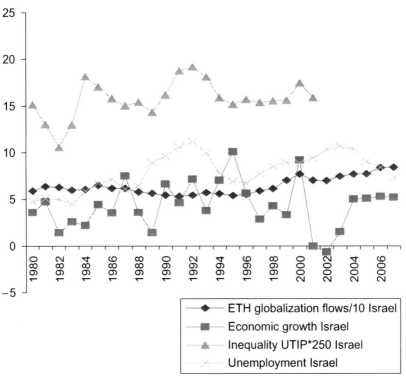

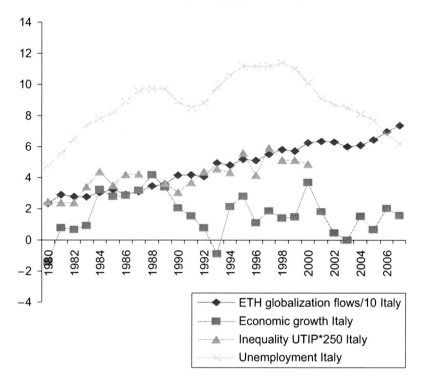

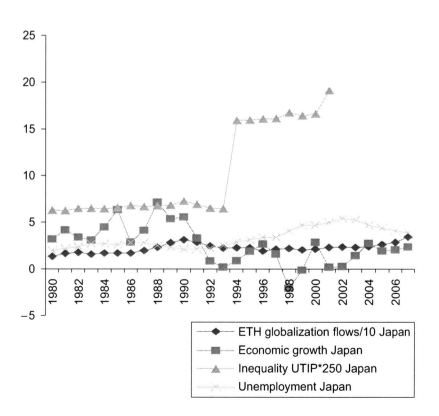

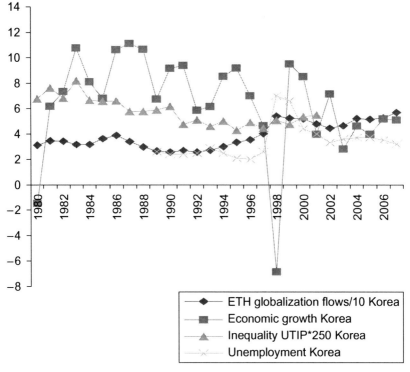

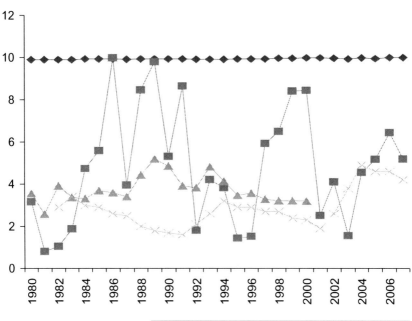

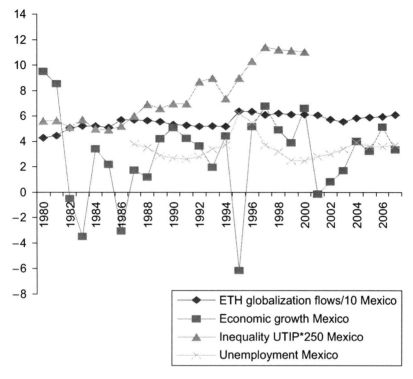

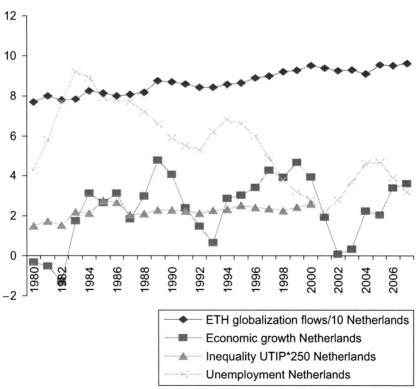

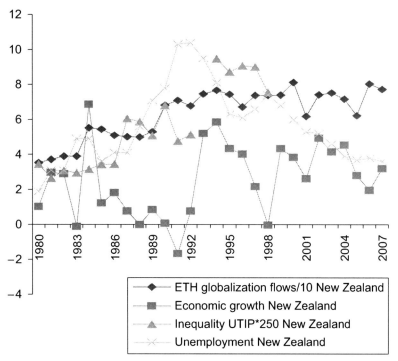

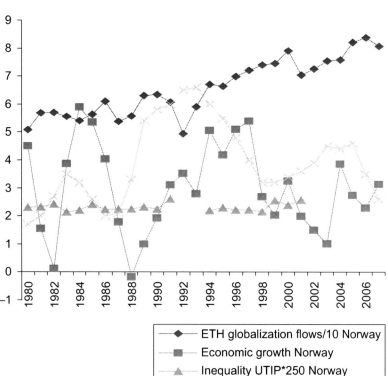

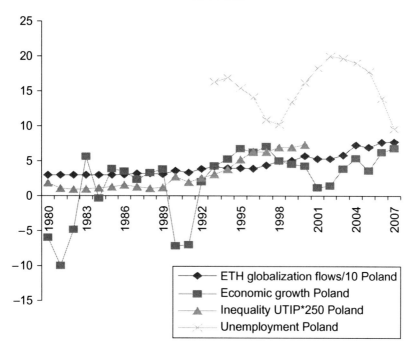

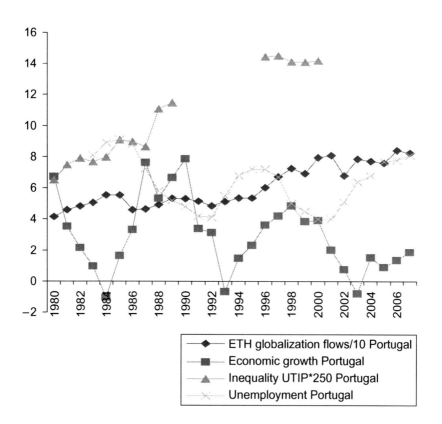

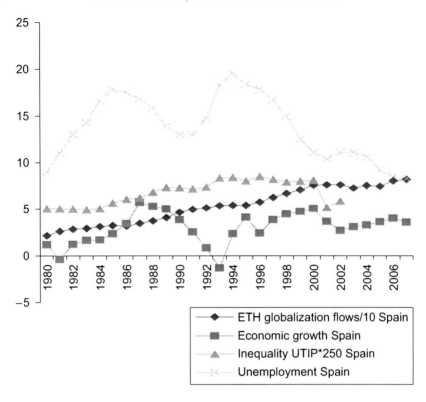

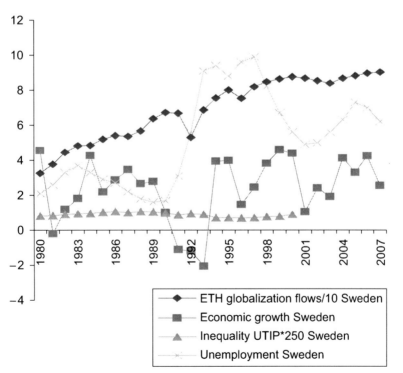

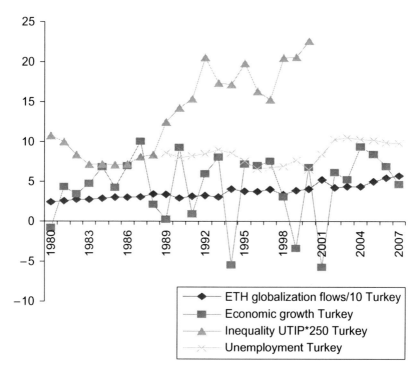

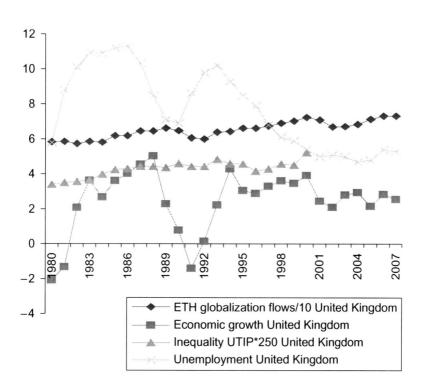

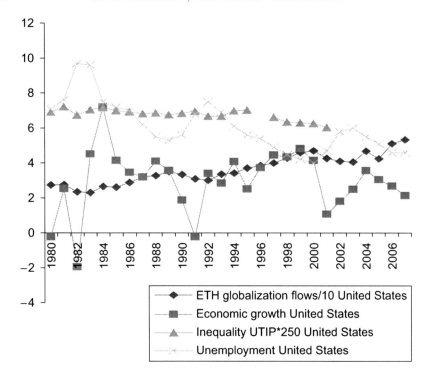

Appendix 4: The Dynamics of Globalization and Inequality since 1970 in Some Major Developing Economies and in the World System as a Whole

Sources:

Globalization: ETH Zurich globalization time series data, http://globalization.kof. ethz.ch/static/rawdata/globalization_2010_short.xls (data downloaded January 2010).

Inequality: See above, Theil index of inequality, based on the University of Texas inequality project, http://utip.gov.utexas.edu/data.html (data downloaded January 2010).

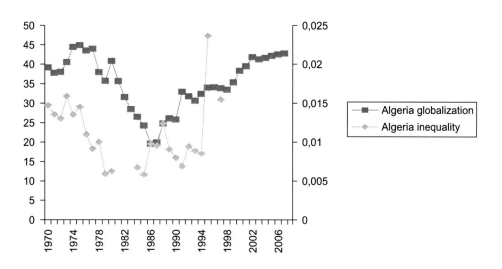

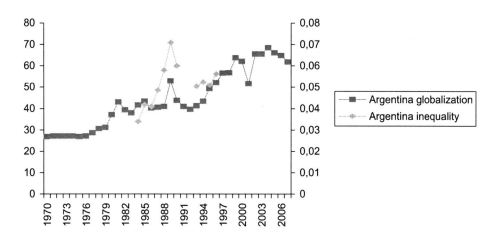

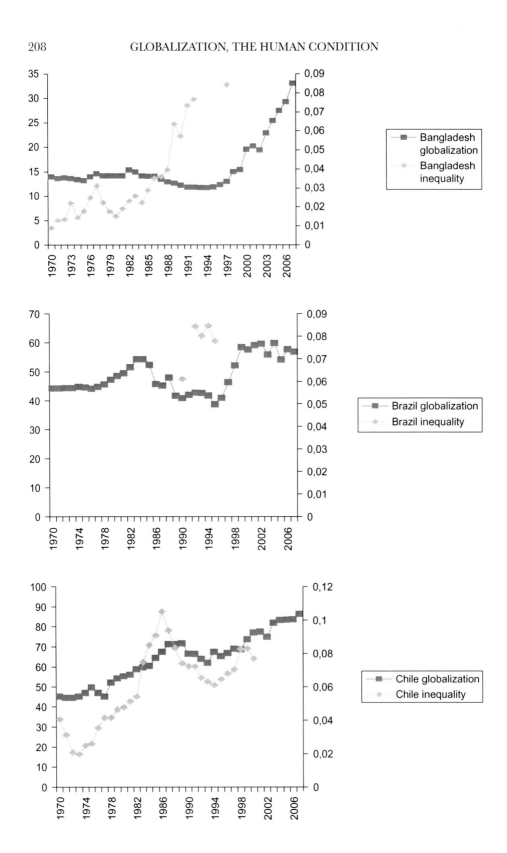

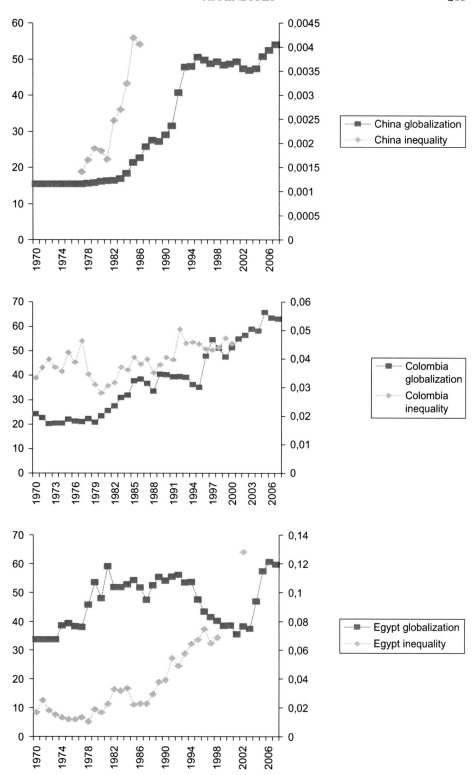

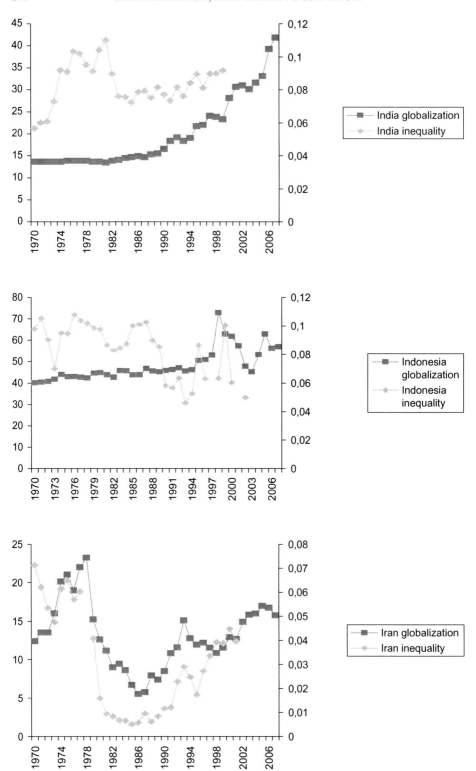

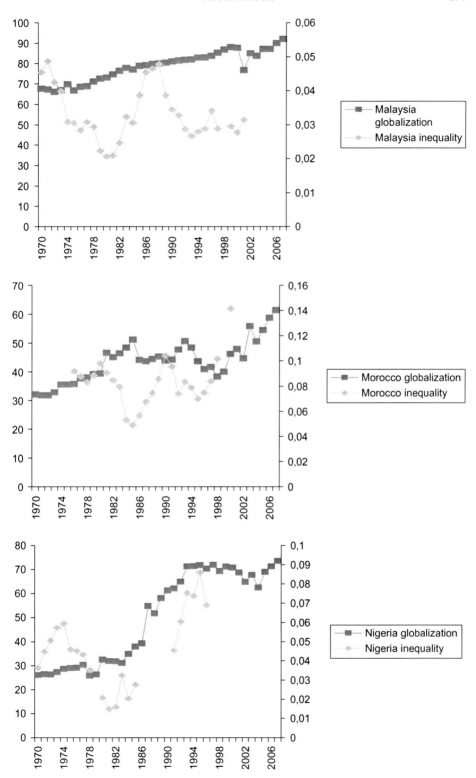

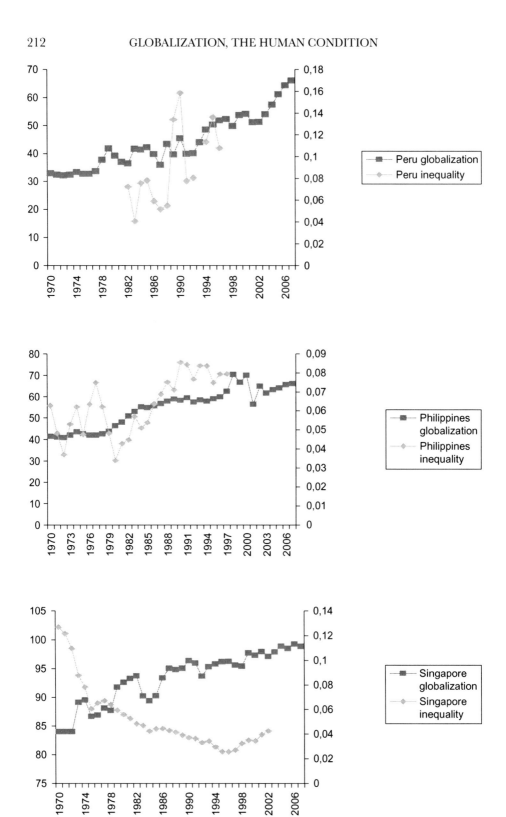

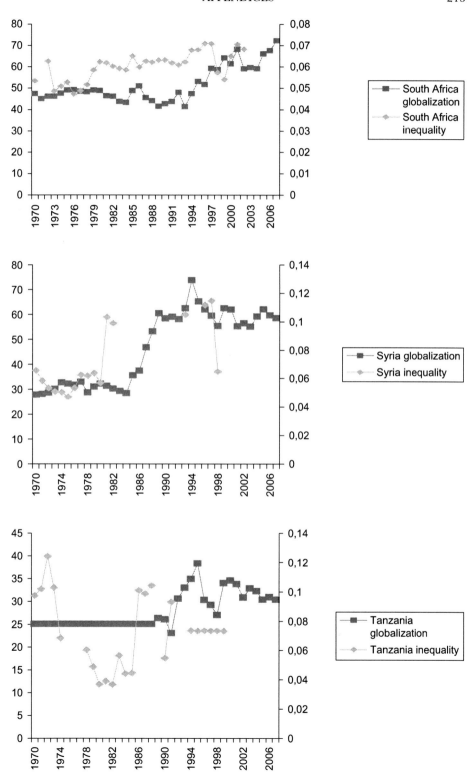

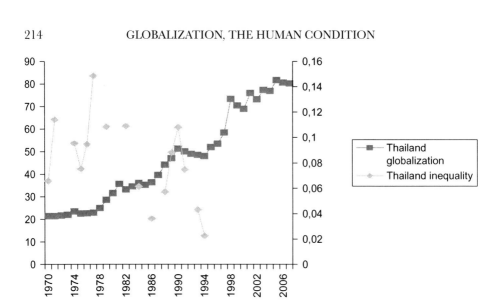

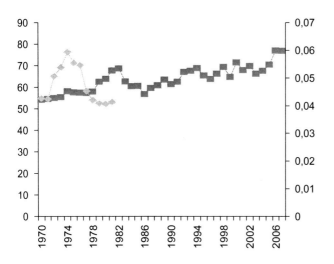

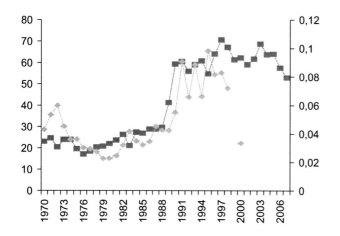 

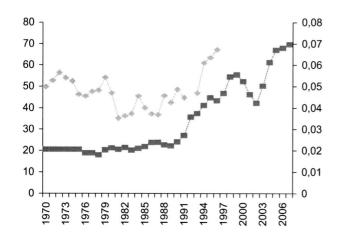 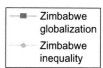

Appendix 5: A Non-parametric Global Development Index, Based on 35 Variables

	Non-parametric – 35 equal weights	Non-parametric, weighting each dimension equally	Democracy	Economic growth	Environment	Gender	Human development	R&D	Social cohesion
	Overall 35 development index	Overall 35 development index, based on 7 dimensions	Overall 35 development index, based on 7 dimensions	Overall 35 development index, based on 7 dimensions	Overall 35 development index, based on 7 dimensions	Overall 35 development index, based on 7 dimensions	Overall 35 development index, based on 7 dimensions	Overall 35 development index, based on 7 dimensions	Overall 35 development index, based on 7 dimensions
Albania	0.585	0.543	0.449	0.418	0.794	0.558	0.787	0.068	0.725
Algeria	0.519	0.497	0.271	0.435	0.713	0.527	0.702	0.063	0.764
Angola	0.392		0.224	0.465	0.597	0.595	0.16	0.002	
Antigua and Barbuda	0.554		0.649	0.294	0.857		0.852	0	0.818
Argentina	0.663	0.617	0.581	0.312	0.831	0.757	0.85	0.229	0.761
Armenia	0.509	0.496	0.39	0.283	0.651	0.477	0.714	0.092	0.865
Australia	0.73	0.724	0.914	0.328	0.654	0.778	0.962	0.515	0.915
Austria	0.756	0.731	0.889	0.288	0.823	0.753	0.949	0.477	0.938
Azerbaijan	0.499	0.506	0.226	0.638	0.652	0.49	0.615	0.101	0.818
Bahamas	0.635	0.622	0.791	0.232	0.925	0.76	0.827	0	0.818
Bahrain	0.556	0.596	0.571	0.448	0.782	0.493	0.897	0.115	0.864
Bangladesh	0.496	0.496	0.321	0.531	0.617	0.485	0.523	0.029	0.936
Barbados	0.657	0.668	0.799	0.282	0.966	0.771	0.914	0.175	0.773
Belarus	0.561	0.574	0.285	0.301	0.704	0.751	0.752	0.257	0.965
Belgium	0.726	0.705	0.863	0.275	0.734	0.78	0.938	0.458	0.888
Belize	0.61	0.557	0.563	0.392	0.761	0.624	0.807	0	0.75

Benin	0.477	0.474	0.513	0.446	0.628	0.433	0.319	0.015	0.958
Bhutan	0.548		0.354	0.6	0.75		0.56	0	0.932
Bolivia	0.566	0.52	0.506	0.417	0.738	0.593	0.64	0.163	0.582
Bosnia and Herzegovina	0.501		0.372	0.24	0.735		0.692	0	0.295
Botswana	0.521	0.477	0.706	0.504	0.642	0.608	0.322	0.02	0.533
Brazil	0.623	0.567	0.558	0.345	0.848	0.632	0.79	0.094	0.706
Brunei Darussalam	0.508	0.573	0.399	0.313	0.851	0.584	0.913	0.065	0.386
Bulgaria	0.615	0.591	0.592	0.273	0.714	0.712	0.774	0.187	0.881
Burkina Faso	0.452	0.452	0.372	0.462	0.6	0.504	0.282	0.003	0.938
Burundi	0.4		0.235	0.407	0.611		0.2	0.004	0.937
Cambodia	0.493	0.479	0.31	0.428	0.674	0.558	0.435	0.012	0.938
Cameroon	0.441	0.426	0.193	0.407	0.674	0.51	0.314	0.021	0.861
Canada	0.729	0.721	0.925	0.319	0.656	0.774	0.957	0.512	0.905
Cape Verde	0.571		0.615	0.448	0.892		0.768	0	0.477
Cen African Republic	0.39		0.314	0.401	0.665		0.179	0.007	0.453
Chad	0.391	0.414	0.217	0.424	0.587	0.392	0.297	0.003	0.977
Chile	0.681	0.642	0.812	0.418	0.765	0.666	0.854	0.193	0.785
China	0.575	0.571	0.283	0.671	0.704	0.583	0.774	0.101	0.881
Colombia	0.614	0.554	0.432	0.34	0.814	0.674	0.81	0.106	0.669
Comoros	0.438		0.408	0.346	0.879		0.569	0.004	0.545
Congo	0.448		0.259	0.452	0.708		0.345	0	
Congo (Democratic Republic of)	0.41		0.157	0.639	0.629		0.198	0	
Costa Rica	0.716	0.659	0.764	0.374	0.897	0.748	0.919	0.072	0.838

(Continued)

	Non-parametric – 35 equal weights	Non-parametric, weighting each dimension equally	Overall 35 development index, based on 7 dimensions	Overall 35 development index, based on 7 dimensions	Overall 35 development index, based on 7 dimensions	Overall 35 development index, based on 7 dimensions	Overall 35 development index, based on 7 dimensions	Overall 35 development index, based on 7 dimensions	Overall 35 development index, based on 7 dimensions
	Overall 35 development index	**Overall 35 development index, based on 7 dimensions**	**Democracy**	**Economic growth**	**Environment**	**Gender**	**Human development**	**R&D**	**Social cohesion**
Côte d'Ivoire	0.434		0.269	0.446	0.785		0.252	0.031	0.871
Croatia	0.64	0.6	0.582	0.289	0.798	0.694	0.842	0.129	0.366
Cuba	0.629	0.593	0.227	0.44	0.823	0.741	0.854	0.11	0.955
Cyprus	0.649	0.628	0.751	0.383	0.761	0.61	0.915	0.091	0.886
Czech Republic	0.643	0.621	0.734	0.278	0.689	0.672	0.877	0.165	0.935
Denmark	0.761	0.744	0.961	0.276	0.741	0.825	0.939	0.526	0.939
Djibouti	0.431		0.409	0.465	0.658		0.406	0.003	0
Dominica	0.617		0.849	0.381	0.921		0.835	0	0.75
Dominican Republic	0.624	0.575	0.549	0.404	0.802	0.7	0.778	0.104	0.688
Ecuador	0.616	0.547	0.467	0.307	0.772	0.723	0.784	0	0.775
Egypt	0.537	0.5	0.271	0.453	0.763	0.426	0.736	0	0.852
El Salvador	0.593	0.551	0.521	0.337	0.737	0.679	0.749	0.079	0.754
Equatorial Guinea	0.351		0.252	0.365	0.988		0.378	0.011	0.455
Eritrea	0.421		0.33	0.427	0.82		0.45	0.006	
Estonia	0.612	0.598	0.695	0.181	0.63	0.719	0.79	0.264	0.909
Ethiopia	0.432	0.444	0.346	0.562	0.522	0.473	0.268	0.006	0.928

Fiji	0.585	0.572	0.599	0.321	0.811	0.616	0.774	0	0.886
Finland	0.794	0.769	0.953	0.232	0.784	0.954	0.956	0.592	0.91
France	0.731	0.702	0.853	0.289	0.783	0.79	0.929	0.389	0.882
Gabon	0.487		0.364	0.371	0.852		0.536	0.036	0.591
Gambia	0.504	0.508	0.333	0.462	0.824	0.673	0.416	0.006	0.844
Georgia	0.513	0.504	0.353	0.387	0.689	0.482	0.66	0.158	0.8
Germany	0.74	0.706	0.88	0.217	0.799	0.815	0.921	0.431	0.882
Ghana	0.549	0.523	0.528	0.499	0.713	0.619	0.453	0.014	0.834
Greece	0.652	0.632	0.725	0.322	0.696	0.65	0.906	0.248	0.876
Grenada	0.563		0.566	0.347	0.973		0.778	0	0.659
Guatemala	0.576	0.536	0.442	0.376	0.78	0.575	0.736	0.038	0.805
Guinea	0.425		0.272	0.447	0.631		0.342	0.004	0.915
Guinea-Bissau	0.418		0.356	0.369	0.743		0.204	0	0.86
Guyana	0.599	0.56	0.543	0.458	0.751	0.748	0.653	0.043	0.727
Haiti	0.433		0.179	0.34	0.649		0.437	0	0.702
Honduras	0.579	0.548	0.476	0.376	0.701	0.672	0.722	0.066	0.822
Hong Kong, China (SAR)	0.626		0.529	0.278	0.731		0.927	0.293	0.89
Hungary	0.653	0.631	0.767	0.284	0.735	0.674	0.803	0.241	0.91
Iceland	0.741	0.711	0.953	0.166	0.779	0.929	0.969	0.223	0.955
India	0.536	0.525	0.525	0.545	0.688	0.377	0.565	0.052	0.922
Indonesia	0.557	0.538	0.331	0.444	0.744	0.617	0.689	0.066	0.874
Iran	0.508	0.482	0.335	0.448	0.62	0.457	0.704	0.003	0.81
Ireland	0.734	0.707	0.893	0.196	0.759	0.808	0.953	0.425	0.916
Israel	0.693	0.684	0.708	0.304	0.738	0.687	0.924	0.557	0.872
Italy	0.674	0.656	0.762	0.246	0.725	0.658	0.925	0.381	0.896
Jamaica	0.611	0.573	0.571	0.269	0.78	0.695	0.76	0.074	0.859
Japan	0.685	0.674	0.862	0.232	0.724	0.656	0.936	0.359	0.947

(Continued)

	Overall 35 development index (Non-parametric – 35 equal weights)	Overall 35 development index, based on 7 dimensions (Non-parametric, weighting each dimension equally)	Democracy	Economic growth	Environment	Gender	Human development	R&D	Social cohesion
Jordan	0.563	0.542	0.345	0.456	0.758	0.539	0.739	0.13	0.825
Kazakhstan	0.533	0.522	0.27	0.332	0.643	0.727	0.657	0.141	0.882
Kenya	0.455	0.457	0.29	0.436	0.656	0.587	0.321	0.012	0.893
Korea (Republic of)	0.618	0.586	0.62	0.332	0.705	0.524	0.879	0.096	0.947
Kuwait	0.524		0.496	0.346	0.565	0.534	0.865	0.096	
Kyrgyzstan	0.549	0.541	0.279	0.367	0.718	0.738	0.604	0.188	0.893
Laos	0.538		0.166	0.519	0.768		0.555	0	0.963
Latvia	0.63	0.605	0.638	0.124	0.737	0.773	0.78	0.29	0.894
Lebanon	0.525		0.312	0.471	0.656		0.699	0.194	
Lesotho	0.472	0.465	0.555	0.407	0.87	0.82	0.278	0.011	0.315
Libya	0.495		0.219	0.368	0.784		0.831	0.224	
Lithuania	0.64	0.608	0.672	0.113	0.771	0.737	0.802	0.241	0.921
Luxembourg	0.633	0.619	0.828	0.27	0.666	0.681	0.937	0.041	0.909
Macedonia	0.539	0.5	0.497	0.296	0.635	0.634	0.767	0.111	0.558
Madagascar	0.512	0.496	0.523	0.338	0.634	0.674	0.406	0.009	0.89
Malawi	0.493	0.476	0.419	0.55	0.664	0.602	0.268	0	0.827
Malaysia	0.591	0.567	0.508	0.321	0.761	0.566	0.809	0.129	0.377
Maldives	0.516	0.52	0.37	0.394	0.97	0.519	0.707	0	0.682

Mali	0.468	0.452	0.509	0.479	0.637	0.458	0.262	0.007	0.81
Malta	0.599	0.588	0.554	0.339	0.759	0.606	0.898	0.098	0.864
Mauritania	0.457	0.443	0.332	0.444	0.554	0.551	0.487	0.016	0.718
Mauritius	0.619	0.622	0.711	0.432	0.891	0.634	0.837	0.051	0.795
Mexico	0.607	0.577	0.557	0.29	0.745	0.624	0.849	0.099	0.873
Moldova	0.574	0.549	0.459	0.212	0.728	0.707	0.694	0.127	0.919
Mongolia	0.59	0.573	0.673	0.464	0.612	0.694	0.63	0.152	0.782
Morocco	0.54	0.518	0.349	0.485	0.748	0.487	0.669	0.046	0.845
Mozambique	0.472	0.48	0.437	0.509	0.521	0.749	0.207	0.001	0.935
Myanmar	0.486		0.092	0.548	0.76		0.525	0.052	0.864
Namibia	0.508	0.432	0.602	0.35	0.661	0.698	0.426	0.026	0.264
Nepal	0.513	0.489	0.409	0.454	0.709	0.478	0.515	0.02	0.839
Netherlands	0.761	0.735	0.95	0.243	0.785	0.815	0.942	0.475	0.932
New Zealand	0.772	0.764	0.933	0.312	0.716	0.867	0.943	0.662	0.916
Nicaragua	0.598	0.57	0.507	0.357	0.726	0.716	0.744	0.052	0.887
Niger	0.415		0.331	0.441	0.599		0.231	0.006	0.824
Nigeria	0.436	0.432	0.231	0.415	0.645	0.54	0.287	0.018	0.89
Norway	0.793	0.778	0.926	0.321	0.74	0.963	0.968	0.564	0.965
Oman	0.536		0.48	0.455	0.759	0.492	0.866	0.038	
Pakistan	0.475	0.456	0.308	0.434	0.691	0.311	0.523	0	0.928
Panama	0.674	0.626	0.661	0.465	0.818	0.701	0.853	0.16	0.727
Papua New Guinea	0.532		0.502	0.447	0.78		0.493	0.009	0.875
Paraguay	0.588	0.537	0.424	0.338	0.784	0.702	0.765	0.045	0.703
Peru	0.621	0.585	0.522	0.481	0.782	0.677	0.729	0.131	0.775
Philippines	0.631	0.582	0.484	0.359	0.72	0.781	0.718	0.142	0.867
Poland	0.662	0.64	0.699	0.374	0.718	0.704	0.848	0.28	0.859
Portugal	0.677	0.645	0.835	0.259	0.736	0.701	0.862	0.26	0.86

(Continued)

	Non-parametric— 35 equal weights	Non-parametric, weighting each dimension equally	Overall 35 development index, based on 7 dimensions	Overall 35 development index, based on 7 dimensions	Overall 35 development index, based on 7 dimensions	Overall 35 development index, based on 7 dimensions	Overall 35 development index, based on 7 dimensions	Overall 35 development index, based on 7 dimensions	Overall 35 development index, based on 7 dimensions
	Overall 35 development index	**Overall 35 development index, based on 7 dimensions**	**Democracy**	**Economic growth**	**Environment**	**Gender**	**Human development**	**R&D**	**Social cohesion**
Qatar	0.485	0.564	0.348	1	0.34	0.396	0.845	0.112	0.909
Romania	0.59	0.568	0.557	0.262	0.7	0.649	0.772	0.124	0.911
Russia	0.568	0.558	0.407	0.224	0.69	0.675	0.717	0.302	0.886
Rwanda	0.435		0.242	0.515	0.646		0.225	0.006	0.976
Saint Kitts and Nevis	0.519		0.717	0.324	0.804		0.844	0	
St. Lucia	0.543		0.775	0.296	0.795		0.822	0.116	0.523
St. Vincent and the Grenadines	0.562		0.612	0.353	0.93		0.803	0	0.545
Samoa	0.565		0.569	0.472	0.868		0.793	0.049	0.886
São Tomé and Príncipe	0.57		0.613	0.515	0.948		0.575	0	0.614
Saudi Arabia	0.52	0.511	0.307	0.355	0.725	0.407	0.813	0.104	0.864
Senegal	0.525	0.518	0.518	0.441	0.69	0.59	0.462	0.016	0.911
Seychelles	0.516		0.501	0.231	0.898		0.875	0	0.886
Sierra Leone	0.362		0.317	0.47	0.58		0.102	0.009	0.466
Singapore	0.616	0.605	0.575	0.194	0.778	0.6	0.916	0.28	0.89
Slovakia	0.641	0.609	0.662	0.348	0.749	0.679	0.824	0.138	0.862
Slovenia	0.698	0.671	0.79	0.333	0.787	0.68	0.899	0.28	0.931

Solomon Islands	0.475		0.409	0.411	0.715		0.632	0	0.273
South Africa	0.555	0.516	0.638	0.349	0.633	0.846	0.445	0.1	0.6
Spain	0.714	0.687	0.829	0.275	0.746	0.774	0.95	0.357	0.878
Sri Lanka	0.623	0.589	0.498	0.461	0.774	0.72	0.737	0.022	0.909
Sudan	0.363		0.103	0.516	0.511		0.436	0.03	
Suriname	0.586	0.594	0.701	0.416	0.895	0.65	0.763	0.031	0.705
Swaziland	0.354		0.245	0.372	0.69		0.266	0.023	0.546
Sweden	0.815	0.792	0.98	0.27	0.819	0.923	0.961	0.671	0.919
Switzerland	0.773	0.744	0.93	0.262	0.829	0.807	0.957	0.493	0.928
Syria	0.516	0.493	0.226	0.43	0.706	0.535	0.755	0.027	0.773
Tajikistan	0.497	0.502	0.24	0.352	0.662	0.653	0.588	0.063	0.953
Tanzania	0.489	0.48	0.407	0.522	0.63	0.632	0.257	0.002	0.914
Thailand	0.62	0.596	0.597	0.316	0.752	0.665	0.742	0.161	0.942
Timor-Leste	0.417		0.535	0.6				0	
Togo	0.408		0.296	0.361	0.635		0.366	0.016	
Trinidad and Tobago	0.607	0.584	0.63	0.409	0.633	0.763	0.754	0.029	0.869
Tunisia	0.588	0.553	0.416	0.477	0.777	0.543	0.765	0.099	0.793
Turkey	0.508	0.491	0.43	0.28	0.67	0.424	0.726	0.078	0.825
Turkmenistan	0.42		0.14	0.476	0.577		0.614	0	0.907
Uganda	0.498	0.494	0.26	0.556	0.674	0.72	0.324	0.012	0.913
Ukraine	0.544	0.534	0.457	0.176	0.63	0.655	0.715	0.198	0.907
United Arab Emirates	0.509	0.525	0.485	0.319	0.535	0.468	0.882	0.054	0.932
United Kingdom	0.74	0.722	0.893	0.266	0.748	0.783	0.926	0.539	0.901

(Continued)

	Non-parametric – 35 equal weights	Non-parametric, weighting each dimension equally	Overall 35 development index, based on 7 dimensions	Overall 35 development index, based on 7 dimensions	Overall 35 development index, based on 7 dimensions	Overall 35 development index, based on 7 dimensions	Overall 35 development index, based on 7 dimensions	Overall 35 development index, based on 7 dimensions	Overall 35 development index, based on 7 dimensions
	Overall 35 development index	Overall 35 development index, based on 7 dimensions	Democracy	Economic growth	Environment	Gender	Human development	R&D	Social cohesion
United States of America	0.742	0.751	0.888	0.289	0.664	0.773	0.929	0.819	0.89
Uruguay	0.671	0.631	0.736	0.378	0.792	0.676	0.844	0.165	0.829
Uzbekistan	0.514	0.517	0.148	0.564	0.595	0.696	0.641	0	0.975
Vanuatu	0.486		0.492	0.418	0.787		0.71	0	
Venezuela	0.568	0.546	0.445	0.25	0.684	0.664	0.799	0.13	0.843
Vietnam	0.571	0.561	0.264	0.512	0.743	0.648	0.768	0.043	0.946
Yemen	0.433	0.418	0.241	0.542	0.623	0.216	0.471	0	0.836
Zambia	0.449	0.431	0.383	0.46	0.659	0.52	0.179	0.01	0.303
Zimbabwe	0.387	0.367	0.18	0.201	0.602	0.528	0.173	0.017	0.869

Appendix 6: A Non-parametric Global Development Index, Based on 30 Variables and Its Multivariate Determinants

1 Human Development Index
2 Combined Failed States Index
3 Gender empowerment index
4 Global footprint
5 Infant mortality (2005)
6 Environmental Performance Index (EPI)
7 Happy life years
8 Life expectancy (years)
9 Tertiary enrolment ratio
10 CO_2 per capita
11 Life satisfaction (0–10)
12 Civil and political liberty violations
13 Female survival, probability of surviving to age 65
14 Global tolerance index
15 Per capita world-class universities
16 Crisis Performance Factor
17 Rule of law
18 Closing overall gender gap
19 Democracy measure
20 Economic growth IMF prediction growth rate in 2010
21 Avoiding net trade of ecological footprint gha per person
22 Closing the economic gender gap
23 Happy Planet Index (HPI)
24 Economic growth, 1990–2005
25 Unemployment rate
26 Carbon emissions per million US dollars GDP
27 ESI
28 Quintile share income difference between richest and poorest 20 per cent
29 Closing the political gender gap
30 ln (number of people per million inhabitants 1980–2000 killed by natural disasters per year + 1)

	Overall 35 development index	Rank in world society on the global development index, based on 35 variables	Overall global development index, based on 30 variables	Rank in world society on the global development index, based on 30 variables	Human Development Index (HDI) value 2004	Rank in world society, according to the UNDP HDI
Albania	0.585	71	0.612	66	0.784	71
Algeria	0.519	110	0.523	118	0.728	99
Angola	0.392	168	0.389	172	0.439	157
Antigua and Barbuda	0.554	91	0.607	68	0.808	58
Argentina	0.663	28	0.687	28	0.863	36
Armenia	0.509	120	0.543	107	0.768	79
Australia	0.730	15	0.744	14	0.957	3
Austria	0.756	8	0.776	8	0.944	14
Azerbaijan	0.499	127	0.527	116	0.736	97
Bahamas	0.635	38	0.644	41	0.825	51
Bahrain	0.556	89	0.557	98	0.859	39
Bangladesh	0.496	130	0.513	124	0.530	134
Barbados	0.657	30	0.672	32	0.879	31
Belarus	0.561	87	0.572	92	0.794	65
Belgium	0.726	17	0.744	15	0.945	12
Belize	0.610	58	0.619	62	0.751	93
Benin	0.477	139	0.490	140	0.428	159
Bhutan	0.548	94	0.567	95	0.538	132
Bolivia	0.566	82	0.581	87	0.692	112
Bosnia and Herzegovina	0.501	126	0.548	104		
Botswana	0.521	108	0.538	111	0.570	128
Brazil	0.623	46	0.632	51	0.792	67
Brunei	0.508	122	0.504	130	0.871	34

Bulgaria	0.615	54	0.628	54	0.816	54
Burkina Faso	0.452	147	0.453	149	0.342	170
Burundi	0.400	167	0.419	167	0.384	165
Cambodia	0.493	133	0.497	137	0.583	126
Cameroon	0.441	150	0.444	158	0.506	140
Canada	0.729	16	0.739	16	0.950	6
Cape Verde	0.571	77	0.622	59	0.722	103
Cen African Republic	0.390	170	0.410	168	0.353	168
Chad	0.391	169	0.402	170	0.368	167
Chile	0.681	23	0.688	26	0.859	38
China	0.575	75	0.590	80	0.768	78
Colombia	0.614	55	0.626	55	0.790	68
Comoros	0.438	151	0.477	142	0.556	129
Congo	0.448	149	0.477	143	0.520	137
Congo (Democratic Republic of)	0.410	165	0.429	166	0.391	163
Costa Rica	0.716	18	0.735	17	0.841	48
Côte d'Ivoire	0.434	154	0.463	146	0.421	160
Croatia	0.640	37	0.655	38	0.846	44
Cuba	0.629	42	0.638	43	0.826	50
Cyprus	0.649	33	0.667	33	0.903	29
Czech Republic	0.643	34	0.656	37	0.885	30
Denmark	0.761	6	0.786	6	0.943	15
Djibouti	0.431	158	0.451	150	0.494	144
Dominica	0.617	51	0.688	27	0.793	66
Dominican Republic	0.624	44	0.636	47	0.751	92
Ecuador	0.616	52	0.635	48	0.765	81
Egypt	0.537	100	0.542	108	0.702	108
El Salvador	0.593	64	0.602	72	0.729	98

(Continued)

	Overall 35 development index	Rank in world society on the global development index, based on 35 variables	Overall global development index, based on 30 variables	Rank in world society on the global development index, based on 30 variables	Human Development Index (HDI) value 2004	Rank in world society, according to the UNDP HDI
Equatorial Guinea	0.351	175	0.407	169	0.653	118
Eritrea	0.421	160	0.445	156	0.454	153
Estonia	0.612	56	0.626	56	0.858	40
Ethiopia	0.432	157	0.431	164	0.371	166
Fiji	0.585	72	0.591	79	0.758	88
Finland	0.794	2	0.818	2	0.947	9
France	0.731	14	0.745	13	0.942	16
Gabon	0.487	135	0.525	117	0.633	121
Gambia	0.504	125	0.505	129	0.479	151
Georgia	0.513	117	0.541	110	0.743	95
Germany	0.740	12	0.753	11	0.932	21
Ghana	0.549	92	0.560	97	0.532	133
Greece	0.652	32	0.663	35	0.921	24
Grenada	0.563	85	0.613	65	0.762	83
Guatemala	0.576	74	0.586	82	0.673	115
Guinea	0.425	159	0.445	157	0.445	156
Guinea-Bissau	0.418	162	0.443	159	0.349	169
Guyana	0.599	61	0.606	69	0.725	100
Haiti	0.433	156	0.467	145	0.482	150
Honduras	0.579	73	0.585	85	0.683	114
Hong Kong, China (SAR)	0.626	43	0.678	30	0.927	23
Hungary	0.653	31	0.667	34	0.869	35
Iceland	0.741	10	0.774	9	0.960	2
India	0.536	102	0.572	93	0.611	123

Indonesia	0.557	88	0.569	94	0.711	105
Iran	0.508	124	0.500	135	0.746	94
Ireland	0.734	13	0.762	10	0.956	4
Israel	0.693	21	0.713	21	0.927	22
Italy	0.674	26	0.691	24	0.940	18
Jamaica	0.611	57	0.632	52	0.724	101
Japan	0.685	22	0.698	22	0.949	7
Jordan	0.563	84	0.566	96	0.760	85
Kazakhstan	0.533	103	0.538	112	0.774	77
Kenya	0.455	146	0.455	147	0.491	147
Korea (Republic of)	0.618	50	0.638	44	0.912	26
Kuwait	0.524	107	0.523	119	0.871	33
Kyrgyzstan	0.549	93	0.551	103	0.705	107
Laos	0.538	99	0.576	90	0.553	130
Latvia	0.630	41	0.654	39	0.845	45
Lebanon	0.525	106	0.557	99	0.774	75
Lesotho	0.472	142	0.448	154	0.494	145
Libya	0.495	131	0.548	105	0.798	62
Lithuania	0.640	36	0.662	36	0.857	41
Luxembourg	0.633	39	0.639	42	0.945	13
Macedonia	0.539	98	0.555	101	0.796	64
Madagascar	0.512	118	0.504	131	0.509	139
Malawi	0.493	132	0.501	133	0.400	162
Malaysia	0.591	65	0.604	70	0.805	59
Maldives	0.516	112	0.538	113	0.739	96
Mali	0.468	144	0.478	141	0.338	171
Malta	0.599	62	0.604	71	0.875	32
Mauritania	0.457	145	0.443	160	0.486	149

(Continued)

	Overall 35 development index	Rank in world society on the global development index, based on 35 variables	Overall global development index, based on 30 variables	Rank in world society on the global development index, based on 30 variables	Human Development Index (HDI) value 2004	Rank in world society, according to the UNDP HDI
Mauritius	0.619	49	0.624	58	0.800	61
Mexico	0.607	60	0.620	60	0.821	53
Moldova	0.574	76	0.586	83	0.694	111
Mongolia	0.590	66	0.592	77	0.691	113
Morocco	0.540	97	0.546	106	0.640	120
Mozambique	0.472	143	0.474	144	0.390	164
Myanmar	0.486	136	0.518	122	0.581	127
Namibia	0.508	123	0.506	128	0.626	122
Nepal	0.513	116	0.532	114	0.527	135
Netherlands	0.761	7	0.783	7	0.947	11
New Zealand	0.772	5	0.793	5	0.936	20
Nicaragua	0.598	63	0.608	67	0.698	109
Niger	0.415	164	0.438	162	0.311	173
Nigeria	0.436	152	0.440	161	0.448	155
Norway	0.793	3	0.816	3	0.965	1
Oman	0.536	101	0.523	120	0.810	55
Pakistan	0.475	141	0.500	136	0.539	131
Panama	0.674	25	0.691	25	0.809	56
Papua New Guinea	0.532	104	0.574	91	0.523	136
Paraguay	0.588	69	0.601	73	0.757	89
Peru	0.621	47	0.635	49	0.767	80
Philippines	0.631	40	0.638	45	0.763	82
Poland	0.662	29	0.675	31	0.862	37
Portugal	0.677	24	0.694	23	0.904	28

Qatar	0.485	138	0.451	151	46
Romania	0.590	67	0.601	74	60
Russia	0.568	81	0.581	88	63
Rwanda	0.435	153	0.451	152	154
St. Kitts and Nevis	0.519	111	0.585	86	52
St. Lucia	0.543	96	0.596	75	69
St. Vincent and the Grenadines	0.562	86	0.620	61	86
Samoa	0.565	83	0.618	63	73
São Tomé and Príncipe	0.570	79	0.625	57	124
Saudi Arabia	0.520	109	0.512	125	74
Senegal	0.525	105	0.531	115	152
Seychelles	0.516	113	0.586	84	47
Sierra Leone	0.362	173	0.374	174	172
Singapore	0.616	53	0.638	46	25
Slovakia	0.641	35	0.653	40	42
Slovenia	0.698	20	0.720	20	27
Solomon Islands	0.475	140	0.516	123	125
South Africa	0.555	90	0.553	102	117
Spain	0.714	19	0.733	18	19
Sri Lanka	0.623	45	0.632	53	91
Sudan	0.363	172	0.380	173	138
Suriname	0.586	70	0.592	78	87
Swaziland	0.354	174	0.369	175	142
Sweden	0.815	1	0.845	1	5
Switzerland	0.773	4	0.794	4	10
Syria	0.516	114	0.512	126	104
Tajikistan	0.497	129	0.501	134	119
Tanzania	0.489	134	0.494	139	158

(Continued)

	Overall 35 development index	Rank in world society on the global development index, based on 35 variables	Overall global development index, based on 30 variables	Rank in world society on the global development index, based on 30 variables	Human Development Index (HDI) value 2004	Rank in world society, according to the UNDP HDI
Thailand	0.620	48	0.634	50	0.784	70
Timor-Leste	0.417	163	0.450	153		
Togo	0.408	166	0.431	165	0.495	143
Trinidad and Tobago	0.607	59	0.614	64	0.809	57
Tunisia	0.588	68	0.595	76	0.760	84
Turkey	0.508	121	0.520	121	0.757	90
Turkmenistan	0.420	161	0.446	155	0.724	102
Uganda	0.498	128	0.496	138	0.502	141
Ukraine	0.544	95	0.556	100	0.774	76
United Arab Emirates	0.509	119	0.503	132	0.839	49
United Kingdom	0.740	11	0.753	12	0.940	17
United States of America	0.742	9	0.728	19	0.948	8
Uruguay	0.671	27	0.680	29	0.851	43
Uzbekistan	0.514	115	0.510	127	0.696	110
Vanuatu	0.486	137	0.542	109	0.670	116
Venezuela	0.568	80	0.578	89	0.784	72
Vietnam	0.571	78	0.587	81	0.709	106
Yemen	0.433	155	0.432	163	0.492	146
Zambia	0.449	148	0.454	148	0.407	161
Zimbabwe	0.387	171	0.390	171	0.491	148

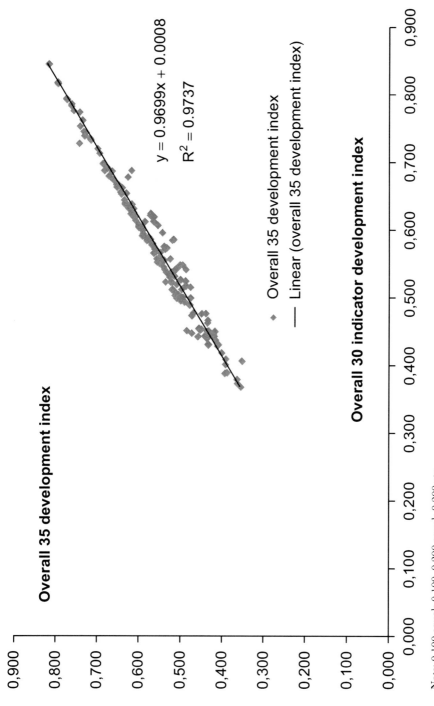

Overall 35 development index

y = 0.9699x + 0.0008
$R^2 = 0.9737$

• Overall 35 development index
—— Linear (overall 35 development index)

Overall 30 indicator development index

Note: 0,100 equals 0.100, 0,200 equals 0.200 etc.

Determinants:

Independent variable	B	Standard error	Beta	t-value	Error p.
Constant	0.257	0.353		0.729	0.468
Percentage of women in government, all levels	0.001	0.001	0.081	1.673	0.097
2000 economic freedom score	0.003	0.001	0.253	4.223	0.000
Annual population growth rate, 1975–2005 (%)	−0.024	0.005	−0.264	−4.427	0.000
ln GDP per capita	0.008	0.083	0.076	0.092	0.927
ln GDP per capita^2	0.001	0.005	0.143	0.175	0.861
MNC outward investments (stock) per GDP	0.002	0.001	0.183	3.232	0.002
MNC PEN – stock of inward FDI per GDP	0.000	0.000	−0.095	−1.845	0.068
Openness Index, 1990 (export share per GDP + import share per GDP)	0.000	0.000	−0.166	−3.224	0.002
UNDP Education Index	0.132	0.054	0.220	2.429	0.017
Years of membership in EMU (2010)	0.004	0.002	0.081	1.485	0.141

adj R^2 = 80.0%; df = 114; F = 46.479, error p. = .000

Appendix 7: The Sources for the Cross-national Data Collection

All the variables are contained in http://www.hichemkaroui.com/?p=2017 and http://www.hichemkaroui.com/?p=2383#more-2383 (both accessed 31 December 2011).

This data set combines the most up-to-date data on the social, economic, political and environmental effects of globalization. The dataset in Excel format is freely available and draws on the following sources:

	Variable label	Source
1	Combined Failed States Index	http://www.fundforpeace.org/web/index.php?option=com_content&task=view&id=452&Itemid=900
2	Civil and political liberty violations	ESI, Yale/Columbia http://sedac.ciesin.columbia.edu/es/esi/
3	Closing economic gender gap	http://www.weforum.org/en/Communities/Women Leaders and Gender Parity/GenderGapNetwork/index.htm
4	Closing educational gender gap	http://www.weforum.org/en/Communities/Women Leaders and Gender Parity/GenderGapNetwork/index.htm
5	Closing health and survivial gender gap	http://www.weforum.org/en/Communities/Women Leaders and Gender Parity/GenderGapNetwork/index.htm
6	Closing of global gender gap overall score 2009	http://www.weforum.org/en/Communities/Women Leaders and Gender Parity/GenderGapNetwork/index.htm
7	Closing political gender gap	http://www.weforum.org/en/Communities/Women Leaders and Gender Parity/GenderGapNetwork/index.htm
8	Corruption avoidance measure	ESI, Yale/Columbia http://sedac.ciesin.columbia.edu/es/esi/
9	Country share in top world 500 universities	University of Shanghai http://www.arwu.org/
10	Crisis Performance Factor	Calculated from the IMF and UNDP. IMF prognosis April 2009

(Continued)

	Variable label	Source
11	Democracy measure	ESI, Yale/Columbia http://sedac.ciesin.columbia.edu/es/esi/
12	Ecological footprint (gha per capita)	Happy Planet Index website http://www.happyplanetindex.org/learn/download-report.html
13	Economic growth IMF prediction growth rate in 2009	IMF http://www.imf.org/external/datamapper/index.php
14	Economic growth IMF prediction growth rate in 2010	IMF http://www.imf.org/external/datamapper/index.php
15	Economic growth in real terms per capita, per annum, 1990–2005	UNDP Human Development Report Office http://hdr.undp.org/en/statistics/data/
16	Environmental Performance Index (EPI)	EPI, Yale/Columbia http://epi.yale.edu/Home
17	Environmental Sustainability Index (ESI)	Yale/Columbia ESI website http://sedac.ciesin.columbia.edu/es/esi/
18	Female survival, probability of surviving to age 65	Calculated from UNDP Human Development Report Office http://hdr.undp.org/en/statistics/data/
19	Gender empowerment index value	UNDP Human Development Report Office http://hdr.undp.org/en/statistics/data/
20	Global tolerance index	Calculated from World Values Survey http://www.worldvaluessurvey.org/
21	Happy life years	Happy Planet Index website http://www.happyplanetindex.org/learn/download-report.html
22	Happy Planet Index (HPI)	Happy Planet Index website http://www.happyplanetindex.org/learn/download-report.html
23	Human Development Index (HDI) value 2004	UNDP Human Development Report Office http://hdr.undp.org/en/statistics/data/
24	Infant mortality (2005)	UNDP Human Development Report Office http://hdr.undp.org/en/statistics/data/
25	Labour force participation rate of migrants (both sexes)	UNDP HDR 2009 http://hdr.undp.org/xmlsearch/reportSearch?y=*&c=g&t=*&k=
26	Life expectancy (years)	Happy Planet Index website http://www.happyplanetindex.org/learn/download-report.html
27	Life satisfaction (0–10)	Happy Planet Index website http://www.happyplanetindex.org/learn/download-report.html

(Continued)

	Variable label	Source
28	Net exports of ecological footprint gha per person	Global Footprint Network at http://www.footprintnetwork.org/images/uploads/Ecological_Footprint_Atlas_2009.pdf
29	Per capita world-class universities	Calculated from the data of this work
30	Quintile share income difference between richest and poorest 20 per cent	UNDP Human Development Report Office http://hdr.undp.org/en/statistics/data/
31	Rule of law	Yale/Columbia ESI website (see above)
32	Tertiary enrolment	Nationmaster Sydney http://www.nationmaster.com/index.php
33	Total unemployment rate of immigrants (both sexes)	UNDP *HDR 2009* http://hdr.undp.org/xmlsearch/reportSearch?y=*&c=g&t=*&k=
34	Unemployment rate	United Nations Statistics http://unstats.un.org/unsd/Demographic/Products/socind/unemployment.htm
35	Cyclones – average number of tropical cyclones per year	http://www.undp.org/cpr/disred/rdr.htm
36	ln (number of people per million inhabitants 1980–2000 killed by natural disasters per year + 1)	http://www.undp.org/cpr/disred/rdr.htm
37	Tertiary emigration rate	UNDP *HDR 2009* http://hdr.undp.org/xmlsearch/reportSearch?y=*&c=g&t=*&k=
38	Droughts – average number of droughts per year	http://www.undp.org/cpr/disred/rdr.htm
39	Earthquakes – average number of earthquakes per year	http://www.undp.org/cpr/disred/rdr.htm
40	Carbon emissions per million US dollars GDP	ESI, Yale/Columbia http://sedac.ciesin.columbia.edu/es/esi/
41	Carbon emissions per capita	ESI, Yale/Columbia http://sedac.ciesin.columbia.edu/es/esi/
42	Percentage of women in government, all levels	UNDP *HDR 2000* http://hdr.undp.org/xmlsearch/reportSearch?y=*&c=g&t=*&k=
43	Percentage of world population	Calculated from UNDP Human Development Report Office http://hdr.undp.org/en/statistics/data/
44	2000 economic freedom score	Heritage Foundation http://www.heritage.org/Index/

(Continued)

	Variable label	Source
45	Absolute latitude	Easterly, William, New York University – Stern School of Business, Department of Economics, May 2000 'The Middle Class Consensus and Economic Development', World Bank Policy Research Working Paper No. 2346, available at: http://papers.ssrn.com/sol3/papers.cfm?abstract_id=630718. Data in Excel – format still retrievable best from a Google search, entering the words 'easterly POLRIGHTS98' at the site http://www.cgdev.org/. The address of the site is given as www.cgdev.org/doc/…/easterly/easterly_consensusdata.xls. Alternatively, a Google search using the search profile words 'easterly_consensusdata.xls' also yields the data set.
46	Annual population growth rate, 1975–2005 (%)	Calculated from UNDP Human Development Report Office http://hdr.undp.org/en/statistics/data/
47	Comparative price levels (US = 1.00)	Calculated from UNDP (GDP curr/GDP PPP) UNDP Human Development Report Office http://hdr.undp.org/en/statistics/data/
48	Foreign savings rate	UNDP *HDR 2000* http://hdr.undp.org/xmlsearch/reportSearch?y=*&c=g&t=*&k=
49	FPZ (free production zones) employment as a percentage of total population	Calculated from ILO http://www.ilo.org/public/english/dialogue/sector/themes/epz/epz-db.pdf
50	ln GDP per capita	UNDP *HDR 2000* http://hdr.undp.org/xmlsearch/reportSearch?y=*&c=g&t=*&k=
51	ln GDP per capita^2	UNDP *HDR 2000* http://hdr.undp.org/xmlsearch/reportSearch?y=*&c=g&t=*&k=
52	Membership of the Islamic Conference	OIC http://www.oic-oci.org/
53	Military expenditure per GDP	UNDP Human Development Report Office http://hdr.undp.org/en/statistics/data/
54	Military personnel rate ln (MPR + 1)	US CIA https://www.cia.gov/library/publications/the-world-factbook/geos/us.html
55	MNC outward investments (stock) per GDP	UNCTAD http://www.unctad.org/sections/dite_dir/docs/wir2007_instock_gdp_en.xls. In addition: http://www.unctad.org/sections/dite_dir/docs/wir2007_instock_gdp_en.xls. Furthermore http://www.unctad.org/sections/dite_dir/docs/wir2007_instock_gdp_en.xls. In addition http://www.unctad.org/Templates/Page.asp?intItemID=3198&lang=1 and http://www.unctad.org/en/docs/wir2008_en.pdf and http://www.unctad.org/Templates/Page.asp?intItemID=3277&lang=1

(Continued)

	Variable label	**Source**
56	MNC PEN – stock of inward FDI per GDP	UNCTAD http://www.unctad.org/sections/dite_dir/docs/wir2007_instock_gdp_en.xls. In addition: http://www.unctad.org/sections/dite_dir/docs/wir2007_instock_gdp_en.xls. Furthermore http://www.unctad.org/sections/dite_dir/docs/wir2007_instock_gdp_en.xls. In addition http://www.unctad.org/Templates/Page.asp?intItemID=3198&lang=1 and http://www.unctad.org/en/docs/wir2008_en.pdf and http://www.unctad.org/Templates/Page.asp?intItemID=3277&lang=1
57	MNC PEN: DYN MNC PEN 1995–2005	UNCTAD http://www.unctad.org/sections/dite_dir/docs/wir2007_instock_gdp_en.xls. In addition: http://www.unctad.org/sections/dite_dir/docs/wir2007_instock_gdp_en.xls. Furthermore http://www.unctad.org/sections/dite_dir/docs/wir2007_instock_gdp_en.xls. In addition http://www.unctad.org/Templates/Page.asp?intItemID=3198&lang=1 and http://www.unctad.org/en/docs/wir2008_en.pdf and http://www.unctad.org/Templates/Page.asp?intItemID=3277&lang=1
58	Openness Index, 1990 (export share per GDP + import share per GDP)	Calculated from UNDP Human Development Report Office http://hdr.undp.org/en/statistics/data/
59	Population density	https://www.cia.gov/library/publications/the-world-factbook/
60	Public education expenditure per GNP	UNDP Human Development Report Office http://hdr.undp.org/en/statistics/data/
61	UNDP Education Index	UNDP Human Development Report Office http://hdr.undp.org/en/statistics/data/
62	Worker remittance inflows as a percentage of GDP	UNDP *HDR 2009* http://hdr.undp.org/xmlsearch/reportSearch?y=*&c=g&t=*&k=
63	Immigration – share of population 2005 (%)	UNDP *HDR 2009* http://hdr.undp.org/xmlsearch/reportSearch?y=*&c=g&t=*&k=
64	Muslim population share per total population	Nationmaster Sydney http://www.nationmaster.com/index.php
65	Net international migration rate, 2005–2010	UNDP *HDR 2009* http://hdr.undp.org/xmlsearch/reportSearch?y=*&c=g&t=*&k=
66	Years of membership in the EU (2010)	Website of the European Commission: http://ec.europa.eu/index_en.htm and EU Scadplus http://europa.eu/legislation_summaries/index.htm, as well as http://www.state.gov/

(Continued)

	Variable label	**Source**
67	Years of membership in EMU (2010)	Website of the European Commission: http://ec.europa.eu/index_en.htm and EU Scadplus http://europa.eu/legislation_summaries/index.htm, as well as http://www.state.gov/
68	Social security expenditure per GDP average 1990s (ILO)	ILO http://www-ilo-mirror.cornell.edu/public/english/protection/socfas/research/stat/table14.htm
69	Overall 30 variable development index	Calculated from this work
70	Overall 35 variable development index	Calculated from this work
71	Overall 35 variable development index, based on 7 dimensions	Calculated from this work
72	Avoiding net trade of ecological footprint gha per person	Calculated from this work

A Commented Guide to the Literature: Major International Studies in Peer-Reviewed Social Science Journals about Globalization and Other Preconditions of Policy Success or Failure for the Nine 'European Union 2020 Guidelines' (compiled from Cambridge Scientific Abstracts and the Social Sciences Citation Index)

Author	Year	Title	Source	Research design focused on	Pro-globalization approach inherent in European Commission thinking	EU-2020 guideline
Alderson, A. S. and Nielsen, F.	2002	Globalization and the great U-turn: Income inequality trends in 16 OECD countries	*American Journal of Sociology* 107.5 (2002): 1244–99	Inequality	Partially rejected	Promoting social inclusion and combating poverty
Alderson, A. S. and Nielsen, F.	1999	Income inequality, development, and dependence: A reconsideration	*American Sociological Review* 64.4 (1999): 606–31	Economic growth, inequality	Rejected	Improving the business and consumer environment and modernizing the industrial base
Babones, Salvatore and Zhang, Xi	2008	Heterogeneity in the global South in the relationship between income inequality and foreign trade	*International Review of Modern Sociology* 34.1 (2008): 95–108	Inequality	Partially rejected	Promoting social inclusion and combating poverty
Barbieri, Katherine and Reuveny, Rafael	2005	Economic globalization and civil war	*Journal of Politics* 67.4 (2005): 1228–47	Civil war	Confirmed	x

(*Continued*)

Author	Year	Title	Source	Research design focused on	Pro-globalization approach inherent in European Commission thinking	EU-2020 guideline
Beckfield, Jason	2006	European integration and income inequality	*American Sociological Review* 71.6 (2006): 964–85	Income inequality	Confirmed	Promoting social inclusion and combating poverty
Boehmer, U. and Williamson, J. B.	1996	The impact of women's status on infant mortality rate: A cross-national analysis	*Social Indicators Research* 37.3 (1996): 333–60	Infant mortality	Rejected	Promoting social inclusion and combating poverty
Bornschier, Volker	1983	World economy, level development and income distribution: An integration of different approaches to the explanation of income inequality	*World Development* 11.1 (1983): 11–20	Income inequality	Rejected	Promoting social inclusion and combating poverty
Bornschier, Volker	1980	Multinational corporations, economic policy and national development in the world system	*International Social Science Journal* 32.1 (1980): 158–72	Economic growth	Rejected	Improving the business and consumer environment and modernizing the industrial base

Bornschier, Volker; Chase-Dunn, Christopher; Rubinson, Richard	1978	Cross-national evidence of the effects of foreign investment and aid on economic growth and inequality: A survey of findings and a reanalysis	*American Journal of Sociology* 84.3 (1978): 651–83	Economic growth, income inequality	Rejected	Improving the business and consumer environment and modernizing the industrial base
Bradshaw, Y. W.	1993	Borrowing against the future: children and Third World indebtedness	*Social Forces* 71.3 (1993): 629–56	Child survival, childhood immunization, economic growth, prevalence of health attendants, adequate nutrition, balanced urbanization	Rejected	Promoting social inclusion and combating poverty
Bradshaw, Y. W. and Schafer, J.	2000	Urbanization and development: The emergence of international nongovernmental organizations amid declining states	*Sociological Perspectives* 43.1 (2000): 97–116	Overurbanization, economic growth, and access to safe water	Rejected	Increasing labour market participation and reducing structural unemployment
Bussmann, Margit; de Soysa, Indra; Oneal, John R.	2005	The effect of globalization on national income inequality	*Comparative Sociology* 4.3–4 (2005): 285–312	Income inequality	Confirmed	Promoting social inclusion and combating poverty

(Continued)

Author	Year	Title	Source	Research design focused on	Pro-globalization approach inherent in European Commission thinking	EU-2020 guideline
Bussmann, Margit and Schneider, Gerald	2007	When globalization discontent turns violent: Foreign economic liberalization and internal war	*International Studies Quarterly* 51.1 (2007): 79–97	Political violence, instability	Partially rejected	Promoting social inclusion and combating poverty
Clark, R.	2008	Dependency, network integration, and development	*Sociological Perspectives* 51.3 (2008): 629–48	Economic growth, tertiary school expansion	Rejected	Improving the business and consumer environment and modernizing the industrial base
Crenshaw, E.	1992	Cross-national determinants of income inequality: A replication and extension using ecological-evolutionary theory	*Social Forces* 71.2 (1992): 339–63	Income inequality	Confirmed	Promoting social inclusion and combating poverty
Crenshaw, E. and Ameen, A.	1994	The distribution of income across national populations: Testing multiple paradigms	*Social Science Research* 23.1 (1994): 1–22	Income inequality	Partially rejected	Promoting social inclusion and combating poverty
Davenport, C.	1995	Assessing the military's influence on political repression	*Journal of Political and Military Sociology* 23.1 (1995): 119–44	Repression	Partially rejected	Promoting social inclusion and combating poverty

Dick, Ch. and Jorgenson, A. K.	2010	Sectoral foreign investment and nitrous oxide emissions: A quantitative investigation	*Society and Natural Resources* 23.1 (2010): 71–82	Nitrous oxide emissions	Rejected	Improving resource efficiency and reducing greenhouse gases emissions
Dixon, W. J. and Boswell, T.	1996	Dependency, disarticulation, and denominator effects: Another look at foreign capital penetration	*American Journal of Sociology* 102.2 (1996): 543–62	Economic growth, decapitalization, income inequality	Rejected	Improving the business and consumer environment and modernizing the industrial base
Dutt, A. K.	1997	The pattern of direct foreign investment and economic growth	*World Development* 25.11 (2007): 1925–36	Economic growth	Confirmed	Improving the business and consumer environment and modernizing the industrial base
Ehrhardt-Martinez, Karen; Crenshaw, Edward M.; Jenkins, J. Craig	2002	Deforestation and the environmental Kuznets curve: A cross-national investigation of intervening mechanisms	*Social Science Quarterly* 83.1 (2002): 226–43	Deforestation	Confirmed	Improving resource efficiency and reducing greenhouse gases emissions
Firebaugh, Glenn	1992	Growth effects of foreign and domestic investment	*American Journal of Sociology* 98.1 (1992): 105–30	Economic growth	Confirmed	Improving the business and consumer environment and modernizing the industrial base

(Continued)

Author	Year	Title	Source	Research design focused on	Pro-globalization approach inherent in European Commission thinking	EU-2020 guideline
Firebaugh, Glenn and Beck F. D.	1994	Does economic growth benefit the masses? Growth, dependence, and welfare in the Third World	*American Sociological Review* 59 (1994): 631–53.	Economic growth, inequality	Confirmed	Improving the business and consumer environment and modernizing the industrial base
Glasberg, D. S. and Ward, K. B.	1993	Foreign debt and economic growth in the world-system	*Social Science Quarterly* 74.4 (1993): 703–20	Economic growth	Partially rejected	Improving the business and consumer environment and modernizing the industrial base
Gustafsson, B. and Johansson, M.	1999	In search of smoking guns: What makes income inequality vary over time in different countries?	*American Sociological Review* 64.4 (1999): 585–605	Income inequality	Partially rejected	Promoting social inclusion and combating poverty
Hafner-Burton, Emilie M.	2005	Right or robust? The sensitive nature of repression to globalization	*Journal of Peace Research* 42.6 (2005): 679–98	Human rights	Partially rejected	Promoting social inclusion and combating poverty

Author	Year	Title	Source	Variable	Result		Description
Herkenrath, Mark and Bornschier, Volker	2002	Transnational corporations in world development: Still the same harmful effects in an increasingly globalized world economy?	International Sociological Association, Brisbane, Australia, 2002	Economic growth, income inequality	Rejected	x	Improving the business and consumer environment and modernizing the industrial base
Huang, Jie and Slomczynski, Kazimierz M.	2003	The dimensionality and measurement of economic dependency: A research note	International Journal of Sociology 33.4 (2003): 82–98	Interaction of dependency variables	Confirmed		
Jenkins, J. Craig and Schock, Kurt	2003	Political process, international dependence, and mass political conflict: A global analysis of protest and rebellion, 1973–1978	International Journal of Sociology 33.4 (2003): 41–63	Protest and rebellion	Confirmed		Promoting social inclusion and combating poverty
Jorgenson, A. K.	2003	Consumption and environmental degradation: A cross-national analysis of the ecological footprint	Social Problems 50.3: 374–94	Ecological footprint	Rejected		Improving resource efficiency and reducing greenhouse gases emissions

(Continued)

Author	Year	Title	Source	Research design focused on	Pro-globalization approach inherent in European Commission thinking	EU-2020 guideline
Jorgenson, A. K.	2007	Does foreign investment harm the air we breathe and the water we drink? A cross-national study of carbon dioxide emissions and organic water pollution in less-developed countries, 1975 to 2000	*Organization & Environment* 20.2 (2007): 135–57	Carbon dioxide emissions; emission of organic water pollutants	Rejected	Improving resource efficiency and reducing greenhouse gases emissions
Jorgenson, A. K.	2006	Unequal ecological exchange and environmental degradation: A theoretical proposition and cross-national study of deforestation, 1990–2000	*Rural Sociology* 71.4 (2006): 685–712	Deforestation	Rejected	Improving resource efficiency and reducing greenhouse gases emissions
Jorgenson, A. K. and Burns, T. J.	2007	The political-economic causes of change in the ecological footprints of nations, 1991–2001: A quantitative investigation	*Social Science Research* 36.2 (2007): 834–53	Growth of ecological footprint	Rejected	Improving resource efficiency and reducing greenhouse gases emissions

Author	Year	Title	Publication	Topic	Status	Theme
Jorgenson, A. K.; Dick, C.; Mahutga, M. C.	2007	Foreign investment dependence and the environment: An ecostructural approach	*Social Problems* 54.3 (2007): 371–94	Nitrogen oxides, volatile organic compounds, carbon monoxide, and carbon dioxide gas	Rejected	Improving resource efficiency and reducing greenhouse gases emissions
Jorgenson, A. K.	2008	Structural integration and the trees: An analysis of deforestation in less-developed countries, 1990–2005	*Sociological Quarterly* 49.3 (2008): 503–27	Deforestation	Rejected	Improving resource efficiency and reducing greenhouse gases emissions
Jorgenson, A. K.	2004	Uneven processes and environmental degradation in the world-economy	*Human Ecology Review* 11.2 (2004): 103–17	Ecological footprint	Rejected	Improving resource efficiency and reducing greenhouse gases emissions
Jorgenson, A. K.	2005	Unpacking international power and the ecological footprints of nations: A quantitative cross-national study	*Sociological Perspectives* 48.3 (2005): 383–402	Ecological footprint	Rejected	Improving resource efficiency and reducing greenhouse gases emissions
Jorgenson, A. K.	2006	Global warming and the neglected greenhouse gas: A cross-national study of the social causes of methane emissions intensity, 1995	*Social Forces* 84.3 (2006): 1779–98	Greenhouse gas emissions	Rejected	Improving resource efficiency and reducing greenhouse gases emissions

(Continued)

Author	Year	Title	Source	Research design focused on	Pro-globalization approach inherent in European Commission thinking	EU-2020 guideline
Jorgenson, A. K.	2009	Political-economic integration, industrial pollution and human health: A panel study of less-developed countries, 1980–2000	*International Sociology* 24.1 (2009): 115–43	Industrial organic water pollution, infant mortality	Rejected	Improving resource efficiency and reducing greenhouse gases emissions
Jorgenson, A. K.	2007	Foreign direct investment and pesticide use intensity in less-developed countries: A quantitative investigation	*Society and Natural Resources* 20.1 (2007): 73–83	Pesticide consumption	Rejected	Improving resource efficiency and reducing greenhouse gases emissions
Jorgenson, A. K.	2009	The transnational organization of production, the scale of degradation, and ecoefficiency: A study of carbon dioxide emissions in less-developed countries	*Human Ecology Review* 16.1 (2009): 64–74	Total carbon dioxide emissions and emissions per unit of production	Rejected	Improving resource efficiency and reducing greenhouse gases emissions
Jorgenson, A. K.	2004	Global inequality, water pollution, and infant mortality	*Social Science Journal* 41.2 (2004): 279–88	Water pollution, infant mortality	Rejected	Improving resource efficiency and reducing greenhouse gases emissions

Author	Year	Title	Source	Variable	Result	Policy recommendation
Jorgenson, A. K. and Burns, T.J.	2004	Globalization, the environment, and infant mortality: A cross-national study	Humboldt Journal of Social Relations 28.1 (2004): 7–52	Water pollution, infant mortality	Rejected	Improving resource efficiency and reducing greenhouse gases emissions
Jorgenson, A. K. and Kuykendall, Kennon A.	2008	Globalization, foreign investment dependence and agriculture production: Pesticide and fertilizer use in less-developed countries, 1990–2000	Social Forces 87.1 (2008): 529–60	Pesticide and fertilizer use	Rejected	Improving resource efficiency and reducing greenhouse gases emissions
Kaya, Y.	2010	Globalization and industrialization in 64 developing countries, 1980–2003	Social Forces 88.3 (2010): 1153–82	Manufacturing employment	Partially rejected	Increasing labour market participation and reducing structural unemployment
Kentor, J.	2001	The long term effects of globalization on income inequality, population growth, and economic development	Social Problems 48.4 (2001): 435–55	Income inequality, population growth and economic development	Rejected	Promoting social inclusion and combating poverty
Kentor, J.	1998	The long-term effects of foreign investment dependence on economic growth, 1940–1990	American Journal of Sociology 103.4 (1998): 1024–46	Economic growth	Rejected	Improving the business and consumer environment and modernizing the industrial base

(Continued)

Author	Year	Title	Source	Research design focused on	Pro-globalization approach inherent in European Commission thinking	EU-2020 guideline
Kentor, J. and Boswell, T.	2003	Foreign capital dependence and development: A new direction	*American Sociological Review* 68.2 (2003): 301–13	Economic growth	Partially rejected	Improving the business and consumer environment and modernizing the industrial base
Kentor, J. and Jorgenson, A. K.	2010	Foreign investment and development an organizational perspective	*International Sociology* 25.3 (2010): 419–41	Economic growth	Partially rejected	Improving the business and consumer environment and modernizing the industrial base
Kick, Edward L.; Davis, Byron L.; Lehtinen, Marlene; Burns, Thomas J.	2000	World-system position, national political characteristics and economic development outcomes	*Journal of Political and Military Sociology* 28.1 (2000): 131–55	Economic growth	Partially rejected	Improving the business and consumer environment and modernizing the industrial base
Kukreja, Sunil	1991	The relationship between transnational penetration, militarization, debt dependence, and political exclusion	*International Review of Modern Sociology* 21.1 (1991): 131–62	Political exclusion, debt dependence	Partially rejected	Promoting social inclusion and combating poverty

Author	Year	Title	Source	Variable	Result	Policy
Kurzman, C.; Werun, R.; Burkhart, R. E.	2002	Democracy's effect on economic growth: A pooled time-series analysis, 1951–1980	*Studies in Comparative International Development* 37.1 (2002): 3–33	Economic growth	Confirmed	Improving the business and consumer environment and modernizing the industrial base
Lawrence, Kirk S.	2009	The thermodynamics of unequal exchange	*International Journal of Comparative Sociology* 50.3–4 (2009): 335–9	Energy use	Rejected	Improving resource efficiency and reducing greenhouse gases emissions
Lee, Cheol-Sung	2005	Income inequality, democracy, and public sector size	*American Sociological Review* 70.1 (2005): 158–81	Income inequality	Rejected	Promoting social inclusion and combating poverty
Lee, Cheol-Sung; Nielsen, Francois; Alderson, Arthur S.	2007	Income inequality, global economy and the state	*Social Forces* 86.1 (2007): 77–111	Income inequality	Partially rejected	Promoting social inclusion and combating poverty
Lena, H. F. and London, B.	1993	The political and economic determinants of health outcomes: A cross-national analysis	*International Journal of Health Services* 23.3 (1993): 585–602	Life expectancy, mortality, health and welfare	Rejected	Promoting social inclusion and combating poverty
London, B. and Ross, R. J. S.	1995	The political sociology of foreign direct investment: Global capitalism and capital mobility, 1965–1980	*International Journal of Comparative Sociology* 36.3–4 (2005): 198–218	Foreign direct investment	Rejected	Improving the business and consumer environment and modernizing the industrial base

(Continued)

Author	Year	Title	Source	Research design focused on	Pro-globalization approach inherent in European Commission thinking	EU-2020 guideline
Longo, Stefano and York, Richard	2008	Agricultural exports and the environment: A cross-national study of fertilizer and pesticide consumption	*Rural Sociology* 73.1 (2008): 82–104	Fertilizer and pesticide consumption	Rejected	Improving resource efficiency and reducing greenhouse gases emissions
Mahuga, Matthew C.	2006	The persistence of structural inequality? A network analysis of international trade, 1965–2000	*Social Forces* 84.4 (2006): 1863–89	Economic growth	Rejected	Improving the business and consumer environment and modernizing the industrial base
Mahuga, Matthew C.; Bandelj, Nina	2008	Foreign investment and income inequality: The natural experiment of Central and Eastern Europe	*International Journal of Comparative Sociology* 49.6 (2008): 429–54	Inequality	Rejected	Promoting social inclusion and combating poverty
Meyer, Lisa B.	2003	Economic globalization and women's status in the labor market: A cross-national investigation of occupational sex segregation and inequality	*Sociological Quarterly* 44.3 (2003): 351–83	Occupational sex segregation and occupational inequality	Rejected	Promoting social inclusion and combating poverty; increasing labour market participation and reducing structural unemployment

Author	Year	Title	Source	Variable	Status	Category
Mills, Melinda	2009	Globalization and inequality	*European Sociological Review* 25.1 (2009): 1–8	Inequality	Rejected	Promoting social inclusion and combating poverty
Moore, Spencer; Teixeira, Ana C.; Shiell, Alan	2006	The health of nations in a global context: Trade, global stratification, and infant mortality rates	*Social Science & Medicine* 63.1 (2006): 165–78	Infant mortality	Rejected	Promoting social inclusion and combating poverty
Morris, Theresa M.	1999	The global economy and changes in the determinants of cross-national income inequality	*Social Thought & Research* 22 (1999): 183–214	Income inequality	Rejected	Promoting social inclusion and combating poverty
Mostafa, M. M.	2010	A Bayesian approach to analyzing the ecological footprint of 140 nations	*Ecological Indicators* 10.4 (2010): 808–17	Ecological footprint	Rejected	Improving resource efficiency and reducing greenhouse gases emissions
Mostafa, M. M.	2010	Clustering the ecological footprint of nations using Kohonen's self-organizing maps	*Expert Systems with Applications* 37.4 (2010): 2747–55	Ecological footprint per capita	Rejected	Improving resource efficiency and reducing greenhouse gases emissions
Mostafa, M. M. and Nataraajan, R.	2009	A neuro-computational intelligence analysis of the ecological footprint of nations	*Computational Statistics and Data Analysis* 53.9 (2009): 3516–31	Ecological footprint	Rejected	Improving resource efficiency and reducing greenhouse gases emissions

(Continued)

Author	Year	Title	Source	Research design focused on	Pro-globalization approach inherent in European Commission thinking	EU-2020 guideline
Neumayer, Eric and de Soysa, Indra	2006	Globalization and the right to free association and collective bargaining: An empirical analysis	*World Development* 34.1 (2006): 31–49	Process-related standards of a right to free association and collective bargaining	Confirmed	Promoting social inclusion and combating poverty
Nugent, Colleen and Shandra, John M.	2009	State environmental protection efforts, women's status, and world polity: A cross-national analysis	*Organization & Environment* 22.3 (2009): 293–310	Environmental protection efforts	Rejected	Improving resource efficiency and reducing greenhouse gases emissions
Oneal, John R.	2003	Measuring interdependence and its Pacific benefits: A reply to Gartzke & Li	*Journal of Peace Research* 40.6 (2003): 721–5	Dyadic interactions of nations/ peace or war	Confirmed	x
Pattnayak, Satya R.	1999	Source of investment and economic growth rate in non-core countries: A re-analysis	*International Review of Modern Sociology* 29.1 (1999): 35–54	Economic growth	Confirmed	Improving the business and consumer environment and modernizing the industrial base

Payne, Caroline L.	2009	Bringing home the bacon or not? Globalization and government respect for economic and social rights	*Human Rights Review* 10.3 (2009): 413–29	Economic and social rights	Partially rejected	Promoting social inclusion and combating poverty
Ragin, C. C. and Bradshaw, Y. W.	1992	International economic dependence and human misery, 1938–1980: A global perspective	*Sociological Perspectives* 35.2 (1992): 217–47	Physical quality of life	Rejected	Promoting social inclusion and combating poverty
Reuveny, Rafael and Li, Quan	2003	Economic openness, democracy, and income inequality: An empirical analysis	*Comparative Political Studies* 36.5 (2003): 575–601	Income inequality	Partially rejected	Promoting social inclusion and combating poverty
Rice, James	2008	Material consumption and social well-being within the periphery of the world economy: An ecological analysis of maternal mortality	*Social Science Research* 37.4 (2008): 1292–1309	Maternal mortality	Rejected	Promoting social inclusion and combating poverty
Richards, David L.; Gelleny, Ronald D.; Sacko, David H.	2001	Money with a mean streak? Foreign economic penetration and government respect for human rights in developing countries	*International Studies Quarterly* 45.2 (2001): 219–39	Human rights	Confirmed	Promoting social inclusion and combating poverty

(Continued)

Author	Year	Title	Source	Research design focused on	Pro-globalization approach inherent in European Commission thinking	EU-2020 guideline
Roberts, Wade T.	2005	The uneven globalization of civil society organizations and the consequences for cross-national disparities in human development	*International Journal of Sociology and Social Policy* 25.1–2 (2005): 118–44	International nongovernmental organizational ties	Confirmed	x
Robinson, T. D. and London, B.	1991	Dependency, inequality, and political violence – A cross-national analysis	*Journal of Political and Military Sociology* 19.1 (1991): 119–56	Political violence, income inequality	Partially rejected	Promoting social inclusion and combating poverty
Sanderson, Matthew R. and Kentor, Jeffrey	2008	Foreign direct investment and international migration: A cross-national analysis of less-developed countries, 1985–2000	*International Sociology* 23.4 (2008): 514–39	Outward migration	Rejected	Increasing labour market participation and reducing structural unemployment
Schofer, Evan	2004	Cross-national differences in the expansion of science, 1970–1990	*Social Forces* 83.1 (2004): 215–48	National science infrastructure (factor analytical weighting of various science indicators, including publications per capita)	Confirmed	x

Author	Year	Title	Journal	Variable	Confirmed	Goal
Schofer, Evan and Meyer, John W.	2005	The worldwide expansion of higher education in the twentieth century	Sociological Review 70.6 (2005): 898–920	Higher education enrolment		Optimizing support for R&D and innovation, strengthening the knowledge triangle and unleashing the potential of the digital economy
Shandra, J. M.; Leckband, C.; McKinney, L. A; London, B.	2009	Ecologically unequal exchange, world polity, and biodiversity loss: A cross-national analysis of threatened mammals	International Journal of Comparative Sociology 50.3–4 (2009): 285–310	Threatened mammal species	Rejected	Improving resource efficiency and reducing greenhouse gases emissions
Shandra, J. M.; London, B.; Williamson, J. B.	2003	Environmental degradation, environmental sustainability, and over urbanization in the developing world: A quantitative, cross-national analysis	Sociological Perspectives 46.3 (2003): 309–29	Overurbanization	Rejected	Increasing labour market participation and reducing structural unemployment
Shandra, John M.	2007	Economic dependency, repression, and deforestation: A quantitative, cross-national analysis	Sociological Inquiry 77.4 (2007): 543–71	Deforestation	Rejected	Improving resource efficiency and reducing greenhouse gases emissions

(Continued)

Author	Year	Title	Source	Research design focused on	Pro-globalization approach inherent in European Commission thinking	EU-2020 guideline
Shandra, John M.	2007	International nongovernmental organizations and deforestation: Good, bad, or irrelevant?	*Social Science Quarterly* 88.3 (2007): 665–89	Deforestation	Rejected	Improving resource efficiency and reducing greenhouse gases emissions
Shandra, John M.; Leckband, Christopher; London, Bruce	2009	Ecologically unequal exchange and deforestation: A cross-national analysis of forestry export flows	*Organization & Environment* 22.2 (2009): 208–29	Deforestation	Rejected	Improving resource efficiency and reducing greenhouse gases emissions
Shandra, John M.; Shandra, Carrie L.; London, Bruce	2010	Do non-governmental organizations impact health? A cross-national analysis of infant mortality	*International Journal of Comparative Sociology* 51.1–2 (2010): 137–64	Infant mortality	Rejected	Promoting social inclusion and combating poverty
Shandra, John M.; Shandra, Carrie L.; London, Bruce	2008	Women, non-governmental organizations, and deforestation: a cross-national study	*Population and Environment* 30.1–2 (2008): 48–72	Deforestation	Rejected	Improving resource efficiency and reducing greenhouse gases emissions
Shandra, John M.; Shor, Eran; London, Bruce	2009	World polity, unequal ecological exchange, and organic water pollution: A cross-national analysis of developing nations	*Human Ecology Review* 16.1 (2009): 53–63	Organic water pollution	Rejected	Improving resource efficiency and reducing greenhouse gases emissions

Author	Year	Title	Citation	Variable	Decision	Policy
Shandra, John M.; London, Bruce; Whooley, Owen P.; Williamson, John B.	2004	International nongovernmental organizations and carbon dioxide emissions in the developing world: A quantitative, cross-national analysis	*Sociological Inquiry* 74.4 (2004): 520–45	Carbon dioxide emissions	Rejected	Improving resource efficiency and reducing greenhouse gases emissions
Shandra, John M.; London, Bruce; Williamson, John B.	2003	Environmental degradation, environmental sustainability, and overurbanization in the developing world: A quantitative, cross-national analysis	*Sociological Perspectives* 46.3 (2003): 309–29,	Overurbanization	Rejected	Increasing labour market participation and reducing structural unemployment
Shandra, John M.; Nobles, Jenna E.; London, Bruce; Williamson, John B.	2005	Multinational corporations, democracy and child mortality: A quantitative, cross-national analysis of developing countries	*Social Indicators Research* 73.2 (2005): 267–93	Child mortality	Rejected	Promoting social inclusion and combating poverty
Shandra, John M.; Nobles, Jenna; London, Bruce; Williamson, John B.	2004	Dependency, democracy, and infant mortality: A quantitative, cross-national analysis of less developed countries	*Social Science & Medicine*, 59.2 (2004): 321–33	Infant mortality	Rejected	Promoting social inclusion and combating poverty

(Continued)

Author	Year	Title	Source	Research design focused on	Pro-globalization approach inherent in European Commission thinking	EU-2020 guideline
Shandra, John M; Shor, Eran; London, Bruce	2008	Debt, structural adjustment, and organic water pollution	*Organization & Environment* 21.1 (2008): 38–55	Organic water pollution	Rejected	Improving resource efficiency and reducing greenhouse gases emissions
Shen, C. and Williamson, J. B.	2001	Accounting for cross-national differences in infant mortality decline (1965–1991) among less developed countries: Effects of women's status, economic dependency, and state strength	*Social Indicators Research* 53.3 (2001): 257–88	Infant mortality decline	Rejected	Promoting social inclusion and combating poverty
Shen, C. and Williamson, J. B.	1997	Child mortality, women's status, economic dependency, and state strength: A cross-national study of less developed countries	*Social Forces* 76.2 (1997): 667–700	Child mortality	Rejected	Promoting social inclusion and combating poverty
Shen, C. and Williamson, J. B.	1999	Maternal mortality, women's status, and economic dependency in less developed countries: a cross-national analysis	*Social Science & Medicine* 49.2 (1999): 197–214	Maternal mortality	Rejected	Promoting social inclusion and combating poverty

					Confirmed	Improving the business and consumer environment and modernizing the industrial base
de Soysa I. and Oneal J. R.	1999	Boon or bane? Reassessing the productivity of foreign direct investment	American Sociological Review 64.5 (1999): 766–82	Economic growth		
Spencer, Moore	2006	Peripherality, income inequality, and life expectancy: Revisiting the income inequality hypothesis	International Journal of Epidemiology 35.3 (2006): 623–32;	Life expectancy	Rejected	Promoting social inclusion and combating poverty
Tausch, Arno	2007	Quantitative world system studies contradict current Islamophobia: World political cycles, global terrorism, and world development	Alternatives: Turkish Journal of International Relations 6.1–2 (2007): 15–81	11 indicators of development	Rejected	Majority of the 9 guidelines
Tausch, Arno	2005	Is Islam really a development blockade?	Insight Turkey 7.1 (2005): 124–35	14 indicators of development	Rejected	Majority of the 9 guidelines
Tausch, Arno	2003	Social cohesion, sustainable development and Turkey's accession to the European Union: Implications from a global model	Alternatives: Turkish Journal of International Relations 2.1 (2003): 1–41	14 indicators of development	Rejected	Majority of the 9 guidelines
Timberlake, Michael and Williams, Kirk R.	1987	Structural position in the world-system, inequality, and political violence	Journal of Political and Military Sociology 15.1 (1987): 1–15	Political violence, inequality	Rejected	Promoting social inclusion and combating poverty

(Continued)

Author	Year	Title	Source	Research design focused on	Pro-globalization approach inherent in European Commission thinking	EU-2020 guideline
Tsai, Ming-Chang	2007	Does globalization affect human well-being?	*Social Indicators Research* 81.1 (2007): 103–26	Human Development Index, inflation, unemployment, rapid urbanization, state revenue, social spending	Partially rejected	Promoting social inclusion and combating poverty
Tsai, Ming-Chang	2006	Macro-structural determinants of political freedom in developing countries: A cross-national analysis	*Social Indicators Research* 76.2 (2006): 317–40	Political freedom	Confirmed	Promoting social inclusion and combating poverty
Tsai, Ming-Chang	2006	Economic and non-economic determinants of poverty in developing countries: Competing theories and empirical evidence	*Canadian Journal of Development Studies / Revue canadienne d'etudes du developpement* 27.3 (2006): 267–85	Poverty below $1/$2 a day	Confirmed	Promoting social inclusion and combating poverty
Van Rossem, R.	1996	The world system paradigm as general theory of development: A cross-national test	*American Sociological Review* 61.3 (1996): 508–27	Development performance	Confirmed	Majority of the 9 guidelines

Weede, Erich	1981	Dependency theories and economic growth: A cross-national study	*Koelner Zeitschrift fuer Soziologie und Sozialpsychologie* 33.4 (1981): 690–707	Economic growth	Confirmed	Improving the business and consumer environment and modernizing the industrial base
Weede, Erich	1981	The military, multinational corporations, and the economy: A cross-national study with particular reference to developing nations	*Schweizerische Zeitschrift fuer Soziologie/Revue Suisse de sociologie* 7.1 (1981): 113–27	Economic growth, income inequality	Confirmed	Improving the business and consumer environment and modernizing the industrial base
Weede, Erich and Tiefenbach, Horst	1981	Three dependency explanations of economic growth: A critical evaluation	*European Journal of Political Research* 9.4 (1981): 391–406	Economic growth, income inequality	Confirmed	Improving the business and consumer environment and modernizing the industrial base
Williamson, J. B. and Boehmer, U.	1997	Female life expectancy, gender stratification, health status, and level of economic development: A cross-national study of less developed countries	*Social Science & Medicine* 45.2 (1997): 305–17	Female life expectancy	Rejected	Promoting social inclusion and combating poverty

(Continued)

Author	Year	Title	Source	Research design focused on	Pro-globalization approach inherent in European Commission thinking	EU-2020 guideline
Wimberley, Dale W.	1998	Investment dependence and food consumption in the third world: A cross-national study	Rural Sociological Society, 1989	Per capita calorie and protein consumption	Rejected	Promoting social inclusion and combating poverty
Wimberley, Dale W. and Bello R.	1992	Effects of foreign investment, exports and economic growth on Third World food consumption	*Social Forces* 70.4 (1992): 895–921	Food consumption	Rejected	Promoting social inclusion and combating poverty

REFERENCES

A. T. Kearney, Inc. and the Carnegie Endowment for International Peace. 2002. 'Globalization's Last Hurrah?' *Foreign Policy*, January/February, 38–51.

_____. 2003. 'Measuring Globalization: Who's Up, Who's Down?' *Foreign Policy*, January/February, 60–72.

Addison, T. B. Guha-Khasnobis and G. Mavrotas (eds). 2006. 'FDI to Developing Countries: The Unfinished Agenda'. *The World Economy* 29(1).

Addison, T. and A. Heshmati. 2004. 'The New Global Determinants of FDI to Developing Countries'. *Research in Banking and Finance* 4: 151–86.

Ades, A. F. and E. L. Glaeser. 1999. 'Evidence on Growth, Increasing Returns and the Extent of the Market'. *Quarterly Journal of Economics* 114(3): 1025–45.

Agénor, P. R. 2003. 'Does Globalisation Hurt the Poor?' Washington DC: World Bank. Unpublished manuscript. http://www-wds.worldbank.org/external/default/WDSContentServer/WDSP/IB/2002/11/22/000094946_02111304010527/additional/134534322_20041117181619.pdf (accessed 14 February 2012).

Aghion, Ph. and P. Howitt. 1992. 'A Model of Growth through Creative Destruction'. *Econometrica* 60(2): 323–51.

Ake C. 1974. 'Modernization and Political Instability: A Theoretical Exploration'. *World Politics* 26(4): 576–91.

Alderson, A. S. 1999. 'Income Inequality, Development, and Dependence: A Reconsideration'. *American Sociological Review* 64(4): 606–31.

Alderson, A. S. and J. Beckfield. 2004. 'Power and Position in the World City System'. *American Journal of Sociology* 109(4): 811–51.

Alderson, A. S. and F. Nielsen. 2002. 'Globalization and the Great U-turn: Income Inequality Trends in 16 OECD Countries'. *American Journal of Sociology* 107(5): 1244–99.

Alesina, A. and E. La Ferrara. 2005. 'Ethnic Diversity and Economic Performance'. *Journal of Economic Literature* 43: 721–61.

Al-Mutavkkil, A., A. Heshmati and J.-S. Hwang. 2009. 'Development of Telecommunication and Broadcasting Infrastructure Indices at the Global Level'. *Telecommunication Policy* 33: 176–9.

Altman, M. and M. P. McDonald. 2001. 'Choosing Reliable Statistical Software'. *PS: Political Science & Politics* 34(3): 681–7.

Amin, S. 1976. *Unequal Development: An Essay on the Social Formations of Peripheral Capitalism*. New York: Monthly Review Press.

_____. 1994. *Re-reading the Postwar Period: An Intellectual Itinerary*, trans. Michael Wolfers. New York: Monthly Review Press.

_____. 1997. *Die Zukunft des Weltsystems. Herausforderungen der Globalisierung. Herausgegeben und aus dem Franzoesischen uebersetzt von Joachim Wilke*. Hamburg: VSA.

An, C. B. and S. H. Jeon. 2006. 'Demographic Change and Economic Growth: An Inverted-U Shape Relationship'. *Economics Letters* 92(3): 447–54.

Andersen, T. M. and T. T. Herbertsson. 2003. 'Measuring Globalization'. IZA Discussion Paper No. 817. Bonn: IZA.

Archibugi, D. and A. Coco. 2004. 'A New Indicator of Technological Capabilities for Developed and Developing Countries (ArCo)'. *World Development* 32(4): 629–54.

Archibugi, D., M. Denni and A. Filippetti. 2009. 'The Technological Capabilities of Nations: The State of Art of Synthetic Indicators'. *Technological Forecasting and Social Change* 76: 917–31.

Arrighi, G. 1995. *The Long 20th Century. Money, Power, and the Origins of Our Times.* London, New York: Verso.

Arrow, K. J. 1951. *On Mandelbaums Study of the Industrialization of Backward Areas.* Santa Monica, CA: Rand Corporation.

Attinà, F. 2002. *La politica di sicurezza e difesa dell'Unione europea: il cammino europeo dopo il trattato di Amsterdam.* Gaeta: Artistic and Publishing Company.

_____. 2003a. 'Organisation, Competition and Change of the International System'. *International Interactions* 16(4): 317.

_____. 2003b. 'The Euro-Mediterranean Partnership Assessed: The Realist and Liberal Views'. *European Foreign Affairs Review* 8(2): 181–99.

_____. 2004. 'The Barcelona Process, the Role of the European Union and the Lesson of the Western Mediterranean'. *Journal of North African Studies* 9(2): 140–52.

_____. 2005. 'State Aggregation in Defence Pacts: Systematic Explanations'. Jean Monnet Working Papers in Comparative and International Politics, Jean Monnet Centre EuroMed, Department of Political Studies, University of Catania. http://www.fscpo.unict.it/EuroMed/jmwp56.pdf (accessed 14 February 2012).

Babones, S. and X. Zhang. 2008. 'Heterogeneity in the Global South in the Relationship between Income Inequality and Foreign Trade'. *International Review of Modern Sociology* 34(1): 95–108.

Bakir, E. and A. Campbell. 2006. 'The Effect of Neo-Liberalism on the Fall in the Rate of Profit in Business Cycles'. *Review of Radical Political Economics* 38(3): 365–73.

Balassa, B. 1964. 'The Purchasing Power Parity Doctrine: A Reappraisal'. *Journal of Political Economy* 72: 584–96.

Bandelji, N. 2009. 'The Global Economy as Instituted Process: The Case of Central and Eastern Europe'. *American Sociological Review* 74(1): 128–49.

Barbieri, K. and R. Reuveny. 2005. 'Economic Globalization and Civil War'. *Journal of Politics* 67(4): 1228–47.

Barro, R. J. 1991. 'Economic Growth in a Cross Section of Countries'. *Quarterly Journal of Economics* 106(2): 407–43.

_____. 1996. 'Democracy and Growth'. *Journal of Economic Growth* 1(1): 1–27.

_____. 1998. *Determinants of Economic Growth: A Cross-Country Empirical Study.* Lionel Robbins Lectures. Cambridge, MA: MIT Press.

_____. 2003. 'Economic Growth in a Cross Section of Countries'. *International Library of Critical Writings in Economics* 159(1): 350–86.

Barro, R. J. and J.-W. Lee. 2000. 'International Data on Educational Attainment: Updates and Implications'. Centre for International Development at Harvard University, CID Working Paper 42.

Barro, R. J. and X. Sala-i-Martin. 2003. *Economic Growth,* 2nd ed. Cambridge, MA: MIT Press.

Batou, J. and H. Szlajfer (eds). 2009. *Western Europe, Eastern Europe, and World Development, 13th–18th Centuries: Collection of Essays of Marian Małowist.* Leiden and Boston: Brill.

Bauer, O. 1936. *Zwischen zwei Weltkriegen? Die Krise der Weltwirtschaft, der Demokratie und des Sozialismus.* Bratislava: E. Prager.

Beckfield, J. 2006a. 'Does Income Inequality Harm Health? New Cross-National Evidence'. *Journal of Health and Social Behavior* 45(3): 231–48.

_____. 2006b. 'European Integration and Income Inequality'. *American Sociological Review* 71(6): 964–85.

Beer, L. 1999. 'Income Inequality and Transnational Corporate Penetration'. *Journal of World-Systems Research* 5(1): 1–25.

Bernhard, M. and H. Szlajfer. 1995. *From the Polish Underground: Selections from Krytyka, 1978–1993.* University Park: Pennsylvania State University Press.

Bhaduri, A. K. and J. Steindl. 1983. *The Rise in Monetarism as a Social Doctrine.* London: Thames Polytechnic.

Bhandari, A. K. and A. Heshmati. 2007. 'Measurement of Globalization and its Variations Among Countries, Regions and Over Time'. In *Roadmap to Bangalore? Globalization, the EU's Lisbon Process and the Structures of Global Inequality*, ed. A. Heshmati and A. Tausch, 69–108. Hauppage, NY: Nova Science.

Bloom, D. and D. Canning. 2004. 'Global Demographic Change: Dimensions and Economic Significance'. NBER Working Paper 10817.

_____. 2007. 'Commentary: The Preston Curve 30 Years On: Still Sparking Fires'. *International Journal of Epidemiology*. http://ije.oxfordjournals.org/cgi/content/full/dym079v1 (accessed 14 February 2012).

Bloom, D. and J. D. Sachs. 1998. 'Geography, Demography and Growth in Africa'. *Brookings Papers on Economic Activity* 2: 207–95.

Bloom, D., D. Canning and J. Sevilla. 2003. *The Demographic Dividend: A New Perspective on the Economic Consequences of Population Change*. Santa Monica, CA: Rand Corporation.

Bobróvnikov, A. V. 2004. *Makrocikly v Ekonomike stran Latinskoj Ameriki* [Macrocycles in the economies of Latin American countries]. Moskva: Inst. Latinskoj Ameriki.

Boccara, P. 1977. *Études sur le Capitalisme Monopoliste d'État, sa Crise et son Issue*. Paris: Éditions sociales.

_____. 1983. 'Cycles Longs Mutations Technologiques et Originalité de la Crise de Structure'. *Issues: Cahiers de Recherches de la Revue Economie et Politique/Espaces Marx*. 1983 (2/3): 6–60.

_____. 1987. 'Les Cycles Longs et la Longue Phase de Difficultés en Cours: Population et Finance'. *Issues: Cahiers de Recherches de la Revue Economie et Politique/Espaces Marx*. 1987, 3 (29): 3–45.

_____. 1993. 'Poussées Périodiques de la Pensée sur les Cycles Longs, Récurrence et Irréversibilité: de l'Apparition des Fluctuations de Période Kondratieff vers leur mise en cause Radicale'. *Economies et Sociétés: Cahiers de l'ISMEA* 27 (7–8): 73–139.

_____. 2008. *Transformations et Crise du Capitalisme Mondialisé: Quelle Alternative?* Paris: Le Temps des Cerises.

_____. 2009. 'Paul Boccara: "We must incriminate the basic rules of capitalism"', trans. Christine A. *L'Humanité, English edition*. http://www.humaniteinenglish.com/spip.php?article1186 (accessed 14 February 2012).

Boccara, P., L. C. Treviño and O. Weinstein. 1983. *Cycles longs, mutations et crise*. Paris: Institut de Recherches Marxistes.

Boehmer, U. and J. B. Williamson. 1996. 'The Impact of Women's Status on Infant Mortality Rate: A Cross-national Analysis'. *Social Indicators Research* 37(3): 333–60.

Bornschier, V. 1975. 'Abhängige Industrialisierung und Einkommensentwicklung'. *Schweizerische Zeitschrift für Soziologie* 1(1): 67–105.

_____. 1976. *Wachstum, Konzentration und Multinationalisierung von Industrieunternehmen*. Frauenfeld and Stuttgart: Huber.

_____. 1980a. 'Multi-national Corporations, Economic Policy and National Development in the World System'. *International Social Science Journal* 32(1): 158–72.

_____. 1980b. *Multinationale Konzerne, Wirtschaftspolitik und nationale Entwicklung im Weltsystem*, with contributions by Thanh-Huyen Ballmer-Cao et al. Frankfurt and New York: Campus.

_____. 1981. 'Dependent Industrialization in the World Economy: Some Comments and Results Concerning a Recent Debate'. *Journal of Conflict Resolution* 25(3): 371–400.

_____. 1982. 'The World Economy in the World System. Structure Dependence and Change'. *International Social Science Journal* 34(1): 38–59.

_____. 1983. 'World Economy, Level Development and Income Distribution: An Integration of Different Approaches to the Explanation of Income Inequality'. *World Development* 11(1): 11–20.

_____. 1996. *Western Society in Transition*. New Brunswick, NJ: Transaction Publishers.

_____. (ed.) 2000. *State-building in Europe: The Revitalization of Western European Integration*. Cambridge and New York: Cambridge University Press.

_____. 2002. 'Changing Income Inequality in the Second Half of the 20th Century: Preliminary Findings and Propositions for Explanations'. *Journal of World-Systems Research* 8(1): 100–27.

_____. 2005. *Culture and Politics in Economic Development*. London and New York, NY: Routledge.

Bornschier, V. and T. H. Ballmer-Cao. 1979. 'Income Inequality: A Cross-national Study of the Relationships between MNC-Penetration, Dimensions of the Power Structure and Income Distribution'. *American Sociological Review* 44(3): 438–506.

Bornschier, V. and Ch. K. Chase-Dunn. 1985. *Transnational Corporations and Underdevelopment*. New York: Praeger.

Bornschier, V., Ch. K. Chase-Dunn and R. Rubinson. 1978. 'Cross-national Evidence of the Effects of Foreign Investment and Aid on Economic Growth and Inequality: A Survey of Findings and a Reanalysis'. *American Journal of Sociology* 84(3): 651–83.

Bradshaw, Y. W. 1993. 'Borrowing Against the Future: Children and Third World Indebtedness'. *Social Forces* 71(3): 629–56.

Bradshaw, Y. W. and J. Schafer. 2000. 'Urbanization and Development: The Emergence of International Non-governmental Organizations amid Declining States'. *Sociological Perspectives* 43(1): 97–116.

Brand, U. 2005. *Gegen-Hegemonie. Perspektiven globalisierungskritischer Strategien*. Hamburg: VSA.

Brand, U. and Ch. Görg. 2003. *Postfordistische Naturverhaltnisse: Konflikte um genetische Ressourcen und die Internationalisierung des Staates*. Muenster: Westfaelisches Dampfboot.

Brand, U. and W. Raza (eds). 2003. *Fit fur den Postfordismus?: Theoretisch-politische Perspektiven des Regulationsansatzes*. Muenster: Westfaelisches Dampfboot.

Brand, U., A. Demirovic, Ch. Görg and J. Hirsch (eds). 2001. *Nichtregierungsorganisationen in der Transformation des Staates*. Muenster: Westfaelisches Dampfboot.

Brand, U., A. Brunnengräber and L. Schrader. 2000. *Global governance: Alternative zur neoliberalen Globalisierung?* Muenster: Westfaelisches Dampfboot.

Brand, U., Ch. Görg, J. Hirsch and M. Wissen. 2008. *Conflicts in Environmental Regulation and the Internationalisation of the State: Contested Terrains*. London: Routledge.

Brzoska, M. and P. Lock. 1992. *Restructuring of Arms Production in Western Europe*. Oxford and New York: Oxford University Press.

Brzoska, M. and Th. Ohlson. 1986. *Arms Production in the Third World*. London and Philadelphia: Taylor & Francis.

———. 1987. *Arms Transfers to the Third World, 1971–85*. Oxford and New York: Oxford University Press.

Brzoska, M. and F. S. Perason. 1994. *Arms and Warfare: Escalation, De-escalation, and Negotiation*. Columbia, SC: University of South Carolina Press.

Bussmann, M. and G. Schneider. 2007. 'When Globalization Discontent Turns Violent: Foreign Economic Liberalization and Internal War'. *International Studies Quarterly* 51(1): 79–97.

Bussmann, M., I. de Soysa and J. R. Oneal. 2005. 'The Effect of Globalization on National Income Inequality'. *Comparative Sociology* 4(3–4): 285–312.

Cardoso, F. H. 1977. 'El Consumo de la Teoría de la Dependencia en los Estados Unidos'. *El Trimestre Economico* 44(173/1): 33–52.

———. 1979. *Development under Fire*. Mexico City: Instituto Latinoamericano de Estudios Transnacionales, DEE/D/24 i, Mayo (Mexico 20 D. F., Apartado 85-025).

Cardoso, F. H. and E. Faletto. 1971. *Dependencia y desarrollo en América Latina*. Mexico D.F.: Editorial Siglo I.

CEPAL/ECLAC. 2002. *Globalización y Desarrollo*. Santiago de Chile: United Nations Economic Commission for Latin America. http://www.eclac.cl/cgi-bin/getProd.asp?xml=/publicaciones/xml/6/10026/P10026.xml&xsl=/tpl/p9f.xsl&base=/MDG/tpl/top-bottom.xsl (accessed 14 February 2012).

Chanda, A. and L. Putterman. 2007. 'Early Starts, Reversals and Catch-up in the Process of Economic Development'. *Scandinavian Journal of Economics* 109(2): 387–413.

Chang, M. L. 2004. 'Growing Pains: Cross-National Variation in Sex Segregation in Sixteen Developing Countries'. *American Sociological Review* 69(1): 114–37.

Chase-Dunn, Ch. K. 1975. 'The Effects of International Economic Dependence on Development and Inequality: A Cross-national Study'. *American Sociological Review* 40(4): 720–38.

Cheol-Sung, L, F. Nielsen and A. S. Alderson. 2007. 'Income Inequality, Global Economy and the State'. *Social Forces* 86(1): 77–111.

Ciccone, A. and M. Jarocinski. 2008. 'Determinants of Economic Growth. Will Data Tell?' European Central Bank Working Paper Series 852. http://www.ecb.int/pub/pdf/scpwps/ecbwp852.pdf (accessed 14 February 2012).

Clark, R. 2008. 'Dependency, Network Integration, and Development'. *Sociological Perspectives* 51(3): 629–48.

Clauss, G. and H. Ebner. 1978. *Grundlagen der Statistik. Fuer Psychologen, Paedagogen und Soziologen.* Berlin: Volk and Wissen.

Coleman, J. S. 1965. *Education and Political Development.* Princeton: Princeton University Press.

Conceição, P. and J. K. Galbraith. 2000. 'Constructing Long and Dense Time Series of Inequality Using the Theil Index'. *Eastern Economic Journal* 26(1): 61–74.

Constant, A., L. Gataullina, K. F. Zimmermann and L. Zimmermann. 2006. 'Clash of Cultures: Muslims and Christians in the Ethnosizing Process'. German Institute for Economic Research Discussion Paper 628, Berlin, October 2006. http://ideas.repec.org/p/diw/diwwpp/dp628.html (accessed 14 February 2012).

Crenshaw, E. 1992. 'Cross-National Determinants of Income Inequality: A Replication and Extension Using Ecological-Evolutionary Theory'. *Social Forces* 71(2): 339–63.

Crenshaw, E. and A. Ameen. 1994. 'The Distribution of Income across National Populations: Testing Multiple Paradigms'. *Social Science Research* 23(1): 1–22.

Crowly, A. M., J. Rauch, S. Seagrave and D. A. Smith. 1998. 'Quantitative Cross-national Studies of Economic Development: A Comparison of the Economics and Sociology Literatures'. *Studies in Comparative International Development* 33(2): 30–58.

Davenport, C. 1995. 'Assessing the Military's Influence on Political Repression'. *Journal of Political and Military Sociology* 23(1): 119–44.

de Soysa, I. and E. Neumayer. 2005. 'False Prophet, or Genuine Saviour? Assessing the Effects of Economic Openness on Sustainable Development, 1980–99'. *International Organization* 59(3): 731–72.

de Soysa, I. and J. Oneal. 1999. 'Boon or Bane? Reassessing the productivity of foreign direct investment'. *American Sociological Review* 64(3): 766–82.

Decancq, K. and M. A. Lugo. 2008. 'Setting Weights in Multi-dimensional Indices of Well-being'. Working Paper, Department of Economics, University of Oxford, May 2008.

Delors, J. 1992. *Our Europe: The Community and National Development,* trans. Brian Pearce. London and New York: Verso.

Devezas, T. C. (ed.) 2006. *Kondratieff Waves, Warfare and World Security.* Amsterdam: IOS Press.

Devezas, T. C. and J. T. Corredine. 2001. 'The Biological Determinants of Long-Wave Behaviour in Socio-economic Growth and Development'. *Technological Forecasting and Social Change* 68(1): 1–57.

Devezas, T. C. and G. Modelski. 2003. 'Power Law Behaviour and World System Evolution: A Millennial Learning Process'. *Technological Forecasting and Social Change* 70(9): 819–59.

Devezas, T. C., H. A. Linestone and H. J. S. Santos. 2005. 'The Growth Dynamics of the Internet and the Long-Wave Theory'. *Technological Forecasting and Social Change* 72(8): 913–35.

Di Marco, L. E. (ed.) 1972. *International Economics and Development: Essays in Honour of Raúl Prebisch.* New York: Academic Press.

Dick, Ch. and A. K. Jorgenson. 2010. 'Sectoral Foreign Investment and Nitrous Oxide Emissions: A Quantitative Investigation'. *Society and Natural Resources* 23(1): 71–82.

Dixon, W. J. and T. Boswell. 1996. 'Dependency, Disarticulation, and Denominator Effects: Another Look at Foreign Capital Penetration'. *American Journal of Sociology* 102(2): 543–62.

Dollar, D. and R. Gatti. 1999. 'Gender Inequality, Income and Growth: Are Good Times Good for Women?' World Bank Policy Research Report on Gender and Development (1). Washington DC: World Bank.

Dowrick, S. and J. Quiggin. 1997. 'Convergence in GDP and Living Standards: A Revealed Preference Approach'. *American Economic Review* 67(1): 41–64.

Dreher, A. 2005. 'Does Globalization Affect Growth? Empirical Evidence from a New Index'. Department of Economics, University of Konstanz, unpublished manuscript. (Published later in 2006 in *Applied Economics* 38(10): 1091–1110.)

Dreher, A., G. Noel and P. Martens. 2008. *Measuring Globalization: Gauging its Consequence*. New York: Springer.

Durlauf, St. N., A. Kourtellos and Ch. M. Tan. 2008. 'Are any Growth Theories Robust?' *Economic Journal* 118(1): 329–46.

Dutt, A. K. 1997. 'The Pattern of Direct Foreign Investment and Economic Growth'. *World Development* 25(11): 1925–36.

Easterly, W. 2000. 'The Middle Class Consensus and Economic Development'. World Bank Policy Research Paper No. 2346. Available via SSRN: http://ssrn.com/abstract=630718; data available at http://www.cgdev.org/doc/expert%20pages/easterly/easterly_consensusdata.xls in Excel format (accessed 14 February 2012).

———. 2002. 'Inequality Does Cause Underdevelopment: New Evidence'. Center for Global Development Working Paper 1, January. http://papers.ssrn.com/sol3/papers.cfm?abstract_id=999973 (accessed 14 January 2012).

Easterly, W. and R. Levine. 1997. 'Africa's Growth Tragedy: Policies and Ethnic Divisions'. *Quarterly Journal of Economics* 112(4): 1203–50.

Edwards, S. 1997. 'Openness, Productivity and Growth: What do we really know?' NBER Working Paper (5978). Cambridge, MA: National Bureau of Economic Research.

Ehrhardt-Martinez, K., E. M. Crenshaw and J. C. Jenkins. 2002. 'Deforestation and the Environmental Kuznets Curve: A Cross-National Investigation of Intervening Mechanisms'. *Social Science Quarterly* 83(1): 226–43.

Eide, A. and M. Thee. 1980. *Problems of Contemporary Militarism*. New York: St. Martin's Press.

Elola, J., A. Daponte and V. Navarro. 1995. 'Health Indicators and the Organization of Health-Care Systems in Western Europe'. *American Journal of Public Health* 85(10): 1397–1401.

Escudier, J.-L. 1993. 'Kondratieff et l'Histoire Économique Française ou la Rencontre Inachevée'. *Annales. Économies, Sociétés, Civilisations* 48(2): 359–83.

Eur-Lex. 2005. 'Communication to the Spring Council: "Working Together for Growth and Jobs – A New Start for the Lisbon Strategy"'. http://eur-lex.europa.eu/LexUriServ/LexUriServ.do?uri=COM:2005:0024:FIN:en:PDF (accessed 14 February 2012).

European Commission. 2003. 'Joint Report on Social Exclusion Summarising the Results of the Examination of the National Action Plans for Social Inclusion 2003–2005'. Brussels: European Commission. http://eur-lex.europa.eu/LexUriServ/LexUriServ.do?uri=COM:2003:0773:fin:en:pdf (accessed 14 February 2012).

———. 2005a. 'The Economic Costs of non-Lisbon. A Survey of the Literature on the Economic Impact of Lisbon-type Reforms'. http://ec.europa.eu/economy_finance/publications/publication966_en.pdf (accessed 14 February 2012).

———. 2005b. 'A New Start for the Lisbon Strategy'. http://europa.eu/legislation_summaries/employment_and_social_policy/community_employment_policies/c11325_en.htm (accessed 16 March 2012).

———. 2007. 'Growing Regions, growing Europe: Fourth report on economic and social cohesion'. http://ec.europa.eu/regional_policy/sources/docoffic/official/repor_en.htm and http://ec.europa.eu/regional_policy/sources/docoffic/official/reports/cohesion4/index_en.htm (including main regional data) (accessed 14 February 2012).

European Roundtable of Industrialists (ERT). 2001. 'European Pensions. An Appeal for Reform. Pension Schemes that Europe Can Really Afford'. Brussels: ERT.

Fahey, T., Christopher T. Whelan and Bertrand Maître. 2005. *First European Quality of Life Survey: Income inequalities and deprivation*. Dublin: European Foundation for the Improvement of Living and Working Conditions.

Firebaugh, G. 1992. 'Growth Effects of Foreign and Domestic Investment'. *American Journal of Sociology* 98(2): 105–30.

_____. 1996. 'Does Foreign Capital Harm Poor Nations? New Estimates Based on Dixon and Boswell's Measures of Capital Penetration'. *American Journal of Sociology* 102(3): 563–75.

_____. 1999. 'Empirics of World Income Inequality'. *American Journal of Sociology* 104(Spring): 1597–1630.

_____. 2000a. 'Observed Trends in Between-Nation Income Inequality, and Two Conjectures'. *American Journal of Sociology* 106(Summer): 215–21.

_____. 2000b. 'Trends in Between-Nation Income Inequality'. *Annual Review of Sociology* 26: 323–39.

_____. 2004. 'Does Industrialization No Longer Benefit Poor Countries? A Comment on Arrighi, Silver, and Brewer, 2003'. *Studies in Comparative International Development* 39(Spring): 99–105.

Firebaugh, G. and F. Beck. 1994. 'Does Economic Growth Benefit the Masses? Growth, Dependence, and Welfare in the Third World'. *American Sociological Review* 59(Autumn): 631–53.

Firebaugh, G. and B. Goesling. 2004. 'Accounting for the Recent Decline in Global Income Inequality'. *American Journal of Sociology* 110(Autumn): 283–312.

Foster, J. B. and H. Szlajfer (eds). 1984. *The Faltering Economy: The Problem of Accumulation under Monopoly Capitalism*. New York: Monthly Review Press.

Franco-Giraldo, A., M. Palma and C. Alvarez-Dardet. 2006. 'The Effect of Structural Adjustment on Health Conditions in Latin America and the Caribbean, 1980–2000'. *Revista Panamericana de Salud Publica* 19(5): 291–9.

Frank, A. G. 1967. *Capitalism and Underdevelopment in Latin America: Historical Studies of Chile and Brazil*. New York: Monthly Review Press.

_____. 1983. 'World System in Crisis'. In *Contending Approaches to World System Analysis*, ed. W. R. Thompson, 27–42. Beverly Hills: Sage.

_____. 1990. 'Revolution in Eastern Europe: Lessons for Democratic Social Movements (and Socialists?)'. *Third World Quarterly* 12(2): 36–52.

_____. 1998. *ReOrient: Global Economy in the Asian Age*. Berkeley: University of California Press.

Frankel, J. A. and D. Romer. 1999. 'Does Trade Cause Growth?' *American Economic Review* 89(3): 379–99.

Froebel, F. 1980. *The New International Division of Labour: Structural Unemployment in Industrialised Countries and Industrialisation in Developing Countries*. Cambridge and New York: Cambridge University Press; Paris: Editions de la Maison des Sciences de l'Homme.

Furtado, C. 1963. *The Economic Growth of Brazil: A Survey from Colonial to Modern Times*, trans. R. W. de Aguiar and E. C. Drysdale. Berkeley: University of California Press.

_____. 1964. *Development and Underdevelopment*, trans. by R.W. de Aguiar and E. C. Drysdale. Berkeley: University of California Press.

_____. 1976. *Economic Development of Latin America: Historical Background and Contemporary Problems*, trans. S. Macedo. Cambridge and New York: Cambridge University Press.

_____. 1983. *Accumulation and Development: the Logic of Industrial Civilization*, trans. Suzette Macedo. Oxford: M. Robertson.

Furukawa, M. 2005. 'Factor Analysis of Attributive Determinants for Life Expectancy and Infant Mortality Rate with Recipient Country Data in Consideration of Socio-economic Environment'. *Nippon eiseigaku zasshi. Japanese Journal of Hygiene* 60(3): 335–44.

Galalp, H. 1989. 'The Stages and Long-Cycles of Capitalist Development'. *Review of Radical Political Economics* 21(4): 83–92.

Galbraith, J. K. 1999. 'Globalization and Pay'. *Proceedings of the American Philosophical Society* 143(2):178–86.

_____. 2007. 'Maastricht 2042 and the Fate of Europe: Toward Convergence and Full Employment'. International Policy Analysis Unit, Friedrich-Ebert-Stiftung.

_____. 2009. 'Inequality, Unemployment and Growth: New Measures for Old Controversies'. *Journal of Economic Inequality* 7(2): 189–206.

Galbraith, J. K. and E. Garcilazo. 2004. 'Unemployment, Inequality and the Policy of Europe, 1984–2000'. *Banca Nazionale del Lavoro Quarterly Review* 8(228): 3–28.

_____. 2005. 'Pay Inequality in Europe 1995–2000: Convergence Between Countries and Stability Inside'. *European Journal of Comparative Economics* 2(2): 139–75.

Galbraith, J. K. and H. Kum. 2003. 'Inequality and Economic Growth: A Global View Based on Measures of Pay'. *CESifo Economic Studies* 49(4): 527–56.

_____. 2005. 'Estimating the Inequality of Household Incomes: A Statistical Approach to the Creation of a Dense and Consistent Global Data Set'. *Review of Income and Wealth* 51(1): 115–43.

Galbraith, J. K., P. Conceição and P. Ferreira. 1999. 'Inequality and Unemployment in Europe: The American Cure'. *New Left Review* 237: 28–51.

Galbraith, J. K., O. Giovannoni and A. J. Russo. 2007. 'The Fed's Real Reaction Function: Monetary Policy, Inflation, Unemployment, Inequality – and Presidential Politics'. Levy Institute of Bard College Working Paper 511.

Gallup, J. L. and J. D. Sachs, with A. D. Mellinger. 1999. 'Geography and Economic Development'. In *Annual World Bank Conference on Development Economics 1998*, ed. Boris Pleskovic and Joseph E. Stiglitz. Washington DC: World Bank. (Also published in *International Regional Science Review* 22(2): 179–232.)

Galtung, J. 1971. 'A Structural Theory of Imperialism'. *Journal of Peace Research* 8(2): 81–117.

_____. 1982. *Kapitalistische Großmacht Europa oder Die Gemeinschaft der Konzerne?* Reinbek near Hamburg: Rowohlt TB-V.

Ghobara, H. A., P. Huth and B. Russett. 2004. 'Comparative Public Health: The Political Economy of Human Misery and Well-Being'. *International Studies Quarterly* 48(1): 73–94.

Glasberg, D. S. and K. B. Ward. 1993. 'Foreign Debt and Economic Growth in the World-System'. *Social Science Quarterly* 74(4): 703–20.

Goesling, B. and G. Firebaugh. 2004. 'The Trend in International Health Inequality'. *Population and Development Review* 30(Spring): 131–46.

Goldstein, J. S. 1985. 'Basic Human Needs: The Plateau Curve'. *World Development* 13(5): 595–609.

_____. 1988. *Long Cycles: Prosperity and War in the Modern Age*. New Haven: Yale University Press.

Greene, W. H. 2008. *Econometric Analysis*, 6th ed. Upper Saddle River, NJ: Prentice Hall.

Grier, K. B. and G. Tullock. 1989. 'An Empirical Analysis of Cross-National Economic Growth'. *Journal of Monetary Economics* 24(2): 259–76.

Griffith-Jones, St. and O. Sunkel. 1986. *Debt and Development Crises in Latin America: The End of an Illusion*. Oxford: Clarendon Press; New York: Oxford University Press.

Grupp, H. and M. E. Mogee. 2004. 'Indicators of National Science and Technology Policy: How Robust are Composite Indicators?' *Research Policy* 33: 1373–84.

Guger A., M. Marterbauer and E. Walterskirchen. 2004. *Growth Policy in the Spirit of Steindl and Kalecki*. WIFO Working Paper 240. http://ewald.walterskirchen.wifo.ac.at/ (accessed 9 March 2012).

_____. 2006a. 'Growth Policy in the Spirit of Steindl and Kalecki'. *Metroeconomica* 57(3): 428–42.

_____. 2006b. 'Zur Aktualität der Politischen Ökonomie von Josef Steindl'. *Kurswechsel* 4: 18–26. http://www.beigewum.at/wordpress/wp-content/uploads/018_alois_guger_markus_marterbauer_ewald_walterskirchen.pdf (accessed 14 February).

Gustafsson, B. and M. Johansson. 1999. 'In Search of Smoking Guns: What Makes Income Inequality Vary Over Time in Different Countries?' *American Sociological Review* 64(4): 585–605.

Gylfason, Th. 2001. 'Natural Resources, Education, and Economic Development'. *European Economic Review* 45(4–6): 847–59.

Hafner-Burton, E. M. 2005. 'Right or Robust? The Sensitive Nature of Repression to Globalization'. *Journal of Peace Research* 42(6): 679–98.

Hall, R. E. and Ch. I. Jones. 1999. 'Why Do Some Countries Produce so Much More Output per Worker than Others?' *Quarterly Journal of Economics* 114(1): 83–116.

Hamid, A. 2007. 'Military Expenditures and Inequality: Empirical Evidence from Global Data'. *Defence and Peace Economics* 18(6): 519–35.

Hatton, T. J. and J. A. Williamson. 2009. 'Vanishing Third World Emigrants?' Harvard University, Department of Economics. http://www.economics.harvard.edu/faculty/williamson/files/VanishingHWpaperFeb2809.pdf (accessed 14 February 2012).

Heinemann, F., Andreas Ammermüller, Jürgen Egeln et al. 2004. *Eignung von Strukturindikatoren als Instrument zur Bewertung der ökonomischen Performance der EU-Mitgliedstaaten unter besonderer Berücksichtigung von Wirtschaftsreformen – Evaluierung der EU-Strukturindikatoren und Möglichkeit ihrer Weiterentwicklung.* Zentrum für Europäische Wirtschaftsforschung (ZEW – Centre for European Economic Research), Final Report to the Federal Ministry of Finance, Research Contract 5/04. http://ftp.zew.de/pub/zew-docs/div/ZEW_Strukturindikatoren_lang_rev.pdf. English-language short version available at http://ftp.zew.de/pub/zew-docs/div/ZEW_Strukturindikatoren_kurz_en_rev.pdf (accessed 14 February 2012).

Herkenrath, M. and V. Bornschier. 2003. 'Transnational Corporations in World Development – Still the Same Harmful Effects in an Increasingly Globalized World Economy?' *Journal of World-Systems Research* 9(1): 105–39.

Herkenrath, M., C. Koenig, H. Scholtz and Th. Volken. 2005. 'Convergence and Divergence in the Contemporary World System: An Introduction'. *International Journal of Comparative Sociology* 46(5–6): 363–82.

Heshmati, A. 2003. *Measurement of a Multidimensional Index of Globalization and its Impact on Income Inequality.* Helsinki: United Nations University, World Institute for Development Economics Research.

_____. 2006a. 'Measurement of a Multi-Dimensional Index of Globalization'. *Global Economy Journal* 6(2): 1–28.

_____. 2006b. 'The Relationship between Income Inequality Poverty, and Globalization'. In *The Impact of Globalization on the World's Poor*, ed. M. Nissanke and E. Thorbecke, 59–93. Basingstoke: Palgrave Macmillan.

_____. 2006c. 'The World Distribution of Income and Income Inequality: A Review of the Economic Literature'. *Journal of World-Systems Research* 12(1): 60–107.

_____. 2007. *Global Trends in Income Inequality.* Hauppauge, NY: Nova Science.

Heshmati, A. and S. C. Lee. 2010. 'The Relationship between Globalization, Economic Growth and income Inequality'. *Journal of Globalization Studies* (Moscow) 1(2): 87–117.

Heshmati, A. and J.-E. Oh. 2006. 'Alternative Composite Lisbon Development Strategy Indices: A Comparison of EU, USA, Japan and Korea'. *European Journal of Comparative Economics* 3(2): 133–70.

Heshmati, A. and A. Tausch (eds). 2007. *Roadmap to Bangalore? Globalization, the EUs Lisbon Process and the Structures of Global Inequality.* Hauppauge, NY: Nova Science.

Heshmati, A., A. Tausch and C. Bajalan. 2008. 'Measurement and Analysis of Child Well-Being in Middle and High Income Countries'. *European Journal of Comparative Economics* 5(2): 227–49.

Hettne, B., A. Inotai and O. Sunkel (eds). 2000. *The New Regionalism and the Future of Security and Development. Foreword by Giovanni Andrea Cornia.* Basingstoke: Macmillan, in association with UNU/WIDER.

Hodler, R. 2004. 'The Curse of Natural Resources in Fractionalized Countries'. Economics Department, University of Bern. http://www.gsoep.de/documents/dokumentenarchiv/17/41536/Paper-132.pdf (accessed 15 February 2012).

Hoell, O. and A. Tausch. 1980. 'Austria and the European Periphery'. In *European Studies of Development*, ed. J. de Bandt, P. Mandi and D. Seers, 28–37: London: Macmillan.

HOLLIS Catalog, Harvard University Library, available at: http://hollis.harvard.edu/advancedsearch/advancedsearch.html.

Hotelling, H. 1933. 'Analysis of a Complex of Statistical Variables into Principal Components'. *Journal of Educational Psychology* 24: 417–41 and 498–520.

Huang, J. and K. M. Slomczynski. 2003. 'The Dimensionality and Measurement of Economic Dependency: A Research Note'. *International Journal of Sociology* 33 (4): 82–98.

Huntington, S. P. 1968. *Political Order in Changing Societies.* New Haven: Yale University Press.

_____. 1996. *The Clash of Civilizations and the Remaking of World Order.* New York: Simon & Schuster.

IMF. 2009. World Economic Outlook database. http://www.imf.org/external/pubs/ft/weo/2009/01/weodata/download.aspx (accessed 15 February 2012).

Inglehart, R. T. 1990. *Culture Shift in Advanced Industrial Societies*. Princeton: Princeton University Press.
_____. 2007. 'The Worldviews of Islamic Publics in Global Perspective'. In *Values and Perceptions of the Islamic and Middle Eastern Publics*, ed. M. Moaddel, 25–46. Basingstoke: Palgrave Macmillan.

Inglehart, R. T. and P. Norris. 2003a. *Rising Tide: Gender Equality and Cultural Change Around the World*. Cambridge and New York: Cambridge University Press.
_____. 2003b. 'The True Clash of Civilizations'. *Foreign Policy*, Spring. http://www.globalpolicy. org/component/content/article/162/27604.html (accessed 15 February 2012).

Ito, K. 1993. *Encyclopedic Dictionary of Mathematics*. Cambridge, MA and London: MIT Press.

Jackson, D. J. and E. F. Borgatta (eds). 1981. *Factor Analysis and Measurement in Sociological Research. A Multi-Dimensional Perspective*. London and Beverly Hills: Sage.

Jamison, D. T., M. Sandbu and J. Wang. 2001. 'Cross-country Variation in Mortality Decline, 1962–87: The Role of Country-Specific Technical Progress'. Background Paper for Working Group One, WHO Commission on Macroeconomics and Health. http://www.emro.who.int/ cbi/pdf/CountryMortalityDecline.pdf (accessed 15 February 2012).

Jenkins, C. K. and K. Schock. 2003. 'Political Process, International Dependence, and Mass Political Conflict: A Global Analysis of Protest and Rebellion, 1973–1978'. *International Journal of Sociology* 33(4): 41–63.

Jenkins, J. C. and S. J. Scanlan. 2001. 'Food Security in Less Developed Countries, 1970 to 1990'. *American Sociological Review* 66(5): 718–44.

Jenkins, J. C., S. J. Scanlan and L. Peterson. 2007. 'Military Famine, Human Rights, and Child Hunger'. *Journal of Conflict Resolution* 51(6): 823–47.

Jessop, B. 1990. 'Regulation Theories in Retrospect and Prospect'. *Economy and Society* 19(2): 153–216.

Jessop, B. and N.-L. Sum. 2006. *Beyond the Regulation Approach: Putting Capitalist Economies in Their Place*. Cheltenham: Edward Elgar.

Jorgenson, A. K. 2003. 'Consumption and Environmental Degradation: A Cross-national Analysis of the Ecological Footprint'. *Social Problems* 50(3): 374–94.
_____. 2004a. 'Global Inequality, Water Pollution, and Infant Mortality'. *Social Science Journal* 41(2): 279–88.
_____. 2004b. 'Uneven Processes and Environmental Degradation in the World-Economy'. *Human Ecology Review* 11(2): 103–17.
_____. 2005. 'Unpacking International Power and the Ecological Footprints of Nations: A Quantitative Cross-national Study'. *Sociological Perspectives* 48(3): 383–402.
_____. 2006a. 'Global Warming and the Neglected Greenhouse Gas: A Cross-national Study of the Social Causes of Methane Emissions Intensity, 1995'. *Social Forces* 84(3): 1779–98.
_____. 2006b. 'Unequal Ecological Exchange and Environmental Degradation: A Theoretical Proposition and Cross-national Study of Deforestation, 1990–2000'. *Rural Sociology* 71(4): 685–712.
_____. 2007a. 'Does Foreign Investment Harm the Air We Breathe and the Water We Drink? A Cross-National Study of Carbon Dioxide Emissions and Organic Water Pollution in Less-Developed Countries, 1975 to 2000'. *Organization & Environment* 20(2): 135–57.
_____. 2007b. 'Foreign Direct Investment and Pesticide Use Intensity in Less-Developed Countries: A Quantitative Investigation'. *Society and Natural Resources* 20(1): 73–83.
_____. 2008. 'Structural Integration and the Trees: An Analysis of Deforestation in Less-Developed Countries, 1990–2005'. *Sociological Quarterly* 49(3): 503–27.
_____. 2009a. 'Foreign Direct Investment and the Environment, the Mitigating Influence of Institutional and Civil Society Factors, and Relationships between Industrial Pollution and Human Health'. *Organization & Environment*. 22(2): 135–57.
_____. 2009b. 'Political-Economic Integration, Industrial Pollution and Human Health: A Panel Study of Less-Developed Countries, 1980–2000'. *International Sociology* 24(1): 115–43.
_____. 2009c. 'The Sociology of Unequal Exchange in Ecological Context: A Panel Study of Lower-Income Countries, 1975–2000'. *Sociological Forum* 24(1): 22–46.

_____. 2009d. 'The Transnational Organization of Production, the Scale of Degradation, and Ecoefficiency: A Study of Carbon Dioxide Emissions in Less-Developed Countries'. *Human Ecology Review* 16(1): 64–74.

Jorgenson, A. K. and T. J. Burns. 2004. 'Globalization, the Environment, and Infant Mortality: A Cross-National Study'. *Humboldt Journal of Social Relations* 28(1): 7–52.

_____. 2007. 'The Political-Economic Causes of Change in the Ecological Footprints of Nations, 1991–2001: A Quantitative Investigation'. *Social Science Research* 36(2): 834–53.

Jorgenson, A. K. and B. Clark. 2009. 'The Economy, Military, and Ecologically Unequal Exchange Relationships in Comparative Perspective: A Panel Study of the Ecological Footprints of Nations, 1975–2000'. *Social Problems* 56(4): 621–46.

Jorgenson, A. K. and K. A. Kuykendall. 2008. 'Globalization, Foreign Investment Dependence and Agriculture Production: Pesticide and Fertilizer Use in Less-developed Countries, 1990–2000'. *Social Forces* 87(1): 529–60.

Jorgenson, A. K., K. Austin and Ch. Dick. 2009. 'Ecologically Unequal Exchange and the Resource Consumption/Environmental Degradation Paradox'. *International Journal of Comparative Sociology* 50(3–4): 263–84.

Jorgenson, A. K., C. Dick and M. C. Mahutga. 2007. 'Foreign Investment Dependence and the Environment: An Ecostructural Approach'. *Social Problems* 54(3): 371–94.

Jourdon, Ph. 2008. 'Does the Study of Kondratieff Cycles Help Us to Know More about the Social Nature of Money?' *Entelequia. Revista Interdisciplinar* 6: 95–122. http://www.eumed.net/entelequia/en.art.php?a=06a06 (accessed 15 February 2012).

Kaldor, M. 1983. *The World Military Order the Impact of Military Technology on the Third World*. London: Macmillan.

Kalecki, M. 1943. 'Political Aspects of Full Employment'. *Political Quarterly* 14(4): 322–31.

_____. 1966. *Studies in the Theory of Business Cycles, 1933–1939*. New York: A.M. Kelley.

_____. 1968a. *Theory of Economic Dynamics; an Essay on Cyclical and Long-Run Changes in Capitalist Economy*. New York: Monthly Review Press.

_____. 1968b. 'Trend and Business Cycles Reconsidered'. *Economic Journal* 78(310): 263–76.

_____. 1971. *Selected Essays on the Dynamics of the Capitalist Economy 1933–1970*. Cambridge: Cambridge University Press.

_____. 1979. *Essays on Developing Economies*, with an introduction by Professor Joan Robinson. Hassocks: The Harvester Press.

_____. 1996. 'The Maintenance of Full Employment after the Transition Period: A Comparison of the Problem in the United States and United Kingdom'. *International Labour Review* 135(3–4): 359–65. Reprinted from *International Labour Review* 52 (1945).

Kalecki, M. and G. R. Feiwel. 1972. *The Last Phase in the Transformation of Capitalism*. New York: Monthly Review Press.

Kamarck, A. M. 1976. *The Tropics and Economic Development: A Provocative Inquiry into the Poverty of Nations*. Baltimore: Johns Hopkins University Press.

Kang, S. M. 2002. 'A Sensitivity Analysis of the Korean Composite Environmental Index'. *Ecological Economics* 43: 159–74.

Kaplan, M. 1974. 'The Power Structure in International Relations'. *International Social Science Journal* 26(1): 95–108.

Katz, S. 2006. 'Indicators for Complex Innovation Systems'. *Research Policy* 35(7): 893–909.

Kawachi, I, and B. P. Kennedy. 1997. 'Socio-economic Determinants of Health. Health and Social Cohesion: Why Care About Income Inequality?' *British Medical Journal* 314(7086): 1037–40.

Kawachi, I., B. P. Kennedy and R. G. Wilkinson. 1999. 'Crime: Social Disorganization and Relative Deprivation'. *Social Science & Medicine* 48(6): 719–31.

Kawachi, I., B. P. Kennedy, K. Lochner and D. Prothrow-Stith. 1997. 'Social Capital, Income Inequality, and Mortality'. *American Journal of Public Health* 87(9): 1491–98.

Kaya, Y. 2010. 'Globalization and Industrialization in 64 Developing Countries, 1980–2003'. *Social Forces* 88(3): 1153–82.

Keller, K. R. I., P. Poutvaara and A. Wagener. 2006. 'Military Draft and Economic Growth in OECD Countries'. IZA Discussion Paper No. 2022. http://ssrn.com/abstract=892346 (accessed 15 February 2012).

Kentor, J. 1998. 'The Long-Term Effects of Foreign Investment Dependence on Economic Growth, 1940–1990'. *American Journal of Sociology* 103(4): 1024–46.

_____. 2001. 'The Long Term Effects of Globalization on Income Inequality, Population Growth, and Economic Development'. *Social Problems* 48(4), Special Issue on Globalization and Social Problems: 435–55.

Kentor, J. and T. Boswell. 2003. 'Foreign Capital Dependence and Development: A New Direction'. *American Sociological Review* 68(2): 301–13.

Kentor, J. and A. K. Jorgenson. 2010. 'Foreign Investment and Development: An Organizational Perspective'. *International Sociology* 25(3): 419–41.

Kentor, J. and D. Kick. 2008. 'Bringing the Military Back In: Military Expenditures and Economic Growth 1990 to 2003'. *Journal of World-Systems Research* 14(2): 142–72.

Kerbo, H. 2005. 'Foreign Investment and Disparities in Economic Development and Poverty Reduction: Comparative-Historical Analysis of the Buddhist Countries of Southeast Asia'. *International Journal of Comparative Sociology* 46(5–6): 425–59.

Kick, E. L., B. L. Davis, M. Lehtinen and T. J. Burns. 2000. 'World-System Position, National Political Characteristics and Economic Development Outcomes'. *Journal of Political and Military Sociology* 28(1): 131–55.

Kim, J. O. and Ch. W. Mueller. 1978. *Factor Analysis. Statistical Methods and Practical Issues.* Beverly Hills and London: Sage.

Klasen, St. 1999. 'Does Gender Inequality Reduce Growth and Development? Evidence from Cross-Country Regressions'. World Bank, Development Research Group/Poverty Reduction and Economic Management Network.

Klitgaard, R. and J. Fedderke. 1995. 'Social Integration and Disintegration: An Exploratory Analysis of Cross-country Data'. *World Development* 23(3): 357–69.

Kohler, G. and A. Tausch. 2003. *Global Keynesianism: Unequal Exchange and Global Exploitation.* Huntington, NY: Nova Science.

Kohr, L. 1957. *The Breakdown of Nations.* New York: Rinehart.

_____. 1958. 'The Velocity Theory of Population'. *Land Economics* 34(2): 178–81.

_____. 1960. 'The History of the Common Market'. *Journal of Economic History* 20(3): 441–54.

_____. 1977. *The Overdeveloped Nations: the Diseconomies of Scale.* New York: Schocken Books.

_____. 1992. 'Leopold Kohr on the Desirable Scale of States'. *Population and Development Review* 18(4): 745–50.

Kormendi, R. C. and P. Meguire. 1985. 'Macroeconomic Determinants of Growth: Cross-country Evidence'. *Journal of Monetary Economics* 16(2): 141–63.

Kornai, J. 2005. 'The Great Transformation of Central Eastern Europe: Success and Disappointment'. Presidential Address, I. E. A. 14th World Congress, Marrakech, Morocco, 29 August. http://www.economics.harvard.edu/faculty/kornai/files/Pres_Address_Morocco.pdf (accessed 15 February 2012).

Korotayev, A. V. and S. V. Tsirel. 2010. 'A Spectral Analysis of World GDP Dynamics: Kondratieff Waves, Kuznets Swings, Juglar and Kitchin Cycles in Global Economic Development, and the 2008–2009 Economic Crisis'. *Structure and Dynamics* 4(1). http://www.escholarship.org/uc/item/9jv108xp (accessed 15 February 2012).

Kotz, D. M. 2009. 'The Financial and Economic Crisis of 2008: A Systemic Crisis of Neoliberal Capitalism'. *Review of Radical Political Economics* 41(3): 305–17.

Krasilshchikov, V. 2008. *The Rise and Decline of Catching up Development. An Experience of Russia and Latin America with Implications for Asian Tigers,* 2nd ed. Entelequia. Revista Interdisciplinar, eBook. http://www.eumed.net/entelequia/en.lib.php?a=b008 (accessed 15 February 2012).

Krugman, P. R. 1990. *Rethinking International Trade.* Cambridge, MA: MIT Press.

_____. 1994. *Peddling Prosperity: Economic Sense and Nonsense in the Age of Diminished Expectations*. New York: W. W. Norton.

_____. 2003. *The Great Unravelling: From Boom to Bust in Three Scandalous Years* Camberwell, Vic.: Penguin.

Kukreja, S. 1991. 'The Relationship Between Transnational Penetration, Militarization, Debt Dependence, and Political Exclusion'. *International Review of Modern Sociology* 21(1): 131–62.

Kurzman, C., R. Werun and R. E. Burkhart. 2002. 'Democracy's Effect on Economic Growth: A Pooled Time-Series Analysis, 1951–1980'. *Studies in Comparative International Development* 37(1): 3–33.

Kuznets, S. 1940. 'Schumpeter's Business Cycles'. *American Economic Review* 30(2): 157–69.

_____. 1955. 'Economic Growth and Income Inequality'. *American Economic Review* 45(1): 1–28.

_____. 1976. *Modern Economic Growth: Rate, Structure and Spread*. New Haven: Yale University Press.

Laver, M. and K. A. Shepsle. 1999. 'Understanding Government Survival: Empirical Exploration or Analytical Models?' *British Journal of Political Science* 29(2): 395–401.

Lavoie, M. 1996. 'Traverse, Hysteresis, and Normal Rates of Capacity Utilization in Kaleckian Models of Growth and Distribution'. *Review of Radical Political Economics* 28(4): 113–47.

Lawrence, K. S. 2009. 'The Thermodynamics of Unequal Exchange'. *International Journal of Comparative Sociology* 50(3–4): 335–59.

Lee, Ch.-S. 2005. 'Income Inequality, Democracy, and Public Sector Size'. *American Sociological Review* 70(1): 158–81.

Lee, Ch.-S., F. Nielsen and A. S. Alderson. 2007. 'Income Inequality, Global Economy and the State'. *Social Forces* 86(1): 77–111.

Lee, K. 2009. 'Towards a Reformulation of Core/Periphery Relationship: A Critical Reappraisal of the Trimodality of the Capitalist World-Economy in the Early 21st Century'. *Perspectives on Global Development and Technology* 8(2–3): 263–94.

Lena, H. F. and B. London. 1993. 'The Political and Economic Determinants of Health Outcomes. A Cross-national Analysis'. *International Journal of Health Services* 23(3): 585–602.

Letukas, L. and J. Barnshaw. 2008. 'A World-System Approach to Post-Catastrophe International Relief'. *Social Forces* 87(2): 1063–87.

Levine, R. E. and D. Renelt. 1992. 'Sensitivity Analysis of Cross-Country Growth Regressions'. *American Economic Review* 82(4): 942–63.

Li, Q. and A. Resnick. 2003. 'Reversal of Fortunes: Democratic Institutions and Foreign Direct Investment Inflows to Developing Countries'. *International Organization* 57(1): 175–211.

Library of Congress, available at http://catalog.loc.gov/cgi-bin/Pwebrecon.cgi?DB=local&PAGE= First.

Lockwood, B. 2004. 'How Robust is the Foreign Policy/Kearney Globalization Index?' *The World Economy* 27: 507–23.

Lockwood, B. and M. Redoano. 2005. 'The CSGR Globalization Index: An Introductory Guide'. CSGR Working Paper 155/04. http://www2.warwick.ac.uk/fac/soc/csgr/ (accessed 15 February 2012).

London, B. and R. J. S. Ross. 1995. 'The Political Sociology of Foreign Direct Investment – Global Capitalism and Capital Mobility, 1965–1980'. *International Journal of Comparative Sociology* 36(3–4): 198–218.

Longo, S. and R. York. 2008. 'Agricultural Exports and the Environment: A Cross-national Study of Fertilizer and Pesticide Consumption'. *Rural Sociology* 73(1): 82–104.

Louçã, F. 1997. *Turbulence in Economics: An Evolutionary Appraisal of Cycles and Complexity in Historical Processes*. Cheltenham, UK and Lyme, NH: Edward Elgar.

_____. 1999. 'Nikolai Kondratiev and the Early Consensus and Dissensions about History and Statistics'. *History of Political Economy* 31(1): 169.

Louçã, F. and J. Reijnders (eds) 1999. *The Foundations of Long Wave Theory: Models and Methodology*. Northampton, MA: Edward Elgar.

Luxemburg, R. 1964. *The Accumulation of Capital*. New York: Monthly Review Press.

Lynch, J., G. D. Smith, S. Harper, M. Hillemeier, N. Ross, G. A. Kaplan and M. Wolfson. 2004. 'Is Income Inequality a Determinant of Population Health?' *Milbank Quarterly* 82(1): 5–99.

Macinko, J. A., L. Y. Shi and B. Starfield. 2004. 'Wage Inequality, the Health System, and Infant Mortality in Wealthy Industrialized Countries, 1970–1996'. *Social Science & Medicine* 58(2): 279–92.

Mackenbach, J. P., A. E. Kunst, A. E. J. M. Cavelaars et al. 1997. 'Socio-economic Inequalities in Morbidity and Mortality in Western Europe'. *Lancet* 349(9066): 1655–59.

Mahler, V. A. 2001. 'Economic Globalization, Domestic Politics and Income Inequality in the Developed Countries: A Cross-National Study'. Luxembourg Income Study Working Paper 273.

Mahutga, M. C. 2006. 'The Persistence of Structural Inequality? A Network Analysis of International Trade, 1965–2000'. *Social Forces* 84(4): 1863–89.

Mahutga, M. C. and N. Bandelji. 2008. 'Foreign Investment and Income Inequality: The Natural Experiment of Central and Eastern Europe'. *International Journal of Comparative Sociology* 49(6): 429–54.

Mandel, E. 1995. *Long Waves of Capitalist Development: A Marxist Interpretation*. London: Verso.

Mandelbaum, K. 1945. *The Industrialisation of Backward Areas*. Oxford: B. Blackwell.

Mankiw, N. G., D. Romer and D. N. Weil. 1992. 'A Contribution to the Empirics of Economic Growth'. *Quarterly Journal of Economics* 107(2): 407–37.

Marglin, S. and J. Schor. 1990. *Golden Age of Capitalism, Reinterpreting the Post-war Experience*. Oxford: Oxford University Press.

Mariategui, J. C. 1959–70. *Obras completas*, with María Wiesse, Alberto Tauro and Armando Bazán. Lima: Biblioteca Amauta.

Marmot, M. and R. G. Wilkinson. 2001. 'Psychosocial and Material Pathways in the Relation between Income and Health: A Response to Lynch et al.' *British Medical Journal* 322(7296): 1233–36.

Marterbauer, M. and E. Walterskirchen. 2006. 'Neglecting Demand and Cycle in the Euro Area'. Austrian Institute for Economic Research, WIFO Working Papers No. 268. http://ewald.walterskirchen.wifo.ac.at/fileadmin/homepage_walterskirchen/files/2006/Demand_cycle_2006.pdf (accessed 15 February 2012).

Masters, W. A. and M. S. McMillan. 2000. 'Climate and Scale in Economic Growth'. WPS/2000–13, Centre for the Study of African Economies, University of Oxford. http://www.csae.ox.ac.uk/workingpapers/pdfs/20-13text.pdf (accessed 15 February 2012).

McGuire, J. W. 1998. 'Labour Union Strength and Human Development in East Asia and Latin America'. *Studies in Comparative International Development* 33(4): 3–34.

Meko, D. 2009. 'GEOS 585A, Applied Time Series Analysis'. University of Arizona. http://www.ltrr.arizona.edu/~dmeko/geos585a.html (accessed 15 February 2012).

Meyer, L. B. 2003. 'Economic Globalization and Women's Status in the Labour Market: A Cross-National Investigation of Occupational Sex Segregation and Inequality'. *Sociological Quarterly* 44(3): 351–83.

Mills, M. 2009. 'Globalization and Inequality'. *European Sociological Review* 25(1): 1–8.

Moaddel, M. 1994. 'Political Conflict in the World Economy: A Cross-national Analysis of Modernization and World-System Theories'. *American Sociological Review* 59(2): 276–303.

———. 1996. 'The Social Bases and Discursive Context of the Rise of Islamic Fundamentalism: The Cases of Iran and Syria'. *Sociological Inquiry* 66(3): 330–55.

———. 1998. 'Religion and Women: Islamic Modernism versus Fundamentalism'. *Journal for the Scientific Study of Religion* 37(1): 108–30.

———. 2002. 'The Study of Islamic Culture and Politics: An Overview and Assessment'. *Annual Review of Sociology* 28: 359–86.

———. 2004. 'The Future of Islam After 9/11'. *Futures* 36(9): 961–77.

———. 2005. *Islamic Modernism, Nationalism, and Fundamentalism: Episode and Discourse*. Chicago: University of Chicago Press.

Moore, S., A. C. Teixeira and A. Shiell. 2006. 'The Health of Nations in a Global Context: Trade, Global Stratification, and Infant Mortality Rates'. *Social Science & Medicine* 63(1): 165–78.

Moran, T. 2005. 'Kuznets's Inverted U-Curve Hypothesis: The Rise, Demise, and Continued Relevance of a Socioeconomic Law'. *Sociological Forum* 20(2): 209–44.

Morris, T. M. 1999. 'The Global Economy and Changes in the Determinants of Cross-National Income Inequality'. *Social Thought and Research* 22: 183–214.

Mosley, H. 1979. 'Review Essays: Monopoly Capital and the State: Some Critical Reflections on O'Connor's Fiscal Crisis of the State'. *Review of Radical Political Economics* 11(1): 52–61.

Mostafa, M. M. 2010. 'A Bayesian Approach to Analyzing the Ecological Footprint of 140 Nations'. *Ecological Indicators* 10(4): 808–17.

Mostafa, M. M. 2010. 'Clustering the Ecological Footprint of Nations Using Kohonen's Self-Organizing Maps'. *Expert Systems with Applications* 37(4): 2747–55.

Mostafa, M. M. and R. Nataraajan. 2009. 'A Neuro-computational Intelligence Analysis of the Ecological Footprint of Nations'. *Computational Statistics and Data Analysis* 53(9): 3516–31.

Murshed, S. M. (ed.) 2002. *Globalization, Marginalization and Development*. London and New York: Routledge.

Murshed, S. M. and K. Raffer (eds). 1993. *Trade, Transfers, and Development: Problems and Prospects for the Twenty-First Century*. Aldershot, UK and Brookfield, VT: Edward Elgar.

Myrdal, G. 1957. *Economic Theory and Underdeveloped Regions*. London: Duckworth.

_____. 1968. *Asian Drama: An Inquiry into the Poverty of Nations*. New York: Pantheon; Harmondsworth: Penguin.

_____. 1970. *The Challenge of World Poverty: A World Anti-poverty Program in Outline*, foreword by Francis O. Wilcox. New York: Pantheon Books.

Nagakawa, T. 2006. *Business Fluctuations and Cycles*. Hauppauge, NY: Nova Science.

Navarro, V. and L. Y. Shi. 2001. 'The Political Context of Social Inequalities and Health'. *Social Science & Medicine* 52(3): 481–91.

Neumayer, E., I. de Soysa. 2006. 'Globalization and the Right to Free Association and Collective Bargaining: An Empirical Analysis'. *World Development* 34(1): 31–49.

Neutel, M. and A. Heshmati. 2006. 'Globalisation, Inequality and Poverty Relationships: A Cross Country Evidence'. IZA Discussion Paper No. 2223. http://papers.ssrn.com/sol3/papers.cfm?abstract_id=921391 (accessed 15 February 2012).

Nomiya, D. 2007. 'The Demise of Comparative Sociology? Globalization and its Shadow'. *International Journal of Japanese Sociology* 16(1): 35–47.

Noorbakhsh, F. 1998. 'The Human Development Index: Some Technical Issues and Alternative Indices'. *Journal of International Development* 10: 589–605.

Norris, P. and R. Inglehart. 2004. *Sacred and Secular: Religion and Politics Worldwide*. Cambridge and Melbourne: Cambridge University Press.

Nugent, C. and J. M. Shandra. 2009. 'State Environmental Protection Efforts, Women's Status, and World Polity: A Cross-national Analysis'. *Organization and Environment* 22(3): 293–310.

O'Hara, P. A. 1994. 'An Institutionalist Review of Long Wave Theories: Schumpeterian Innovation, Modes of Regulation, and Social Structures of Accumulation'. *Journal of Economic Issues* 28(2): 489–500.

_____. 2000. *Marx, Veblen and Contemporary Institutional Political Economy: Principles and Unstable Dynamics of Capitalism*. Cheltenham, UK and Northampton, MA: Edward Elgar.

_____. 2001. 'Long Waves of Growth and Development'. In *Encyclopedia of Political Economy*, ed. P. A. O'Hara, 673–7. London and New York: Routledge.

_____. 2003a. 'Principles of Political Economy: Integrating Themes from the Schools of Heterodoxy'. Global Political Economy Research Unit Working Paper, Economics Department, Curtin University. http://pohara.homestead.com/files/principles.doc (accessed 15 February 2012).

———. 2003b. 'Recent Changes to the IMF, WTO and SPD: Emerging Global Mode of Regulation or Social Structure of Accumulation for Long Wave Upswing?' *Review of International Political Economy* 10(3): 481–519.

———. 2003c. 'Deep Recession and Financial Instability or a New Long-Wave of Economic Growth for US Capitalism? A Regulation School Approach'. *Review of Radical Political Economics* 35(1): 18–43.

———. 2004a. 'A New Family-Community Social Structures of Accumulation for Long Wave Upswing in the United States'. *Forum for Social Economics* 34(2): 51–80.

———. 2004b. 'Cultural Contradictions of Global Capitalism'. *Journal of Economic* 38(2): 413–20.

——— (ed.) 2004c. *Global Political Economy and the Wealth of Nations: Performance, Institutions, Problems, and Policies.* New York: Routledge.

———. 2005a. 'Contradictions of Neo-liberal Globalisation: The Importance of Ideologies and Values in Political Economy'. *Journal of Interdisciplinary Economics* 16(3): 341–65.

———. 2005b. *Growth and Development in the Global Political Economy: Social Structures of Accumulation and Modes of Regulation.* Oxford and New York: Routledge.

Oneal, J. R. 2003. 'Measuring Interdependence and Its Pacific Benefits: A Reply to Gartzke & Li'. *Journal of Peace Research* 40(6): 721–5.

Owen, A. L. and St. Wu. 2007. 'Is Trade Good for your Health?' *Review of International Economics* 15(4): 660–82.

Palma-Solis, M. A., C. Alvarez-Dardet Díaz, A. Franco-Giraldo, I. Hernández-Aguado and S. Pérez-Hoyos. 2009. 'State Downsizing as a Determinant of Infant Mortality and Achievement of Millennium Development Goal Four'. *International Journal of Health Services* 39(2): 389–403.

Papadopoulos, F. and P. Tsakloglou. 2003. 'Social Exclusion in the EU: A Capability-Based Approach'. Unpublished paper.

Papageorgiou, Ch., A. Savvides and M. Zachariadis. 2007. 'International Medical Technology Diffusion'. *Journal of International Economics* 72(2): 409–27.

Pattnayak, S. R. 1999. 'Source of Investment and Economic Growth Rate in Non-Core Countries: A Re-Analysis'. *International Review of Modern Sociology* 29(1): 35–54.

Payne, C. L. 2009. 'Bringing Home the Bacon or Not? Globalization and Government Respect for Economic and Social Rights'. *Human Rights Review* 10(3): 413–29.

Pearson, K. 1901. 'On Lines and Planes of Closest Fit to Systems of Points in Space'. *Philosophical Magazine* 6(2): 559–72.

Perroux, F. 1961. *L'Économie du XXe siècle.* Paris: P.U.F.

———. 1965. *La pensée économique de Joseph Schumpeter: les dynamiques du capitalisme.* Geneva: Droz.

———. 1973. *Pouvoir et économie.* Paris: Bordas.

———. 1983. *A New Concept of Development: Basic Tenets.* London: Croom and Helm.

Pettersson, Th. 2007. 'Muslim Immigrants in Western Europe: Persisting Value Differences or Value Adaption'. In *Values and Perceptions of the Islamic and Middle Eastern Publics*, ed. M. Moaddel, 71–104. Basingstoke: Palgrave Macmillan.

Polanyi, K. [1944] 1957. *The Great Transformation: The Political and Economic Origins of Our Time.* Boston: Beacon Press.

Prebisch, R. 1950. *The Economic Development of Latin America and its Principal Problems.* Lake Success, NY: United Nations Department of Economic Affairs.

———. 1983. 'The Crisis of Capitalism and International Trade'. *ECLAC Review/Revista de la CEPAL* 20(Summer): 51–74.

———. 1988. 'Dependence, Development, and Interdependence'. In *The State of Development Economics*, ed. G. Ranis and T. P. Schultz, 31–41. Oxford: Basil Blackwell.

Prebisch, R. et al. 1983. *Problemas Econó micos del Tercer Mundo.* Buenos Aires: Editorial de Belgrano.

Preston, S. H. 2007. 'Response: On the Changing Relation between Mortality and Level of Economic Development'. *Int. J. Epidemiol.* 36(3): 502–503.

Raffer, K. 1987. *Unequal Exchange and the Evolution of the World System: Reconsidering the Impact of Trade on North-South Relations*. Basingstoke: Macmillan.

Raffer, K. and H. W. Singer. 1996. *The Foreign Aid Business: Economic Assistance and Development Co-operation*. Cheltenham, UK and Brookfield, VT: Edward Elgar.

_____. 2001. *The Economic North-South Divide: Six Decades of Unequal Development*. Cheltenham, UK and Northampton, MA: Edward Elgar.

Ragin, C. C. and Y. W. Bradshaw. 1992. 'International Economic Dependence and Human Misery, 1938–1980: A Global Perspective'. *Sociological Perspectives* 35(2): 217–47.

Rennstich, J. K. 2002. 'The New Economy, the Leadership Long Cycle and the Nineteenth K-Wave'. *Review of International Political Economy* 9(1): 150–82.

_____. 2007. 'Is globalization self-organizing?' In *Globalization as Evolutionary Process. Modelling Global Change*, ed. G. Modelski, T. C. Devezas, W. R. Thompson, 74–107. London and New York: Routledge.

Reuveny, R. and Q. Li . 2003. 'Economic Openness, Democracy, and Income Inequality: An Empirical Analysis'. *Comparative Political Studies* 36(5): 575–601.

Reuveny, R. and W. W. Thompson. 2004. 'World Economic Growth, Systemic Leadership, and Southern Debt Crises'. *Journal of Peace Research* 41(1): 5–24.

Rice, J. 2008. 'Material Consumption and Social Well-Being Within the Periphery of the World Economy: An Ecological Analysis of Maternal Mortality'. *Social Science Research* 37(4): 1292–1309.

Richards, D. L., R. D. Gelleny and D. H. Sacko. 2001. 'Money with a Mean Streak? Foreign Economic Penetration and Government Respect for Human Rights in Developing Countries'. *International Studies Quarterly* 45(2): 219–39.

Roberts, W. T. 2005. 'The Uneven Globalization of Civil Society Organizations and the Consequences for Cross-National Disparities in Human Development'. *International Journal of Sociology and Social Policy* 25(1–2): 118–44.

Robinson, T. D. and B. London. 1991. 'Dependency, Inequality, and Political Violence – A Cross-national Analysis'. *Journal of Political and Military Sociology* 19(1): 119–56.

Rodgers, G. B. 1979. 'Income and Inequality as Determinants of Mortality: An International Cross-section Analysis'. *Population Studies* 33(2): 343–51.

Rodriguez, F. and D. Rodrik. 2001. 'Trade Policy and Economic Growth: A Sceptics Guide to the Cross-national Evidence'. In *NBER Macroeconomics Annual 2000*, ed. B. S. Bernanke and K. Rogoff. Cambridge, MA: MIT Press.

Rosenstein-Rodan, P. N. 1964. *Capital Formation and Economic Development*. London: Allen & Unwin.

Ross, R. J. S. 2004. *Slaves to Fashion: Poverty and Abuse in the New Sweatshops*. Ann Arbor: University of Michigan Press.

Rothgeb, J. M. 1995. 'Investment Penetration, Agrarian Change, and Political Conflict in Developing Countries'. *Studies in Comparative International Development* 30(4): 46–62.

Rothschild, K. W. 1944. 'The Small Nation and World Trade'. *Economic Journal* 54(213): 26–40.

_____. 1950. *The Austrian Economy Since 1945*. London: Royal Institute of International Affairs.

_____. 1954. *The Theory of Wages*. Oxford: Blackwell.

_____. 1957. 'Der Lohnanteil am Gesamteinkommen: einige Bemerkungen zu einem umstrittenen Problem'. *Weltwirtschaftliches Archiv* 78(2): 157–202.

_____. 1958. 'Einkommensbildung und Einkommensverteilung'. *Weltwirtschaftliches Archiv* 80(2): 53–8.

_____. 1959. 'The Limitations of Economic Growth Models'. *Kyklos* 12(4): 567–88.

_____. 1964. 'Surveys of Foreign Post-war Developments in Economic Thought'. *American Economic Review* 54(2): 1–55.

_____. 1965. 'Theme and Variations, Remarks on the Kaldorian Distribution Formula'. *Kyklos* 18(4): 652–69.

_____ (ed.) 1971. *Power in Economics: Selected Readings*. Harmondsworth: Penguin.

_____. 1993. *Ethics and Economic Theory: Ideas, Models, Dilemmas.* Aldershot: Edward Elgar.

_____. 1994. *Employment, Wages, and Income Distribution: Critical Essays in Economics.* London and New York: Routledge.

_____. 1995. *Economic Method, Theory and Policy: Selected Essays of Kurt W. Rothschild*, ed. J. E. King. Aldershot, UK and Brookfield, VT: Edward Elgar.

_____. 2000a. 'Europe and the USA: Comparing what with what?' *Kyklos* 53(3): 249–64.

_____. 2000b. 'The Economic Consequences of Rolling Back the Welfare State'. *Kyklos* 53(2): 203–4.

_____. 2001. 'The Reluctant Rebel or Glamour and Poverty of the Homo Oeconomicus'. *Kyklos* 54(2–3): 445–52.

_____. 2003. 'What the Future Holds. Insights from Social Science'. *Kyklos* 56(1): 117–20.

_____. 2009. 'A Nostalgic Retrospect on a Debate on Various Aspects of Welfare Economics'. *European Journal of the History of Economic Thought* 16(4): 559–74.

Rubinson, R. 1976. 'The World Economy and the Distribution of Income within States: A Cross-national Study'. *American Sociological Review* 41(4): 638–59.

Sachs, J. D. and A. M. Warner. 2001. 'The Curse of Natural Resources'. *European Economic Review* 45 (4–6): 827–38.

Sala-i-Martin, X. 1997. 'I Just Ran Two Million Regressions'. *American Economic Review* 87(2), Papers and Proceedings of the Hundred and Fourth Annual Meeting of the American Economic Association, May 1997: 178–83.

Sala-i-Martin X., G. Doppelhofer and R. I. Miller. 2004. 'Determinants of Long-term Growth: A Bayesian Averaging of Classical Estimates (BACE) Approach'. *American Economic Review* 94(4): 813–35.

Samuelson, P. 1964. 'Theoretical Notes on Trade Problems'. *Review of Economics and Statistics* 46: 145–54.

Sanderson, M. 2010. 'International Migration and Human Development in Destination Countries: A Cross-National Analysis of Less-Developed Countries, 1970–2005'. *Social Indicators Research* 96(1): 59–83.

Sanderson, M. R. and J. Kentor. 2008. 'Foreign Direct Investment and International Migration: A Cross-National Analysis of Less-Developed Countries, 1985–2000'. *International Sociology* 23(4): 514–39.

_____. 2009. 'Globalization, Development and International Migration: A Cross-National Analysis of Less-Developed Countries, 1970–2000'. *Social Forces* 88(1): 301–36.

Schofer, E. 2004. 'Cross-national Differences in the Expansion of Science, 1970–1990'. *Social Forces* 83(1): 215–48.

Schofer, E. and J. W. Meyer. 2005. 'The Worldwide Expansion of Higher Education in the Twentieth Century'. *Sociological Review* 70(6): 898–920.

Schofer, E., F. O. Ramirez and J. W. Meyer. 2000. 'The Effects of Science on National Economic Development, 1970 to 1990'. *American Sociological Review* 65(6): 866–87.

Schumacher, E. F. 1973a. *Small is Beautiful: Economics as if People Mattered.* New York: Harper & Row.

_____. 1973b. 'Western Europe's Energy Crisis: A Problem of Life-Styles'. *Ambio* 2(6) 'Energy in Society: A Special Issue': 228–32.

_____. 1976. 'Patterns of Human Settlement'. *Ambio* 5(3): 91–7.

_____. 1977. *A Guide for the Perplexed.* New York: Harper & Row.

Schumpeter, J. A. [1908] 2009. *Wesen und Hauptinhalt der Theoretischen Nationalökonomie.* Republished as *The Nature and Essence of Economic Theory.* Rutgers, NJ: Transaction Publishers.

_____. [1912] 1969. *Theorie der Wirtschaftlichen Entwicklung.* Republished as *The Theory of Economic Development: An Inquiry into Profits, Capital, Credit, Interest, and the Business Cycle*, trans. Redvers Opie. London and Oxford: Oxford University Press.

_____. 1939. *Business Cycles. A Theoretical, Historical, and Statistical Analysis of the Capitalist Process.* New York and London: McGraw-Hill Book Company.

_____. 1942. *The Process of Creative Destruction*. London: Unwin.

_____. [1950] 1975. *Capitalism, Socialism and Democracy*, 3rd ed. New York and London: Harper & Row.

_____. 1954. *History of Economic Analysis*. New York: Oxford University Press.

Seers, D. (ed.) 1981. *Dependency Theory: A Critical Reassessment*. London: Pinter.

Seers, D. and Ostrom, K. (eds). 1983. *The Crises of the European Regions*. London: Macmillan, in association with the European Association of Development Institutes.

Seers, D., B. Schaffer and M.-L. Kiljunen. 1979. *Underdeveloped Europe: Studies in Core-Periphery Relations*. Atlantic Highlands, NJ: Humanities Press.

Seers, D. and C. Vaitsos, assisted by M.-L. Kiljunen. 1980. *Integration and Unequal Development: The Experience of the EEC*. London: Macmillan.

Shandra, J. M. 2007a. 'Economic Dependency, Repression, and Deforestation: A Quantitative, Cross-National Analysis'. *Sociological Inquiry* 77(4): 543–71.

_____. 2007b. 'International Nongovernmental Organizations and Deforestation: Good, Bad, or Irrelevant?' *Social Science Quarterly* 88(3): 665–89.

Shandra, J. M., C. Leckband and B. London. 2009. 'Ecologically Unequal Exchange and Deforestation: A Cross-National Analysis of Forestry Export Flows'. *Organization & Environment* 22(2): 208–29.

Shandra, J. M., C. Leckband, L. A. McKinney and B. London. 2009. 'Ecologically Unequal Exchange, World Polity, and Biodiversity Loss A Cross-National Analysis of Threatened Mammals'. *International Journal of Comparative Sociology* 50(3–4): 285–310.

Shandra, J. M., B. London, O. P. Whooley and J. B. Williamson. 2004. 'International Nongovernmental Organizations and Carbon Dioxide Emissions in the Developing World: A Quantitative, Cross-National Analysis'. *Sociological Inquiry* 74(4): 520–45.

Shandra, J. M., B. London and J. B. Williamson. 2003. 'Environmental Degradation, Environmental Sustainability, and Over-urbanization in the Developing World: A Quantitative, Cross-National Analysis'. *Sociological Perspectives* 46(3): 309–29.

Shandra, J. M., J. E. Nobles, B. London and J. B. Williamson. 2004. 'Dependency, Democracy, and Infant Mortality: A Quantitative, Cross-national Analysis of Less Developed Countries'. *Social Science & Medicine*, 59(2): 321–33.

_____. 2005. 'Multi-national Corporations, Democracy and Child Mortality: A Quantitative, Cross-national Analysis of Developing Countries'. *Social Indicators Research* 73(2): 267–93.

Shandra, J. M., C. L. Shandra and B. London. 2008. 'Women, Non-governmental Organizations, and Deforestation: A Cross-national Study'. *Population and Environment* 30(1–2): 48–72.

_____. 2010. 'Do Non-governmental Organizations Impact Health? A Cross-national Analysis of Infant Mortality'. *International Journal of Comparative Sociology* 51(1–2): 137–64.

Shandra, J. M., E. Shor and B. London. 2008. 'Debt, Structural Adjustment, and Organic Water Pollution'. *Organization and Environment* 21(1): 38–55.

_____. 2009. 'World Polity, Unequal Ecological Exchange, and Organic Water Pollution: A Cross-national Analysis of Developing Nations'. *Human Ecology Review* 16(1): 53–63.

Shaw J. W., W. C. Horace and R. J. Vogel. 2005. 'The Determinants of Life Expectancy: an Analysis of the OECD Health Data'. *Southern Economic Journal* 71(4): 768–83.

Shen, C. and J. B. Williamson. 1997. 'Child Mortality, Women's Status, Economic Dependency, and State Strength: A Cross-national Study of Less Developed Countries'. *Social Forces* 76(2): 667–700.

_____. 1999. 'Maternal Mortality, Women's Status, and Economic Dependency in Less Developed Countries: A Cross-national Analysis'. *Social Science and Medicine* 49(2): 197–214.

_____. 2001. 'Accounting for Cross-national Differences in Infant Mortality Decline 1965–1991 Among Less Developed Countries: Effects of Women's Status, Economic Dependency, and State Strength'. *Social Indicators Research* 53(3): 257–88.

Silverberg, G. 2005. 'When is a Wave a Wave? Long Waves as Empirical and Theoretical Constructs from a Complex Systems Perspective'. Maastricht: MERIT – Infonomics Research

Memorandum series. http://www.merit.unu.edu/publications/rmpdf/2005/rm2005-016.pdf (accessed 14 February 2012).

———. 2007. 'Long Waves: Conceptual, Empirical and Modelling Issues'. In *Elgar Companion to Neo-Schumpeterian Economics*, ed. Horst Hanusch and Andreas Pyka, 800–19. Cheltenham: Edward Elgar.

Singa Boyenge, J.-P. 2007. 'ILO Database on Export Processing Zones (Revised)'. ILO Working Paper 251, Sectoral Activities Programme. Geneva: International Labour Office (ILO).

Singer, H. W. 1975. *The Strategy of International Development: Essays in the Economics of Backwardness*, ed. Alec Cairncross and Mohinder Puri. London: Macmillan.

Singer, H. W. and J. A. Ansari. 1988. *Rich and Poor Countries: Consequences of International Economic Disorder*. London and Boston: Unwin Hyman.

Singer, H. W. and S. Roy. 1993. *Economic Progress and Prospects in the Third World: Lessons of Development Experience Since 1945*. Aldershot, UK and Brookfield, VT: Edward Elgar.

Singer, P. I. 1970. *Dinamica Populacional e Desenvolvimento. O Papel do Crescimento Populacional no Desenvolvimento Economico*. São Paulo: Edicoes CEBRAP.

———. 1975. *Estudos Sobre a População Brasileira*. São Paulo: CEBRAP.

———. 1976. *A Crise do Milagre: Interpretação Crítica da Economia Brasileira*. Rio de Janeiro: Paz e Terra.

Soares, R. R. 2007. 'On the Determinants of Mortality Reductions in the Developing World'. *Population and Development Review* 33(2): 247–87.

Spencer, M. 2006. 'Peripherality, Income Inequality, and Life Expectancy: Revisiting the Income Inequality Hypothesis'. *International Journal of Epidemiology* 35(3): 623–32.

SPSS. 2007. *Statistical Package for the Social Sciences, User Guide*. Version 14.

———. 2008. *Statistical Package for the Social Sciences, User Guide*. Version 15.

Steindl, J. 1952. *Maturity and Stagnation in American Capitalism*. Oxford: Basil Blackwell.

———. 1979. 'Stagnation Theory and Stagnation Policy'. *Cambridge Journal of Economics* 1979(3): 1–14.

———. 1988. Diskussionsbeitrag zur EG-Frage. *Kurswechsel*, 4(3): 3–7.

———. 1990. *Economic Papers 1941–88*. Basingstoke: MacMillan.

Stiglitz, J. 2002. *Globalization and its Discontents*. New York: W. W. Norton.

Stoneman, C. 1975. 'Foreign Capital and Economic Growth'. *World Development* 3(1): 11–26.

Sturm, J.-E. and J. de Haan. 2005. 'Determinants of Long-term Growth: New Results Applying Robust Estimation and Extreme Bounds', Research Paper Series 12, Thurgauer Wirtschaftsinstitut, University of Konstanz. http://kops.ub.uni-konstanz.de/bitstream/handle/urn:nbn:de:bsz:352-opus-16757/TWI_res12.pdf?sequence=1 (accessed 14 February 2012); later published in *Empirical Economics* 30(3): 597–617.

Sumner, A. 2005. 'Is Foreign Direct Investment Good for the Poor? A Review and Stocktake'. *Development in Practice* 15(3–4): 269–85.

Sunkel, O. 1966. 'The Structural Background of Development Problems in Latin America'. *Weltwirtschaftliches Archiv* 97(1): 22–63.

———. 1973. 'Transnational Capitalism and National Disintegration in Latin America'. *Social and Economic Studies* 22(1): 132–76.

———. 1978. 'The Development of Development Thinking'. In *Transnational Capitalism and National Development. New Perspectives on Dependence*, ed. J. J. Villamil, 19–30. Hassocks: Harvester Press.

———. 1993. *Consolidation of Chiles Democracy and Development: the Challenges and the Tasks*. Brighton: Institute of Development Studies.

———. 1994. *Rebuilding Capitalism: Alternative Roads after Socialism and Dirigisme*. Ann Arbor: University of Michigan Press.

——— (ed.) 2003. *Development from Within: Toward a Neo-structuralist Approach for Latin America*. Boulder, CO: L. Rienner.

Sunkel, O. and P. Paz. 1970. *El Subdesarrollo Latinoamericano y la Teoría del Desarrollo*. Madrid: Siglo Veintiuno de España.

Sutcliffe B. and A. Glyn. 1999. 'Still Underwhelmed: Indicators of Globalization and Their Misinterpretation'. *Review of Radical Political Economics* 31(1): 111–32.

Sweezy, P. M. 1971. *Theorie der Kapitalistischen Entwicklung.* Frankfurt: Suhrkamp.

Szlajfer, H. (ed.) 1990. *Economic Nationalism in East-Central Europe and South America: 1918–1939. Le Nationalisme Économique en Europe du Centre-Est et en Amérique du Sud.* Geneva: Librairie Droz.

Tausch, A. 2003a. 'Social Cohesion, Sustainable Development and Turkeys Accession to the European Union'. *Alternatives: Turkish Journal of International Relations* 2(1): 1–41.

———. 2003b. 'The European Union: Global Challenge or Global Governance? Fourteen World System Hypotheses and Two Scenarios on the Future of the Union'. In *Globalization: Critical Perspectives*, ed. Gernot Kohler and Emilio José Chaves, 93–197: Hauppauge, NY: Nova Science.

———. 2004. 'Europe, the Muslim Mediterranean and the End of the Era of Global Confrontation'. *Alternatives: Turkish Journal of International Relations* 3(4): 1–29.

———. 2005. 'Is Islam really a development blockade?' Ankara Center for Turkish Policy Studies, ANKAM. *Insight Turkey* 7(1): 124–35.

———. 2007a. 'Европейский союз : град на холме и Лиссабонская стратегия [European Union: City on a Hill and Lisbon Strategy]'. *Mirovaja ekonomika i meždunarodnyje otnošenija* 50(3): 65–72.

———. 2007b. 'Quantitative World System Studies Contradict Current Islamophobia: World Political Cycles, Global Terrorism, and World Development'. *Alternatives: Turkish Journal of International Relations* 6(1–2): 15–81.

———. 2007c. *The City on the Hill? The Latin Americanization of Europe and the Lost Competition with the USA.* Amsterdam: Rozenberg and Dutch University Press.

———. 2007d. 'War Cycles'. *Social Evolution and History (Moscow)* 6(2): 39–74.

———. 2008a. *Multi-cultural Europe: Effects of the Global Lisbon Process: Muslim Population Shares and Global Development Patterns 1990–2003 in 134 countries.* New York: Nova Science.

———. 2008b. 'Разрушительное созидание? (Рассуждения в духе Шумпетера о некоторых трендах и Лиссабонском процессе в Европе) [Destructive Creation (Schumpeter-Style Reasonings on Some Trends and Lisbon Process in Europe)]'. *Mirovaja ekonomika i meždunarodnyje otnošenija* 51(10): 34–41.

———. 2010a. 'Passive Globalization and the Failure of the European Union's Lisbon Strategy, 2000–2010: Some New Cross-National Evidence'. *Alternatives: Turkish Journal of International Relations* 9(1): 1–91.

———. 2010b. 'Paul Boccara's analysis of global capitalism, the return of the Bourbons, and the breakdown of the Brussels/Paris neo-liberal consensus'. *Entelequia. Revista Interdisciplinar* 12(Fall): 105–47. http://www.eumed.net/entelequia/en.art.php?a=12a06 (accessed 14 February 2012).

Tausch, A. and Chr. Ghymers. 2006. *From the Washington Towards a Vienna Consensus? A Quantitative Analysis on Globalization, Development and Global Governance.* Hauppauge, NY: Nova Science.

Tausch, A. and P. Herrmann. 2001. *Globalization and European Integration.* Huntington, NY: Nova Science.

Tausch, A. and A. Heshmati. 2005. 'Turkey and the Lisbon Process: A Short Research Note on the Position of Turkey on a New Lisbon Strategy Index (LSI)'. *Insight Turkey, Ankara* 8(1): 7–18.

Tausch, A. and M. Moaddel. 2009. *What 1.3 Billion Muslims Really Think: An Answer to a Recent Gallup Study, Based on the 'World Values Survey'*, foreword by M. Moaddel. Hauppauge, NY: Nova Science.

Tausch, A. and F. Prager. 1993. *Towards a Socio-Liberal Theory of World Development.* Basingstoke and New York: Macmillan/St. Martin's Press.

Tausch, A., A. Heshmati A. and C. Bajalan. 2010. 'On the Multi-variate Analysis of the "Lisbon Process"'. In *History and Mathematics: Processes and Models of Global Dynamics*, ed. L. E. Grinin, A. V. Korotayev, P. Herrmann and A. Tausch, 92–137. Volgograd: 'Uchitel' Publishing House.

Timberlake, M. and K. R. Williams. 1987. 'Structural Position in the World-System, Inequality, and Political Violence'. *Journal of Political and Military Sociology* 15(1): 1–15.

Tsai, M.-Ch. 1999. 'State Power, State Embeddedness, and National Development in Less Developed Countries: A Cross-National Analysis'. *Studies in Comparative International Development* 33(4): 66–88.

_____. 2006a. 'Economic and Non-economic Determinants of Poverty in Developing Countries: Competing Theories and Empirical Evidence'. *Canadian Journal of Development Studies/Revue Canadienne Detudes du Developpement* 27(3): 267–85.

_____. 2006b. 'Macro-structural Determinants of Political Freedom in Developing Countries: A Cross-national Analysis'. *Social Indicators Research* 76(2): 317–40.

_____. 2007. 'Does Globalization Affect Human Well-Being?' *Social Indicators Research* 81(1): 103–26.

Tsai, P.-L. 1995. 'Foreign Direct Investment and Income Inequality: Further Evidence'. *World Development* 23(3): 469–83.

_____. 1998. 'The States Interest Seeking and Economic Stagnation in the Third World: Cross-National Evidence'. *Sociological Quarterly* 39(1): 101–18.

Ueberla, K. [1968] 1971. *Faktorenanalyse. Eine Systematische Einfuehrung fuer Psychologen, Mediziner, Wirtschafts- und Sozialwissenschaftler*, 2nd ed. Berlin, Heidelberg, New York: Springer.

United Nations (current issues). *United Nations Human Development Report.* New York and Oxford: Oxford University Press.

United Nations Conference on Trade and Development (current issues). *World Investment Report.* New York and Geneva: United Nations.

United Nations Development Programme. 2004. *A Global Report. Reducing Disaster Risk. A Challenge for Development.* New York: United Nations Development Programme, Bureau for Crisis Prevention and Recovery.

Van Rossem, R. 1996. 'The World System Paradigm as a General Theory of Development: A Cross-national Test'. *American Sociological Review* 61(3): 508–27.

Vernengo, M. 2006. 'Technology, Finance, and Dependency: Latin American Radical Political Economy in Retrospect'. *Review of Radical Political Economics* 38(4): 551–68.

Wallerstein, I. 2000. *The Essential Wallerstein.* New York: The New Press.

Warner, R. 1998. *Spectral Analysis of Time-Series Data.* New York: Guilford Press.

Weede, E. 1970. 'Zur Methodik der kausalen Abhängigkeitsanalyse (Pfadanalyse) in der nichtexperimentellen Forschung'. *Kölner Zeitschrift für Soziologie und Sozialpsychologie* 22: 532–50.

_____. 1972. 'Zur Pfadanalyse: Neuere Entwicklung, Verbesserungen, Ergänzungen'. *Kölner Zeitschrift für Soziologie und Sozialpsychologie* 24: 101–17.

_____. 1977. *Hypothesen, Gleichungen und Daten: Spezifikations- und Meßprobleme bei Kausalmodellen für Daten aus einer und mehreren Beobachtungsperioden*, vol. 1 Kronberg/Taunus: Monographien Sozialwissenschaftliche Methoden (ZUMA).

_____. 1980a. 'Beyond Misspecification in Sociological Analyses of Income Inequality'. *American Sociological Review* 45: 497–501.

_____. 1980b. 'Militär, Multis und Wirtschaft'. *Schweizerische Zeitschrift für Soziologie* 7: 113–27.

_____. 1981a. 'Dependency Theories and Economic Growth: A Cross-National Study'. *Koelner Zeitschrift fur Soziologie und Sozialpsychologie* 33(4): 690–707.

_____. 1981b. 'The Military, Multi-national Corporations, and the Economy: A Cross-national Study with Particular Reference to Developing Nations'. *Schweizerische Zeitschrift fur Soziologie. Revue suisse de sociologie* 7(1): 113–27.

_____. 1983. 'Military Participation Ratio. Human Capital Formation and Economic Growth: A Cross-national Analysis'. *Journal of Political and Military Sociology* 11: 11–29.

_____. 1985. *Entwicklungsländer in der Weltgesellschaft.* Opladen: Westdeutscher Verlag.

_____. 1986. 'Rent Seeking, Military Participation and Economic Performance in LDCs'. *Journal of Conflict Resolution* 30: 291–314.

_____. 1993. 'The Impact of Military Participation on Economic Growth and Income Inequality: Some New Evidence'. *Journal of Political and Military Sociology* 21: 241–58.

_____. 1999. 'Future Hegemonic Rivalry between China and the West?' In *The Future of Global Conflict*, ed. V. Bornschier and Ch. K. Chase-Dunn, 244–62, London, Thousand Oaks, CA and New Delhi: Sage.

_____. 2002. 'Impact of Intelligence and Institutional Improvements on Economic Growth'. *Kyklos* 55(3): 361–80.

_____. 2004. 'Does Human Capital Strongly Affect Economic Growth Rates? Yes, But Only If Assessed Properly'. *Comparative Sociology* 3(2): 115–34.

Weede, E. and W. Jagodzinski. 1977. 'Einführung in die Konfirmatorische Faktorenanalyse'. *Zeitschrift für Soziologie* 6: 315–33.

_____. 1980. 'Weltpolitische und ökonomische Determinanten einer ungleichen Einkommensverteilung. Eine international vergleichende Studie'. *Zeitschrift für Soziologie* 9: 132–48.

Weede, E. and H. Tiefenbach. 1981a. 'Correlates of the Size Distribution of Income in Cross-national Analyses'. *Journal of Politics* 43(4): 1029–41.

_____. 1981b. 'Some Recent Explanations of Income Inequality: An Evaluation and Critique'. *International Studies Quarterly* 25: 255–82.

_____. 1981c. 'Three Dependency Explanations of Economic Growth: A Critical Evaluation'. *European Journal of Political Research* 9(4): 391–406.

Wei, W. W. 2006. *Time Series Analysis: Univariate and Multi-variate Methods.* Boston, MA: Pearson/ Addison Wesley.

Wickrama, Th., N. Bikask and K. A. S. Wickrama. 2003. 'The Influence of Women's Status, Economic Development and Dependency on Infant Mortality in Developing Countries: The Ceiling and Moderating Effects of the Level of Economic Development'. *Journal of Contemporary Sociology* 40: 239–54.

Wilkinson, R. G. 1992a. 'For Debate – Income Distribution and Life Expectancy'. *British Medical Journal* 304(6820): 165–8.

_____. 1992b. 'National Mortality Rates: The Impact of Inequality'. *American Journal of Public Health* 82(8): 1082–84.

_____. 1997. 'Socio-economic determinants of health. Health inequalities: Relative or absolute material standards?' *British Medical Journal* 314(7080): 591–5.

Wilkinson, R. G. and K. E. Picket. 2006. 'Income Inequality and Population Health: A Review and Explanation of the Evidence'. *Social Science & Medicine* 62(7): 1768–84.

Williamson, J. A. 2002. 'Is Protection Bad for Growth? Will Globalization Last? Looking for Answers in History'. Presented at the 13th IEHA Congress, Buenos Aires. http://www.economics.harvard. edu/faculty/williamson/files/Is_Protection_Bad.pdf (accessed 14 February 2012).

Williamson, J. B. and U. Boehmer. 1997. 'Female Life Expectancy, Gender Stratification, Health Status, and Level of Economic Development: A Cross-national Study of Less Developed Countries'. *Social Science & Medicine* 45(2): 305–17.

Wimberley, D. W. 1998. 'Transnational Corporate Investment and Food in the Third World: A Cross-national Analysis'. *Rural Sociology* 56(3): 406–31.

Wimberley, D. W. and R. Bello. 1992. 'Effects of Foreign Investment, Exports and Economic Growth on Third World Food Consumption'. *Social Forces* 70(4): 895–921.

Wolpin, M. D. 1986. *Militarization, Internal Repression and Social Welfare in the Third World.* London: Croom Helm.

Woolhandler, S. and D. U. Himmelstein. 1985. 'Militarism and Mortality. An International Analysis of Arms Spending and Infant Death Rates'. *Lancet* 8442: 1375–78.

Worldcat catalogue system, available at http://www.worldcat.org/advancedsearch.

Yotopoulos, P. A. 1996. *Exchange Rate Parity for Trade and Development: Theory, Tests, and Case Studies* Cambridge and New York: Cambridge University Press.

Yotopoulos, P. A. and Y. Sawada. 2005. 'Exchange Rate Misalignment: A New Test of Long-Run PPP Based on Cross-country Data'. CIRJE Discussion Paper CIRJE-F-318, Faculty of Economics, University of Tokyo. http://www2.e.u-tokyo.ac.jp/cemano/research/DP/ documents/coe-f-58.pdf (accessed 14 February 2012).

INDEX OF PERSONS
AND AUTHORSHIPS

INDEX OF SUBJECTS
AND COUNTRIES

Dominican Republic 36n24, 72n12, 111,
128, 130, 144, 149, 227
DYN measure of dynamic change over
time xi, 189–90; *see also* growth of
MNC penetration over time (DYN
MNC PEN)

ecological footprint (gha per capita) xvi,
xix, xxix, 51, 67–8, 75n17, 76, 76n18,
113n29, 125–6, 163, 236
economic cycles 101, 139
economic freedom xx, xxxvi, xxxix, xli, 40,
71, 73–4, 81, 83–6, 106, 108, 111–3,
120, 136–8, 159, 162, 164, 167,
171–2, 181, 234, 237
economic growth xvi–xxi, xxiv, xxvii,
xli–xlii, 1–6, 18–20, 23–4, 28, 37, 40,
41n29, 42–3, 42n31, 45, 45n37, 46,
46n38–9, 47–8, 47n39, 48n44, 49n44,
52, 55, 62–4, 66–71, 73, 73n14, 75–7,
75n18, 80, 82, 84–6, 88–9, 91–4,
97–9, 100–2, 104–5, 107–9, 113n30,
114n30, 123–5, 127–8, 134, 139–41,
147, 156, 163, 166–8, 185–206, 216,
218, 220, 222, 224–5, 236, 241–7,
251–4, 256, 263, 265–6
Ecuador 36, 72n12, 128, 130, 144,
149–50, 218, 227
Egypt 36n24, 38, 72n12, 132, 145,
149–50, 209, 218, 227
El Salvador 33, 36, 72n12, 98n8, 111, 128,
130, 142, 148–50, 218, 227
electoral fractionalization in 1985
(ELF85) xi
Environmental Sustainability Index (ESI)
xi, xvii, xxi, 51, 55n62, 76–7, 81, 90,
93, 111, 126–7, 163, 236
Environmental Performance Index (EPI)
xi, xvii, xxi, 51, 55n62, 76–7, 95–6,
101–4, 126–7, 163, 169, 225, 236
Equatorial Guinea 72n12, 128, 134,
143, 228
Eritrea 36n24, 72n12, 133, 146, 218, 228
Estonia xi, 72n12, 95n5, 98n8, 112, 118,
128, 130, 134–5, 146–7, 218, 228
ETH Zurich (Swiss Federal Institute of
Technology Zurich) xi–xii, 3, 6,
191, 207

Ethiopia 38, 72n12, 133, 142, 149, 151,
218, 228
ethno-linguistic fractionalization 70
EU-15 xi, 3–6
EU-2020 xi, xvi, xix, xxi–xxii, xxv,
xxx–xxxiii, xxxvii, xxxix, 3, 12, 14,
18, 28, 36, 41, 56, 65, 72–3, 75,
75n18, 77, 81, 123–6, 128, 134, 156,
241–2, 244, 246, 248, 250, 252, 254,
256, 258, 260, 262, 264, 266
EU-2020 development index: *see* global
development index
euro xi, xix, xxi–xxii, xxix, xl, 4, 7, 11–13,
17, 22, 75, 136, 159
euro area xix, 4, 7, 11–12, 17, 75
Euro-Lex xi
European Commission ix–xi, xvii,
xxii–xxiii, xxix, xxxvii, xxxix, xl, 2,
2n5, 3n6, 9–10, 9n1, 12, 14, 18, 20,
24, 47, 56, 75, 81, 122, 136, 156,
158n3, 239–242, 244, 246, 248, 250,
252, 254, 256, 258, 260, 262, 264, 266
European Monetary Union (EMU) xi,
xxxix, 1, 74, 82, 98–99, 110, 113n29,
136–8, 156, 159, 162, 170, 234, 240
European Roundtable of Industrialists
(ERT) xi
European Union (EU) ix, xi–xii, xv, xviii,
xxii–xxiv, xxvii, xxix, xxxvii, xlii, 1–4,
9–10, 10n2, 11–16, 18, 22–4, 24n11,
25n15, 56, 82, 88, 98–9, 109–10, 112,
121, 124, 128, 134, 140–1, 147–8,
155–7, 162, 177, 239–40, 241–66

F (statistical test) xi, 73n13, 79–81,
79n3, 106n12, 107nn15–17,
108nn18–19, 109n20, 110nn22–4,
111nn25–6, 112n27–8, 116nn31–4,
117n35, 118nn36–8, 119nn39–41,
120nn42–5, 121n47, 135n3, 137,
152–3, 164–84, 234
Failed States Index: *see* Combined Failed
States Index
female survival, probability of surviving to
age 65 xvii, xxiii, xlii, 76–7, 80, 94–6,
99, 102–4, 116, 126–7, 158, 163,
173–4, 225, 236
Fiji 36n24, 72n12, 131, 145, 148–9, 219, 228

Lightning Source UK Ltd.
Milton Keynes UK
UKOW050617310512

193673UK00002B/3/P